Cold War Asia

InterConnections: The Global Twentieth Century

Renata Keller, Julia F. Irwin, Christopher McKnight Nichols, and Jayita Sarkar, *editors*

This series is home to innovative global, international, and transregional histories of the long twentieth century. Our books emphasize interactions and connections across three principal areas of inquiry: governments, militaries, and nonstate actors, including businesses; international organizations, nation-states, and individuals; and foreign and domestic policies. The series showcases work that transcends conventional geographic, temporal, and disciplinary borders, offering fresh and original perspectives on the making of the contemporary world.

A complete list of books published in the InterConnections series is available at https://uncpress.org/series/interconnections-the-global-20th-century.

Cold War Asia
Unlearning Narratives,
Making New Histories

· ·

EDITED BY
MASUDA HAJIMU

The University of North Carolina Press Chapel Hill

© 2025 The University of North Carolina Press
All rights reserved
Set in Charis by Westchester Publishing Services
Manufactured in the United States of America

Library of Congress Cataloging-in-Publication Data

Names: Masuda, Hajimu, editor.
Title: Cold War Asia : unlearning narratives, making new histories / edited by Masuda Hajimu.
Other titles: InterConnections.
Description: Chapel Hill : University of North Carolina Press, [2025] | Series: Interconnections: The Global Twentieth Century | In chapter 6's title, Kisho Tsuchiya's "Theorizing Southeast Asia's Cold War: Timor in 1974–75", the word "Cold" is deliberately crossed out. | Includes bibliographical references and index.
Identifiers: LCCN 2025001940 | ISBN 9781469686301 (cloth ; alk. paper) | ISBN 9781469686318 (pbk. ; alk. paper) | ISBN 9781469683119 (ebook) | ISBN 9781469687841 (pdf)
Subjects: LCSH: Cold War—History. | Cold War—Social aspects—Asia. | Cold War—Historiography. | Asia—History, Military—20th century. | Asia—Social conditions—20th century. | BISAC: HISTORY / Modern / 20th Century / Cold War | POLITICAL SCIENCE / International Relations / Diplomacy
Classification: LCC DS33.3 .C554 2025 | DDC 909.825—dc23/eng/20250304
LC record available at https://lccn.loc.gov/2025001940

Cover art: *Hmong Soldiers of the CPT with a Thai student*. Courtesy of Comrade Chart Saelee.

For product safety concerns under the European Union's General Product Safety Regulation (EU GPSR), please contact mailto:gpsr@mare-nostrum.co.uk or write to The University of North Carolina Press and Mare Nostrum Group B.V., Mauritskade 21D, 1091 GC Amsterdam, The Netherlands.

Contents

List of Illustrations, ix

Foreword, xi
ODD ARNE WESTAD

Acknowledgments, xv

Introduction, 1
Reconceptualizing the Cold War: On-the-Ground Experiences in Asia
MASUDA HAJIMU

Part I
Social Warfare

1 Terror in East Java, 23
 The NU versus PKI Conflict before and after September 30, 1965
 IMAM MUHTAROM

2 Islam and Communism in West Java, 44
 The Cold War and Sociocultural Polarization in Indonesia, 1945–65
 MATTHEW WOOLGAR

3 Assimilation of Ethnic Chinese in Cold War Thailand, 1948–57, 73
 CUI FENG

4 Voices of the Voiceless, 91
 The Cold War and the Hmong in Northern Thailand, 1965–82
 PRASIT LEEPREECHA

Part II
Local Imaginings and Identity Politics

5   Reconsidering the Naxalite Movement, 115
    *Local and Social Experiences of the Cold War in
    Kerala, India, in the 1960s*
    MUHAMMED KUNHI MAHIN UDMA

6   Theorizing Southeast Asia's ~~Cold~~ War, 143
    Timor in 1974–75
    KISHO TSUCHIYA

7   Anti-Vietnamese Xenophobia as the Vernacular Expression
    of Anticommunism in 1950s Laos, 174
    Rethinking (Not Removing) Our Cold War Lens
    SIMON CREAK

Part III
Individual Hope, Negotiation, and Trauma

8   Bodyguards of the US Military?, 205
    The Voices of US-Educated Okinawans, 1949–72
    KINUKO MAEHARA-YAMAZATO

9   The Voices of Young Vietnamese Women Volunteers
    during the Vietnam War, 231
    LUONG THI HONG

10 The Red Guards in Burma, 1960s–80s, 252
    An Oral History
    BIN YANG

11 Afterlife of Cold War Memories, 274
    *Familial Transmission of Martial Law–Era Memories
    in the Post–Cold War Philippines*
    MARY GRACE R. CONCEPCION

12 Letter to Granddad, 299
    Tracing the Life of a Leftist during the Malayan Emergency, 1948–60
    SIM CHI YIN

Reflections

13 The Long, Hot Cold Wars of Asia—and Latin America, 307
   ALAN McPHERSON

14 An Archipelagic Turn, 319
   Islands as Method in Understanding Cold War Asia
   TAOMO ZHOU

15 The Cold War in Asia, 328
   DAVID C. ENGERMAN

   Contributors, 335

   Index, 339

Illustrations

Map

0.1 Map of Asia (until 1991), xx

Figures

1.1 The graves of Makarabis and his wife, with other five victims, at Soro Public Cemetery, Blitar, East Java, Indonesia, 35

4.1 Hill-tribe resettlement site of Phu Lomlo in 1965, 99

4.2 Hmong soldiers of the CPT with a Thai student, 101

4.3 Young Hmong and Mien (Yao) Hill Tribe volunteer soldiers in Pratu Pha Training Camp, Lampang Province, 1971, 106

5.1 Mr. Ayinnor Vasu, 121

5.2 Mr. Kunnel Krishnan, 135

6.1 FRETILIN pamphlet's cartoon, "UDT and APODETI are agents of imperialism," 156

7.1 "Ha, ha, ha! Come and die for no reason!" *Nak Rop Lao*, 1950, 184

7.2 "Peace" path or "death" path? *Nak Rop Lao*, 1950, 185

7.3 "Take him to our country." *Nak Rop Lao*, 1950, 186

7.4 "Whoa! The Lao will turn completely Vietnamese!" *Nak Rop Lao*, 1950, 187

7.5 "We must help each other achieve independence." *Nak Rop Lao*, 1950, 187

7.6 Vietminh arsonists. *Nak Rop Lao*, 1950, 188

7.7 "Pancha-Shila or coexistence 'translated into Vietnamese and Chinese.'" *Lao Hakxa Sat*, 1959, 192

7.8 "The Vietminh are at your disposal." *Echo de la liberté*, 1961, 193

8.1 Okinawan students departing for the United States on July 15, 1952, 211

8.2 Golden Gate Club members' meeting with General Paul Caraway, high commissioner of the USCAR, on March 11, 1961, 214

Foreword

ODD ARNE WESTAD

Once, not very long ago, I spoke with a family of farmers in China's southern Guangdong Province about their experiences over the course of the parents' and grandparents' lives. We first talked about how the era of economic reform had changed their fortunes. They had been poor and now they felt moderately wealthy. Several of them had been to Hong Kong on package tours, and one young couple had stayed at a resort in the Philippines, though it was a bit unclear to them exactly where they had been. They were chided by one of the grandparents. He had been born in Indonesia and arrived in China in 1962 as a refugee. Having been a sailor, he knew the Southeast Asian archipelagoes well, though he had not been there for fifty years. In China he had married into a farming family. Being a farmer in Guangdong seemed a better occupation, even in the immediate wake of the Great Leap disaster, than being a Chinese sailor in an increasingly unfriendly sea.

Then one of the uncles spoke up. He had been a soldier along the Sino-Vietnamese border during the brief war in 1979. Being proud of his service, he believed that China had been defending its territory against attack. Those Vietnamese, he said, they really hate us Chinese. Then he asked me why that was so. The Indonesian-born grandfather answered on my behalf. "It is all those countries," he said. "Those people did not used to have countries of their own. Then they suddenly got them. And then we became their enemy, because they did not like China being so big and powerful. It is all about that."[1]

I remembered this conversation when I was reading the chapters of the wonderfully rich collection that Masuda Hajimu has put together. In the memory of so many people, all across Asia, the experience of the Cold War is summoned in a thousand different ways and with thousands of different implications. Just as it does not make sense to divide people by exclusionary identities or fragmentary politics, the contributors to this volume argue that it does not make sense to simply look at the Cold War as imported into Asia or understand it from the top down. As Masuda reminds us in his own work, building, among others, on the great Korean Cold War anthropologist Heonik Kwon, it is the variety of experiences of that era that ordinary Asians carry with them that gives it significance in terms of politics, social affairs, and day-to-day behavior.[2] It is very likely that future Cold War research on Asian topics will be based, at least in part, on such insights, and that it therefore will help us put together a much fuller picture of Asian history in the final half of the twentieth century.[3]

This book is an excellent starting point for such explorations. I do not know whether the exclusion of China, Korea, and Japan (except Okinawa) from the discussion here was deliberate, but the approach does allow for more of a focus on Southeast Asia. And in many ways the exclusions therefore help with understanding some of the voices that are usually not heard in discussions of Cold War Asia, especially various postcolonial experiences and different conceptual understandings of the Cold War, as the volume's title indicates. One issue that comes out very clearly in the chapters on Indonesia, Timor, Laos, and Thailand especially is how syncretic Asian Cold War concepts could be, how much of history and place they encompassed, and, as Masuda points out in his introduction, how "social warfare" became a distinct area of Cold War operations in one Asian region after another.[4]

Another issue that comes out in several chapters is the emphasis on women and gender as categories of analysis. This, it seems to me, is increasingly a crucial aspect of how we view Cold War Asia (to use Masuda's preferred term). Gender relations went through dramatic changes in most countries in Asia during the late twentieth century, and Cold War social warfare played an integral part in these changes, as we see in the chapters on Vietnam and Burma.

There are a number of other dimensions that could be discussed, but let me mention a final one here: the issue of memory and memorialization. The chapters on the post–Cold War Philippines and on reaching out to an exiled and martyred grandfather in China are remarkable examples of how to communicate with the past.[5] On the issue of memory, as well, Cold War Asia stands out as remarkably fertile ground for research, as the conversation with which I open this foreword also indicates.

The program Masuda outlines at the end of his introduction will be debated for a long time among Cold War historians and historians of contemporary Asia. As with all programmatic statements, its relevance will be in its implementation. The need to practice grassroots history, through both archival research and interviews, is obviously there, as is the need to integrate the study of emotions into our understanding of history.[6] The authors contributing to this volume all, in their different ways, show us how we can gain more ground in advancing toward these and other historiographical aims. But it will be up to the many whom this collection inspires to bring us closer to the realization of such an ambitious program.

Notes

1. Conversation with nine members and three generations of a family in Guangdong Province, May 2019.

2. Hajimu Masuda, *Cold War Crucible: The Korean Conflict and the Postwar World* (Cambridge, MA: Harvard University Press, 2015); and Heonik Kwon, *The Other Cold War* (New York: Columbia University Press, 2010).

3. For further indications of recent directions in the study of the Cold War in Asia, see Christopher Goscha and Christian Ostermann, eds., *Connecting Histories: Decolonization and the Cold War in Southeast Asia, 1945–1962* (Stanford, CA: Stanford University Press, 2009); and Tsuyoshi Hasegawa, ed., *The Cold War in East Asia, 1945–1991* (Stanford, CA: Stanford University Press, 2011).

4. Here it is possible to compare research on Cold War Asia with the recent flourishing of literature on the Latin American Cold War; see, for example, Thomas C. Field, Stella Krepp, and Vanni Pettinà, eds., *Latin America and the Global Cold War* (Chapel Hill: University of North Carolina Press, 2020).

5. I must note, with pride, that Sim Chi Yin, the world-renowned artist and photographer who contributed the text on locating the memorial to her grandfather in China, was once my student in London.

6. For a tour de force in the use of oral history sources to do grassroots Cold War history, see Artemy M. Kalinovsky, *Laboratory of Socialist Development: Cold War Politics and Decolonization in Soviet Tajikistan* (Ithaca, NY: Cornell University Press, 2018). For a discussion of the study of emotions in international affairs, see Barbara Keys and Claire Yorke, "Personal and Political Emotions in the Mind of the Diplomat," *Political Psychology* 40, no. 6 (2019): 1235–49.

Acknowledgments

For invaluable help with my collaborative research projects spanning five years, I am in debt to many. At the National University of Singapore (NUS), I hosted a series of two international conferences and three online workshops, under the title "Reconceptualizing the Cold War: On-the-Ground Experiences in Asia," from 2019 to 2022. Although there was no shortage of new research on the Cold War, a history of the Cold War that focuses on Asia from East and Southeast Asia to South Asia, that looks into ordinary people's grassroots experiences, that combines oral history and archival research approaches in multiple local languages, and that raises fundamental questions concerning the very nature of the Cold War, was, I thought, still lacking. That is why I set out to gather a group of scholars willing to explore new perspectives on Cold War histories and contribute to the creation of a new digital archive of oral history collections concerning the Cold War and decolonization in Asia, which is now available at https://rcw-asia.com. I would like to thank all who responded to my initial call for papers. Our conferences, obviously, could not cover all of Asia, and, as such, this volume is not comprehensive in its coverage of the region, which is massive in size and diverse in terms of social, cultural, political, and historical settings. Nevertheless, I hope this collection of essays will inspire further studies of the Cold War and of Asia from a social point of view.

I am grateful to all who participated in our conferences and workshops. In addition to those whose work appears in this volume, Chen Yongming, Cheng Yi-meng, Jason Ng Sze Chieh, Chong Ujong, David E. Gilbert, Vannessa Hearman, Paula Hendrikx, Phianphachong Intarat, S. Hajirah Junaid, Sujane Kanparit, Kao Dan-hua, Hema Kiruppalini, Covell Meyskens, Robert Moisa, Sherzod Muminov, May Ngo, Nguyen Diu-Huong, Uyen Nguyen, Ricky C. Ornopia, Mythri P U, Pa Kuan Huai, Vatthana Pholsena, Morragotwong Phumplab, Elgin Glenn Salomon, Juliette Sendra, Savina Sirik, Veronica Sison, Appridzani Syahfrullah, Tan Teng Phee, Siti Zainatul Umarah, Xiyan Wang, Beiyu Zhang, and Zhiyu Zhang participated in these forums and contributed to the development of our projects. I am grateful to Sayaka Chatani, Simon Richard Creak, Fang-Tze Hsu, Akiko Ishii,

Seung-Joon Lee, Wei Yi Leow, Samson Lim, Joey Long, Seng Guo Quan, Iqbal Singh Sevea, and Taomo Zhou for reading early drafts of papers and providing invaluable comments.

I also extend my special thanks to my projects' former postdoc fellows, Kisho Tsuchiya, Chien-Wen Kung, and Muhammed Kunhi, as well as to our overseas researchers and research assistants who collected and contributed their oral history collections to our archive: Rina Hong and Chong Ujong (Japan and Korea); Chen Yishen, Chen Yongming, Cheng Yimeng, and Cui Feng (China); Megumi Hagiwara and Chen Yiwen (Taiwan); Socheat Nhean, Soeung Bunly, and Soun Ponleu (Cambodia); Ngatini (Vietnam); Phianphachong Intarat (Thailand); Pa Kuan Huai (Malaysia); Dominique Lucagbo, Christian Lemuel Magaling, Elgin Glenn R. Salomon, and Veronica Sison (the Philippines); Khairunnisa, Robert Moisa, Imam Muhtarom, Juliette Sendra, Appridzani Syahfrullah, Siti Zaainatul Umaroh, and Satriono Priyo Utomo (Indonesia); Muhammed Kunhi and Mythri P U (India); and Arivarun Anbualagan, Syahrul Anuar, Foo Yong Xiang, Bing Hongjian, Joshua Lim, and Jeremy Tan (Singapore).

Looking back, our projects have their origin in the conference I organized at NUS in 2016, "Unlearning Cold War Narratives: Toward Alternative Understandings of the Cold War World," through which I met amazing scholars from across the world, including David C. Engerman, Alan McPherson, and Taomo Zhou, who also agreed to contribute their reflection essays to this volume. Special thanks to Heonik Kwon, whom I met at this conference and who invited me to take part in his "Beyond the Cold War, Toward a Community of Asia" project and supported my work tremendously. I am grateful to the Korean Studies Promotion Service of the Academy of Korean Studies (AKS-2016-LAB-2250005). Many thanks also to Odd Arne Westad for agreeing to write a foreword to this volume, Mark Bradley and Brad Simpson for commenting on an early draft of my introductory chapter, Jay Winston for patiently reading all chapters and helping me to polish the manuscript, and Amron Lehte for compiling the index. At the University of North Carolina Press (UNCP), Debbie Gershenowitz has been a wonderful editor who has kept encouraging me as I worked on this volume. I am also grateful to Alexis Dumain and Valerie Burton, as well as the broader UNCP editing, design, and marketing staff—Alyssa Brown, Iris Levesque, Mary Caviness, Lindsay Starr, and Liz Orange Lane—for helping this book to come to life. Thanks also to the two external reviewers who provided detailed and valuable feedback on an early draft.

Last but not least, I would like to thank my home institution, NUS, for generously sponsoring our projects. An Academic Research Fund Tier 2 grant (MOE2018-T2-1-138) supported our conferences, digital archive, and staffing, and a subsequent Academic Research Fund Tier 1 grant (FY2022-FRC1-004) helped with the development of this volume and the collection of primary materials. Likewise, I owe the success of these projects to warm support from colleagues and staff in the Department of History at NUS. Eileen Shen Yanling has worked on various matters ranging from conference organization to financial issues with remarkable efficiency, for which I am most grateful. Finally, my deepest gratitude goes to the contributors to this volume, who enthusiastically responded to my call and joined the team, and who wrote, rewrote, and then revised their drafts at least once or twice, and in some cases more than three times, and patiently remained committed throughout these projects over many years. I am very fortunate to be able to work with such remarkable people.

Cold War Asia

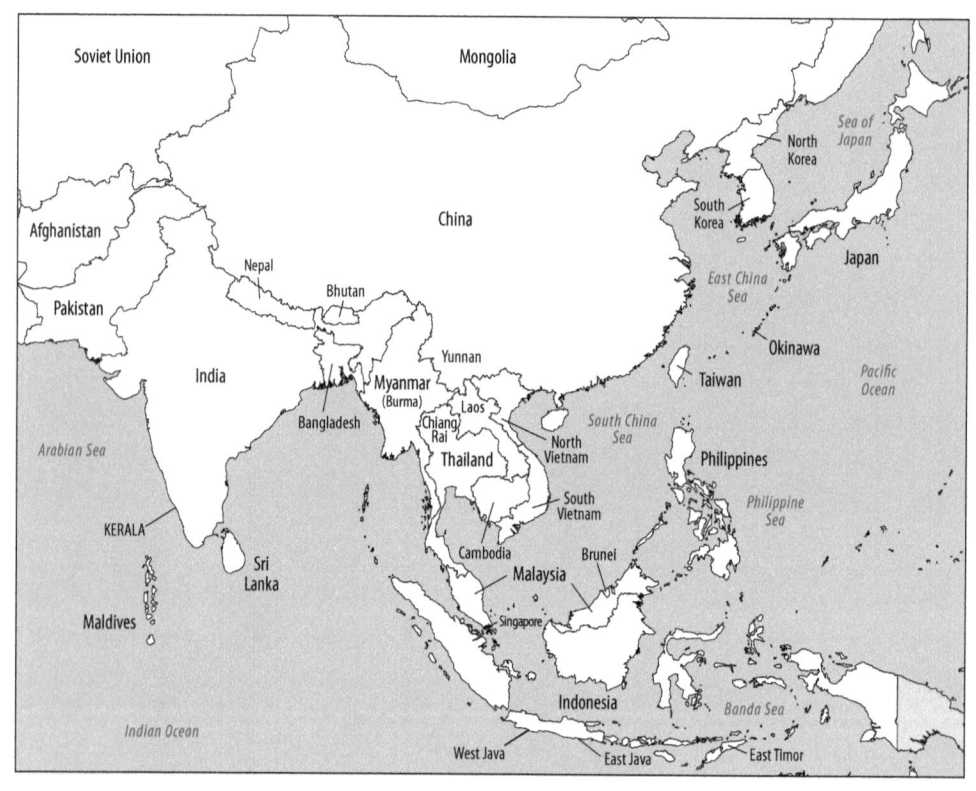

MAP 0.1 Map of Asia (until 1991).

Introduction
Reconceptualizing the Cold War:
On-the-Ground Experiences in Asia

••

MASUDA HAJIMU

A few years ago, I received a message from an old friend. In it, she complained about recent situations in Cold War studies: "I have been frustrated for several years by the claim that people are doing a new kind of Cold War studies, because none of it seems new." Seeing her message, which listed several "recent" (but not "new") tendencies, I had ambivalent thoughts. First, I thought that she probably missed some of the most interesting developments in the field, or perhaps had been underestimating their significance. And yet, a casual and poignant remark she dropped stayed in my mind: "Is there anything else that seems new to you?" It stuck in my mind precisely because I agreed with her in that I felt a similar deep frustration.

In fact, this current situation has been simultaneously encouraging and depressing. It is encouraging because studies of the Cold War have been truly flourishing and diversifying over the past two decades.[1] In particular, with the increase in multilingual and multiarchival research, recent studies have encompassed histories of almost all regions of the globe, from Latin America to Asia, the Middle East, and Africa.[2] Because of this, the Cold War has stopped being viewed as a subfield of US history, and has come to be seen as part of a growing global and international history. In addition, with the prevalence of social and cultural approaches, Cold War studies are no longer confined within the framework of conventional diplomatic history. A myriad of topics has come to be considered relevant: gays and lesbians, white supremacism, Buddhism, evangelicalism, and Mexican and Chinese immigrants, as well as Hollywood, jazz, parenting, miniskirts, and even vaginal orgasms and impotence, among many others.[3]

Concurrently emerging in the 2000s were several significant interventions in Cold War history: a domestic politics turn, a religious turn, a Latin America turn, a development turn, and an imperial turn, as well as growing interests in childhood, sexuality, and immigration, in addition to already prevailing attention to race, gender, and labor. For instance, while the significance of domestic politics had been emphasized for a long time, it was "slighted" in the 1990s due to the dominance of two major trends mentioned above: internationalization and the social and cultural turn.[4] It was in the 2000s that a growing number of scholars, such as Fredrik Logevall, recast a spotlight on the roles of domestic politics during the Cold War.[5] Another critical development was Latin American specialists' interventions in the previously bipolar or US-centric paradigms of Cold War studies. Such scholars focused on the crossroads between Cold War history and Latin America's domestic politics, social conflicts, and postcolonial histories, underscoring the notion of Latin America's "long Cold War," which had occurred arguably since the turn of the twentieth century.[6]

Then, with growing attention to the "roots" or "prehistory" of the Cold War in the interwar period or even the late nineteenth century, the basic periodization of the Cold War has become less distinct.[7] What this blurring suggests is that the nature of the Cold War itself has become less obvious. What is noteworthy in the literature in the twenty-first century is that the time when scholars had a clear axis of contention is long gone, and that the focus of questions has shifted from the Cold War's origins to its nature. Now, the question is no longer only "Who began it?" but also "How did it work?" and then "What was it?" Thus, it is not surprising that this has also been a time when a number of scholars have raised more fundamental questions, attempting to reconceptualize the Cold War in terms of, for instance, decolonization, developmentalism, postcolonial histories, social mechanisms, and ordinary people's wars.[8] In short, Cold War literature in the twenty-first century can be characterized by continuous expansion and diversification, with the rises of new "turns" and focuses, which, at least at a glance, should be considered encouraging and even heartwarming.

And yet, the current situation in the field is somewhat depressing, as well. If we can characterize this recent trend as one of diversification, it is also a process of fractionalization and disconnection of research. In other words, what we have seen in recent years is an increasing tendency toward a division of labor among scholars, and, as a result, consolidation of conventional narratives. Let me explain. First, a surge of literature along the lines of internationalization—or "new Cold War history"—has revealed policymakers' decision-making processes not only in Washington but also in Moscow, Beijing, and other places in the world. Along this line, we've learned that many third world leaders were not merely puppets of superpowers but had their own purposes and calculations.[9] Obviously, we've learned a lot. But these scholars' focuses are almost always on policymakers and policymaking processes. In addition, while we've learned about quite a few cases of "tails-wagging-dogs" phenomena, these anecdotes have usually been presented as additions to existing conventional Cold War narratives, rather than challenges to them.

Second, we've observed a surge of literature along the lines of the social and cultural turn. However, until very recently, such studies have tended to focus mostly on the United States and Europe. Much more problematic is that they have usually focused exclusively on the *effects* of the Cold War on society, culture, and the daily lives of ordinary people. In this approach, which I call the "Cold War as weather," the Cold War appears merely as a given phenomenon—like weather conditions—rather than a result of social and historical construction. As such, while we have surely learned a lot of details about how the Cold War impacted society and culture, these studies are presented more like additions rather than challenges to conventional Cold War frameworks. Third, there has been a trend quite similar to this "Cold War as weather" approach among Asian history specialists who have explored how the Cold War spread to Asia, how it impacted Asia, and how Asian societies were mobilized during the Cold War.[10] I would call this "the Cold War *in* Asia" approach, in the sense that it more or less describes the Cold War as weather over Asia, without raising much in the way of questions or interventions as to the conventional frameworks of the Cold War, itself.[11]

What is even more problematic is that these studies have usually been conducted separately, and, as a result, a particular kind of impression has been further solidified: that is, policymakers' conduct shaped the Cold War, which, in turn, had enormous aftereffects on societies and ordinary people's daily lives, and Asia was an end recipient of the global confrontation. Such a narrative is simplistic, as well as problematic. First, as long as we continue to accept it, we will continue to view society, culture, and ordinary people's daily lives as passive entities under a global and political conflict. And, thus, we will not be able to think about how they might have conditioned and shaped the ways in which the Cold War world was made. Second, as long as we continue to view Asia as a passive recipient of the global confrontation, we will continue to accept this American-centric (or Western-centric) perspective. And, thus, we will not be able to imagine how Asia, like other parts of the world, might have participated in the making of the Cold War world.

In a sense, recent Cold War scholarship has ended up accepting the most traditional social view and worldview, which puts high-ranking policymakers at the tops of their societies, and the West at the center of the world. To put it more bluntly, this is the century-old great men's narrative, as well as a Western-centric model. While observing a trend of expansion and diversification, what we have seen is, disappointingly, a process of fractionalization and disconnection of research, which has unintentionally contributed to solidifying some of the most traditional views.

Cold War Historiography at the Crossroads

It is interesting to note that, since the mid-2010s, a number of hardcore diplomatic historians—mostly Europeanists—have begun raising deep concerns about the state of the field. One example is Holger Nehring's deep frustration over "intellectual and methodological pluralism" and its consequential "decentering of the field away from its military and diplomatic core." He complains that the meaning of "Cold War" as a concept has been "diluted" because the term lurks everywhere and can be applied to almost everything. Dismissing the recent "cultural-turn" scholarship as conceptually fuzzy and methodologically vague, Nehring laments, "While attracting attention from many different fields and profiting from interdisciplinary inspirations, Cold War studies have lost a clear object of enquiry and a clear conceptualization of what it is that constitutes their subject."[12]

By the same token, Federico Romero's field-survey article, "Cold War Historiography at the Crossroads," views the field as "diluted" because it has become too broad, too diverse, and too inclusive, including almost everything that happened in the second half of the twentieth century. Thus, Romero urges scholars to focus more specifically on the distinct core of the Cold War, suggesting that it be defined as an ideological conflict centered in Europe, and advocating for further research on Europe.[13] Historiographically speaking, therefore, the status of the field in recent years can be summarized as a crossroads of divergence and convergence.

Where should we go? One way is to retreat from the trend of expansion and diversification and focus on the conventional core of the Cold War in Europe, as advocated by Nehring and Romero. The problem with that approach is that we would lose an opportunity to contemplate the meanings of the Cold War much more seriously and fundamentally. To do so would, in turn, help to sustain conventional Cold War narratives that depict policymakers as the sole protagonists who shaped the Cold War, which, in turn, had an enormous impact on ordinary people's lives, in this particular order. In fact, this has been a deeply rooted assumption from the time of the Cold War and since, which has been further cemented not just by internationalist scholarship but, more importantly, by the social and cultural turn scholarship that is narrowly focused on the Cold War's impact on society and culture, without considering the reverse. Nevertheless, if we retreat from this current of expansion and diversification, the field simply reverts to the shape it had before the 1990s.

What has been missing for more than two decades is an effort to analyze the meanings of various findings on diverse topics and, in doing so, to reconsider a big question concerning what the Cold War really was. What we can (and perhaps should) do is not to dismiss social- and cultural-turn literature, nor to retreat from such attempts, but to reassess the essence of the Cold War, itself, not just through examining policymakers' conduct, but by investigating what happened in societies and among people. In other words, the recent surge of literature on a variety of topics suggests a need for a new approach to discussing the nature of the Cold War not just as an international political event, but as a socially constructed phenomenon. To explore such an approach, questions we can consider are as follows:

- What was actually being fought over in the name of the Cold War?
- What kinds of local conflicts, whether social, cultural, gender, ethnic, religious, economic, or generational, existed underneath the Cold War confrontation?
- In what ways did local people observe, imagine, appropriate, and even take advantage of Cold War situations?
- What kinds of emotions were carried through in the form of ideology, whether communism or anticommunism?
- What are the commonalities among hosts of events that might appear irrelevant to one another at a glance?
- What kinds of dynamics can we see in Cold War Asia, and in what ways can we use Cold War Asia as a method to reconsider the Cold War itself?

Reconceptualizing the Cold War

With this end in mind, I set up a project titled "Reconceptualizing the Cold War: On-the-Ground Experiences in Asia," which aims at the creation of an oral history archive for the purpose of reconsidering the Cold War and decolonization in Asia.[14] Its primary goals are to capture the emotions, enthusiasms, and fears of the era, and to explore experiences and memories of ordinary people who witnessed various kinds of real and imagined wars across Asia. Our oral history project in Asia—in a sense, an attempt at history from below, and from Asia—will be an important and useful corrective to conventional histories of the Cold War and decolonization, which have largely emphasized superpowers' and political leaders' conduct, with generally a Western-centric perspective.[15]

Through this project, we aim to draw attention toward the existence of "many Cold Wars," or, more precisely, many wars that were imagined as parts of the global Cold War—as one of our contributors, Kisho Tsuchiya, puts it—which took place on the ground for various purposes.[16] I hope that this attempt will shed a light on various social and local tensions that have been obscured under standard narratives. In a sense, this is an attempt to unlearn conventional narratives that we have been long accustomed to. This, however, does not mean forgetting or ignoring the Cold War. Inherently, the process of unlearning involves the process of learning something new. Thus, what I hope to do through unlearning dominant Cold War narratives is to encourage historians and scholars in other disciplines to rethink what the Cold War really was, and therefore to reconsider the postwar and postcolonial histories of the twentieth century.

As such, this volume—the fruit of numerous conversations and dozens of collaborative projects in the past several years—intends to offer a standpoint from which we can reconceptualize experiences of the Cold War and reconsider twentieth-century history as a whole. It takes readers to the villages of rural Java, to the jungles of northern Thailand, and to the Indigenous tribal communities in Kerala, and shows how what we have called the Cold War world locally took shape and materialized through ordinary people's imaginings and appropriations on the ground. All chapters are based on oral history interviews and/or archival research conducted in Japan, China, Vietnam, Laos, Thailand, Malaysia, Singapore, the Philippines, Indonesia, East Timor, and India. Our authors conducted research in local languages, including not just relatively well-known Asian languages such as Chinese, Japanese, Vietnamese, Lao, Thai, and Indonesian, but a more diverse array of local languages such as Malayalam (southern India), Hmong (northern Thailand), and Tetum (East Timor). This means that the book in itself provides rich, original historical records, which are, in many cases, presented to an English-language audience for the first time.

Furthermore, with its focus on ordinary people's experiences on the ground, the book provides firsthand and grassroots narratives of major historical events that have been, more or less, associated with the Cold War. These include the Chinese Revolution, the Cultural Revolution, the Vietnam War, the Indonesian Mass Killings of 1965–66, Marcos's Martial Law in the

Philippines, and the Naxalite movement in India. Each chapter shows how ordinary people viewed and experienced these events, and how they translated and appropriated Cold War politics as vehicles for their own social struggles and culture wars on the ground. Thus, in short, the book offers empirically rich and substantial accounts of the history of Asia in the second half of the twentieth century, seen in a new light.

Our focus on ordinary people's experiences does not mean that we simply add new information to existing Cold War narratives. Rather, this approach forces us to reconsider what the Cold War was. Simply put, the Cold War has appeared to be an international political conflict precisely because we have usually assumed that political leaders and government officials were its protagonists. However, once we regard ordinary people as protagonists, the nature of the event cannot be the same. As such, this book is an endeavor toward unlearning conventional Cold War narratives and reconsidering the nature of the Cold War from a societal perspective. Readers will close this book with a new perspective through which to reconsider not only the history of the Cold War but that of the twentieth century in general, and the ways in which the world is viewed and understood today.

Chapter Summaries

This volume consists of three parts. Part I, from chapters 1 to 4, deals with what I call "social warfare," that is, ordinary people's social conflicts and culture wars on the ground, which were, though, often fought under the banners of the Cold War logics. While these chapters focus on different subjects, they delve deeper into what were, in reality, gender, religious, ethnic, and economic tensions, thus raising the following questions: What was actually being fought over among grassroots populations in the name of the Cold War? What kinds of local tensions existed underneath the Cold War confrontation?

Chapter 1, "Terror in East Java: The NU versus PKI Conflict before and after September 30, 1965," examines the Indonesian Mass Killings of 1965–66, focusing on villages in rural areas of East Java, Indonesia. Based on oral history interviews with both victims and perpetrators, Imam Muhtarom shows that the conflict was highly complex and its roots were deeply local, and that the issue was not just an ideological conflict between communists and anticommunists, nor a reflection of superpowers' power politics, but involved local and historical contentions among social groups in those villages, such as tensions concerning religion, economic inequality, and gender relationships.

Chapter 2, "Islam and Communism in West Java: The Cold War and Sociocultural Polarization in Indonesia, 1945–65," also explores the Indonesian Mass Killings, with a longer time span and from a religious angle. Based on oral history and archival materials, Matthew Woolgar challenges the widespread assumption that communism and Islam were inherently and completely incompatible, showing that the Indonesian Communist Party (PKI) had emphasized that it was not anti-Islam and supported freedom of religion, and that various groups' leaders tried to cooperate in the 1950s, despite a general tendency toward tension between the PKI and Muslim groups. The chapter argues that religion was not a passive object of Cold War influences, but rather an integral element in the matrix of cultural, social, and political tensions that constituted the Cold War world.

Chapter 3, "Assimilation of Ethnic Chinese in Cold War Thailand, 1948–57," looks into another site of social contention often waged underneath Cold War logics: ethnic tensions. Drawing on oral history interviews with overseas Chinese in Thailand, Cui Feng shows how anti-Chinese sentiment among the Thai population increased in momentum with the rise of Cold War politics, and how Thai ruling elites made full use of such anti-Chinese and anticommunist sentiments to implement a harsher assimilation policy for ethnic Chinese. The chapter concludes that Cold War politics accelerated the assimilation of ethnic Chinese, contributing to homogenizing and nation-building processes in post–World War II Thailand.

Chapter 4, "Voices of the Voiceless: The Cold War and the Hmong in Northern Thailand, 1965–82," continues an examination of the crossroads between Cold War politics and ethnic and identity politics, with a focus on an ethnic minority in Thai society: the Hmong people, who reside in the jungle and border areas of northern Thailand. Based on Hmong-language oral history interviews with elder Hmong who joined both sides of the Cold War politics, Prasit Leepreecha describes the Hmong's ambivalent Cold War experiences. On the one hand, the Cold War tremendously harmed the Hmong because it divided them into two opposing sides, leaving painful memories that still haunt Hmong communities. On the other hand, the Hmong were able to actually take advantage of the global Cold War rivalry in their own local struggles for social justice and equal treatment, transforming themselves from a marginalized and discriminated "hill tribe" into one of the most prominent minorities in Thailand.

Part II, from chapters 5 to 7, of course includes elements of social warfare, like the chapters described above, but focuses more on how local people imagined what were actually multiple local conflicts as parts of a global confrontation, and how they utilized Cold War rhetoric in their own struggles at home, ranging from centuries-old caste discrimination to civil war and generational tensions, and to ethnic and identity politics. They ask, In what ways did local people observe, imagine, appropriate, and even take advantage of Cold War situations?

Chapter 5, "Reconsidering the Naxalite Movement: Local and Social Experiences of the Cold War in Kerala, India, in the 1960s," turns our eyes to the southern part of India, looking into what has been commonly regarded merely as a radical communist—or Maoist—movement: the Naxalite movement in the state of Kerala in the late 1960s. Based on extensive Malayalam-language oral history interviews and other materials, Muhammed Kunhi Mahin Udma pays particular attention to historically deep-rooted conflicts between the *Janmi* (landed aristocratic) and lower-caste *Adivasi* (Indigenous tribal) communities, and examines how Cold War rhetoric functioned in transforming the caste-based system of exploitation and discrimination in the region. Taking a societal viewpoint, the chapter concludes that the early history of the Naxalite movement in Kerala, to a large extent, is the history of *Adivasi* community people's resistance against *Janmis'* exploitation and discrimination.

Chapter 6, Kisho Tsuchiya's "Theorizing Southeast Asia's C̶o̶l̶d̶ War: Timor in 1974–75," deliberates about the nature of the Cold War in Southeast Asia through examining the civil war in Portuguese Timor in 1975, which was then described by foreign observers as the "Cuba of Southeast Asia," in which opposing sides described themselves as "communists" and "anticommunists." It traces how Timorese and Southeast Asian people imagined what were actually multiple local conflicts as parts of one global conflict, and how, because of such imaginings, they ended up inviting international reactions and interventions into the region. This chapter proposes the term "the C̶o̶l̶d̶ War"—crossing out "Cold" but leaving it in place—to clarify the local and actual (hot) nature of warfare on the ground, while, at the same time, highlighting the unerasable traces of the global conflict within local conflicts. As such, it intends to offer a theoretical standpoint for viewing Southeast Asia's Cold War as a *simulacrum* constructed by local leaders and peoples' simulations of the global confrontation between capitalist and communist camps.

Chapter 7, Simon Creak's "Anti-Vietnamese Xenophobia as the Vernacular Expression of Anticommunism in 1950s Laos: Rethinking (Not Removing) Our Cold War Lens," explores the ways in which local expressions of anti-Vietnamese xenophobia functioned as a vernacular form of anticommunism in Cold War Laos. It first examines the historical roots of this xenophobia in the colonial era, and then analyzes anti-Vietnamese fear and racism in a series of anticommunist political cartoons in the 1950s. The chapter argues that, while the fear of Vietnamese expansion pre- and post-dated the Cold War itself, the Lao fear of the Vietnamese should not be seen as a purely national phenomenon. It further argues that, rather than removing the "Cold War lens," scholars should carefully reapply it to illuminate experiences and productions of the Cold War in the global south, and to recognize their diversity.

Part III, from chapters 8 to 12, turns our eyes to ordinary individuals' life stories, looking into their decisions, motivations, negotiations, and reflections. While these chapters have their own subjects, they inspect ordinary individuals' voices and emotions seriously, instead of simply assuming them to be those of the indoctrinated. Thus, these chapters ask, What kinds of emotions were carried through in the form of ideology, whether communist or anticommunist?

Chapter 8, "Bodyguards of the US Military? The Voices of US-Educated Okinawans, 1949–72," looks into US-occupied Okinawa, which was often dubbed "Cold War Island," with particular attention to the life stories of Okinawans who received US military scholarships to study in the United States. While such programs have been commonly considered merely parts of the US cultural Cold War strategy or continuations of a typical colonial practice, Kinuko Maehara-Yamazato delves deeper into Okinawans' perspectives and motivations, exploring how they took advantage of this educational opportunity for their own needs and hopes. This chapter shows that, while these Okinawans did take advantage of the US study-abroad program to access higher education and travel beyond Okinawa, as well as to move upward in society and forge new identities, they did not always become pro-American, nor did their social roles directly reflect anticommunist ideology, as has often been imagined.

Chapter 9, Luong Thi Hong's "The Voices of Young Vietnamese Women Volunteers during the Vietnam War," continues to explore the issue of individual hopes and negotiations in the Cold War world, with a particular focus on Vietnamese women volunteers during the Vietnam War. Drawing on oral history interviews and archival materials in northern Vietnam, it captures individuals' voices and feelings concerning their decisions to join volunteer forces and to go to battlefields. It shows the diverse experiences and motivations of ordinary Vietnamese women, thus challenging conventional narratives that describe these women simply as "heroic young women" of the national liberation, or as "victims" of Cold War politics.

Chapter 10, Bin Yang's "Red Guards in Burma, 1960s–80s: An Oral History," also scrutinizes the issue of individual decisions and experiences, with a particular focus on Mao's China, through tracing the lives of five former Red Guards in Yunnan who had been dispatched to rural villages on the Sino-Burmese frontier in order to join the armed forces led by the Communist Party of Burma. While conventional top-down and macroview accounts have tended to emphasize revolutionary will and dedication, this oral history of former Red Guards personalizes their individual decisions, experiences, and reflections on their common revolutionary journey. The chapter shares vivid details of daily life in Yunnan and Burma, showing how family backgrounds and pragmatic considerations shaped key decisions, and how individual believers in Mao's China contributed to the making (and unmaking) of the Cold War world on the ground.

Chapter 11, Mary Grace R. Concepcion's "Afterlife of Cold War Memories: Familial Transmission of Martial Law–Era Memories in the Post–Cold War Philippines," turns our eyes toward the contemporary Philippines, exploring the shaping and transmission of memories concerning the Martial Law era in the 1970s and 1980s. The focus, however, is not on conventional venues of memory production, such as mass media, museums, education, or cultural productions; rather, the chapter looks into a much more intimate venue of memory production: family. Based on oral history interviews, it examines how memories of the Martial Law era under the Marcos regime were transmitted from former activist parents to their children, how such memories were received by those activists' children who do not have their own memories of the era, and how such memories have functioned in their lives and in Philippine society afterwards. In the end, the chapter discusses why such memories of the Cold War still matter today.

Chapter 12, "Letter to Granddad: Tracing the Life of a Leftist during the Malayan Emergency, 1948–60," is an exceptional one, as it is just an 1,800-word epistolary note. In this imagined letter, Sim Chi Yin introduces her decade-long journey through southern China, Hong Kong, Malaysia, Thailand, and Singapore to retrace the footprints of her grandfather, whose life her family avoided talking about for over six decades. It gives a glimpse of her grandfather's life and family trauma, as well as the family's amnesia concerning him, and her attempt to recover forgotten family history. This text, usually read out as a performance lecture by Sim, is also the basis of a theater performance she is making.[17]

In the final section, Alan McPherson, Taomo Zhou, and David C. Engerman share their broader points of view, reflecting on the meanings and implications of these chapters, and discussing possible ways to reconsider histories of Cold War Asia, the Cold War, and, more broadly, the twentieth century in general.

Five Suggestions

While each author has a different viewpoint, as this is an anthology, I have five overall suggestions for reconceptualizing the Cold War. The first is to use "social warfare" as a category of analysis. While we have been accustomed to view the second half of the twentieth century through Cold War and/or decolonization frameworks, various conflicts and tensions have been obscured under the standard narratives of the Cold War and decolonization. This emphasis differs chapter by chapter, but this book, overall, looks into social tensions and conflicts, as well as ordinary people's disagreements among themselves, which in many cases evolved underneath the banners of the Cold War. What we are hoping for is to analyze various kinds of social warfare on the ground, and to think about what was shared among them even as they appeared completely irrelevant to one another at a glance. Then, based on such observation and analysis of many cases, we should be able to reconsider what the essence of the phenomenon we call the Cold War was.

In doing so, we can go beyond Matthew Connelly's important suggestion in 2000 to "take off the Cold War lens."[18] While many scholars followed this call, what we saw tended to be stories of anticolonial struggles and decolonization processes, often with emphases on local elites' efforts, which went more or less nicely along the lines of respective countries' national histories. To go beyond such an impasse, thus, we need to accept that it is not enough just to take off the Cold War lens. More important is what we look at and how we approach it afterwards. In other words, what we suggest in this book is not simply to replace the stories of the Cold War with those of decolonization, but to more carefully and consciously look at what is going on in societies and among people. That is why we are advocating the use of social warfare as a category of analysis, and that is why this book emphasizes the importance and usefulness of an oral history approach, asking questions such as, In what ways did ordinary people observe, appropriate, and even take advantage of Cold War situations? What kinds of emotions—hope, fear, irritation, and so on—were carried through in the form of Cold War ideologies and logics? In order to examine these points, we need to ask people who witnessed and experienced the era.

And that is the second suggestion: that is, to pay more attention to ordinary people's emotions—hopes and dreams, fears and irritations—as well as their everyday struggles and various choices. To be sure, we have a lot of literature that focuses on how the Cold War impacted ordinary people's lives and their ways of thinking. However, such studies have tended to describe ordinary people as mere recipients of given situations, rather than as creators of such situations. Likewise, we have quite a lot of literature that deals with the roles played by ideology and propaganda. But in these studies, too, ordinary people are often absent, or described merely as recipients of such ideology and propaganda. But wasn't it ordinary people's emotive support that brought ideology and propaganda alive? Wasn't it ordinary people who made them appealing and impactful through their choices to follow them? That's why our project emphasizes the importance and usefulness of an oral history approach, asking, What kinds of emotions were carried through in the form of ideology, whether communist or anticommunist? What was actually being fought over among grassroots populations in the name of the Cold War?

In saying "ordinary people," we do not limit the term to describing those who were leftist or progressive. Nor do we limit it to those who were oppressed or victimized in societies, or those who heroically resisted and fought against state powers. While we do include these kinds of people, we are even more interested in the voices of "ordinary people" who tended to be the majorities in societies, who often cooperated with states in the making or recovery of social order, and who often became perpetrators, rather than victims, in suppressing and silencing minorities' demands and challenges.[19] As we can see in Imam Muhtarom's chapter, for instance, some of those interviewed were even killers themselves (who appear in his chapter under pseudonyms), as well as those who took advantage of Cold War logics.

If these first two suggestions are about reconsideration of analytical categories and primary objects of research, my third is about how to approach them. What I'm suggesting through examining social warfare and ordinary people is to explore what was happening on the ground in the name of the Cold War and, based on such observation and analysis of many cases, to reconsider what was the essence of the phenomenon we call the Cold War. Thus, my third suggestion is to consciously use this kind of approach—an *inductive*, as opposed to *deductive* analysis—to the Cold War world. Some might feel puzzled since, generally speaking, almost all historians, with the exception of hardcore Marxists, usually use inductive reasoning.

And yet, if we look at the Cold War world and the literature on it, what we may call Cold War deduction is everywhere. One typical example is the permeation of Cold War categorical thinking since the time of the Cold War and even today. This way of thinking maintains that the world was divided into two camps in the post–World War II period, that there was a rise of communist parties in, say, India or Japan or Indonesia, and that members of those parties had to be communists working for the purposes of Moscow. This type of categorical thinking that ignores local situations and historical contexts has appeared almost everywhere, whether in Japan or China, Thailand or the Philippines, Indonesia or India.

Another type of Cold War deduction can be seen in the literature of what I have called the "Cold War as weather" approach. After all, many studies have positioned themselves with a particular mindset to find elements of the Cold War in society, culture, and ordinary people's everyday lives, and, of course, they can find such things. But what's missing are things considered irrelevant to the Cold War by those studies. What I'd like to suggest, therefore, is to consciously avoid such Cold War deductive mindsets and, through numerous oral history projects, to explore what was actually going on and what was actually being fought over among populations in the name of the Cold War. In doing so, thus, we can reconsider inductively what the essence of the phenomenon we call the Cold War was.

Thinking about the three suggestions I have discussed—namely, the focus on social warfare and ordinary people's emotions, and an inductive approach—some would assume that the project's primary aim is to look at locally specific and contrasting realities in Asia, as Heonik Kwon astutely advocated in 2010.[20] That's basically correct, and that's what we're doing. But our ultimate aim is not just concerned with detailing and specifying local situations in order to argue that Asia had different experiences of the Cold War. Rather, the book's primary aim is to use Asia as a method for unlearning conventional Cold War narratives and reconceptualizing the Cold War world itself, which is my fourth suggestion.

For this kind of analysis that regards Asia as a method, I would suggest using the framework of "Cold War Asia" (or "Cold War Thailand," etc.), rather than that of "the Cold War *in* Asia" (or "the Cold War *in* Thailand," etc.). This is because, when we use the framework of "the Cold War in Asia," we tend to depict the Cold War as weather and cannot, therefore, raise fundamental questions about its nature. Moreover, when we use the "Cold War *in* Asia" framework, we tend to seek for local specificities, which were supposedly different from the "original" version of the Cold War in the Western world. The danger is that, in doing so, we actually help maintain the conventional, "original" version of the Cold War in the Western world, while simply adding the supplemental information that Asia had different experiences.

Analysis of "Cold War Asia" can still leave space for reconsideration of its adjective ("Cold War"). In taking this approach, we can still discuss the point that the issues that mattered most for many people might have had less to do with the global US-USSR confrontation than with social, cultural, and individual struggles at home. In fact, this is the point that reveals a parallel to what Alan McPherson has called a paradox in Latin American Cold War studies: "The more historians find out about the Cold War in the hemisphere, the more the Cold War itself fades to the background."[21] In this way, "Cold War Asia" as a method can open a path toward comparative and global analysis in the reconsideration of, for instance, "Cold War Latin America," "Cold War America," and the "Cold War world" in general.

Last but not least is a crucial issue concerning the oral history approach itself, which directly involves the politics of memories. To be sure, many people remember the past in ways they want to. The shape of memories will change depending on contemporary political and social situations. Thus, a question might arise concerning how reliable they are as historical sources. However, I don't think these issues, in themselves, should hinder the use of an oral history approach. To begin with, without collecting considerable quantities of voices and memories, we cannot even begin discussing the politics of memories. Much more fundamentally, the nature of oral history as something based on a shaky ground is actually a good reminder for us that any kind of history is, after all, a hypothesis, a transitional attempt based on limited and fragmented sources.

And this is actually my fifth suggestion: that perhaps we can simply accept this. In saying this, I intend to maintain a distance from two major tendencies in the fields of memories studies and historical studies that concern issues with memories. One approach is an earlier depiction of memory as being something "genuine" but buried under official and text-based history, claiming the need to rescue memory from history. Another approach is more like a historians' counteroffensive, pointing out the precarious and nebulous nature of memory, and arguing for the need to save history from memory. Although these approaches might appear to be in conflict, they are actually in agreement in the sense that they share a positivist view that they can reach truth, a conclusion, whether through the line of memory or history. However, do we really need to choose either stance? Probably not. There is nothing wrong with accepting and being self-conscious about the nature of history as fragmented, transitional, and hypothetical.

And we do not need to lament this recognition as a sad sign of relativism. Rather I would like to see it as a sign of what historians can do today in the age of relativism and in this age of backlash against it. What we have been doing, in a sense, is to relativize the importance of Cold War narratives in post–World War II history and try to look at the socially constructed nature of the political world through examining social warfare and ordinary people's everyday struggles. In other words, it has been an attempt to think about the roles of imagination in the construction of social reality and the needs and functions of such "reality" on the ground and among people. In this process—which can be termed the process of learning and unlearning of Cold War histories—what I have come to notice is a dangerous function of "history": that is, to simplify complex situations, to shorten lengthy stories, and to offer it all as a digestible package. In other words, at worst, once spread widely among the large portion of populations, any "reality" or "history" can function as a social device to block people from thinking further through providing easy answers.

This awareness is important because it helps us to be sensitive and careful about the imagined and constructed nature of our reality and our history, and its social functions in our world, today. In other words, what I would suggest is that, instead of trying to fight the tide of relativism, we might be able to actually incorporate it in order to foster individuals who can observe and think for themselves in the oceans of information, without simply believing in dominant and authoritative narratives. And that's the ability we really need in this age of relativism, and in this age of fake news. In that sense, I believe that our oral history project, with its diverse set of individuals in a wide political spectrum, will be a valuable repository of encouragements, as well as alarms, for people today.

Finally, I should discuss how our studies relate to emotions history, which itself has been a thriving field, particularly since the early 2000s. To be honest, however, when I began thinking about this project back in 2016—perhaps the peak period of the so-called emotional turn in the discipline of history—I did not see it as particularly relevant to our work. The "emotional turn" seemed distant from it, I thought initially, because much such work focuses on theoretical and methodological debates on what emotions are, whether they are universal or socially constructed, and so forth, without much looking into actual people's conduct and emotions on the ground.

Nevertheless, while preparing and setting up our online archive of oral history collections that are full of ordinary people's everyday feelings and conduct, and while discussing and reading each contributor's chapters and Taomo Zhou's insightful reflection essay, I have come to think that our work aiming at unlearning conventional Cold War narratives and reconceptualizing the meanings of the Cold War actually shares a great deal of awareness with emotions history. After all, we too are trying to move away from dominant understandings of the Cold War as essentially a product of reason and rationality, whether as a result of realpolitik, ideology, or class struggle.

Instead, as I have done in my previous work, our work takes a serious view of the roles played by emotions across Cold War Asia, as in the cases of, for example, Lao people's indignation at the destabilization of social harmony, and Indonesians' anger about disruption of gender norms. We also show how such emotions were often expressed and utilized through Cold War rhetoric, and how the ways in which such emotions were expressed differed depending on time and political regimes.

Therefore, if I am allowed to boost the significance of our project, I can say that we are already ahead of the "emotional turn." In a sense, we are actually *doing* emotions history, though not in the sense of tracing a history of particular emotions over time, but through incorporating diverse emotions as an indispensable element in the histories of the Cold War and twentieth century in general. This book, thus, coincidentally becomes a response to one prominent emotions history scholar's recent lament: "If there is currently a deficiency in the field [of the history of emotions], it is in the lack of empirical works that substantiate the stated aims of the field's ancients."[22] With empirically rich and substantial accounts, and incorporating ordinary people's emotions, this is a book that not only is about Cold War history and Asian history, but exemplifies emotions history at work.

Notes

1. For discussion of recent Cold War historiography, see, for example, Masuda Hajimu, "The Early Cold War: Studies of Cold War America in the Twenty-First Century," in *A Companion to U.S. Foreign Relations: Colonial Era to the Present*, ed. Christopher R. W. Dietrich (Hoboken, NJ: Wiley Blackwell, 2020), 2:632–51. For earlier historiographical discussions, see, for instance, Odd Arne Westad, *Reviewing the Cold War: Approaches, Interpretations, and Theory* (London: Frank Cass, 2000);

and Rana Mitter and Patrick Major, eds., *Across the Blocs: Cold War Cultural and Social History* (London: Frank Cass, 2004).

2. The Cold War International History Project (CWIHP) at the Woodrow Wilson Center, first led by James G. Hershberg and then by Christian F. Ostermann, has played a particularly important role in collecting and releasing a massive amount of formerly unavailable documents from the "other" side of the Cold War since the 1990s.

3. For more detail, see Masuda, "Early Cold War." For earlier discussions on the cultural turn, see, for example, Christian G. Appy, *Cold War Constructions: The Political Culture of United States Imperialism, 1945-1966* (Amherst, MA: University of Massachusetts Press, 2000); and Joel Isaac and Duncan Bell, *Uncertain Empire: American History and the Idea of the Cold War* (New York: Oxford University Press, 2012).

4. Andrew Johnstone, "Before the Water's Edge: Domestic Politics and U.S. Foreign Relations," *Passport* 45, no.3 (2015): 25-29.

5. See, for instance, Fredrik Logevall, "A Critique of Containment," *Diplomatic History* 28, no. 4 (2004): 473-99; and Campbell Craig and Fredrik Logevall, *America's Cold War: The Politics of Insecurity* (Cambridge, MA: Belknap Press, 2009).

6. See, for instance, Gilbert M. Joseph and Daniela Spenser, *In from the Cold: Latin America's New Encounter with the Cold War* (Durham, NC: Duke University Press, 2008); Greg Grandin and Gilbert M. Joseph, *A Century of Revolution: Insurgent and Counterinsurgent Violence during Latin America's Long Cold War* (Durham, NC: Duke University Press, 2010); and Virginia Garrard-Burnett, Mark Atwood Lawrence, and Julio E. Moreno, *Beyond the Eagle's Shadow: New Histories of Latin America's Cold War* (Albuquerque: University of New Mexico Press, 2013). For the similar but much broader "decolonization turn" literature, see, for instance, Christopher E. Goscha and Christian Ostermann, *Connecting Histories: Decolonization and the Cold War in Southeast Asia* (Stanford, CA: Stanford University Press, 2009); and Leslie James and Elisabeth Leake, *Decolonization and the Cold War: Negotiating Independence* (London: Bloomsbury, 2015).

7. Odd Arne Westad, *The Cold War: A History* (New York: Basic Books, 2017).

8. See, for instance, Matthew Connelly, "Taking Off the Cold War Lens: Visions of North-South Conflict during the Algerian War for Independence," *American Historical Review* 105, no. 3 (2000): 739-69; Nick Cullather, *The Hungry World: America's Cold War Battle against Poverty in Asia* (Cambridge, MA: Harvard University Press, 2010); Heonik Kwon, *The Other Cold War* (New York: Columbia University Press, 2010); and Masuda Hajimu, *Cold War Crucible: The Korean Conflict and the Postwar World* (Cambridge, MA: Harvard University Press, 2015), respectively.

9. Ang Cheng Guan, *Southeast Asia's Cold War: An Interpretive History* (Honolulu: University of Hawai'i Press, 2018); and Goscha and Ostermann, *Connecting Histories*.

10. Such literature includes Tuong Vu and Wasana Wongsurawat, *Dynamics of the Cold War in Asia: Ideology, Identity, and Culture* (New York: Palgrave Macmillan, 2009); Zheng Yangwen, Hong Liu, and Michael Szonyi, *The Cold War in Asia: The Battle for Hearts and Minds* (Boston: Brill, 2010); and Tsuyoshi Hasegawa, *The Cold War in East Asia, 1945-1991* (Stanford, CA: Stanford University Press, 2011). These

studies generally assume the "Cold War as weather" approach, searching for a regional development and variation of the Cold War in Asia, as opposed to our attempt to use Cold War Asia as a method to reconsider the Cold War itself. Also, none of these studies examine ordinary people's experiences. The only exception that attempts to challenge conventional Cold War narratives is Jadwiga E. Pieper Mooney and Fabio Lanza, *De-centering Cold War History: Local and Global Change* (New York: Routledge, 2013). While not solely focusing on Asia, *De-centering Cold War History* shares a fundamental interest with us in the sense that it challenges Cold War master narratives that focus on superpower politics by shedding light on local-level experiences and regional initiatives that were crucial to the making of a Cold War world. However, the book discusses Asia only in passing (three chapters out of ten deal with Asia), and it does not intend to raise a fundamental question concerning the very nature of the Cold War, as we will in our book. Therefore, although there is no shortage of books on the Cold War, there is no history of the Cold War that looks into ordinary people's grassroots experiences and raises a fundamental question concerning the very nature of the Cold War. In this volume, while we do have chapters that deal with topics concerning China and Japan, it is true that we do not have chapters on Korea and Taiwan and instead focus more on South and Southeast Asia, specifically Indonesia, Thailand, Laos, Vietnam, Malaya, the Philippines, East Timor, and India. The reason for this choice is a historiographical one. Simply put, there have been quite a few studies concerning the Cold War in East Asia, while not much work has focused on South and Southeast Asia, at least not until recently. Thus, we put relatively heavier weight on areas which have received relatively less attention.

11. Fortunately, there have been a series of publications that challenge such conventional trends. See, for example, Zach Fredman, *The Tormented Alliance: American Servicemen and the Occupation of China, 1941–1949* (Chapel Hill: University of North Carolina Press, 2022); and Brian Cuddy and Fredrik Logevall, *The Vietnam War in the Pacific World* (Chapel Hill: University of North Carolina Press, 2022).

12. Nehring, "What Was the Cold War?" *English Historical Review* 127:527 (2012), 923.

13. Romero, "Cold War Historiography at the Crossroads," *Cold War History* 14:4 (2014), 685–703.

14. The research was supported by an Academic Research Fund Tier 2 grant (MOE2018-T2-1-138). In 2022, we launched an online archive of oral history collections at https://rcw-asia.com/. Currently, we have uploaded more than two hundred oral history interview transcripts in English translation (as well as in the original languages, in some cases).

15. For detailed discussions on the meanings of the oral history approach itself, see Robert Perks and Alistair Thomson, *The Oral History Reader*, 3rd ed. (New York: Routledge, 2016); and Paul Richard Thompson and Joanna Bornat, *The Voice of the Past: Oral History*, 4th ed. (New York: Oxford University Press, 2017).

16. See chapter 6 in this volume: Kisho Tsuchiya, "Theorizing Southeast Asia's Cold War: Timor in 1974–1975"; also see Masuda Hajimu and Sidnei Munhoz, "Many Cold Wars: Re-conceptualizing the Post–WWII World," *Esboços* 23, no. 36 (2017).

17. Video documentation of Sim's performance lecture at the Asia Art Archive in America, in December 2022, is available at https://www.aaa-a.org/programs/sim-chi-yin-methods-of-memory-time-travels-in-the-archives.

18. Connelly, "Cold War Lens," 739–69.

19. For discussions of such "ordinary people," see, for example, Yoshiaki Yoshimi, *Grassroots Fascism: The War Experience of the Japanese People*, trans. Ethan Mark (New York: Columbia University Press, 2015); Robert Gellately, *Backing Hitler: Consent and Coercion in Nazi Germany* (New York: Oxford University Press, 2001); and Wendy Z. Goldman, *Terror and Democracy in the Age of Stalin: The Social Dynamics of Repression* (New York: Cambridge University Press, 2007).

20. Kwon, *Other Cold War*, 6–7.

21. Garrard-Burnett, Lawrence, and Moreno, *Beyond the Eagle's Shadow*, 307.

22. Rob Boddice, *The History of Emotions* (Manchester: Manchester University Press, 2017), 217.

Part I **Social Warfare**

1 Terror in East Java
The NU versus PKI Conflict before
and after September 30, 1965

IMAM MUHTAROM

The Indonesian Mass Killings of 1965–66 was the bloodiest series of events that ever occurred in Indonesia. In this historical massacre, which evolved quickly following the failed coup in Jakarta on September 30, 1965, that resulted in the murder of six anticommunist Indonesian generals, as well as General Suharto's swift countercoup and rise to power, more than 500,000 (and possibly more than one million) people were killed without trial.[1] Those massacred included members of *Partai Komunis Indonesia* (hereafter PKI; Communist Party of Indonesia), as well as those of various leftist organizations that were considered to be affiliated or sharing ideological inclinations with the PKI—namely, *Barisan Tani Indonesia* (hereafter BTI; Indonesian Peasant's Front), *Gerakan Wanita Indonesia* (hereafter Gerwani; Indonesian Women's Movement), *Pemuda Rakyat* (People's Youth), *Lembaga Kesenian Rakyat* (hereafter Lekra; Institute of People's Culture), and *Sentral Organisasi Buruh Seluruh Indonesia* (hereafter SOBSI; Central Organization of Indonesian Workers).

These killings were carried out by the army, as well as by members of civilian militias, such as *Partai Nasional Indonesia* (hereafter PNI; Nationalist Party of Indonesia), as well as *Nahdlatul Ulama* (hereafter NU; Revival of the Ulama)—the largest Islamic organization in Indonesia.[2] The highest numbers of casualties were seen in Central Java and East Java Provinces. This was not only because of the dense population of Java and the relative success of the PKI in this region in previous elections.[3] Much more importantly, there was a pattern of systematic massacres that involved the high command of the army in Jakarta, regional army commanders, noncommunist parties, and right-wing mass organizations.[4] Such a pattern of cooperation between the army and right-wing civilian organizations in massacring communists and communist sympathizers was clearly seen in East Java's Blitar Regency, and particularly in the Siwi subdistrict, as we will see in detail below. In this area, the NU right-wing organization, together with the military, attacked and massacred members of the PKI and other organizations that were considered to be affiliated with the PKI, following the failed coup and General Suharto's swift countercoup.

What we need to keep in mind, however, is that portents of such violence appeared long before the eruption of the bloody events following September 30, 1965. As a matter of fact, the relationship between the PKI (and its affiliated organizations) and the NU had been already deteriorating in many senses. Even in rural areas of the Siwi subdistrict, these two groups had been increasingly hostile to one another, chiefly concerning issues of mass struggles, land ownership, and the production sharing system between poor peasants and rice field owners. These problems brought hope and anxiety simultaneously to the people of this region amid a feud between the PKI and NU groups. Hope was held among the large segment of peasants and small farmers who joined and sympathized with the PKI. They believed that there would be change for the betterment of their lives, both socially and economically. At the same time, anxiety and anger were common among the segment of landlords and others who tended to be Islamic members of the NU group. They were concerned about the PKI's blasphemy toward the God they respected. These problems led these two groups to a sharp conflict, eventually touching off massacres of PKI members and their affiliates, often conducted by NU groups' adherents. Thus, while recent English-language scholarship tends to focus on the roles played by the Indonesian army, there is a possibility to go beyond existing analyses and explore further.[5]

Focusing on the villages of the southern region of the Siwi subdistrict, this chapter examines the evolution of the PKI's conflict with the NU before and after September 30, 1965. It shows that the PKI-NU conflict was highly complex, that its roots were deeply local, and that the issue was not just a reflection of superpowers' power politics, nor an ideological conflict between communists and anticommunists, even though it could not be separated completely from an ideological framework. This chapter argues that the conflict occurred not just between the army and the PKI but also among social groups in these villages, and that it involved local and historical contentions among those social groups, concerning, for example, religion, economic inequality, and gender relationships. In a sense, the 1965–66 conflict can be seen as a culmination of what Masuda Hajimu calls "social warfare." While it was fought under "anticommunist" and "communist" banners, with the NU and its affiliates on the one hand, and PKI and their affiliates on the other, the crux of the matter was ordinary people's disagreements. As we will see below, such divisions deepened at every religious lecture held by the NU, and at every opening remark at art performances held by Lekra. The culmination of such disagreements was the tragedy after September 30, 1965, in which dozens of people were killed in southern Siwi and tens of thousands across Indonesia.

In this way, this chapter makes use of Masuda's idea regarding reconceptualization of the Cold War, which suggests that discussions of Cold War politics cannot be confined solely within the narrow framework of policy and diplomacy analysis, and that such discussions should incorporate analysis of ordinary people who made Cold War discourses alive and meaningful, and who made the Cold War world real and irrefutable even while geographically living far from the centers of Cold War politics.[6] The chapter utilizes oral history sources in addition to more traditional primary and secondary sources. In obtaining oral history data, I have conducted interviews with people currently living in rural areas of south Siwi who directly experienced the terror in this area following September 30, 1965.[7]

South Siwi Before 1965: Social and Historical Background

Villages in south Siwi had been within the influence of Javanese culture. The first generations of people who came to the area in large numbers were migrants from Central Java, particularly from the Yogyakarta and Kedu areas, which were then centers of Javanese culture under the Kingdom of Yogyakarta and the Kingdom of Solo.[8] These migrants were said to have moved from Central to East Java after their defeat in the Java War (1825-30) by Dutch colonial troops.[9] In terms of religion, these Javanese people were Muslims but practiced a syncretic version of Islam. They had great respect for their ancestors because they believed in ancestors as figures who would help them to find the way to salvation in the afterlife.[10] Since ancestors were believed to play a role in this world, too, the Javanese people attached great importance to various kinds of rituals and performances concerning the day of birth, circumcision, marriage, and the death of family members, as well as harvest and planting, building houses, and digging wells.[11] In short, almost all activities in a life cycle required rituals. As we will see below, they also enjoyed and took a serious view of performing arts in the form of shadow puppets, man puppets, *jaranan* (dances), and *ludruk* (traditional plays), all of which were not just entertainment but contained elements of ritual.

The majority of the rural population in south Siwi engaged in farming, and they could be classified into three groups: peasants without paddy fields, small farmers with little pieces of land for their own farming, and landlords whose vast fields were cultivated by other poor peasants. The first two groups greatly outnumbered the last one. Peasants' lives in rural south Siwi from the 1940s to 1960s remained largely poor and underdeveloped, since, at that time, the rice harvest was only once a year.[12] There were no factory-produced chemical fertilizers that could be used. Their daily diet was coarse fare, such as bulgur, which was considered a type of meal for horses. The rice they harvested was not for them to eat every day because it was for sale to make money for buying the cheaper, coarse fare. Such conditions of poverty had continued in south Siwi from the Dutch colonial period to the World War II era, as well as from the post–World War II period until the early 1960s.

This is why the rural population welcomed the PKI. Many thought that the PKI cared about the problems faced by the large segment of peasants. It was already present in Siwi at the time of the Dutch military aggression in 1947, and it joined in the national struggle to expel the Dutch from Siwi.[13] After the liberation war, the PKI emphasized programs that were in line with problems faced by rural residents in south Siwi, the majority of whom were poor worker peasants.[14] One of the greatest burdens imposed on south Siwi peasants was the *mertelu* system, which was a traditional agreement between peasants and rice field landlords. Under this system, rice field owners got two-thirds of the yield, while peasants got only one-third. Much worse, production costs were borne by peasants, while landowners contributed only fertilizers.[15] In other words, all costs of seedlings, cultivating the land, caring for rice plants, irrigation, and harvesting were borne by the peasants themselves. One oral history interviewee recalled the problems many peasants faced in Jambeng village and its surroundings: "Peasants were often cheated. Some peasants were loaned hulled rice when it was wet and asked to return it with the dry grain. However, even though both were one quintal, the yield and the money would be different, when the grain was dry or wet. This kind of fraud was carried out by landlords to their peasants. Thus, peasants suffered more and more."[16]

In fact, the need for agrarian reform had been one of the greatest concerns of the government for more than a decade since the independence of Indonesia was declared in 1945. The state's efforts seemed to be bearing fruit in 1960 when President Sukarno passed two agrarian reform–related laws— *Undang-Undang Bagi Hasil* (UUBH; Production Sharing Law) and *Undang-Undang Pokok Agraria* (UUPA; Basic Agrarian Law). The former aimed to regulate agreements between landlords and peasants, while the latter aimed to regulate the ownership of agricultural land, both under terms favorable to peasants. These were long-awaited laws that were designed to improve the economic situation of peasants and small farmers.

Keeping in step with these government programs, the PKI's efforts to defend peasants' interests became more visible than ever in the early 1960s. While the PKI had been actively incorporating peasants and small farmers since its reorganization in 1951 under the leadership of D. N. Aidit, the party further made the issue of agriculture its main priority in 1960, with a simple, eye-catching slogan: "Land for peasants." Along this line, the party and its affiliated organization, Barisan Tani Indonesia, began promoting the implementation of the Production Sharing Law in every region where the BTI was influential.[17] As we will see below, however, such efforts triggered social tensions—and the escalation of PKI-NU conflicts, in the end—because the interests of peasants and small farmers that the PKI was determined to promote were in direct confront with those of landlords, who tended to be adherents of the NU and PNI groups.

That said, such a rise of social tensions in the first half of the 1960s was not preordained, nor was the eventual PKI-NU conflict, let alone the mass killings of PKI members and sympathizers in 1965, doomed to happen. In fact, while PKI and NU groups' members increasingly insulted each other *within* their own internal meetings and activities, once outside their organizations, they lived together, exchanged greetings as usual, and continued to respect their neighboring lives. An example of such mutual respect can be seen among the youth members of the PKI-affiliated Pemuda Rakyat, the NU-affiliated Islamic youth organization *Ansor* (The Helpers), and the PNI's youth organization, *Pemuda Marhaen* (Marhaen's Youth), when all were serving as members of the *Hansip* (*Pertahanan Sipil*; Civilian Defense Guards) in their own villages. In Hansip units—that is, auxiliary units of the Indonesian military at the village level—all members wore the same uniform, and there were few disputes over politics or ideology.[18] Such mutual respect was shown among the three organizations when they worked together in cleaning their streets and villages under the banner of Nasakom programs, as well.[19]

This was possible because many people still retained a sense of community as members of one culture, namely that of Java, sharing Javanese customs and traditions, despite disagreements over politics and ideology. Let us look at an example to see how Javanese cultural customs and rituals transcended political disputes. In Degan hamlet, Gajo village, there was a custom among villagers of visiting their elder, Sani, a sort of shaman, when they faced difficulties involving work or health. Sani welcomed such villagers and prayed for them. Then, the villager usually gave him sugar or a little money as an expression of gratitude. In the neighborhood of south Siwi, Sani had been known as an NU figure. However, he continued to help villagers who asked for help, regardless of his political stance against the PKI. In short, villagers might have different opinions with different political affiliations, but they shared a sense of community in terms of Javanese culture. As such, ridicule and contempt due to the differences in political stances were dampened by this traditional relationship, at least until 1965. Then, how did such coexistence collapse, and why?

Social and Cultural Tensions

One significant reason for the deterioration of the PKI-NU relationship involved the PKI's (and its affiliated BTI's) aggressive strategy of unilaterally occupying rice fields belonging to the rich and forcefully implementing the Basic Agrarian Law and Production Sharing Law of 1960 in the countryside—practices known as "unilateral actions." Such actions were, at least partly, expressions of peasants' and small farmers' disappointment with the slow pace of the implementation of the two agrarian laws. The problem was that, while they were enacted in 1960, those laws were not implemented for years at the village level.[20] Such a delay prompted peasants to implement the laws themselves, with the support of the PKI and BTI. With such "unilateral actions," the PKI and BTI secured a foothold in the hearts of rural communities. However, these actions generated resentment among wealthy rice field owners who were opposed to the implementation of the new agrarian laws.[21] In this way, the PKI's "unilateral actions" immediately touched off physical confrontations between peasants supported by the PKI and BTI, on the one hand, and landlords who had been supported by NU-affiliated organizations, such as Ansor and its multipurpose brigade, Banser (*Barisan Ansor Serbaguna*; Ansor Multi-Purpose Brigade), on the other.

The unilateral actions took place in all villages in south Siwi. In Soro village, for instance, approximately twenty-five peasants, supported by the PKI, the BTI, and Pemuda Rakyat, took part in an action in village landlord Haji Tengas's rice fields. These peasants came from the same village's Mentaraman hamlet, led by a local PKI member named Iwak. NU-affiliated Ansor members were present to monitor the peasants' unilateral action.[22] A similar action took place in Gajo village's Bere hamlet. In this case, peasants, as well as the PKI and its affiliated groups' members, forcibly harvested a crop of yellow rice. Knowing about PKI groups' planning of unilateral action beforehand, Ansor members were on alert, gathering from not just neighboring areas but faraway subdistricts. On this occasion, Ansor and Banser members let the PKI groups carry out the forcible rice harvesting, waiting for the proper time for a counterattack. They waited for the harvesting work to be done and, thus, watched peasants cutting the rice stalks, knocking off the rice seeds, and lifting rice sacks to the side of the road. Ansor and Banser members, led by a man named Sarjoti, attacked when a pile of rice bags was neatly arranged on the roadside to be transported. (The peasants conducted their unilateral action far from accessible roads for bicycles or carts.) On being suddenly raided, the peasants and their supporters ran away. The crops on the roadside were then taken back to the owner of the rice fields.[23]

In the same village's Degan hamlet, peasants and their supporters took a similar unilateral action by forcibly harvesting a crop of yellow rice. The rice field belonged to a landlord named Sino, and was located on the north side of the current Degan hamlet mosque. In this case, too, the action was conducted by both local PKI members and those coming from faraway subdistricts. Observing this, Ansor members were angry. All Ansor members in the Siwi area were deployed to repel the unilateral action, and eventually they succeeded.[24] Members of the NU, as well as Ansor and Banser, insisted that the unilateral actions promoted by the PKI, the BTI, and Pemuda Rakyat were wrong, because they were inappropriate acts of breaking the property rights of others, violating the order and morality of religion and state.[25]

Apart from such unilateral actions in rural villages, another kind of activity that sowed seeds of discord between PKI and NU groups was *ludruk* performances—traditional stage performances that focused on everyday people's life stories and struggles. What angered the NU group were plays that were adopted on the ludruk stage, with titles such as *Lahire Gustiallah* (Birth of God), *Matine Gustiallah* (Death of God), and *Gustiallah Mantu* (God performs marriage).[26] NU members were outraged and felt humiliated by such performances in which the God they glorified was trampled. This anger later provided a strong justification for the NU groups' massacre of PKI-affiliated people.

Seeing the rapid growth of the PKI and its affiliated organizations in Siwi, members of NU groups did not remain silent. To compete with these performances organized by Lekra and Pemuda Rakyat, NU groups developed a performing arts group called *Lesbumi* (*Lembaga Seni-Budaya Muslim*

Indonesia; Indonesian Moslem Art-Culture Institute), which was intended to convey Islamic teachings. Lesbumi performed a drama called *Tablo*. One interviewee, Sudi Subidi, who was a chairman of the Lesbumi in Siwi subdistrict, recalled, "The story is the history of the prophet, the history of the traces of *khulafaur rashidin* (four friends of the prophet), the traces of the heroes of Islam. The goal is to include faith [Islam] through art. The history of the prophet, the history of Islamic heroes such as Umar bin Khattab, Teuku Umar. Yes, it was like ludruk, but the play is about Islamic heroes."[27]

Such performances of *Tablo*, together with the orchestra, martial arts, and *hadrah* and *dangdut* dance and music performances, which were all modified in line with Islamic teachings, were expressions of NU members' souls' callings against the perceived insults launched by the PKI. They were intended to counteract the influence of communist ideology. NU groups' members voluntarily participated in the performing arts as well as joining in confrontational actions in the fields to counter unilateral actions launched by PKI groups. They did not want their followers, particularly the youth, to be influenced by PKI groups' dazzling art performances.

There was, in fact, a reason for such concerns. One interviewee, Sudi Subidi, recalled a certain "lure" that PKI's Lekra had for the youth. He said that the young people of south Siwi villages often joined Lekra just because they liked a sense of "freedom" when gathering and practicing art performances. Among NU members, men and women who were not married couples could not gather freely. In performing arts supported by Lekra, however, men and women could mingle in one place without being separated—a sort of freedom that could not be found in NU groups' performances and gatherings.[28] Thus, NU members thought that those who joined Lekra's performances were improperly escaping the constraints of social and gender norms.

Among the youth, such a slight difference in everyday lives could lead to serious antagonism, including even fierce fistfights between members of PKI and NU groups. In particular, when the issue involved a male-female relationship, such hostility built up quickly because NU youth members did not want to accept "their" girls being flirted with and teased by PKI youths from neighboring villages. One NU member, Sarjoti, who liked fighting and led such an attack, recollected that he even visited Soro village's young men from PKI families, warning them not to try to seduce teenage girls from his village, with his sickles in his hands. He recalled that he did not hesitate to stop PKI kids riding bicycles through his village to spit on their faces.[29]

Such disputes between NU and PKI groups flared up and became increasingly uncontrollable when PKI members trampled, or at least were believed to trample, upon a Koran on a martial arts performing stage. An NU member, Sarjoti of Tegala village in north Siwi, insisted that he still remembered this as an incident that angered NU youth members who were there. Unable to endure this anymore, they brought coffins, meaning that they challenged PKI youth to compete in martial arts to the death on the stage.[30]

That said, one interviewee, Towi, a member of Lekra, denied the allegation that their performances had insulted Islamic beliefs, saying that he never saw such an insulting ludruk staged. Three other interviewees—Simas Langun, the director of ludruk in Jambeng village, as well as Milan and Fiyoso, both leftist sympathizers—also said that no such ludruk was staged. Milan even stated that such an allegation was just a groundless trick created by the winning party for the purpose of bringing down the defeated communist groups.[31]

Whether true or not, however, members of the NU group firmly believed at that time and since that there were ludruk performances that insulted their God. Based on this view, these plays (or the notion of such plays) served as a catalyst for NU members to stand up against the insult to their religion and defend their beliefs. By the climax of the NU's conflict with the PKI, NU members increasingly considered it a jihad to defend their religion. Therefore, the killing of the enemy, namely PKI members, was increasingly considered to be legitimate.

With such enmity as a backdrop, in the villages of the south Siwi area before the September 30, 1965 coup, insults between members of PKI and NU groups escalated through activities such as lectures, internal meetings, and art performances.[32] Both PKI and NU groups simply praised themselves, while slandering the opposing side; NU groups, for instance, praised only Islamic teachings, while PKI groups praised only leftist teachings and Sukarno's leadership.[33] To be sure, as noted above, such mutual insults initially tended to happen only within groups' internal activities, and, once outside, both PKI and NU groups' members met as neighbors and greeted each other as usual, continuing to respect social manners in neighboring life. Yet, by the eve of the September 30, 1965 coup, the standoff between PKI and NU groups had reached a flash point.

Amidst this rising tension, one NU branch leader of Nandes village, whose name was Muhtar, was assaulted, though he fought back and barely survived this attempt at premeditated murder.[34] NU member Sarjoti insisted that even his grandmother was threatened with murder by a PKI leader of

Gajo village, whose name was Sukudu. He recalled, "It was the time when my grandmother went to the mosque. Her veil was opened up with the tip of a sickle, and she was told, 'This person will soon die.' Having received such a threat, my grandmother stopped going to the mosque and immediately returned home. My grandmother told this to me, and I asked her, 'Who did it?' 'Sukudu,' replied my grandmother. Deep down I swore, 'You bastard, Sukudu!'"[35]

According to Sarjoti, this threat was made on September 23, 1965. Around this time, a rumor spread that an Islamic figure of Pace village, Kyai Samut, was also threatened by a PKI member when he was passing by the Soro market and told that he would be soon killed.[36]

If nothing more had happened, these threats and rumors might have been simply forgotten, but one event made them appear as if they were parts of a coherent preparation by the PKI, touching off a chain of tragedy. The event, of course, was the outbreak of the coup in Jakarta on September 30, 1965.

South Siwi after September 30, 1965

The NU-PKI discord reached its culmination when news of the murder of six generals spread across the country. NU members in Siwi took the news as an evil omen of a PKI rebellion, which would occur throughout Indonesia. They thought that it was well planned on all levels, from the central level in Jakarta to the grassroots level in villages. If, in Jakarta, the rebellion involved the killing of army generals, at the village level, they thought, the PKI would aim to kill religious leaders, who were none other than the NU leaders.[37] It was said that the PKI had already made lists of who would be killed in each village. Many believed that a PKI rebellion across the country was an imminent reality, largely due to a mass of disinformation carried out by the army.[38] Siwi NU leader Sudi Subidi still believed in this version of reality decades later, recalling, "In Degan hamlet [at Gajo village], Sani['s] and Tifi['s names] were included [in the PKI's list for killing]. Each PKI branch had made such a list for who should be killed. It even instructed that corpses would be buried at the old hospital. Actually, in the back of the hospital, a large hole was dug to bury the corpses of NU members. It's been prepared as such. I could have been buried there, too."[39]

Whether such a list and instruction actually existed was unclear, and many scholars today, in fact, question the credibility of such an allegation.[40] Nevertheless, many NU members at that time believed that the PKI was indeed planning an organized rebellion across the nation, including the countryside. It was widely believed that the PKI and its affiliated organizations would use all of their local branches to carry out the rebellion, and that the PKI's lists of who should be killed had been found in PKI members' homes in Siwi.[41] Sudi Subidi remembered (and still believed in) the tense situation in south Siwi at that time: "The situation was heated and boiling. We knew that an eruption would be coming; we just did not know when it would come exactly."[42]

It was this background that made NU members welcome the military's request to prepare personnel and get actively involved in preparing and implementing the massacre of the PKI and its affiliated supporters. This can be seen in the NU's actions following the request of the Fifth Military Regional Command, which oversaw the entire East Java Province, to provide personnel to wipe out PKI people. Sudi Subidi recalled his involvement as follows: "Mr. Sanin, the commander of the East Java Military Command [sic], needed the personnel to clean up [the PKI]. So, Ansor members I supervised in three places were used for this cleaning-up campaign. [We] were obliged to provide its members as in other districts. So, posts were made for the Ansor to confront the PKI in East Blitar. In Siwi I set up three posts: in Kabar, in Kaman, and in Sekan. I asked every village branch of the Ansor to provide ten people to work every day and to donate food rations."[43]

Once cooperation between the military and NU had been set up, the massacre of the PKI's and affiliated organizations' members was carried out in an organized manner. The military asked the NU to provide personnel to wipe out the PKI; and the NU's Islamic youth organization, Ansor, particularly its multipurpose brigade, Banser, became the tactical squad of the PKI crackdown on the ground.

The process began with a list established by the military. Based on existing names, the military, together with Banser members, arrested leaders or active figures in the PKI and affiliated organizations.[44] Gajo village's Sarjoti recalled that they did not have any difficulty identifying PKI figures in their village. This was because Banser members already knew very well who was hostile to them, and who was active in the PKI and its affiliated organizations.[45] As we will discuss below, this gave local people, such as Sarjoti, a certain amount of power to utilize the situation by and for themselves.

Once identified and arrested, suspects were sent first to the *Koramil* (Military District Command) or police station, and then to villages to be executed. These suspects—often members of the PKI, BTI, Gerwani, or

Pemuda Rakyat—who were about to be executed were tagged as *jatah* (quota). After being sent to villages, then, it was Banser members in each village who would take care of these "quotas"—that is, kill these people—at the villages' cemeteries. Following the September 30, 1965, incident, Banser members came to be deployed every night to guard their respective villages, wearing their swords. In the village of Soro, for example, *Banser* members stood as village guards in front of local magnate Pak Solah Saji's house on the south side of the Soro Market. One Banser member, Bati, who was on guard at the post, recollected the arrest of Makarabis, a PKI figure in the village, as follows: "Makarabis was caught in Malang City. He was pursued and captured by Kaimi and Sasanu, who were members of the NU. Kaimi was Kiyat's brother from Kamil hamlet in Pace village. Makarabis was chased from alley to alley in Malang City, and, then, caught alive."[46]

According to Bati, Makarabis was first taken to the police station in Siwi, and then sent to Soro village to be executed. The police, in this case, informed the village that they would receive a "quota" of four or five people. Then, around 8:00 p.m., they departed the guard post in front of Solah Saji's house, headed on foot to the Soro village's public cemetery, which was located at the edge of the rice fields and on the side of the Koro River. The distance was approximately 700 meters.

When the Banser members brought their "quota" to the public cemetery, each victim's thumbs were tied together with a string and a stick in front of his or her stomach. This procession of victims was usually led by local Banser members, with the victims walking in the middle, and police and executioners behind them. Banser members at the front used flashlights to light the dirt road. Once the victims arrived at the cemetery, the process of slaughter awaited police orders. This command was in the form of a whistle blow. Then the executioner from Banser would swing a sword at the PKI member's neck from behind. Bati described the scene as follows: "So, when the PKI person walked in, he was cut from behind, right in the back of the neck. So, [the sound was like this:] "cog" [the sound of a sword slashing at the neck] and then "bleg" [the sound of the body falling into a hole in the ground]. Then, "cog," "bleg," "cog," "bleg." . . . [In this way] the corpses collapsed, one by one."[47]

According to Bati, both Makarabis and his wife were fully dressed on that night. The wife's neck was wrapped with a gold necklace, with a bag full of money and gold bracelets on her wrists. It was said that she was a wealthy clothing trader in the village, and also the chairperson of the local Gerwani branch. Makarabis himself was an active PKI member in the village. They

FIGURE 1.1 The graves of Makarabis and his wife, with other five victims, at Soro Public Cemetery, Blitar, East Java, Indonesia. Photo by the author.

were escorted to the Soro public cemetery, where they were slaughtered in turn with swords. Both were put in the same hole and buried with the other six victims that night. According to Bati, one of those six victims was a local PKI member, Iwak, who had been active in mobilizing villagers for the unilateral action in local magnate Haji Tengas's rice field (see figure 1.1).

Such an arrival of a *jatah* from the police station to Soro village occurred once or twice a week. The average "quota" included four or five people, except for the time when the police brought eight suspects, including Makarabis and his wife, as well as Iwak. It is not easy to figure out the accurate number of victims. According to Gajo village's Banser member Sarjoti, Kamil hamlet cemetery in Pace village had the highest number of victims, with sixteen PKI members buried there. He testified that Sopo village's cemetery had nine, Gajo village's Sepan hamlet cemetery had eight, and Nandes village cemetery had ten.[48] However, Syamsul, another Banser member, recalls that Gajo village's Sepan cemetery should have the highest number of victims, with nineteen buried there.[49]

Terror in East Java 35

Another testimony from Sakini, a gravekeeper at Soro village, reveals that the process of execution might have been even crueler and more inhuman, and not as "neat" and "orderly" as Bati recollected above (such as killing each victim, one by one, quickly with a fatal blow on the neck). At that time and since, Sakini has been the caretaker of the Soro village cemetery in place of his uncle. He had been helping his uncle from the early 1960s, and, following September 30, 1965, he, along with his uncle and a neighbor, was forced to dig a hole at the cemetery every time they were notified of the coming of a "quota." He knew he would be killed if he did not obey this order. Sakini described the process of murder at the Soro village public cemetery as follows: "I remember all people who made the arrests. Because they always gave a message [to us] every time victims were about to be killed. It was like, 'Tonight, there is a delivery, make a hole! Find a place!' They stabbed victims at the graveyard's gate. [I remember] a man whose ears were cut, a woman whose genitals were stabbed with a sword. . . . All screaming in pain. And blood was scattered everywhere. Was this proper for humans? I was always screaming in my heart."[50]

Sakini had to clean up blood spilled all over the ground by covering it with soil every time victims were slaughtered. The slaughter was always carried out at the entrance to the cemetery. Thus, he had to drag all of the bodies approximately twenty-five meters from the gate to the holes inside the cemetery he, his uncle, and a neighbor dug. He said, "It's still good for these victims to be picked up and dragged away [from the scene of murder]. . . . This is how they killed him [Mr. Sakini demonstrating for the author]. The hands were tied in front, the legs were also tied. Then the chin was pulled up. Some held it and then others slaughtered. I remember their actions very well."[51]

Sakini still remembered the tense situation at Soro village, in general, and Jaloto hamlet, in particular, where poor peasants' unilateral actions were especially fierce. In that hamlet, adult men left their houses at night to avoid being captured by the Banser groups. If they stayed at home, they could not avoid Banser's ambushes, while, in the fields, they still had a chance to fight back. Thus, many peasants fled to the fields every night. When attacking, Banser group members wore all-black clothes and headbands, with faces blackened with charcoal, and each carrying a sword.

In this hamlet, Banser groups often ambushed suspects' houses on their own initiative, without the military's orders, taking suspects to the cemetery to be murdered. Intriguingly, Jaloto hamlet was not just a place where violence raged most excessively among neighboring areas. It was also a place where the majority of residents were poor peasants, and their mass actions were some of the most aggressive in the region (Iwak, a leading local PKI figure, for instance, came from this hamlet). Furthermore, it was a place where the majority were *abangan*, that is, local Javanese who were Muslims but practicing a much more syncretic version of Islam. These points shed new light on local and social aspects of the massacre.

Banser's Initiatives in the Massacres

The massacres of the PKI and its affiliated members in Siwi were not all based on military instructions. There were massacres carried out by Banser members themselves, which were allowed to happen by the military. Such massacres were carried out in coordination with the village-level *Banser* branches. In order to think about such local and social aspects, let us zoom in on one of the most—or perhaps the most—violent Banser executioner(s), Sarjoti of Gajo village.

Sarjoti was among the personnel specially prepared by the NU to crush the PKI and its affiliated organizations. During the PKI crackdown in 1965, he stayed in a dormitory provided by the NU in Kaman, Siwi, for more than a month. His primary task was to kill members of the PKI and other affiliated organizations. He remembered those days very well. Usually, he began sharpening his sword at the start of the night, around 6:00 p.m., and then, starting at 9:00 p.m., he carried out an operation to kill PKI members and supporters at cemeteries. He admitted in the author's interview that he was the executioner who killed more PKI people than anyone else in Siwi and its surrounding areas.[52]

What Sarjoti did at least partly shows that Banser was acting alone. The arrest and murder of Sanes in Pace village was a representative case carried out by Sarjoti and his four colleagues. The five of them went to Pace village after hearing that Sanes, the village's PKI leader and hamlet's head, had gone berserk, so that the people of Pace village had run away. Sanes was indeed powerful and literally a strong man. When Sanes was urged to surrender, he climbed to the top of a coconut tree, refusing to come down. His teacher of magic was brought to convince him to come down.[53] The Banser members threatened that, if he did not come down, they would kill his teacher. Sanes ignored this threat. Sarjoti then killed Sanes's teacher by breaking his neck. After that, the coconut tree was sawed down from its trunk. Still, Sanes was alive and without the slightest wound. Sarjoti ran a sword through Sanes's body. His stroke was as deft as if his sword was cutting a car tire. Sanes could not move at all. His body was tied around Sarjoti's with ropes. He was pulled and dragged across the barren land, back and forth, east and west, eventually to his death.

Immediately following the murder of Sanes and his teacher, on that very night, Sarjoti and his colleagues drove to Kenan village's Raka hamlet. First, they headed for Siwi, where they stopped by the police station and transferred to a police jeep, and then headed to Raka. Arriving there, they saw five PKI people desperately making a stand on the roof of a house. The roof tiles were already almost completely gone because they were throwing them toward Banser and Ansor members who were trying to catch them. Meanwhile, one PKI suspect was captured and tied to a tree trunk in the yard, while the other four continued occupying the roof. Eventually, however, all five PKI suspects were killed by Sarjoti himself. The one who was tied to a tree was killed when his neck was broken. Another was killed by Sarjoti's fatal punch. The other three were stabbed to death in single combat on the roof of the house, with Sarjoti using his sword while PKI suspects (that is, peasants) resisted in vain with their sickles. Sarjoti recalled in the author's interview, "As soon as we arrived at Raka and got off from their ugly jeep, the police returned to the police station in Siwi. The policeman should have shot the (PKI) members, but he didn't."[54]

In this incident, the police simply allowed PKI members to be beaten and massacred. They "escorted" Sarjoti and his colleagues to the site, which was a form of support. Sarjoti, in fact, did not know why Banser had to kill those PKI people. He said he wondered, "Wasn't it just the military's matter to shoot PKI members directly?" That said, it was Sarjoti himself who took the initiative and actually killed these people. Indeed, he did not forget to give vent to his resentment. Sukudu, who had threatened Sarjoti's grandmother with a sickle when she was about to pray at the mosque, was the first person he killed, by breaking his neck.

Sarjoti's killing record continued. At Bere hamlet in Gajo village, he and his colleagues arrested and killed five PKI members without military intervention. Together with Ansor comrades, he plotted the arrests and murders. At noon they dug a hole in the cemetery. They then conveyed a message to PKI members and affiliated supporters, asking them to join the night guard if they wished to survive. When they left the house on guard patrol, they were arrested and taken to the cemetery, where Sarjoti and his Banser colleagues slaughtered them.[55]

The 1965 massacres also targeted people who were not PKI members. Quite a few executions were for ordinary crimes committed in the past. In

Gajo village's Degan hamlet, for instance, thieves often became targets of murder by local Banser members. These thieves (including those already in prison) were taken away and killed at the cemetery.[56] In Jambeng village, a thief and gambler named Karet was killed by Gajo village Banser members.[57] A similar case occurred in Soro village, where the victim, named Rugi, was killed and thrown into a well. He was not a member of the PKI but was murdered due to a personal grudge within the same village.[58] Another victim in this village was named Magi, who was said to have carried out a massive theft of goats from the Soleh Soka's mosque for revenge after Banser members killed his father and brothers, Saera and Podo, both of whom were thieves.[59]

Furthermore, at the time of the 1965 massacre, threats against *abangan*, nondevout followers of Islam in the southern Siwi countryside, increased. These local Javanese, who had great respect for their ancestors and infused all their behaviors with their local Javanese mysticism, were not active in slaughtering people.[60] Yet, because of their attitudes, they were easily stigmatized as PKI members. To save themselves, they began going to participate in worship in mosques and prayer rooms in the villages of south Siwi, which thus became full of these new arrivals.[61] They become involved in Islamic activities, for example, participating in the weekly recitation of surah Yassin from the Koran on Thursday evenings. Slowly but eventually, they began to leave their previous Javanese rituals.[62]

As a result, cultural scenes gradually but radically changed after 1965. Until 1965, in rural south Siwi, the population of abangan was greater than that of devout followers of a more orthodox version of Islam. However, after 1965, due to fear of being stigmatized as PKI members and communists, many local people turned to Islamic activities. The younger generations in south Siwi villages became more familiar with Islam than various Javanese rituals. Many mosques and *mushalla* (prayer rooms) were built in communist base areas after September 30, 1965. One interviewee, Fiyoso, a survivor of the massacre who was once arrested by NU members and lived a harsh, stigmatized life, called this change a process of Islamization in rural south Siwi.[63]

Conclusion

The Indonesian Mass Killings of 1965 were highly complex events, and their roots were deeply local and historical. Focusing on rural villages in south Siwi in East Java, this chapter has explored the causes and development of this tragedy, with a focus on local and sociocultural contentions among social groups, namely conflicts between the NU and PKI, which existed long before the September 30, 1965, incident. To be sure, the roles played by the military were significant in explaining the nationwide massacres. It was the military that supplied a mass of disinformation so that NU members believed that the PKI was planning a rebellion throughout the country from Jakarta to remote villages, and that PKI members were atheists and had made numerous threats and attacks on leaders of the Muslim community. Based on such (dis)information, NU members in East Java viewed the situation as part of a jihad to defend Islam and the state.

That said, there could have been a bloody conflict in south Siwi even without the presence of the army. In other words, the conflict was a vertical one because it involved the army as the state apparatus, but at the same time, there was a horizontal conflict, which involved various local, social, and cultural struggles on the ground. The involvement of the army made it possible for the massacres to be conducted more systematically and on a more massive scale. Also, the horizontal conflict between the NU and PKI was deeply interrelated with the Cold War situation of the post–World War II period. While the countryside of south Siwi was far removed from the centers of world politics, the PKI and its affiliated groups could be seen as parts of global communist movements, although they had their own characteristics because the idea of communism was translated to the local level. In rural south Siwi, it evolved at the crossroads of Javanese cultural traditions and worldviews, along with Islam's efforts to expand its influence in the region.

On the one hand, influenced by the hope of economic improvement and the egalitarian notions of the large majority of peasants, the idea of communism was enthusiastically welcomed and grew rapidly in rural south Siwi. On the other hand, it was in these same villages that the popularity of communism gave rise to great opposition from other Javanese who tended to be devout Muslims and owners of large rice fields, and who also tended to be supporters of NU groups. Therefore, in this rural area of south Siwi, the idea of communism, as well as the logic of anticommunism, came to be interpreted and utilized locally. The consequence was that communist ideology was stigmatized and made taboo by communities under the logic of anticommunism, with the effect of silencing various horizontal conflicts, whether political, social, economic, cultural, or gender based. If south Siwi's Cold War—that is, communist and anticommunist politics—in reality involved such various struggles among villagers, then such conflicts might continue even today, considering that the idea of communism is still banned by the Indonesian government.

Notes

* I want to thank Masuda Hajimu, Sony Karsono, and M. Syafiq for their comments on this chapter and contribution of materials. I am responsible for all errors.

1. Komisi Nasional Hak Asasi Manusia Republik Indonesia [The Indonesian National Human Rights Commission], *Ringkasan Eksekutif Laporan Penyelidikan Pelanggaran Hak Asasi Manusia Berat* [Executive Summary of the Investigation Report on Gross Human Rights Violations] (Jakarta: Komnas HAM RI, 2012), 25–40.

2. John Roosa, *Buried Histories, The Anticommunist Massacres of 1965–1966* (Madison: University of Wisconsin Press, 2020), 176–77; and Vannessa Hearman, *Unmarked Graves: Death and Survival in the Anti-Communist Violence in East Java, Indonesia* (Singapore: NUS Press, 2018), 75–82.

3. Donald Hindley, "The Communist Party of Indonesia, 1951–1961: A Decade of Aidit Leadership" (PhD thesis, Australian National University, 1961). In Blitar Regency, the PKI gained 40–50 percent of votes in the 1955 elections.

4. Roosa, *Buried Histories*, 20–21.

5. One the roles of the army, see, for instance, Geoffrey Robinson, *The Killing Season: A History of the Indonesian Massacres, 1965–66* (Princeton, NJ: Princeton University Press, 2018); and Jess Melvin, *The Army and the Indonesian Genocide: Mechanics of Mass Murder* (Abingdon, UK: Routledge, 2018).

6. Masuda Hajimu, *Cold War Crucible: The Korean Conflict and The Postwar World* (Cambridge, MA: Harvard University Press, 2015); featured review of *The Cold War: A World History* by Odd Arne Westad, *American History Review* 124, no. 3 (June 2019): 1013–16; and his introductory chapter in this volume, "Reconceptualizing the Cold War: On-the-Ground Experiences in Asia."

7. In this chapter, I have used pseudonyms for the safety and privacy of interviewees.

8. Sakini, interview by the author on October 16 and 24, 2020. Sakini said he was the grandson of a couple from the central part of Java or Central Java Province today. The author is in the fifth generation of a family who moved from Kedu, Central Java Province today, to Pace village, Soro subdistrict.

9. Peter Carey, *Kuasa Ramalan*, trans. Parakitri T. Simbolon, 2nd ed. (Jakarta: Kepustakaan Populer Gramedia with KITLV Jakarta, 2012), 800–828. This is an Indonesian translation of Peter Carey, *The Power of Prophecy: Prince Dipanagara and the End of an Old Order in Java, 1785–1855* (Leiden: KITLV Press, 2007). Also, the personal story of the late Tugi and Tano as told to the author in Soro, Blitar. Tugi and Tano are members of the author's family.

10. Sakini, interviews by the author on October 16 and 24, 2020.

11. Sakini, interviews; Fiyoso, interviews by the author on October 18 and 21, 2020.

12. Sakini, interviews; Fiyoso, interviews.

13. Badul, interview by the author on December 5, 2020.

14. Fiyoso, interviews; this is closely related to the success of the agrarian program and PKI membership recruitment by D. N. Aidit from 1953 to 1955 in the countryside. See Hindley, "The Communist Party of Indonesia, 1951–1961."

15. Fiyoso, interviews; Milan, interview by the author on October 22, 2020; Syamsul, interviews by the author on February 22 and October 24, 2020; Towi, interviews by the author on October 22 and 25, 2020; and Badul, interview.

16. Fiyoso, interviews.

17. Andi Achdian, *Tanah Bagi yang Tak Bertanah: Landreform Pada Masa Demokrasi Terpimpin* (Bogor: Kekal Press, 2008).

18. Bati, interview by the author on March 9, 2020.

19. Milan, interview by the author on October 22, 2020. Nasakom was the acronym for "Nationalism, Religion, and Communism," which was advocated by Sukarno as an attempt to unite different groups of people and their ideologies.

20. Fiyoso, interviews; Achdian, *Tanah Bagi*; and Hesti Rukmiati Wijaya, "Land Tenancy and Labour Contracts in Javanese Agriculture" (PhD thesis, University of Melbourne, 1983).

21. In the UUBH, it is explained that the sharing system for wet soil is 6:4 (6 for cultivators, 4 for rice field owners) and 1:1 for dry land with secondary crops.

22. Bati, interview.

23. Sarjoti, interview by the author on February 23, 2020.

24. Sudi Subidi, interview by the author on March 10, 2020.

25. Sudi Subidi, interview.

26. Sudi Subidi, interview; Sarjoti, interview; Badul, interview.

27. Sudi Subidi, interview.

28. Sudi Subidi, interview.

29. Sarjoti, interview.

30. Sarjoti, interview.

31. Milan, interview.

32. Bati, interview.

33. Fiyoso, interviews; Towi, interviews.

34. Sarjoti, interview.

35. Sarjoti, interview.

36. Badul, interview.

37. Sudi Subidi, interview.

38. Roosa, *Buried Histories*, 61–84; and Saskia E. Wieringa, *Penghancuran Gerakan Perempuan Indonesia*, trans. Hesri Setiawan (Jakarta: Garba Budaya, 1999), which is an Indonesian translation of Saskia E. Wieringa, "The Politization of Gender Relations in Indonesia: The Indonesian Women's Movement and Gerwani until the New Order State" (PhD thesis, University of Amsterdam, 1995).

39. Sudi Subidi, interview. Regarding the digging of holes and the list of names killed by interviewees, these interviewees did not see them firsthand and, therefore, their accounts are doubtful.

40. John Roosa, *Dalih Pembunuhan Massal: Gerakan 30 September dan Kudeta Suharto*, trans. Hesri Setiawan (Jakarta: Institut Sejarah Sosial Indonesia dan Hasta Mitra, 2008), which is an English translation of John Roosa, *Pretext for Mass*

Murder: The September 30th Movement and Suharto's Coup d'État in Indonesia (Madison: University of Wisconsin Press, 2006); and Benedict Anderson and Ruth Benedict, *A Preliminary Analysis of the October 1, 1965 Coup in Indonesia* (Ithaca, NY: Cornell Modern Project, 1971).

41. Sarjoti, interview; Syamsul, interviews.
42. Sudi Subidi, interview.
43. Sudi Subidi, interview.
44. Sudi Subidi, interview.
45. Sarjoti, interview.
46. Bati, interview.
47. Bati, interview.
48. Sarjoti, interview.
49. Syamsul, interviews.
50. Sakini, interviews.
51. Sakini, interviews.
52. Sarjoti, interview.
53. In rural south Siwi at that time there was a teaching of magical arts. The teaching was informal. Some teachers had many students, some only a few.
54. Sarjoti, interview.
55. Sarjoti, interview.
56. Sarjoti, interview.
57. Milan, interview; Syamsul, interviews.
58. Bati, interview.
59. Sakini, interviews.
60. Sakini, interviews.
61. Badul, interview.
62. Fiyoso, interviews.
63. Fiyoso, interviews.

2 Islam and Communism in West Java

The Cold War and Sociocultural Polarization
in Indonesia, 1945–65

MATTHEW WOOLGAR

The term "Cold War" is widely used to mean a pattern of polarization in world affairs shaped by superpower rivalry and a linked ideological struggle between capitalism and communism.[1] However, there has been an increasing recognition that, even during the Cold War, "bipolarity had its limitations," amid various potentially cross-cutting forces.[2] In this context there has been a growing scholarly interest in the relationship between religion and the Cold War.[3] However, the existing literature on this topic has most often focused on diplomatic, institutional and intellectual perspectives.[4] When conditions on the ground are considered, religion is often treated as "an object of the Cold War's impact," part of a broader tendency to view society and culture "as passive entities under the global conflict."[5] This is an important limitation, especially when one considers Masuda Hajimu's argument that to understand the Cold War we need to take into account the mutually constitutive relationship between global developments and "struggles within each society."[6] A recognition of such interactions points to the need to understand "the actors of local and national conflicts, their agency, culture, and politics."[7] It also implies that a wide range of social and cultural conditions need to be investigated to effectively understand the dynamics of the Cold War.

In this context, one can think of the Cold War as constituted by various intersecting processes of social, cultural, and political polarization. Such an approach complements Masuda's concept of "social warfare," with multiple axes of polarization coming to be channeled through "Cold War logics." Questions which might arise include, What drove polarization? What limited it? Along which axes did polarization occur? And how did different forms of polarization interact? These considerations point to the urgency of an approach to the study of religion and the Cold War that incorporates not only diplomatic, institutional, and intellectual dimensions, but experiences at the grassroots. It must engage not only with national elites based in capital cities, but with developments in the provinces. In this vein, studying developments in subnational spaces can be useful for disentangling the "diversity of processes and contexts that feed into, and are impacted by . . . global processes as they developed in specific sites."[8] In this approach, religion is not the passive recipient of external influences, but an integral part of the matrix of social, cultural, and political tensions that constituted the Cold War. Methodologically, this also suggests the importance of an eclectic approach to source material and an ability to integrate archival research with sources such as mass media publications and oral histories.

This chapter pursues such an approach via a case study of West Java, Indonesia, focusing on the 1945–65 period. The chapter first briefly sketches the history of the Indonesian Communist Party (*Partai Komunis Indonesia*, PKI) and reviews historiography relating to Islam and communism in Indonesia. It then outlines developments up to the end of the Indonesian War of Independence in 1949, before exploring some ways that the PKI leaders and local activists navigated the Islamic context of postindependence Indonesia. The chapter then focuses in on the PKI's relations with the main Muslim parties and follows this with an examination of heightened conflict during the mid-1960s. This research is part of a broader project on the Indonesian left in the postwar period and, as such, draws particularly on oral histories and printed sources linked to the PKI and allied mass organizations. Where possible, I have also sought to incorporate perspectives from other groups, drawing on contemporary publications, archival sources, or secondary literature.

Overall, the chapter argues that across the period studied, a broad process of sociocultural polarization took place between the PKI and groups under the banner of Islam. Superpower competition became entangled with these tensions. At the same time, the chapter indicates that communism was not inherently incompatible with Islam; rather, the relationship was varied and contingent. This has sometimes been obscured by a "road to disaster" narrative shaped by a retrospective view of the anti-communist massacres of 1965–66.[9] As such, the chapter also challenges the generalization that "the communist world-view was opposed to religion of any kind, including Islam" by showing how the PKI adapted to an environment wherein Islam was deeply rooted.[10] More broadly, the chapter points to religion as an entry point for a broader approach to the Cold War that engages with the intersection of multiple forms of political, cultural, and social polarization.

Communism and Islam in Indonesia: Historical and Historiographical Context

The PKI emerged in the Netherlands Indies in the early twentieth century but was almost eradicated following a failed uprising in the late 1920s.[11] Refounded shortly after Indonesia declared independence in 1945, it was again almost wiped out in 1948, not long before the final withdrawal of Dutch colonial forces. The party then underwent a period of rapid growth.[12] It finished fourth in Indonesia's first national elections in 1955 and, beginning in the late 1950s, played an increasingly important role in Indonesian political life under President Sukarno's authoritarian "Guided Democracy." By the mid-1960s, the PKI was the largest nonruling communist party in the world.[13] However, in 1965 and 1966 Indonesia experienced one of the most concentrated episodes of anticommunist violence during the Cold War, in which possibly 500,000 people were killed.[14]

In interpreting these developments, there have been differing assessments of the extent of tensions between communism and Islam. Propaganda under the military dictatorship established in the mid-1960s argued that communism was atheistic and fundamentally antithetical to Islam.[15] Among scholars, a conceptual framework laid out by anthropologist Clifford Geertz has proved particularly influential. Geertz argued that Islam in Java was characterized by "syncretism" and delineated between "cultural types," with pious *santri* stressing Islamic dimensions while peasant *abangan* and aristocratic-bureaucratic *priyayi* emphasized syncretic elements.[16] He also saw politics during the period as shaped by this context, with Islamic parties drawing support from among the santri while the PKI was particularly strong among the abangan.[17] Geertz's analysis has subsequently been critiqued, for conflating social and religious categories, taking too narrow a definition of Islam, and drawing oversharp distinctions between his "cultural types."[18] However, a distinction between less observant abangan and more devout santri has remained influential in the scholarship.

This chapter navigates a middle path between scholars who have foregrounded a process of polarization between pious Muslims and communists, and others who are more skeptical of claimed Muslim-communist tensions. Merle Ricklefs notably put a historical twist on Geertz's framework, arguing that the distinction between santri and abangan was "not wrong" but was "historically contingent," shaped by social and cultural developments beginning in the nineteenth century.[19] In his analysis of the postindependence period, he saw increasing "*santri-abangan* polarization and politicization," crystallized though tension between the PKI and Muslim groups and culminating in the violence of 1965-66.[20] However, more recently, a number of scholars have questioned the notion of a sharp division between Islam and communism. Jessica Melvin has critiqued the view that the PKI was seen as an "ideological threat to political Islam," and Lin Hongxuan has highlighted "the remarkable confluence of Islam and Marxism in Indonesia" lasting into the 1950s amid evidence of an "eclectic and open-minded thought process" among Indonesian intellectuals.[21] This chapter argues for a middle ground, acknowledging variation and flexibility in evolving relations between Communism and Islam, but also recognizing an overall trend of sociocultural and political polarization, a tendency reinforced by the broader international context.

West Java is a promising case through which to explore these issues and revise existing interpretations. The analyses deployed by Geertz and Ricklefs focused on the ethnic Javanese in East and Central Java. However, the largest ethnic group in West Java is the Sundanese, an ethnic identity often said to be particularly closely identified with Islam.[22] The province also witnessed especially extensive activity from the Darul Islam uprising, which began in 1949 and involved a guerrilla campaign while calling for an Islamic state, causing severe dislocation in the province until its defeat in the early 1960s.[23] Still, the PKI made significant inroads in West Java: for example, in regional elections in 1957, it gained over one million votes in the province, making it the second largest party.[24] Despite the presence of a sizeable PKI contingent, and a recent history of Islamically inspired political violence in the Darul Islam, in West Java the extent of anticommunist violence of 1965-66 was, relatively speaking, much lower than elsewhere in Java. Around 3,000–10,000 people were killed in the province, compared to approximately 150,000 killed in East Java.[25] An account of communism and Islam during this period in West Java thus does not fit easily with a viewpoint that posits an inevitable conflict between Islam and communism.

Islam and Communism Under Colonial Rule and Revolution

During the late colonial period, there was some evidence of sociocultural polarization emerging in West Java. There were certain parallels to developing santri-abangan divisions that Ricklefs argues were occurring in East and Central Java. Care is needed, however, in transplanting these concepts across ethnic groups. The term "abangan," for example, originates from the Javanese language and was not widely used among the ethnic Sundanese in West Java in the late colonial or early postindependence periods.[26] Moreover, there were indications that the interweaving of Sundanese culture and Islam was particularly durable, as reflected in the great difficulty that Christian missionaries faced in West Java.[27] However, during the early twentieth century West Java did see the emergence of more assertive and intolerant forms of Islam, as well as a reaction against the trend with the appearance of groups advocating a form of spirituality that "they claimed was an authentic Sundanese syncretic creed."[28]

There were tentative signs that new forms of political organization were reinforcing these divisions, but also notable examples of communism and Islam becoming intertwined. The PKI's precursor, the Indies Social Democratic Association (*Indische Sociaal-Democratische Vereeniging*, ISDV), initially worked to build up support within the mass organization known as the Islamic League (*Sarekat Islam*).[29] However by the early 1920s Sarekat Islam had begun imposing "party discipline" and the organization increasingly split into a left-oriented "red" group and a "white" group more closely identifying with political Islam.[30] It was at this time of emerging tensions between communism and political Islam that the PKI seems to have begun gaining substantial ground in parts of rural West Java.[31] However, the break between Islam and communism was not total and irrevocable. Indeed, Lin Hongxuan has pointed out that during this period "conciliatory discourses involving Islam and Communism were surprisingly common."[32] This was particularly evident during an anticolonial uprising in 1926 in Banten, in the far western tip of Java. This rebellion saw a creative combination of Islam and communism and an alliance between PKI activists and Islamic leaders.[33] Following the uprising the PKI was banned, curtailing possibilities for communist mass agitation until the onset of the Indonesian Revolution at the end of World War II.

West Java again witnessed examples of a creative accommodation between communism and Islam during the Indonesian Revolution of 1945–49, as Indonesians of various ideological orientations resisted the return of Dutch colonial forces following the end of World War II. In late 1945, Banten saw the growth of a movement involving religious leaders under the banner of an Islamized communism, although it was quickly suppressed by the Indonesian army.[34] As the revolution progressed, there were signs from elsewhere in West Java that some individuals continued to combine commitments to Islam and communism, and there were examples of the PKI working with Islamic organizations. The self-proclaimed Muslim communist Hasan Raid, for example, was briefly a member of the Islamic militia

Hizbullah in West Java before going on to join the PKI in Central Java, then Jakarta.[35] A Dutch intelligence report in 1946 noted that in Cililin, the local PKI and leaders from the Islamic organization *Masyumi* had good relations, although there seemed to be tensions in nearby areas.[36] Another report from 1948 mentioned a Muslim religious leader as the head of the PKI in the Balaraja area of Tangerang.[37]

However, there were signs of increasing strain as the revolution wore on, with the situation exacerbated by the violent conditions of the revolution on the ground and worsening Cold War tensions at a global level.[38] In late 1947 and early 1948, Indonesian police reports indicated that in parts of West Java the PKI was unable to organize openly because of the strength and hostility of Masyumi.[39] In mid-1948 an apparently forged letter circulated, claiming to be from the head of the PKI in West Java, which instructed cadres to kidnap local Masyumi leaders.[40] There was also a virulent strand of anticommunism in the emerging movement that would ultimately become the Darul Islam revolt, despite some isolated cases of possible cooperation with the PKI.[41] Conditions worsened further after the Madiun Affair in September 1948, which saw significant violence between leftist and Muslim militias in parts of East Java. The conflict emerged amid a crisis that saw local sociocultural cleavages, economic discontent, and intramilitary tensions come together with a national political conflict and an increasingly polarized international context.[42] Although the Madiun Affair was less decisive in shaping communist-Muslim relations than has sometimes been argued, and less directly felt in West Java than in East Java, it did mark a hardening of relations, and its memory would later be repeatedly revived by Muslim groups hostile to the PKI.[43]

Communists Navigating a Muslim Society

In attempting to rebuild the PKI from the ruins following the Madiun Affair, leaders who took over the party in the early 1950s carefully positioned their approach to Islam. Under the new leadership of D. N. Aidit and his allies, the PKI argued that it was not against religion, and emphasized its support for religious freedom.[44] It also aimed to show that the People's Republic of China and the Soviet Union allowed freedom of religion.[45] Aidit even pressed the Soviet Union to give greater consideration to Islam in its diplomatic efforts, arguing that Muslims would be more open to communism if they better understood the situation of Islam in the Soviet Union.[46] By late 1954 the PKI had announced its acceptance of President Sukarno's

"Five Principles" (*Panca Sila*) as the foundation of the state's politics—one of these principles being recognition of a divine power (*Ketuhanan yang Maha Esa*).[47]

The PKI leadership broadly stuck to its position on Panca Sila and freedom of religion through the 1950s and 1960s, occasionally ending up with awkward ideological formulations.[48] For example, on one occasion Aidit argued that "the PKI as a Party is atheist (*a-theis*) . . . but PKI members are varied, there are those who are atheist, there are those who believe in God (*theis*)."[49] However, in general, the party leadership navigated the issue of religious belief with considerable dexterity. This was evident, for example, when Aidit was interviewed in 1964. The PKI "accepts Pancasila," he explained, and this meant that "antireligious propaganda is not permitted but also compulsion in religion is not permitted" as religion was a "personal matter." He recognized that "most of the Indonesian people are Muslim" and "many PKI members embrace religion." The "PKI does not stop its members adhering to a religion as long as they implement the anti-imperial and antifeudal program and politics of the PKI."[50] At a national and local level the PKI advocated for the cooperation of progressive nationalist, Islamic, and communist groups.[51] This resonated with the analysis of President Sukarno, who had long called for "close harmony" between Islam, nationalism, and Marxism.[52] Indeed, from the late 1950s this approach received a boost as Sukarno elaborated the idea of *Nasakom*, an abbreviation for "Nasionalisme, Agama, Komunisme," meaning "nationalism, religion, and communism."[53]

There were also individuals within the PKI who combined their activities with open piety. A number of "red *kyais*" supported the PKI (a *kyai* being a Muslim religious leader, often one who led a religious boarding school). Two of the best known were Kyai Achmad Dasuki Siradj from Central Java, who sat in the constituent assembly for the PKI, and Kyai Mohamad Sabitun, a prominent Ahmadiyah leader who sat in the East Java provincial assembly for the PKI.[54] In West Java during the election campaigns of 1955 and 1957 there were a number of occasions when religious leaders appeared at PKI events to express support for the PKI and condemn Masyumi.[55] This included Kyai Abdullah, a member of the West Java PKI provincial committee, who cited "numerous verses of the Koran" to criticize Masyumi and also "explained the West Java PKI's election manifesto."[56] A communist representative on the a quasi-governmental body called the National Front recalled a local PKI leader who was a "Haji who joined the PKI . . . consequently it had lots of followers [in that area]."[57]

Among mass organizations allied with the PKI there were also pious Muslims. In the mid-1950s researchers interviewed a local leader of the Indonesian Peasant's Front (*Barisan Tani Indonesia*, BTI) in Sukabumi, who was a keen reader of PKI literature, but had been educated in a religious boarding school, sold copies of the Koran for part of his income, and had undertaken the hajj.[58] A member of a trade union allied to the PKI remembered a fellow union member who had gone on the hajj and was "very influential in local meetings because he was also a religious [figure]."[59] Another activist in a left-wing youth group recalled a local PKI leader who was skilled at reciting the Koran.[60] A number of members of the BTI and the People's Youth (*Pemuda Rakyat*; the PKI's youth wing) explained that they had earlier studied at religious boarding schools or knew of others who had.[61]

More broadly, the PKI and allied mass organizations carried out extensive community service activities, which could involve cooperation with Islamic organizations and supporting religious activities, including building and repairing mosques or prayer houses.[62] On some occasions, this may have been a tactical attempt to win over devout Muslims.[63] However, it sometimes also reflected the piety of local activists. A PKI representative in the Bandung city council explained that he supported building places of worship, since "among PKI members are many Muslims," citing a hadith (in Arabic and Indonesian) to the effect that "those who do not pray will surely be tortured by Allah in Hell."[64] Trade unions allied to the PKI campaigned for workers to receive a bonus at the Muslim celebration of Lebaran, as a day that "is honored and celebrated as custom and tradition of the Indonesian Nation which embraces Islam."[65] Mundane activities such as an effort to improve local roads could lead to cooperation between the PKI and Muslim parties.[66] In 1957 the PKI newspaper noted that in some regions "Masyumi people and PKI people work together whitewashing and cleaning prayer houses and mosques, as well as repairing roads and bridges."[67] A member of the People's Youth recalled that when taking part in community service (*gotong royong*) activities they helped various different parts of the community "whether they were from [the Muslim organizations] Nahdlatul Ulama (NU) or Masyumi, wherever they were from, we had to help out."[68] Imam Muhtarom's chapter on East Java in this volume also provides examples of quotidian cooperation between youth groups allied to the PKI and those linked to Muslim parties.[69]

Throughout the 1950s, the Darul Islam rebellion was a particularly important issue in West Java, as guerrilla activity caused ongoing violence and created tens of thousands of refugees in the province. The PKI was vehement in its criticism of the Darul Islam rebels, and activists from West Java were at the forefront on this issue.[70] Many who sympathized with the PKI in the province had been victims of violence committed by Darul Islam or seen it firsthand, and members of the PKI and its allied mass organizations (such as trade unions, youth organizations, and a peasant association) often joined local security operations to defend their villages from attackers.[71] Yet in criticizing Darul Islam the PKI stressed that the party was not anti-Islam, instead emphasizing the humanitarian cost of the insurgency. A journalist described attending a PKI mass meeting in Bogor, West Java, where "the Communist Party doled out clothes and rice to peasants who had been robbed or burned out. . . . To such peasants, the party leaders carefully explain that the party is not in the least anti-Islam. To clinch the argument a pamphlet is distributed . . . written by a Moslem religious leader."[72] Indeed, the head of the PKI in West Java even framed the party's approach to Darul Islam as "defending Islam," explaining that the "Darul Islam [guerrillas] damage religion. The PKI opposes [their] actions which damage religion."[73]

The PKI and Islamic Parties in the 1950s

The staunchest opposition to the PKI from an Islamic political party in the 1950s came from Masyumi, the largest party in West Java. Masyumi attacked the PKI as antireligious, as treacherous foreign agents, and as aspiring totalitarians, reinforcing such claims with frequent references to the Madiun Affair.[74] Tensions were exacerbated by electoral competition approaching the first national elections in 1955.[75] In late 1954 Masyumi's central council declared communists "infidels" (*kafir*), saying that they denied the existence of God, undermined the family by holding wives in common, and violated Islamic property law.[76] West Java was particularly affected as a Masyumi stronghold and because it was home to some of Masyumi's most fiercely anticommunist leaders. It was in West Java that Masyumi firebrand Isa Anshary set up the "Anti Communist Front" to oppose the PKI.[77] So vitriolic were the front's attacks that the West Java PKI reported it to the police for making "slanderous allegations," and some of Masyumi's leadership sought to distance itself from the most extreme rhetoric.[78] Tensions continued throughout the late 1950s, with the PKI's growing influence in national politics a significant factor in Masyumi's involvement in a rebellion in Indonesia's "outer islands" in the late 1950s. Anxiety about the PKI also stimulated Masyumi's increasingly close relationship with the United States, which provided funding to the party during the elections of 1955 and later backed the regional rebels.[79]

The PKI meanwhile carried out a tricky balancing act, criticizing Masyumi while stressing the importance of unity. The PKI newspaper *Harian Rakjat* (People's Daily) spilled much ink complaining about Masyumi and rebutting its propaganda.[80] Yet, the PKI emphasized that it was not attacking Islam but, rather, specific actions of the Masyumi Party, which was alleged to be defending imperialists, landlords, and rebels.[81] The PKI's leader in West Java argued the PKI "are the defenders of Islam, not Masyumi, because Masyumi won't wipe out the Darul Islam guerrillas."[82] Communist leaders painted Masyumi as a disruptive force, complaining during the elections of 1955 that Masyumi was circulating inflammatory literature in West Java, and was trying to interfere with PKI campaign activities.[83] At the same time, individual leaders could have strong political differences yet maintain amicable personal relationships.[84] Moreover, the PKI leadership went out of its way to emphasize openness to cooperation where possible and highlighted potential common ground such as support for the Indonesian integration of West Irian, and for independence struggles in the Middle East.[85] Some of this was a tactical recognition of the PKI's vulnerability, and the PKI was happy to see Masyumi banned in 1960.[86] However, attempts to find common ground also reflected the potentially unifying force of Indonesian nationalism and anti-imperialism.[87] The argument that the PKI's opposition to Masyumi was contingent seems to have resonated at the grassroots. Thus one member of the PKI's youth organization, the People's Youth, recalled that "Masyumi viewed the PKI as its main opponent . . . but the PKI didn't claim to be Masyumi's enemy. The PKI's enemies were imperialism and capitalism, and landlords."[88]

During the 1950s the PKI's relations with the other large Islamic party, the NU, were significantly less confrontational than those with Masyumi. Greg Fealy has argued that a pragmatic theology stressing principles such as the "pursuit of benefit" and "avoidance of harm" inclined the NU "towards caution, flexibility and moderation" in its approach to politics in this period, a tendency reinforced by its concern to maintain its influence in the patronage-wielding Ministry of Religion.[89] Although the NU's leadership was generally wary of the PKI, there were prominent voices that argued that some forms of cooperation with the PKI were necessary.[90] During the 1950s, the NU rarely directly confronted the PKI, much to the exasperation of some Masyumi leaders.[91] During the 1955 national election campaign, the NU equivocated on the possibility of entering a cabinet with the PKI in the future, and although there were tensions over particular issues during the campaign, both parties made an effort to maintain cordial relations.[92] The PKI was also notably effusive in its praise of the NU following the elections, in marked contrast to the communists' continued criticism of Masyumi.[93]

There were hints that the NU was becoming increasingly concerned following the PKI's strong performance in the regional elections of 1957, but even in the late 1950s and early 1960s there were instances of cross-party cooperation.[94] A sign of growing wariness was the NU joining Masyumi in efforts to keep the PKI out of key posts in regional government in West Java following the 1957 elections.[95] However, the PKI and NU still found particular issues they could agree on, including some economic issues and opposition to Dutch rule in West Irian.[96] At times individuals' personal experiences could cut across party lines. In the West Javanese city of Cirebon in the late 1950s, an NU leader struck a deal with the PKI to get himself appointed to a key post, undercutting the other parties. A Bandung newspaper explained that he had been a member of the PKI "before the [Second World] War" and that the PKI's support for him was likely based on their view that he was a "comrade in their struggle, even though he is now in the NU."[97] That there were sometimes good personal relationships on the ground is supported by oral history evidence. A communist representative in the National Front recalled that "I had good relations with the NU, in fact better [than with the Indonesian National Party]."[98]

Within West Java, the closest relationship between the PKI and an Islamic party was with the Indonesian Islamic League Party (*Partai Sarekat Islam Indonesia*, PSII), the heir to the Islamic League, from which the PKI had split in the early 1920s. Although the PSII was smaller than Masyumi and the NU, West Java was one of the PSII's strongest regions, and, in the elections of 1957, it came in fifth in the province.[99] There were clear differences between the party and the PKI, given that the PSII consistently called for a stronger role for Islam in the state.[100] However, tensions between the PSII and Masyumi, as well as the PSII's vigorous anti-imperial nationalism, smoothed cooperation between the PSII and the PKI.[101] There were noticeable echoes between the rhetoric of the PKI and the PSII emphasizing the unity of all political forces in fulfilling Indonesian independence.[102] A number of prominent individuals with ties to West Java linked the PSII and the left, including Haji Tubagus Ahmad Chatib and the prominent female Muslim activist Yati Aruji Kartawinata.[103] Nationally and within West Java, the PKI and PSII could often be found in organizations, committees, and events set up to advance an agenda of anti-imperialism.[104] During the

1955 election the PSII and PKI agreed not to attack each other, and following the election the PKI praised the PSII as representing a "democratic and progressive" political tradition.[105]

As was the case with the NU, there were some signs of increased tension in the PSII as the PKI's growth became more evident at the time of the 1957 regional elections. However, the overall tenor of relations between the PKI and the PSII remained constructive. It is true that the PSII joined the effort to limit the PKI's ability to secure key positions in West Java's regional government in the aftermath of those elections.[106] However, in general, the PSII continued to emphasize cooperation across the political spectrum.[107] For its part, the PKI continued to portray the PSII positively, with the Communist Party newspaper praising the PSII in a report on the PSII's congress in 1962 as "supporting national unity" and showing that "Islamic Parties are not necessarily reactionary."[108] As late as September 1965, the newspaper carried a cartoon celebrating the cooperation between the PKI and the PSII.[109] These relatively warm relations between the two parties are corroborated by oral history testimony. One PKI leader in the region recalled that the "PSII and the PKI's relations were good," while a member of the People's Youth remembered that "the PSII often worked together [with us]."[110] A left-wing teacher, who did not join a party, explained that he saw the appeal of both parties: "I sympathized with the PSII, I sympathized with the PKI."[111]

Growing Conflict in the 1960s

Whilst the PKI's relations with Islamic parties varied, the trend was toward increasing polarization. The PKI's strong showing in the elections of 1955 and 1957 had made Islamic parties increasingly wary of the party, as reflected in efforts to marginalize the PKI in regional governments described above. The banning of Masyumi in 1960 for its involvement in a failed regional rebellion that broke out in the late 1950s removed key Islamic anti-communist voices from the political stage, but US backing for the rebels also reinforced the link between global Cold War polarization and conditions within Indonesia. Accelerating PKI growth in the early 1960s further increased anxieties on the religious right: the PKI's claimed national membership increased from 1,000,000 in 1956 to 3,500,000 in 1965.[112] Within the NU at a national level, a new generation of leaders was emerging who wanted a tougher response to the communist challenge and viewed older leaders as "too soft and diplomatic."[113] The growing influence of a militant strand within the NU was evident when, in 1962, it formed a paramilitary wing, the Ansor Multi-Purpose Brigade (*Barisan Ansor Serbaguna, Banser*), which grew rapidly in the following years.[114] Growing tensions between the PKI and Muslim groups were part of a broader pattern of political polarization under President Sukarno's authoritarian "Guided Democracy." An increasing concentration of power encouraged a "winner-takes-all" mentality among political actors, while Sukarno's emphasis on revolutionary spirit and the rapidly deteriorating economic conditions also raised the political temperature. A deepening crisis in Indochina increased the sense that Southeast Asia was becoming a Cold War flashpoint.

An important element in increasing polarization on the ground was the growing emphasis that PKI leaders placed on agrarian struggle. This was the culmination of a long-term trend in PKI thinking, but it also reflected an increasing Maoist tinge to its revolutionary activism and growing restrictions on the mobilization of industrial workers.[115] There were also signs of cultural differences and socioeconomic polarization becoming entwined. In parts of West Java there was a significant overlap between religious elites and large landholders.[116] A common pattern was for tensions to develop between the BTI and pious Muslim landlords (who were sometimes also local officials) linked to Masyumi.[117] Hostility to former members of Masyumi continued even after the party was banned in 1960. In West Java, individuals linked to Masyumi were also disproportionately targeted in the PKI-backed "unilateral action" land reform campaign that began in late 1963. As one People's Youth member recalled, "We'd target the evil landlords. . . . If they were from the NU, we'd ease off a bit, but if [the land] was owned by a Masyumi man we'd thrash them."[118] Although in West Java ex-Masyumi members were most likely to be targeted by land reform actions, the PKI's relations with the NU also deteriorated. For example, the US embassy noted an NU newspaper reporting "the murder of an Islamic village leader near Tjirebon . . . which was reported to have followed several other acts of violence in that area," with the NU attributing the killing to a "certain peasant organization," a thinly veiled reference to the BTI.[119]

By the mid-1960s, the situation was increasingly tense and rhetoric was becoming more heated. The PKI's national leadership took an increasingly militant tone, with Aidit calling for it to "intensify the revolutionary offensive in all fields."[120] Meanwhile, in West Java, the head of the NU's youth movement, Ansor, proclaimed that the youth group was "God's army," which "would not hesitate to pounce on and tear to pieces those who interfere with them."[121] In urban centers youth groups marched en masse with military-style drum bands and roll calls.[122] In rural areas the impact of land reform actions combined with worsening economic conditions. One People's Youth member recalled things were "heating up" with "prices rising" and "efforts by reactionary groups" who were "working hard to oppose the [agrarian] actions being carried out by the BTI and the People's Youth."[123] A sense of the tension emerges from some of the contemporary reports compiled by BTI activists conducting village research projects across Java in 1965.[124] For example, one team of researchers was forced to flee in the middle of the night (aided by People's Youth members wielding machetes), having being discovered by hostile village authorities.[125]

However, it is also important to recognize that conditions on the ground were far from uniform, either within or between regions. The extent of socioeconomic polarization varied in different areas, and the alignment of cultural and socioeconomic divisions was not exact: as noted above, there were cases in which local BTI leaders were themselves pious Muslims, and some landlords impacted by land reform efforts were aligned to secular parties.[126] Oral history accounts indicate that the extent of tensions differed considerably by locality and some areas were relatively little affected.[127] In addition to differences at local levels, there were broader regional trends: the level of conflict during the land campaign from the end of 1963 was also lower in West Java than in Central and East Java. This seems to have been due to several factors. One was the relatively smaller size of the PKI relative to East and Central Java. Another reason was the strong presence of the army in the villages of West Java following the defeat of the Darul Islam uprising.[128] A third factor was the relative weakness of the NU in West Java relative to some other areas: in East Java in particular, the NU was involved in recurrent and bitter conflicts with the PKI and BTI over land reform efforts, as is reflected in Imam Muhtarom's chapter.[129]

Increasingly tense conditions in the countryside formed part of the context for the anticommunist massacres of 1965–66. However, a growing body of evidence has shown that the violence was not a spontaneous popular outburst against the PKI, as Indonesian military propaganda claimed.[130] Recent studies of the killings of 1965–66 have highlighted the central role played by the Indonesian army, working with the police and the approval and sometimes active support of the United States and its allies.[131] Military propaganda blamed the PKI for an abortive coup attempt, with the alleged plotters branded as "bloodthirsty animals and counterrevolutionary traitors."[132] It also misleadingly portrayed communists and their allies as collectively guilty and as an ongoing threat.[133] Scholars have crucially pointed out that most of the anticommunist killings took the form of "forced disappearances" after prisoners had been detained in military-controlled facilities.[134] For example, Imam Muhtarom's chapter in this volume on events in Blitar in East Java mentions prisoners being dispatched from local military and police command posts for execution. The recurrence of the pattern of forced disappearances from military custody that is found in local studies across the archipelago is hard to explain without some level of coordination having occurred at the national level.[135] Researchers have also highlighted the key role played by the postures of regional army commanders in influencing geographical and temporal patterns of the killings.[136] The caution of West Java military commander General Adjie helps explain why levels of killing were much lower in West Java than Central and East Java.[137]

Whilst the role of the military was crucial, mounting evidence has also confirmed the active involvement of religious groups in the violence.[138] Military propaganda purposely stoked religious hatred, denouncing the "barbarous actions of the atheist PKI."[139] Meanwhile, some influential Muslim leaders enthusiastically argued that anticommunism was part of a holy war.[140] The army worked closely with Muslim militias on the ground in some regions. For example, in East Java the army worked with the NU, some of whose members provide oral history testimony in Imam Muhtarom's chapter.[141] Within West Java, there are secondhand reports of Muslim groups being involved in killing, some in areas where there had been bitter conflicts over land, such as Subang.[142] Moreover, in the Cirebon area a member of a religious youth group admitted participating in killing military detainees.[143] Islamic schools and Muslim organizations encouraged a martial atmosphere. A writer who grew up in a religious boarding school in Tasikmalaya later recalled martial arts training involving machetes taking place in school.[144] In addition to direct involvement in killings, civilians could sometimes provide valuable information. For example, in Ciwidey, to the south of Bandung, a civilian acted as a "guide" for soldiers looking for individuals who were to be arrested and killed.[145] Wariness borne of fighting Darul Islam seems to have been a factor limiting the army's further mobilization of Muslim groups in West Java.[146] However, following a change of personnel in 1966, and a shift to a more aggressive approach, the army may have mobilized some former Darul Islam fighters to take part in the killing.[147]

Conclusion: Polarization, Entanglement, and Contingency

Overall, it was not the case that communism and Islam were inherently and completely incompatible. The PKI emphasized that it was not anti-Islam and supported freedom of religion. Its relations with Muslim organizations varied, from conflict with Darul Islam and tension with Masyumi to warmer relations with the PSII. Even when criticizing Masyumi and Darul Islam, the PKI was careful to differentiate between them and Islam in general. Other cross-cutting elements included the social work of the PKI and its affiliates and the presence of a significant number of pious Muslims within the party.

However, there was a broad tendency over time for tension between the PKI and Muslim groups to increase. This lends some support to Ricklefs's interpretation of the period through the lens of a broader process of cultural polarization that became entwined with politics. Violence during the revolution, and then electoral competition, heightened tensions. Hostility between the PKI and the largest Muslim groups increased as the PKI grew rapidly and the land reform campaign that the PKI backed from late 1963 increased the potential for conflict. Growing tensions in the countryside provide part of the context for the anticommunist violence of 1965–66.

Evolving tensions were exacerbated by superpower rivalries. The Madiun Affair was shaped by growing international polarization as well as local developments, and it had implications for communist-Muslim relations throughout Indonesia. US involvement in the regional rebellion of the late 1950s, along with its support for the army during its campaign of violence against the PKI in 1965–66, also helped fuel polarization and conflict. Allegations that the PKI were agents of Moscow and Masyumi were imperialist stooges (in an old Dutch or new American form) were another ingredient. A growing Maoist tinge to the PKI was a factor in the party's increasing focus on agrarian struggle, which heightened tensions with Muslim groups.

This is not to say that the violence of 1965–66 was spontaneous or inevitable. The military as an institution played a crucial role in driving forward the killings on the ground: many of those killed had been detained in military facilities. With close control of the media from late 1965, the military also sought to cultivate fear and hatred of the PKI through a vicious propaganda campaign that framed the communists as treacherous and as a threat to the nation, moral order, and religion. In doing so it resonated with earlier allegations made by some Muslim groups about the PKI's alleged perfidy and godlessness.

Recent scholarship has rightly rejected stereotyped explanations of the violence as resulting from a supposed Indonesian proclivity toward emotional and "irrational outbursts."[148] Yet there can also be a danger in overdrawing the distinction between reason and emotion, which constantly interact via "'cognitive-affective' thought processes."[149] Anticommunist narratives that facilitated prominent Muslim groups' cooperation with the army designated communists as a serious threat to be feared and detested, partly on the basis they were a threat to religious and moral order. This was also a significant part of the context for the participation of Muslim groups in the killing.

This chapter has argued that a close examination of developments in one province provides an entry point for exploring the Cold War as a process through which multiple forms of polarization became entangled. Religion was not the passive object of Cold War influences, but rather an integral element in the matrix of cultural, social, and political tensions that constituted the Cold War. Such an approach has also demonstrated the need to account for variation and contingency in the evolution of the Cold War. By incorporating perspectives from the grass roots and the provinces, and combining archival, published, and oral history sources, we can see more clearly how conflicts were made—and mitigated—on the ground.

Notes

* In addition to thanking the organizer of, and participants in, the NUS "Reconceptualizing the Cold War" workshop, I would like to thank Michael Yeo, Kevin Fogg, and Lin Hongxuan for reading and commenting on a draft version of this chapter.

1. To take one example, Odd Arne Westad, *The Cold War: A World History* (London: Penguin, 2018), 1–4, describes the Cold War as a "confrontation between capitalism and socialism" and an "international system" marked by "bipolarity."

2. Quotation from Westad, *Cold War*, 7. On the interaction of the left-right struggle with the process of decolonization see Odd Arne Westad, *The Global Cold War: Third World Interventions and the Making of Our Times* (Cambridge: Cambridge University Press, 2007); on the Sino-Soviet split and the third world, see Jeremy Friedman, *Shadow Cold War: The Sino-Soviet Competition for the Third World* (Chapel Hill: University of North Carolina Press, 2015); on the intersection of various forms of identity in shaping violence during the Cold War, see Paul Thomas Chamberlin, *The Cold War's Killing Fields: Rethinking the Long Peace* (New York: Harper, 2018), 15.

3. Useful starting points include Dianne Kirby, ed., *Religion and the Cold War* (Basingstoke, UK: Palgrave, 2003); Philip Muehlenbeck, ed., *Religion and the Cold War: A Global Perspective* (Nashville, TN: Vanderbilt University Press, 2012); and Dianne Kirby, "The Religious Cold War" in Richard H. Immerman and Petra Goedde, eds., *The Oxford Handbook of the Cold War* (Oxford: Oxford University Press, 2016), 540–64.

4. An intellectual and institutional focus was highlighted in Stephen J. Whitfield's review of Kirby, *Religion and the Cold War* in *Journal of Cold War Studies* 8,

no. 1 (2005): 139. The argument broadly applies across the literature cited in endnote 4. One study which points to some ways of broadening approaches to the study of the Cold War and religion is Clemens Six, *Secularism, Decolonisation, and the Cold War in South and Southeast Asia* (London: Routledge, 2018).

5. Masuda Hajimu critiques this approach; see Masuda, "The Early Cold War: Studies of Cold War America in the Twenty-First Century," in Christopher R. W. Dietrich, ed., *A Companion to U.S. Foreign Relations: Colonial Era to the Present* (Hoboken, NJ: Wiley Blackwell, 2020), 2:636–38.

6. Masuda Hajimu, *Cold War Crucible: The Korean Conflict and the Postwar World* (Cambridge, MA: Harvard University Press, 2015), 285.

7. Federico Romero, "Cold War Historiography at the Crossroads," *Cold War History* 14, no. 4 (2014): 693–94. There is, however, a tension between Romero's engagement with such a broad perspective and his desire to recenter the focus of Cold War studies on Europe.

8. John-Paul A. Ghobrial, "Seeing the World Like a Microhistorian," *Past and Present* 242, no. 14 (2019): 8.

9. The quotation comes from Henk Schulte Nordholt, "Indonesia in the 1950s Nation, Modernity, and the Post-colonial State," *Bijdragen tot de Taal-, Land- en Volkenkunde* 167, no. 4 (2011): 386. Schulte Nordholt used the term to critique this persistent narrative.

10. Ben Fowkes, "Unholy Alliance: Muslims and Communists—An Introduction," *Journal of Communist Studies and Transition Politics* 25, no. 1 (2009): 26.

11. The classic account of the PKI's early history is Ruth T. McVey, *The Rise of Indonesian Communism* (Ithaca, NY: Cornell University Press, 1965).

12. On the PKI in the 1950s and 1960s see especially Donald Hindley, *The Communist Party of Indonesia 1951–1963* (Berkeley: University of California Press, 1966); and Rex Mortimer, *Indonesian Communism under Sukarno: Ideology and Politics, 1959–1965* (Ithaca, NY: Cornell University Press, 1974).

13. This ranking is based on membership data from US Department of State Bureau of Intelligence and Research, "World Strength of the Communist Party Organizations," no. 17 (1965): 7–14.

14. An overview of the killings is provided by Geoffrey Robinson, *The Killing Season: A History of the Indonesian Massacres, 1965–66* (Princeton, NJ: Princeton University Press, 2018). On the question of numbers, see Robert Cribb, "How Many Deaths? Problems in the Statistics of Massacre in Indonesia (1965–1966) and East Timor (1975–1980)," in Ingrid Wessel and Georgia Wimhöfer, eds., *Violence in Indonesia* (Hamburg: Abera, 2001), 82–98; and Siddharth Chandra, "New Findings on the Indonesian Killings of 1965–66," *Journal of Asian Studies* 76, no. 4 (2017): 1059–86.

15. For this theme in military newspapers in 1965–66, see John Roosa, *Buried Histories: The Anticommunist Massacres of 1965–1966 in Indonesia* (Madison: University of Wisconsin Press, 2020), 77. A violent attack on a mosque by PKI supporters also takes place at the start of Arifin C. Noer's famous propaganda film *Pengkhianatan G30S/PKI* [The betrayal of the Thirtieth September Movement/Indonesian Communist Party] (1984). For the continued influence of this argument, even after the fall of the military regime, see the following account written

by an Indonesian member of parliament: Abdul Qadir Djaelani, *Komunisme Musuh Islam Sepanjang Sejarah* [Communism the enemy of Islam throughout history] (Jakarta: Yayasan Pengkajian Islam Madinah-Munawwarah, 2000).

16. Clifford Geertz, *The Religion of Java* (Chicago: University of Chicago Press, 1960), 4–6, 40.

17. Clifford Geertz, "Social Context of Economic Change: An Indonesian Case Study" (unpublished working paper, MIT, 1956), 141–44.

18. For example, Donald K. Emmerson, *Indonesia's Elite: Political Culture and Cultural Politics* (Ithaca, NY: Cornell University Press, 1976), 23–24; Mark R. Woodward, *Java, Indonesia and Islam* (Dordrecht: Springer, 2011), chap. 1; and Timothy P. Daniels, *Islamic Spectrum in Java* (Farnham, UK: Ashgate, 2009).

19. M. C. Ricklefs, "The Birth of the Abangan," *Bijdragen tot de Taal-, Land- en Volkenkunde* 162, no. 1 (2006): 35.

20. M. C. Ricklefs, *Islamisation and Its Opponents in Java c. 1930 to the Present* (Singapore: NUS Press, 2012), 496.

21. Melvin, "The Hammer and Sickle on 'Mecca's Veranda'—The Indonesian Communist Party in Aceh, 1920–65," *Indonesia*, no. 108 (2019): 23–40; Lin, "Ummah Yet Proletariat: Islam and Marxism in the Netherlands, East Indies and Indonesia, 1915–1959" (PhD diss., University of Washington, 2020), 132, 318.

22. Lynda Newland, "Under the Banner of Islam: Mobilising Religious Identities in West Java," *Australian Journal of Anthropology* 11, no. 2 (2000): 203.

23. On the Darul Islam uprising see C. van Dijk, *Rebellion Under the Banner of Islam* (The Hague: Martinus Nijhoff, 1981); Chiara Formichi, *Islam and the Making of the Nation: Kartosuwiryo and Political Islam in 20th Century Indonesia* (Leiden: KITLV Press, 2012); and Karl D. Jackson, *Traditional Authority, Islam and Rebellion* (Berkeley: University of California Press, 1980).

24. "Daftar Angka2 Hasil Pemilihan D.P.R.D. Tahun 1957–1958" [Data tables for the results of regional representative council elections in the years 1957–1958] (copies of election results from the Indonesian Election Bureau, available on microfilm at Cornell University Library).

25. For West Java see Harold Crouch, *The Army in Indonesian Politics* (Ithaca, NY: Cornell University Press, 1978), 142; and Ulf Sundhaussen, "The Political Orientations and Political Involvement of the Indonesian Officer Corps" (PhD diss., Monash University, 1972), 694. For East Java, see Chandra, "New Findings."

26. On the term *abangan*, see Ricklefs, "Birth of the Abangan," 35. On the term's nonuse in West Java during this period, see Chaidah S. Bamualim, "Negotiating Islamisation and Resistance: A Study of Religions, Politics and Social Change in West Java from the Early 20th Century to the Present" (PhD diss., Leiden University, 2015), 72. The term *santri* was more widely used, though sometimes had subtly different meanings.

27. Jan Sihar Aritonang and Karel Steenbrink, eds., *A History of Christianity in Indonesia* (Leiden: Brill, 2008), 650–53.

28. Howard M. Federspiel, *Islam and Ideology in the Emerging Indonesian State: The Persatuan Islam (Persis) 1923 to 1957* (Leiden: Brill, 2001); and Bamualim, "Negotiating Islamisation and Resistance," 31.

29. McVey, *Rise of Indonesian Communism*, chap. 5.
30. McVey, *Rise of Indonesian Communism*, 104–5.
31. McVey, *Rise of Indonesian Communism*, 181–82.
32. Lin Hongxuan, "Sickle as Crescent: Islam and Communism in the Netherlands Indies, 1915–1927," *Studia Islamika* 25, no. 2 (2018): 312; on this point more broadly, see also Takashi Shiraishi, *An Age in Motion: Popular Radicalism in Java, 1912–1926* (Ithaca, NY: Cornell University Press, 1990), especially chap. 7; and Oliver Crawford, "Translating and Transliterating Marxism in Indonesia," *Modern Asian Studies* 55, no. 3 (2020): 28–33.
33. Michael C. Williams, *Sickle and Crescent: The Communist Revolt of 1926 in Banten* (Ithaca, NY: Cornell Modern Indonesia Project, 1982).
34. Michael C. Williams, "Banten: 'Rice Debts Will Be Repaid with Rice, Blood Debts with Blood,'" in Audrey Kahin, ed., *Regional Dynamic of the Indonesian Revolution* (Honolulu: University of Hawai'i Press, 1985), 55–81.
35. Hasan Raid, *Pergulatan Muslim Komunis: Otobiografi Hasan Raid* [A communist Muslim's struggle: The autobiography of Hasan Raid] (Yogyakarta: LKPSM-Syarikat, 2001), 62. On Hasan Raid, see also Lin, "Ummah Yet Proletariat," 365–71; C. W. Watson, *Of Self and Injustice: Autobiography and Repression in Modern Indonesia* (Singapore: NUS Press, 2006), chap. 1; and Budiawan, *Mematahkan Perwarisan Ingatan* [Breaking down the inheritance of memory] (Yogayakarta: Elsam, 2004), chap. 4.
36. "Algemeen Inlichtingsrapport Nr. 15 Betreffende Tjimahi en Omstreken, Loopende v/m 6 t/m 16 Mei 1946" [General intelligence report number 15 regarding Cimahi and surroundings, from 6 to 16 May 1946], series 2.10.62 (NEFIS CMI), folder 991, Dutch National Archives (Algemeen Rijksarchief, ARA), The Hague.
37. "Soeasana Banten Dewasa Ini" [The current situation in Banten], attached to a letter from R. S. Soeria Santoso, Secretary of State for Internal Security to Army Commander and Attorney General, July 26, 1948, series 2.10.17 (Procureur Generaal), folder 962, ARA.
38. For violence more broadly in the Indonesian Revolution see the special issue of the *Journal of Genocide Research*, 14, no. 3–4 (2012).
39. "Laporan Tentang Keadaan Didaerah Tasikmalaja Oetara 23 Dec 1947, Kantor Polisi Tasikmalaja Daerah Oetara" [Report regarding the situation in the region of North Tasikmalaya, 23 December 1947, police office of the North Tasikmalaya region] and "Laporan Tentang Keadaan Didaerah Karesidenan Priangan, Kantor Polisi Keresidenan Priangan" [Report regarding the situation in the region of the residency of Priangan, police office of the residency of Priangan] (undated but apparently from December 1947 or January 1948), series RA 26, Kepolisian Negara 1947–1949, folder 495, Indonesian National Archives (Arsip Nasional Republik Indonesia, ANRI), Jakarta.
40. The letter claimed to be from "Partai Kominis Indonesia (P.K.I.) Sectie Djawa Barat" to local branches, dated April 25, 1948, series 2.10.17 (Procureur Generaal), folder 962, ARA. For the plausible suspicion that the document was a forgery by Muslim activists seeking to stoke hostility toward the PKI see "Overgenomen uit

Bp.b-3-26 Juni 1948-B.155.241" [Extract from File Bp.b-3-26 June 1948-.155.241], series 2.10.62 (NEFIS CMI), folder 1622, ARA.

41. Formichi, *Islam*, 173–75. See also appendices 1–3 in B. J. Boland, *The Struggle of Islam in Modern Indonesia* (The Hague: Nijhoff, 1971).

42. For the Madiun Affair and its aftermath, see Ann Swift, *The Road to Madiun: the Indonesian Communist Uprising of 1948* (Ithaca, NY: Cornell Modern Indonesia Project, 1989); Soe Hok Gie, *Orang-orang di Persimpangan Kiri Jalan* [People at a leftward turning point] (Yogyakarta: Bentang, 1997); Larisa Efimova, "Who Gave Instructions to the Indonesian Communist Leader Musso in 1948?" *Indonesia and the Malay World*, 13, no. 90 (2003): 171–89; and Harry A. Poeze, *Madiun 1948, PKI Bergerak* [Madiun 1948, the PKI makes its move] (Jakarta: KITLV-Obor, 2011).

43. For an argument that stresses the decisive impact of the Madiun Affair, see Rémy Madinier, "Lawan dan Kawan (Friends and Foes): Indonesian Islam and Communism During the Cold War (1945–1960)," in Christopher Goscha and Christian Ostermann, eds., *Connecting Histories: Decolonization and the Cold War in Southeast Asia, 1945–1962* (Stanford, CA: Stanford University Press, 2009), 359. Also see Katharine McGregor, "A Reassessment of the Significance of the 1948 Madiun Uprising to the Cold War in Indonesia," *Kajian Malaysia* [*Malaysian Studies*] 27, no. 1–2 (2009): 85–119.

44. For a couple of examples see "Siapa Jang Anti-Agama" [Who is anti-religion], *Bintang Merah* [*Red Star*], 9, no. 5, May 1953; and "Idul Fitri dan Kemerdekaan Beragama" [Eid Al-Fitr and freedom of religion], *Harian Rakjat*, June 1, 1954.

45. "Kaum Muslimin di URSS, Kemerdekaan Agama & Konferensi di Bandung" [Muslims in the USSR, freedom of religion and the Bandung Conference], *Harian Rakjat*, May 29, 1956; and "Delegasi Islam Indonesia—Agama di R.R.T. Bebas Sepenuhnja" [Indonesian Muslim delegation—religion in the PRC is fully free], *Harian Rakjat*, June 5, 1956. This was of course an idealized depiction. For an overview of developments in the People's Republic of China (and Soviet Union) during this period, see Stephen Smith, "On Not Learning from the Soviet Union: Religious Policy in China, 1949–65," *Modern China Studies* 22, no. 1 (2015): 71–98.

46. Ragna Boden, *Die Grenzen der Weltmacht: Sowjetische Indonesienpolitik von Stalin bis Brežnev* [The limits of global power: Soviet Indonesia policy from Stalin to Brezhnev] (Stuttgart: Franz Steiner, 2006), 288.

47. "PKI Menerima Pantjasila Sebagai Dasar Politik Republik Indonesia" [The PKI accepts Pancasila as the political basis of the Republic of Indonesia], *Harian Rakjat*, November 11, 1954.

48. See Mortimer, *Indonesian Communism under Sukarno*, 93–95, on the back-and-forth in the Indonesian press on this issue in the late 1950s and early 1960s.

49. "PKI Bersedia Menerima Pantjasila Tanpa Perubahan" [The PKI is willing to accept Panca Sila without modification], *Harian Rakjat*, October 22, 1957. This is the only time I am aware of Aidit explicitly describing the party as atheist, even in such a qualified way.

50. "DN Aidit Tentang PKI dan Pantjasila, Agama, Perbedaan Pendapat Dalam GKI dll" [DN Aidit on the PKI and Panca Sila, religion, differing views within the international communist movement etc.], *Harian Rakjat*, August 20, 1964.

51. At a national level, see "Memilih Palu-Arit Berarti Memperdjuangkan Terbentuknja Pemerintah Koalisi Nasionalis–Islam–Komunis" [Choosing the hammer and sickle means struggling for the formation of a nationalist–Islamic–communist coalition], *Harian Rakjat*, September 24, 1955; and "Hanja Dengan Persatuan Nasional Berporoskan Nasakom Tuntutan Rakjat Dapat Dilaksanakan" [Only with national unity based on Nasakom can the people's demands be carried out], *Harian Rakjat*, May 26, 1964. From West Java see the comment of the PKI provincial leader Amir Anwar in "Wat de Partijen Ervan Denken" [What the parties think], *De Preangerbode* [*The Preanger Messenger*], October 14, 1955; also see "PKI Djabar—Dengan Poros Nasakom Hantjurkan Kontra-Revolusi" [The West Java PKI—with the foundation of Nasakom, crush the counter-revolution], *Harian Rakjat*, August 20, 1964.

52. Sukarno, "Nationalism, Islam and Marxism," in Sukarno, *Under the Banner of the Revolution* (Jakarta: Publication Committee, 1966), 1:5 (the speech was originally delivered in 1926).

53. For an explanation of the "Nasakom" concept, see Sukarno, "Persatuan Total Dengan Poros Nasakom" [Total unity on the basis of Nasakom] (Jakarta: Departemen Penerangan, 1962).

54. On Achmad Dasuki Siradj see Lin, "Ummah Yet Proletariat," 360–64; on Mohamad Sabitun, see "Mentjoblos Tandagambar [Palu Arit] Berarti Menjokong Partai Jang Diridlo'i Tuhan" [Voting for the hammer and sickle symbol means supporting a party blessed by God]," *Harian Rakjat*, July 10, 1957; and Iskandar Zulkarnain, *Gerakan Ahmadiyah di Indonesia* [The Ahmadiyah movement in Indonesia] (Yogyakarta: LKiS, 2005), 247–48 (admittedly, Kyai Mohamad Sabitun was eventually expelled from the Ahmadiyah for his activities in the PKI).

55. For example, "Rombongan Njoto Disambut Hangat di Tasikmalaja" [Nyoto's group welcomed warmly in Tasikmalaya], *Harian Rakjat*, September 14, 1955; "Rapat Umum PKI di Plered" [A public PKI meeting in Plered], *Harian Rakjat*, September 19, 1955; and "Tjeramah PKI" [A PKI speech], *Harian Rakjat*, August 2, 1957.

56. "M. H. Lukman di Subang" [M. H. Lukman in Subang], *Harian Rakjat*, August 6, 1957; and "Rapat Umum PKI" [A public PKI meeting], *Harian Rakjat*, August 10, 1957.

57. Institut Sejarah Sosial Indonesia (ISSI) Oral History Project '65 (OHP '65), interview 2.18, "Djajadi," Tasikmalaya, April 4, 2001. Names assigned by ISSI are pseudonyms.

58. Cornell University Archives, Indonesia Miscellany, "Desa Political Study (1956)," interview of "H. A. Tandjuddina, Pimpinan Barisan Tani Indonesia" from Sukamanah, Sukabumi. For another example of a BTI hajji from West Java see "Kader BTI Diteror DI" [BTI cadres terrorized by Darul Islam], *Suara Tani* [*The Peasants' Voice*] 10:11 (November 1959).

59. International Institute of Social History, Oral History of the Indonesian Trade Union Movement, tape 11, interview with Didi Wiharnadi.

60. Oral history interview, Tangerang, January 22, 2018.

61. ISSI OHP '65, interview 2.23, "Sudarno" (a BTI member), Cipanas, (2001?); ISSI OHP '65, interview 2.20, "Haryatna" (a People's Youth Member), Tasikmalaya,

April 4, 2001; and oral history interview with a People's Youth member, Banten, April 23, 2018.

62. ISSI OHP '65, interview 2.22, "Kamaludin" (a People's Youth Member), Tasikmalaya, April 3, 2001; "Usaha Membangun BTI" [Efforts to develop the BTI], *Suara Tani*, 9:12, December 1958; and "Bandung: 3 Buah Mesdjid Untuk Rakjat" [Bandung: Three mosques for the people], *Harian Rakjat*, April 15, 1958.

63. In some parts of Indonesia there was a conscious outreach to religious leaders for this reason: see "Pengalaman Tjara Menarik Simpati Kijai2" [Experiences of how to gain the sympathy of Kyais], *Kehidupan Partai* [*Party Life*], May–August 1957.

64. "Risalah Dewan Pemerintah Daerah 1958 II" [Minutes of the regional council, 1958 II], 703, Bandung City Municipal Archive (Arsip Kota Bandung).

65. The quote is from "Sobsi dan Hadiah Lebaran" [Sobsi and Eid al-Fitr bonuses], *Harian Rakjat*, June 19, 1951; see also "Tunjangan Labaran" [Eid al-Fitr bonuses], *Harian Rakjat*, May 9, 1955.

66. For example, see "Gotong Rojong" [Community service], *Harian Rakjat*, May 5, 1955, for the PKI and PSII working together on this in Jatiwangi.

67. "Kerdjasama Masjumi-PKI" [Masyumi-PKI cooperation], *Harian Rakjat*, October 18, 1957.

68. ISSI OHP '65, interview 2.19, "Endin," Tasikmalaya, April 4, 2001.

69. Imam Muhtarom, "Terror in East Java: The NU versus PKI Conflict before and after September 30, 1965," chap. 1 in this volume.

70. "Delegasi Anti-D.I. dari Rakjat Djawa Barat Disambut Hangat di Djakarta" [Anti-Darul Islam delegation from the people of West Java welcomed warmly in Jakarta], *Harian Rakjat*, August 4, 1953; "Pernjataan DPDB BTI Djawa Barat: Gagalkan Rentjana Amnesti Umum Kepada DI–TII" [Statement of the West Java regional leadership council of the BTI: Defeat the planned general amnesty for Darul Islam], *Harian Rakjat*, September 27, 1955; and "DI Mengganas" [Darul Islam on the rampage], *Harian Rakjat*, February 28, 1956.

71. Oral history interview (with a youth organization member), Sukabumi, January 14, 2018; oral history interview (with a youth organization member), Cianjur, January 25, 2018; and oral history interview (with a peasant activist), Kuningan, April 7, 2018.

72. Boyd Compton, "Indonesian Communism: The Ranks Swell," *Institute of Current World Affairs Report*, November 23, 1954.

73. "P.K.I. Pembela Islam" [The PKI are defenders of Islam], *Pikiran Rakjat* [*Thoughts of the People*], October 12, 1953.

74. Madinier, "Kawan dan Lawan," 360–61; see also the many items in the Masyumi periodical *Hikmah* [*Blessing*].

75. On the election campaign, see Kevin William Fogg, "The Fate of Muslim Nationalism in Independent Indonesia" (PhD diss., Yale University, 2012), 329–39.

76. "Putusan Madjlis Sjura Pusat Masjumi Tentang 'Hukum Islam Terhadap Komunisme'" [The decision of Masyumi's central consultative council regarding "Islamic law with regard to communism"], *Hikmah*, January 15, 1955.

77. See Boyd Compton's interview with Isa Anshary in "Muslim Radicalism: The Anti-Communist Front," *Institute of Current World Affairs Report*, May 3, 1955.

78. On the controversy, see "Buktikan Persatuan Segala Golongan" [Prove the unity of all groups], *Harian Rakjat*, January 3, 1955; "Ketua Front Anti Komunis Didengar Keterangannja" [The statement of the chairman of the anticommunist front is heard], *Pikiran Rakjat*, June 18, 1955; and "Sekitar Penuntutan PKI Terhadap Ketua 'Front Anti Komunis'" [On the PKI's legal case against the chairman of the "anticommunist front"], *Harian Rakjat*, June 26, 1955; on subtle differences of emphasis within Masyumi see Fogg, "Fate of Muslim Nationalism," 329–39.

79. On the donation to Masyumi, see the account of CIA officer Joseph Burkholder Smith, *Portrait of a Cold Warrior* (New York: Putnam, 1976), 210. On US involvement in the rebellion in the late 1950s, see Audrey Kahin and George McTurnan Kahin, *Subversion as Foreign Policy: The Secret Eisenhower and Dulles Debacle in Indonesia* (Seattle: University of Washington Press, 1995).

80. For example, "Sumbangan Kepada Propaganda Masjumi" [A contribution to Masyumi's propaganda], *Harian Rakjat*, August 31, 1955; and "Masjumi Kontra Persatuan" [Masyumi against unity], *Harian Rakjat*, September 8, 1955.

81. "Masjumi Mendjelang Pemilihan Umum Dengan Pemalsuan dan Kepalsuan" [Masyumi approaches the general election with fakery and falsehood], *Harian Rakjat*, April 20, 1955; and D. N. Aidit, "Konfrontasi Peristiwa Madiun, Peristiwa Sumatera" [Confronting the Madiun affair, the Sumatra affair], in D. N. Aidit, *Pilihan Tulisan* [Selected works] (Jakarta: Jajasan Pembaruan, 1960), 2:132. For the allegation of Masyumi collusion with Darul Islam, see "Memilih Masjumi Berarti Memilih D.I." [Choosing Masyumi means choosing Darul Islam], *Harian Rakjat*, September 24, 1955; and "Pemimpin Masjumi, wk. ketua DPRDS, 'Residen D.I.' Akan Segera Diadili" [Masyumi leader, vice chair of the provisional regional assembly, "Darul Islam regional leader" will soon go on trial], *Harian Rakjat*, September 2, 1955.

82. "P.K.I. Pembela Islam" [The PKI is the defender of Islam], *Pikiran Rakjat*, October 12, 1953. On the difficulties that Masyumi had in distancing itself from the rebels, see Rémy Madinier, *Islam and Politics in Indonesia* (Singapore: NUS Press, 2015), 161–80.

83. "Sudisman dimuka 20.000 Rakjat Tasikmalaja: Dalam Negera Islam Model DI" [Sudisman in front of 20,000 people in Tasikmalaya: What an Islamic state on the Darul Islam model would look like], *Harian Rakjat*, December 2, 1955; "D.N. Aidit dimuka 100.000 Rakjat Tjirebon" [D. N. Aidit in front of 100,000 people in Cirebon], *Harian Rakjat*, November 16, 1954; and "Waspada Terhadap Kekalapan Reaksi" [Watch out for reactionary fury], *Harian Rakjat*, May 31, 1955.

84. At a national level, see Lin, "Ummah Yet Proletariat," 325–26; a similar argument at a local level was made to me by a trade unionist who worked in Cirebon: oral history interview at Surakarta, February 4, 2018.

85. "DN Aidit: Anggota-anggota Masjumi Tidak Dibikin Dari Batu—Djangan Bosan2 Adjak Anggota2 Masjumi Bersatu Berdasarkan Kepentingan Bersama" [D. N. Aidit: Masyumi members are not made of stone—never tire of inviting Masyumi members to unite based on common interests], *Harian Rakjat*, January 11,

1955; and "Kerdjasama Masjumi-PKI" [Masyumi-PKI cooperation], *Harian Rakjat*, October 18, 1957; see also the letter from the West Java PKI leader Amir Anwar in *Pikiran Rakjat*, November 3, 1955. There is ongoing controversy over nomenclature with regard to the territory that has sometimes been referred to as "West Irian," "Western New Guinea," or "West Papua." My use of West Irian does not imply endorsement of the name but reflects that the term was in common usage.

86. "Hubungan Dengan Belanda Diputuskan, PSI-Masjumi Dibubarkan" [Relations with the Netherlands abrogated, Indonesian socialist party and Masyumi disbanded], *Harian Rakjat*, August 19, 1960.

87. On the role of anti-imperialism in facilitating the interweaving of Islam and Marxism in Indonesia during this period, see Lin, "Ummah Yet Proletariat," 320–21.

88. ISSI OHP '65, interview 2.16, "Suratna," Cipanas, March 15, 2001.

89. Greg Fealy, *Ijtihad Politik Ulama: Sejarah NU 1952–1967* [Ulama and political ijtihad: A history of the Nahdlatul Ulama 1952–1967] (Yogyakarta: LKiS, 2003), 348–49.

90. Lin, "Ummah Yet Proletariat," 354–57.

91. For example, Masyumi's declaration that communists were infidels in *Hikmah*, January 15, 1955, ended with a pointed criticism of the "NU's cooperation with communists."

92. On this ambivalence, see "Vice Premier en Minister van Godsdienst in Bandung" [Vice president and minister of religion in Bandung], *De Preangerbode*, January 10, 1955; "Vice Premier Zet Standpunt van Nahdlatul Ulama Uiteen" [Vice president lays out Nahdlatul Ulama's position], *De Preangerbode*, April 9, 1955; and, more broadly, Madinier, *Islam and Politics in Indonesia*, 145. On maintaining cordial relations, see "Toleransi PKI NU" [PKI-NU tolerance], *Harian Rakjat*, January 25, 1955. Fealy argues that during the election campaign "the only party with which NU was unable to maintain cordial relations was Masyumi." See Fealy, *Ijtihad Politik Ulama*, 187.

93. "Partai-Partai Demokratis Mendapat Kemenangan Jang Mejakinkan" [Democratic parties reach a convincing victory], *Harian Rakjat*, October 1, 1955.

94. Fealy, *Ijtihad Politik Ulama*, 254–55.

95. "Agreement Masjumi, PNI, NU, PSII" [Agreement of Masyumi, Indonesian National Party (Partai Nasional Indonesia, PNI), NU, PSII], *Pikiran Rakjat*, December 27, 1957; and Daniel Lev, "The Transition to Guided Democracy in Indonesia, 1957–1958" (PhD diss., Cornell University, 1964), 138.

96. "Kerdjasama PNI, PKI dan N.U." [Cooperation of PNI, PKI, NU], *Harian Rakjat*, November 15, 1957; and "Pernjataan Bersama PNI, NU dan PKI Sukabumi" [Joint statement of Sukabumi branches of PNI, NU and PKI], *Harian Rakjat*, January 30, 1962.

97. The quote is from "Sjafei Mendjadi Kepala Daerah—Tjalon Dari PNI Dikalahkan—Akibat Kerdjasama NU dan PKI" [Sjafei becomes regional head—candidate from PNI defeated—a result of cooperation between NU and PKI], *Pikiran Rakjat*, February 1, 1958; see also "Kepala Daerah Djadi Rebutan—NU Lebih Akrab Dengan PKI—Dengan Mengorbankan PNI-Masyumi" [Struggle for regional

head position—NU closer to PKI—they Sacrifice PNI and Masyumi], *Pikiran Rakjat*, January 24, 1958.

98. ISSI OHP '65, interview 2.18, "Djajadi," Tasikmalaya, April 4, 2001.

99. "Daftar Angka2."

100. For example, see *PSII dari Tahun ke Tahun* [PSII through the years] ([Jakarta?]: Departemen Penerangan dan Propaganda PSII, 1952); and PSII, *Menjongsong Undang2 Dasar R.I. 1945* [Welcoming the Indonesian Republic's 1945 constitution] (Jakarta: LT-PSII, 1959). I would like to thank Kevin Fogg for making these and other documents relating to the PSII available to me.

101. On tensions between Masyumi and the PSII, see Kevin W. Fogg, *Indonesia's Islamic Revolution* (Cambridge: Cambridge University Press, 2019), chap. 12; and Madinier, *Islam and Politics in Indonesia*, 135–46.

102. For example, compare the preamble to PSII, *Piagam Undang-Undang Dasar Negara Republik Indonesia Menurut Partai Sjarikat Islam Indonesia* [Charter of the Republic of Indonesia's constitution according to the Indonesian Islamic League party] (Jakarta: PSII, 1956); and the statement of the West Java PKI leader Amir Anwar in *Pikiran Rakjat*, November 3, 1955.

103. For Achmad Chatib see Williams, *Sickle and Crescent* and "Banten." On his involvement in the PSII in the early 1950s, see "Geen Sprake van Gratie Abolitie of Amnestie" [No talk of pardon, discharge or amnesty], *De Preangerbode*, June 8, 1951. For biographical data on Yati Aruji Kartawinata, including her activities in West Java, see Syamsudin, *Bunga Rampai Nilai-Nilai Perjuangan Perintis Kemerdekaan di DKI Jakarta* [Anthology of the struggle values of the pioneers of independence of greater Jakarta] (Jakarta: Dinas Sosial Daerah Khusus Ibukota Jakarta, 1987), 3:166–69. On her relationship with the left, see Lin, "Ummah Yet Proletariat," 167–68, 269.

104. For example, "Organisatie van Overleg" [Consultative body], *De Preangerbode*, June 21, 1951; "Kuningan en Irian" [Kuningan and Irian], *De Preangerbode*, January 12, 1955; and "Anti Kolonialistische Bijeenkomst" [Anticolonial meeting], *De Preangerbode*, January 16, 1956.

105. "P.K.I. Sambut Adjakan Fihak P.S.I.I. Untuk Tidak Saling Menjerang" [The PKI welcomes the PSII's proposal to not attack one another], *Harian Rakjat*, April 5, 1955; and "Partai-Partai Demokratis Mendapat Kemenangan Jang Mejakinkan" [Democratic parties reach a convincing victory], *Harian Rakjat*, October 11, 1955.

106. "Agreement Masjumi, PNI, NU, PSII" [Agreement of Masyumi, PNI, NU, PSII], *Pikiran Rakjat*, December 27, 1957.

107. "Kata Harsono Tjokroaminoto—PSII Selalu Bersedia Kerdja Sama Dengan Semua Golongan" [Harsono Tjokroaminoto—The PSII are always prepared to work with all groups], *Pikiran Rakjat*, February 21, 1957; and "Konperensi-Kerdja P.S.I.I. Djawa Barat" [West Java PSII working conference], *Pikiran Rakjat*, June 6, 1961.

108. "Kongres PSII" [PSII congress], *Harian Rakjat*, May 30, 1962.

109. *Harian Rakjat*, September 18, 1965.

110. ISSI OHP '65, interview 2.25, "Rusyana," Cileungsi, July 11, 2001; and ISSI OHP '65, interview 2.16, "Suratna," Cipanas, March 15, 2001.

111. ISSI OHP '65, interview 2.15, "Rahmadin," Cipanas, February 16, 2001.

112. *Bintang Merah*, February–March 1956, 112; and "Tentang PKI, Nasakom, GKI, Singapura, Vietnam dll." [Regarding the PKI, Nasakom, the international communist movement, Singapore, etc.], *Harian Rakjat*, August 20, 1965.

113. Fealy, *Ijtihad Politik Ulama*, 301, quoting an interview with Abdullhak Idris, one of the NU militants.

114. Fealy, *Ijtihad Politik Ulama*, 302–4.

115. For a discussion of the evolution of the PKI's agrarian policy see Mortimer, *Indonesian Communism under Sukarno*, chap. 3 and 7. For resonances with Mao's thought (and their limitations) see Julia Lovell, *Maoism: A Global History* (London: Bodley Head, 2019), 163–68. For a careful analysis of the PKI's relations with PRC leaders during this period see Taomo Zhou, *Migration in the Time of Revolution* (Ithaca, NY: Cornell University Press), 154–56.

116. This was one of the findings of research conducted by BTI activists in 1965, as summarized in Ina Erna Slamet-Velsink, "Views and Strategies of the Indonesian Peasant Movement on the Eve of its Annihilation in 1965–1966" (n.p., 1988). See also Hiroko Horikoshi, "A Traditional Leader in a Time of Change: The Kijaji and Ulama in West Java" (PhD diss., University of Illinois, 1976), 221–27.

117. For example, "Aksi 'Penjerobotan' Padi di Tjimahi" [Actions to "seize" riceland in Cimahi], *Pikiran Rakjat*, June 6, 1955; and "Bukan Kaum Tani, Melainkan Tuantanah jang Memperkosa" [It is not the peasants, but rather the landlord responsible for violations], *Harian Rakjat*, March 7, 1956.

118. Oral history interview, Bandung, February 13, 2018. Notably one of the most serious outbreaks of conflict during the "unilateral action" land reform campaign involved the targeting of a former Masyumi landlord. See "Keterangan DPP BTI Mengenai Peristiwa 'Losari'" [Statement from the BTI central leadership committee regarding the "Losari" affair], *Harian Rakjat*, May 17, 1965.

119. Airgram, Jakarta to Secretary of State, "Joint Weeka No. 31," August 9, 1965, record group (RG) 59, 1964–66, box 2308, POL 2-1, 1-1-65, US National Archives and Records Administration (NARA), College Park, Maryland.

120. "Perhebat Ofensif Revolusioner disegala Bidang" [Intensify the revolutionary offensive in all fields], *Harian Rakjat*, May 12, 1965.

121. "K[e]tua GP Anshor Husny Minwar: Pemuda Ansor Adalah Tentara Tuhan—Tak Akan Segan2 Menerkam Serta Merobek Robek Pengganggunja" [Chairman of the Ansor youth movement Husny Minwar: Ansor youths are God's army—they will not hesitate to pounce on and tear to pieces those who interfere with them], *Pikiran Rakjat*, March 30, 1965. This comment seems to have been a close paraphrase of his words rather than a direct quotation.

122. Hasim Adnan, "Membungkam Deru Bising Drumband di Bumi Parahiyangan" [Silencing the drumband's roar in the Priangan], in Budi Susanto, ed., *Sisi Senyap Politik Bising* [The silent side of roaring politics] (Yogyakarta: Kanisius, 2007), 31–74; and "Pawai Solidaritas—Parpol2 & Ormas2 Islam" [Solidarity parade—Islamic political parties and mass organizations], *Pikiran Rakjat*, July 26, 1965.

123. ISSI OHP '65, interview 2.16, "Suratna," Cipanas, March 15, 2001.

124. Slamet-Velsink, "Views and Strategies." Also see ISSI OHP '65, interview 2.16, "Suratna," Cipanas, March 15, 2001.

125. Slamet-Velsink, "Views and Strategies," 144.

126. "Kaum Tani Dimuka Pengadilan" [Peasants in court], *Harian Rakjat*, June 21, 1957.

127. ISSI OHP '65, interview 2.20, "Haryatna" (a People's Youth Member), Tasikmalaya, April 4, 2001; oral history interview with a BTI activist, Kuningan, April 7, 2018; and oral history interview with People's Youth activist, Sukabumi, January 14, 2018.

128. On the military campaign that saw this shift in the early 1960s, see Sundhaussen, "Political Orientations," 487–89.

129. On PKI-NU clashes over land in East Java, see also Fealy, *Ijtihad Politik Ulama*, 305–12; and Mortimer, *Indonesian Communism under Sukarno*, 317–18.

130. The important point that the "spontaneous" violence narrative is misleading is made in Jess Melvin, *The Army and the Indonesian Genocide: Mechanics of Mass Murder* (Abingdon, UK: Routledge, 2018), 299; and Robinson, *Killing Season*, 123.

131. One the crucial role of the army, see especially Melvin, *Army and the Indonesian Genocide*; and Geoffrey Robinson, "'Down to the Very Roots': The Indonesian Army's Role in the Mass Killings of 1965–66," *Journal of Genocide Research* 19, no. 4 (2017): 465–86. On the role of the police, see Katharine McGregor and Jemma Purdey, "Shining a Light on Police Complicity in 1965," *New Mandala*, November 2, 2015. On Western countries see Bradley Simpson, "International Dimensions of the 1965–68 Violence in Indonesia," in Douglas Kammen and Katharine McGregor, eds., *The Contours of Mass Violence in Indonesia,1965–1968* (Singapore: NUS Press, 2012), 50–74.

132. The quote comes from the army newspaper *Angkatan Bersendjata* [Armed Forces], October 5, 1965. On the complex circumstances surrounding the abortive coup attempt, see John Roosa, *The September 30th Movement and Suharto's Coup d'État in Indonesia* (Madison: University of Wisconsin Press, 2006).

133. Roosa, *Buried Histories*, 64–71, 78–80.

134. John Roosa, "The State of Knowledge About an Open Secret: Indonesia's Mass Disappearances of 1965–66," *Journal of Asian Studies* 75, no. 2 (2016): 292.

135. John Roosa provides a helpful analysis of a number of local studies in his article "Who Knows? Oral History Methods in the Study of the Massacres of 1965–66 in Indonesia," *Oral History Forum d'histoire orale* 33 (2013): 11–26.

136. Robinson, *Killing Season*, 150–51.

137. Robinson, *Killing Season*, 148.

138. Mark Winward, "Capture from Below: Civil-Military Relations during Indonesia's Anticommunist Violence," *Indonesia*, no. 106 (2018), 133.

139. The quote is from "Tuhan tak Perkenankan Orang2 Anti-Tuhan Hidup di Negara Ber-Tuhan" [God does not permit people who are anti-God to live in a godly state], *Angkatan Bersendjata*, December 8, 1965. See also Robinson, *Killing Season*, 166; and Roosa, *Buried Histories*, 77.

140. Robinson, *Killing Season*, 171–73.

141. For a further discussion of the NU in killings in East Java, see Greg Fealy and Katharine McGregor, "Nahdlatul Ulama and the Killings of 1965–66: Religion, Politics and Remembrance," *Indonesia*, no. 89 (2010): 47–50. For challenges in

interpreting oral history accounts of civilian participants on the killings of 1965–66, including NU members, see Roosa, "Who Knows?," 1–4, 11–15.

142. Oral history interview with the son of a BTI member, Sukabumi, January 14, 2018; oral history interview with a member of a left-wing youth group, Cimahi, April 13, 2018; and Telegram from Consulate Surabaya to Embassy Jakarta, November 21, 1965, RG 59, 1964–66, box 2317, POL 23-8, NARA. I would like to thank Douglas Kammen for providing a copy of this telegram and discussing its contents. On Subang in particular, see Sundhaussen, "Political Orientations," 634–35 (although it should be noted that Sundhaussen drew on interviews with army officers who may have played down the military's role in the killings).

143. "Dongkol Lokasi Kuburan Massal di Cirebon" [Dongkol a location of a mass grave in Cirebon], *Media Kajian Strategis Indonesia Global* [Global Indonesian Strategic Studies Media], January 22, 2019.

144. Acep Zamzam Noor, "Sejarah dan Rekonsiliasi Kultural: Pandangan Pesantren" [History and cultural reconciliation: A pesantren perspective], in H. Suparman, *Sebuah Catatan Tragedi 1965: Dari Pulau Buru Sampai ke Mekah* [A note on the 1965 tragedy: From Buru Island to Mecca] (Bandung: Nuansa, 2006), 11–16. Ansor activist Usep Romli recalled similar training going on: "Kisah Usep Romli Melawan PKI di Garut" [Usep Romli's story of fighting the PKI in Garut], *Cendana News*, November 29, 2017.

145. "Jagal Gestok'65 Bandung Selatan Minta Maaf" [Killer from the aftermath of the October 1965 movement from South Bandung asks for forgiveness], YPKP65.org. For references in West Java to civilians handing over alleged communists to the military see also Telegram, Embassy Jakarta to Secretary of State, October 28, 1965, RG 59, 1964–66, box 2318, POL 23-9, NARA; and Horikoshi, "A Traditional Leader in a Time of Change," 335. For this theme more broadly, see Mathias Hammer, "The Organisation of the Killings and the Interaction between State and Society in Central Java, 1965," *Journal of Current Southeast Asian Affairs* 32, no. 3 (2013): 37–62.

146. Such wariness was highlighted in a report from the West German embassy: "Verluste der Indonesischen Bevölkerung Seit 1. Okotober d.J." [Indonesian population losses since 1 October], December 14, 1965, series B37 IB5, vol. 169a, German Diplomatic Archive (Politische Archiv des Auswärtigen Amtes), Berlin.

147. On the role of former Darul Islam fighters and their relation to the military see Solahudin, *The Roots of Terrorism in Indonesia: From Darul Islam to Jema'ah Islamiyah* (Ithaca, NY: Cornell University Press, 2013), 47–49. Former Darul Islam members claimed to have been armed by the army and used to hunt down subversive elements. These claims should be treated skeptically. If they were armed, it was more likely that the army would have used them to kill detainees than send them out to find people. There is also evidence that former fighters later lied about their activities and motives. See Quinton Temby, "Imagining an Islamic State in Indonesia: From Darul Islam to Jemaah Islamiyah," *Indonesia*, no. 89 (2010), 26.

148. Robinson, *Killing Season*, 138.

149. Jonathan Leader Maynard, *Ideology and Mass Killing: The Radicalized Security Politics of Genocides and Deadly Atrocities* (Oxford: Oxford University Press, 2022), 43.

3   Assimilation of Ethnic Chinese
in Cold War Thailand, 1948–57

CUI FENG

Among Southeast Asian countries, the integration of the Chinese in Thailand seemed to be relatively harmonious and thorough, at least at a glance.[1] In fact, today, many young ethnic Chinese in Thailand seem to see themselves as Thai with few conflicting feelings. One interviewee, Foam Ramon, currently studying at Chulalongkorn University in Bangkok, is a good example.[2] As a third-generation Chinese, whose grandparents came from Guangdong Swatow (Shantou), she considers herself a Thai person. She does not speak Chinese. In an interview with the author, she said, "My grandparents are Chinese. They took a boat from China to Bangkok and lived in Chinatown. My grandparents speak the Shantou dialect [of Chinese]. Whenever my grandmother speaks to me in Chinese, I can't understand, so I reply, 'What are you saying?' in the Thai language. I'm Thai. And my grandparents come from China. That's it."[3]

Similar attitudes can be seen in a survey of Thai-Chinese and Indonesian-Chinese students at Jinan University. According to this survey, the number of Thai-Chinese who recognized Thailand as their homeland is much higher than that of Indonesian-Chinese who recognize Indonesia as their homeland.[4] In what ways did the ethnic Chinese in Thailand come to see themselves as Thai, and why? How did they go through the assimilation process?

Research on the assimilation of the Chinese in Thailand, in fact, has a long tradition. As early as the late 1950s, G. W. Skinner discussed Chinese assimilation in Thailand in a positive and hopeful manner, suggesting that anti-Chinese prejudice would cease to exist once the Chinese would come to speak and behave like Thais.[5] Alan Edward Guskin and Richard J. Coughlin came to the same conclusion in the 1960s, that the Chinese had already fully integrated into Thai society.[6] Yet, in recent years, such harmonious models have come under scrutiny. Sittithep Eaksittipong, for example, pointed out in his 2017 dissertation that Skinner's, Guskin's, and Coughlin's research paradigms, which emphasized the assimilable nature of the

Chinese in Thailand, made Chinese assimilation studies in Thailand a political tool serving American strategy in establishing Thailand as an anticommunist fortress in Southeast Asia during the Cold War.[7] Furthermore, Wasana Wongsurawat, in her 2019 book *The Crown and the Capitalists*, examines the complexity and difficulty of the assimilation process from a perspective of social class, and emphasizes the interdependent relationship between Chinese entrepreneurs and Thai ruling elites.[8] While these scholars have approached the issue of assimilation as a collective experience, what about individual experiences?

This chapter addresses the issue of "social warfare" in Thailand, and specifically challenges faced by Thais, concerning the ethnic Chinese population as an obstacle to Thai nation-building. It examines the ways in which overseas Chinese in Thailand were assimilated into Thai society after World War II, showing that the process of assimilation was not necessarily harmonious but in fact quite repressive and often forced, and that individual Chinese had varied reactions to the Thai government's repressive policies.[9] It also emphasizes that anti-Chinese sentiment, which had existed in Thai society for a long time, had significant effects on the many layers of conflicts and disagreements between Thai authorities and the Chinese, between the ordinary Thais and the Chinese, and among the Chinese themselves. The chapter shows that ethnic tension was always a source of trouble, and that such was particularly the case after Thailand began its nation-building process at the end of the nineteenth century.[10] However, as we will see below, in the 1950s, social tensions and concerns about the so-called Chinese problem quickly faded out. This was because the emergence and escalation of the Cold War provided a favorable opportunity for Thai ruling circles to implement a more intense and forcible assimilation policy through the use of "anticommunist" sentiments that were on the rise.

This chapter consists of two sections. The first traces historical conflicts experienced by ethnic Chinese in Thailand from the Rama VI era to the Phibun era. Thai elites believed that the ethnic Chinese were an unstable and undesirable foreign group, whose unique identity was not conducive to construction of the Thai nation-state. Therefore, assimilating them was, they thought, essential to building a powerful and unified Thailand. Thai authorities were also worried that the Chinese political ideologies would affect Thailand's national security because, from the time of the 1911 Chinese Revolution (Xinhai Revolution) to the era of the Cold War, the political orientation of the ethnic Chinese in Thailand had been almost always influenced by what was going on in China. In its second section, this chapter examines how escalation of Cold War tensions provided an opportunity for Thailand to accelerate the assimilation of the ethnic Chinese.

The "Chinese Problem" in Thailand since the Rama VI Era

Chinese people immigrated to Thailand (Siam) over centuries, from the age of the Sukhothai dynasty around the fifteenth century to the time of the Bangkok dynasty (Chakkri dynasty) in the eighteenth century. From the mid-nineteenth century, in particular, many steamship lines launched regular year-round service between southern China's coastal cities and Bangkok, transporting both large amounts of cargo and many passengers on multiple routes. Thus, masses of Chinese then began to arrive in Bangkok and make their livings there. Such a trend continued and even accelerated in the early twentieth century, when massive numbers of Chinese left the coastal region of southern China and came to Thailand to avoid poverty and civil wars. Bangkok became the most important gathering place for Chinese laborers and merchants. Most Chinese in Bangkok were from Chaozhou and spoke only the Teochew dialect in their daily lives.[11] As the number of Chinese immigrants gradually increased, some wealthy Chinese began to worry about the education of the next generation. Some sent their children back to China to study. However, most children chose to stay in Thailand, so that Chinese communities established many Chinese schools in the early twentieth century.

Negative views of the ethnic Chinese emerged among high-ranking officials during the reign of King Rama VI (Vajiravudh), who was on the throne from 1910 to 1925. He firmly believed in a need to establish Thai nationalism and maintained that "nationalism can promote patriotism, and patriotism will become a source of strength for defending the nation."[12] He was the first Thai king educated in the United Kingdom, and he was deeply influenced by Western nationalism in the early twentieth century. Knowing that such a notion was relatively new in the region, he wrote more than 300 articles and books to promote Thai nationalism.[13] One of the most well-known was an article titled "The Jews of the East," in which he harshly criticized the ethnic Chinese in Thailand. The article was published in 1914, just a few years after the 1911 Chinese Revolution. The article condemned the Chinese as greedy and hypocritical, and asserted that they came to Thailand only to make money. According to the article, "These Chinese look like very kind in appearance but are very dark inside. They just want to make a lot of money and send it back to China. They want only rights but don't want civic responsibility in Thailand. They are parasites of Thai society."[14]

In addition to such open and blatant criticism, King Rama VI's private letters reveal that royal family members were deeply suspicious of the Chinese secretly promoting revolutionary republicanism, which could endanger the monarchy. The king, for instance, wrote in a letter on April 21, 1911, "At this time, my ministers and I agree that the government can no longer ignore the Chinese. Now the thinking of the younger generation in Thailand has become somewhat abnormal, since the so-called victory of the Chinese democratic revolution, many Thais have blindly followed the Chinese. The Chinese may adopt various methods to make Thais dissatisfied with the government, and eventually to trigger riots. Then, the Chinese will take the opportunity to take advantage."[15]

King Rama VI believed that the Chinese were not only economically exploiting Thais but sapping Thai employment. In his book *Wake Up Siam*, published in the early 1910s, he described Chinese people taking advantage of and stealing opportunities from Thais, taking a lot of jobs—from retail selling and carpentry to construction work.[16] At the same time, the King believed that Thai people were lazy. He disapproved of the common view that Thai people could not survive without the Chinese and appealed to all Thais to learn to live independently. It is interesting to note that the description of the Chinese in Rama VI's books and articles was strikingly similar to the ways in which Jews were depicted in Europe at that time. As a monarch who received his education in the United Kingdom and aspired to consolidate his rule through nationalism, King Rama VI naturally drew parallels between the Chinese and the Jews, with whom he was familiar in Europe. The king was convinced that the best way to solve the "Chinese problem" was to assimilate ethnic Chinese into Thai society, and that the best way to do so was to eliminate Chinese languages in their communities, though this was not achieved during his reign.

If King Rama VI was the pioneer of Thai nationalism, Phibun Songgram, the prime minister of Thailand from 1938 to 1944 and again from 1948 to 1957, was one of its most significant promoters. From an early age, he was deeply influenced by the notion of Thai nationalism Rama VI promoted, and, during World War II, he implemented even harsher policies to suppress the ethnic Chinese. As Thailand joined the Japanese camp, the Phibun regime became more repressive of the Chinese, while China criticized the

Phibun regime's suppression of the ethnic Chinese and accused the regime of being an accomplice of Japanese imperialists.

Amid such rising tensions, in 1941, the official publication of the Chinese Nationalist Party (*Kuomintang*, KMT) categorized Thailand as a future battlefield for China's anti-Japanese fascist campaign.[17] *Dongnan ribao* (Southeast Daily), an influential KMT newspaper in Zhejiang Province, similarly described Thailand as a "Second Japan in Asia" and Prime Minister Phibun as "the Fascist of Thailand."[18] This article described the Chinese people's sufferings under the Phibun regime as follows: "Phibun increasingly persecutes the overseas Chinese. Thai authorities destroy overseas Chinese culture and then suppress overseas Chinese businesses. . . . In September of this year [1941], the Bangkok government arrested around 5,900 Chinese people for no reason and deported most [to China], banned the boycott of Japanese goods, and blocked all Chinese newspapers."[19]

Even Generalissimo Chiang Kai-shek himself sent a telegram to Phibun urging Thailand to protect the rights, property, and lives of the overseas Chinese.[20] Similarly, a number of diplomats from the Republic of China repeatedly sent messages to the Thai government through various channels, demanding that they stop oppressing the ethnic Chinese, but in vain.[21]

The recurrence of such anti-Chinese policies from the era of King Rama VI to that of Phibun can be best understood when we see it as a cover for the prime objective of Thai ruling elites: the construction of the Thai nation-state. In other words, the actual point in dispute was the conflict and incompatibility of the Chinese ethnic identity with Thai nation-building efforts. Thailand's transformation to modernity was accompanied by the identification of the new nation-state, which would (and should) be different from a traditional Southeast Asian kingdom.[22] In the formation of such a modern Thai state, the shaping of a common enemy played an important role. As in other parts of the world, Thai ruling circles constructed the notion of a nation-state by identifying "us" and "them," and by distinguishing "we" and "others"—that is, "enemies."[23] These "others" could be any group if they were viewed as coming from the "outside," whether they were the British, the Burmese, or the Chinese. In a sense, the Chinese were a sort of scapegoat representing the roles of "others" and "enemies" in the process of nation-state building.

To further complicate this picture, there was popular antagonism between ordinary Thais and the ethnic Chinese. By the early 1940s, anti-Chinese sentiment had already been integrated into various cultural productions and entertainment activities. For example, a newspaper article circa 1940 recorded that there was a park in Bangkok called Coutlin, where people assembled to see drama performances that openly criticized the Chinese.[24] According to the article, every Sunday night, a theater group in Bangkok, called Chapungoon, performed dramas with anti-Chinese themes. One of the popular dramas often performed was titled "Against the Jews of the East."[25]

It is not surprising that such anti-Chinese sentiments among ordinary people eventually turned into violence. This was particularly the case following the end of World War II, when a large number of weapons fell into the hands of ordinary Thais. Suffering through the chaotic economy of the post–World War II period, overseas Chinese businessmen became easy targets of robbery. In fact, according to a Chinese newspaper's reports, in the first week of March 1947, ethnic Chinese were attacked in a large-scale riot in Bangkok. It was reported that, on March 10, rioters stole property worth a total of 700,000 to 800,000 baht from Chinese businessmen.[26] The newspaper in China reported, "Under the influence of [Thai] nationalism, the middle and lower classes in Thailand have a strong anti-Chinese sentiment. The robbers in Thailand attack only the Chinese. Yet, the Thai police do not really try to arrest those bandits. The rampant robberies against the Chinese are not just a mere public security issue; it is an anti-Chinese act in disguise."[27]

Zhongyuan Bao (หนังสือพิมพ์ จงเอี้ยน; Zhongyuan Daily), one of the largest Chinese newspapers in Bangkok, also mentioned that the lives and property of Thai-Chinese had been seriously threatened.[28] As early as January 1947, the Bangkok branch of the Central News Agency (CNA), an official organ of the Republic of China, revealed that local Thai people, with the help of the government, had transferred the management rights of twenty-two Chinese retail rice shops to Thais, which caused the Chinese ambassador to be concerned.[29]

Such anti-Chinese sentiments among local people intensified in combination with the government's assimilation policy toward the ethnic Chinese. Then, dramatic changes took place in Asia in the post–World War II period. In 1949, the Chinese Communist Party (CCP) gained victory, while the KMT retreated to Taiwan. Then, in 1950, the Korean War broke out. Southeast Asian countries were quickly drawn into the political landscape of the Cold War. Prime Minister Phibun was ready to take advantage of this new situation to regain his position and to accelerate the process of suppressing and assimilating the ethnic Chinese in the context of the Cold War.

Repression and Assimilation of Ethnic Chinese in Cold War Thailand

Anti-Chinese sentiment in Thailand did not arise all of a sudden from the Cold War; as we have seen, its roots, at least partly, were in the process of nation-state building in Thailand. However, the development of the Cold War provided a new logic—more frankly, an excuse—that made it possible for the Thai ruling circles and ordinary Thais to accelerate and strengthen the assimilation of the Chinese into their society. Here, two factors should be highlighted. First, with increasing support from the United States, Phibun, who had remade himself as a staunch anticommunist, could return to power.[30] In this second Phibun era, from 1948 to 1957, a number of "anticommunist" policies were implemented: many Chinese schools were closed; a number of Chinese newspapers were banned; the Thai-Chinese economy was severely restricted; and new immigrants from China were largely blocked.

Second, the newly established CCP regime on the mainland and the KMT regime in Taiwan were in a fierce confrontation, and neither side could protect and care for overseas Chinese in southeast Asia.[31] Meanwhile, mainland China launched a series of political movements in the 1950s to clear up remnants of capitalism, while Thailand carried out a series of economic blockades against Communist China. As a result, connections between the ethnic Chinese in Thailand and their homeland were literally severed, giving a further boost to their assimilation. Below, we will analyze how such assimilation processes took place in Cold War Thailand.

Following the return of Prime Minister Phibun Songgram in 1948, a stricter assimilation policy was implemented throughout Thai society. The logic of anticommunist counterinsurgency became the prime rhetoric for promoting assimilation. The historical background that made it possible for such Cold War logic to function was the military confrontation between China and the United States in the Korean War, as well as the waves of communist insurgencies in Southeast Asia, all of which provided a golden opportunity for Phibun to push forward his "anticommunist" politics and the assimilation policies behind it.

Following World War II, communist insurgencies were rapidly on the rise in various places in East and Southeast Asia. In addition, the CCP's victory gave great encouragement to members and sympathizers of the Communist Party of Thailand (CPT), who were largely ethnic Chinese and had strong connections with the CCP.[32] An article published in the CCP's official organ,

Renmin Ribao (People's Daily) on November 21, 1951, showed strong ties between the two parties. In the article, the CPT criticized the Phibun government and US imperialists, stating that they had colluded to suppress the people. The CPT called on the people of the whole of Thailand to unite in fighting for national independence and democracy.[33] The CPT leadership was indeed strongly convinced to follow the aggressive "armed struggle" line. From their perspective, the CCP's victory seemed to show the correct path to liberation for all semicolonial, semifeudal countries, including Thailand.[34] Such a background allowed Phibun to posit a communist victory in China, as well as the existence of ethnic Chinese in Thailand, as a threat.

Prime Minister Phibun never failed to take advantage of popular anticommunist sentiments to promote his Chinese assimilation policies. He said that Chinese immigrants might be entirely banned because "most of the Chinese were supporters of communism."[35] In saying this, he also asserted that the communists would eventually overthrow Thailand's monarchy and constitution, declaring that "the Chinese, White or Red, are a menace if too many of them are permitted to enter the country."[36] Yet, it is clear that Phibun overstated the abilities of communists in Thailand for the purpose of achieving his political goals. In fact, the CPT was not a threat to Thailand in this early Cold War period. Saiyud Kerdphol, a former supreme commander of the Royal Thai Armed Forces, emphasized that Thai officials and the military did not fear the CPT at all because they did not regard it as a real threat to the Bangkok ruling regime.[37] Former KMT officers, who had participated in Thailand's anticommunist counterinsurgency battles, agreed. They pointed out that the CPT's bases were located in the middles of jungles, far away from any small towns or villages. Furthermore, when they were attacked by Thai forces, they simply fled to Laos.[38] Obviously, such small-scale guerrilla warfare launched by CPT guerrillas did not pose any threat to the central government and the monarchy.

Yet, during this period, the Thai government's assimilation policies evolved quickly and extensively from the areas of politics and governance to those of the economy and education. For instance, the Thai government issued a series of administrative regulations to restrict the political rights of overseas Chinese. A person whose father was a foreigner lost the right to vote, as well as being banned from buying land or enrolling in military schools. Also, as local Chinese had organized many left-wing groups in Thailand, from trade unions and newspapers to the CPT, all such organizations became targets of restrictions. The CPT was officially pronounced an illegal party in 1952, and many other Chinese organizations were quickly shut down in the name of anticommunism in the 1950s.[39] Furthermore, the Thai government began restricting the number of Chinese immigrants to Thailand, and began tightening several administrative regulations, both of these intended to limit the influence of the Chinese. For example, the cost of applying for a residence permit for overseas Chinese increased from 20 to 400 baht per year.[40] Also, the government stipulated that anyone with dual nationality was not considered Thai anymore, as many Chinese had held both Chinese and Thai nationality.[41]

In the area of economics, the Thai government attempted to restrict and curb Chinese dominance. Prime Minister Phibun, for instance, issued a new act in 1952, the "Decree of Keeping Jobs (for Thais)," which aimed to ensure jobs for Thais, while limiting the roles of overseas Chinese in the Thai economy. With this decree, the government began restricting the number of Chinese employees in each company so that all companies were required to have at least 50 percent Thai employees. Any Chinese who did not comply with these economic regulations was deported.[42] Furthermore, in 1953, the government issued the "Foreign Exchange Control Law," which set the maximum amount of money—not exceeding 1,000 baht per transaction—that overseas Chinese could remit to China.

Finally, education came to be a central concern of the Thai government. This was because, from the government's perspective, Chinese schools were difficult to control and were considered to be promoting communism as well as the notion of "great China nationalism." Thus, the Phibun government enacted the "Private School Decree" in the 1950s, which aimed to strengthen government control over Chinese schools.[43] Based on this decree, all private Chinese schools had to be registered with the government. The Chinese language could be taught only from grade one to grade four, and Chinese lessons could not exceed ten hours a week. All Chinese schools were required to adopt textbooks that were officially published by the Thai Education Department. Any lessons on Chinese history, Chinese culture, or Chinese folk customs were prohibited. Furthermore, Chinese teachers had to pass a Thai-language exam and be approved by a police official. Obviously, the Thai government regarded education as a part of political and public security; that is why the police department, rather than the education department, was put in charge of managing and monitoring Chinese schools.

The author interviewed several older Chinese who went to Chinese schools during this transition period. One, Tonglaw Amornsiripanich, is a second-generation Chinese, whose parents arrived in Bangkok from Guangdong after a long journey by sea in the 1940s. He said, "In the 1950s, I studied at a Chinese school in Bangkok. I was just a primary school student at the time. The name of the school was 'Cun Zhen,' which means 'keep the truth,' and it was a Chinese Christian school. At first, we studied Chinese history, but never studied Thai history. The textbooks came from Hong Kong and the teachers also came from Hong Kong. Soon after, however, the Thai government began to restrict Chinese schools. Later, we did not learn Chinese at all. We started to take classes in Thai at our Chinese school."[44]

The number of Chinese schools declined dramatically in the 1950s due to the government's increasingly strict control and suppression. Before 1948, there were thousands of Chinese schools but, by 1956, only 195 remained in Thailand.[45] Due to the decline of Chinese schools, Chinese parents began sending their children to local Thai schools. As a result, fewer and fewer Chinese could speak Chinese. According to a study conducted by Huachiew Chalermprakiet University's Chinese-Thai Study Center, in 1948, approximately 180,000 Chinese students were studying in Chinese schools; by 1955, the number had declined to only 50,000.[46] Thus, the ethnic Chinese who grew up in or after the 1950s mostly did not have Chinese educational backgrounds. Generally speaking, their feelings as to being "Chinese" or "China" were not as committed as those of their parents. It is not surprising that these generations of Chinese gradually recognized Thailand as their homeland. During the interview, Tonglaw recalled his feelings about Thailand: "At the end of the 1970s, I stayed in Singapore. At that time, the relationship between Thailand and Vietnam was really terrible. Most of the people thought that Vietnamese troops would occupy Thailand soon. All my Singaporean friends were really worried about me and my family. Whenever I went to church, I always prayed for Thailand."[47]

Obviously, Tonglaw came to have a strong feeling for Thailand when he was a young adult. His parents' homeland, China, was something he learned about from textbooks in his elementary school, but it was no longer his homeland. It became a distant and unfamiliar land for him. Furthermore, from the 1950s, the Thai government began pressing ethnic Chinese to switch their Chinese names to Thai names on official documents. More and more Chinese chose to adopt Thai names and Thai nationality.[48] As their primary concerns shifted from China to Thailand, many ethnic Chinese gradually began integrating themselves into local Thai society.

Let us take a few examples. Mr. Charoen Damahapan was born in a Chinese family in Thailand in October 1948. His family at first gave him a Chinese name, Chen Zimu. However, he was permitted to change his name to the Thai name of Charoen Damahapan in February 1963. Actually, this was not just his decision; his whole family adopted Thai names at the same time.⁴⁹ Another case involves the Pratthachariya family, a wealthy Chinese business family in Bangkok. Their original surname was "Ye." A document the author collected shows that one family member, "Ye Yong," officially changed his name to the Thai name "Sawaeng Pratthaochariya" in April 1958.⁵⁰ While a large majority of ethnic Chinese chose Thai names around this period, a small number of Chinese chose to leave Thailand because they wanted to keep their Chinese names and languages. One such case involves Mr. Lee Yinwen (pseudonym), a businessman living in the city of Hat Yai in southern Thailand before the 1950s. He moved to Penang, Malaysia, with his whole family, in the 1950s, because he did not want to change his Chinese name to a Thai one.⁵¹ He wanted to keep his Chinese identity, as well as Chinese-language education, for the next generations.

Severance of Connections in Cold War Asia

Another important factor that accelerated the assimilation of the ethnic Chinese in Thailand was the actual severance of connections due to the ubiquity of Cold War politics in East and Southeast Asia. To begin with, China set off a series of political campaigns in the 1950s to purge "class enemies" at home. With the spread of extreme leftist politics in China, many ethnic Chinese in Thailand became less and less enthusiastic about returning to China. Many ethnic Chinese lost contact with relatives in China and began feeling psychologically distanced from China.⁵² At the same time, the Thai government was making efforts to block economic exchanges with Communist China. Then, in 1951, the Thai government required the Ministries of Transport and Foreign Affairs to gradually discontinue all modes of communication with China, including shipping, postal services, and telecommunications.⁵³ In 1959, Thai citizens were banned from going to China.⁵⁴

Tonglaw recalled, "My uncle was in Shantou, China, but we lost contact with each other in the late 1950s. I did not find my uncle's family in China until 2015, when I finally got connected again with his son in Shenzhen."⁵⁵ As we can see in this comment, it became more and more difficult for the Chinese in Thailand to maintain contact with their relatives in China, particularly following the escalation of the Cold War. As prominent migrant history scholar Sunil S. Amrith discusses, one of the most important and necessary conditions for maintaining migrants' identification with their homelands is actual connection.⁵⁶ As we have seen, in Cold War Asia, such a connection was almost completely lost, and, as a result, the assimilation of ethnic Chinese in Thailand was further accelerated.

Faced with such suppressive policies, some wealthy and influential Chinese families in Thailand became royalist supporters by actively cooperating with Thai authorities.[57] Quite a few wealthy Chinese men married Thai women, at least partly to secure their social status and networks.[58] On the other hand, ordinary Chinese, who were not so enthusiastic about, if not hostile to, government assimilation policies, were simply regarded as communist sympathizers and thus became targets of stricter restrictions.[59]

One interviewee, Peng Qinglong, a second-generation Chinese who moved back to China with his father in the 1950s, recalled his father's bitter experiences. His father, Peng Shantan, was a teacher in Yela Province in southern Thailand in the late 1940s but lost his job in 1950 due to the spread of anti-Chinese policies.[60] Then, he became a worker at a rubber plantation while using his spare time to teach Chinese to ethnic Chinese children who had lost their schools. Because of such activities, he was constantly harassed by the police, and finally sold all of his property and returned to China in 1957.[61] A Chinese newspaper, *Qiao Shen* (Overseas Chinese Voices), issued in Guangzhou, stated as early as 1949, "Recently, the oppression of the Chinese in Thailand has become more and more serious. Many occupations, such as hairdressing, driving, peddling, accounting, and etc., have prohibited the Chinese from taking part. The unemployment rate for Chinese people has been rapidly increasing. However, China is now struggling in a civil war. Overseas Chinese don't know where they should go."[62]

Amid such a tense environment, the majority of wealthy and influential Chinese families chose to adapt themselves to the government's policies so as to maintain their wealth and social status. Yet, there were different and diverse views among the ethnic Chinese. Some tried to resist assimilation by strengthening their Chinese identities, such as paying more attention to their Chinese names, Chinese languages, and family ties.[63] Others began adopting new identities in order to integrate themselves into Thai society, thus actively assimilating with Thai culture and identity. Such differing views, naturally, caused internal disagreements within these communities. Some Chinese began criticizing other Chinese who actively integrated into Thai society because the former saw the latter as betraying their traditional Chinese identity.[64]

Such tensions could be seen even among my interviewees. Tonglaw, a second-generation Chinese, believed that ethnic Chinese should learn the Thai language and Thai history, instead of learning only Chinese and

Chinese history. He said it would be strange if students learned only Chinese history at school, while not knowing anything about Thai history.⁶⁵ But another second-generation Chinese, whose Chinese name was Zhang Huatai, held a different opinion. He insisted on being Chinese despite his Thai nationality. He called China "the motherland" and Thailand "the second hometown."⁶⁶ He studied at a Chinese school in Chiang Rai in northern Thailand in the 1960s and remembered that the local Thai police always came to his school to check what was taught there. To deal with the police, his school taught in Thai during the daytime while teaching the Chinese language in the evening.

Prasit Leepreecha's chapter in this volume also discusses how the Hmong people in Thailand, against the backdrop of the Cold War, became divided into two factions, fighting each other due to the government's policies toward the Hmong, with one side aligning with the governmental authorities and the other with the CPT.⁶⁷ The situation of the Chinese exhibited some similarity to that of the Hmong; however, the internal conflicts among the Chinese did not escalate to serious confrontation. Although some people, like Zhang Huatai, continued to insist on the importance of learning Chinese and maintaining their Chinese identity, the large majority of ethnic Chinese embarked on the road of assimilation and adapted themselves to government policies, which were often skillfully implemented under the logic of Cold War politics.

By the end of the 1950s, thus, most ethnic Chinese in Thailand were naturalized as Thais, often adopting Thai names. These younger generations of ethnic Chinese gradually integrated into Thai society and actively participated in various businesses and political activities on their own.⁶⁸ To be sure, this does not imply the complete loss of Chinese identity. On the contrary, assimilated Chinese maintain their Chinese identity through religion, ancestor worship, and cultural symbols in specific Chinese festivals while possessing Thai identity in social and everyday life. This phenomenon has been termed "Double Identity."⁶⁹ However, this Chinese identity has assimilated into much of Thai culture and evolved into a purely hybrid cultural symbol, losing its political sensitivity. Looking back, therefore, it is reasonable to say that the Thai government's policies played important roles in the assimilation of ethnic Chinese.

That said, what was at least equally important were the logic of the Cold War, on the one hand, and popular anti-Chinese sentiments, on the other, both of which made it possible for the Thai ruling circles to enforce harsher assimilation policies. In a sense, the assimilation of the Chinese emerged at the crossroads of the historical currents of anti-Chinese politics and contemporary currents of anticommunist politics, which, combined, contributed to the homogenizing and nation-building processes of Thailand in the post–World War II period.

Conclusion

Thailand (Siam) had been in a process of nation-state building since the late nineteenth century, with an emphasis on the unity of the Thai race. As such, the ethnic Chinese had been a "problem" for a long time in the eyes of ruling circles. This was due to the fact that the ruling elites (and ordinary Thais, in general) saw the Chinese as an alien race with their own languages and cultures that were incompatible with the Thai nation-state. Through examining this historical background, this chapter shows that the so-called Chinese problem had remained a thorn in the effort of Thai nation-state building, and that the Thai government had suppressed and tried to assimilate the Chinese since long before the beginning of the Cold War. Then, in the early 1950s, the prevalence of Cold War politics played a decisive role in "solving" such a long-standing problem. Phibun's Thailand remodeled itself into Cold War Thailand, actively adopting anticommunist politics and, in doing so, aggressively carrying out anti-Chinese and proassimilation policies, thus "succeeding" in the making of the homogenized nation-state of Thailand in the post–World War II era through exaggerating the threat of communists (that is, Chinese) to the traditional and supposedly harmonious Thai society.

Furthermore, as we have seen, the Cold War literally severed almost all channels of contact between China and Thailand, and a series of extreme leftist campaigns in China also dampened overseas Chinese's eagerness to return to China, thus contributing to a loss of ethnic identity. As a result, most of the Chinese have integrated themselves into the Thai race in a broad sense and become part of the Thai nation-state through adopting new names, a new language, and a new form of education. That said, there always existed different voices and disagreements even among the ethnic Chinese themselves in the process of assimilation. In addition, there was another layer of conflicts between ethnic Chinese and ordinary people in Thai society. Thus, the government's harsh assimilation policies in the early Cold War period can be seen, at least to some extent, as an extension of grassroots, civilian anti-Chinese sentiments, without which the government could not have executed its policies.

Understanding the history of the ethnic Chinese in Cold War Thailand is useful and constructive because it forces us think more deeply about the functions of the Cold War world, thus opening up a way to reconsider the very nature of the Cold War. Through this examination of Cold War Thailand and the experiences of its ethnic Chinese, we can see how Cold War politics functioned in homogenizing populations and thus building the nation-state of Thailand through assimilating ethnic Chinese. Also, by looking at the ways in which the Cold War intertwined with diaspora politics and ethnic tensions on the ground, we can see that the Cold War was not merely an international confrontation between superpowers, but, in essence, a part of social and cultural conflicts at home that had been going on long before the advent of the Cold War world.

Notes

1. Chansir Disaphol, "Overseas Chinese in Thailand: A Case Study of Chinese Emigres in Thailand in the Twentieth Century" (PhD diss., Tufts University, 2006).

2. Foam Ramon, interview by the author, Bangkok, November 12, 2019.

3. Ramon, interview.

4. Weiguo Chen, "Comparison of National Identity of Chinese Youth in Indonesia, Thailand—A Questionnaire Survey of Chinese Language Institute of Jinan University," *Around Southeast Asia*, 11 (2003), 45–47.

5. William Skinner, *Chinese Society in Thailand: An Analytical History* (Ithaca, NY: Cornell University Press, 1957), 381.

6. Alan Edward Guskin, "Changing Identity: The Assimilation of Chinese in Thailand" (PhD diss., University of Michigan, 1968); and Richard J. Coughlin, *Double Identity: The Chinese in Modern Thailand* (Hong Kong: Hong Kong University Press, 1960).

7. Sittithep Eaksittipong, "Textualizing the 'Chinese of Thailand': Politics, Knowledge, and the Chinese in Thailand during the Cold War" (PhD diss., National University of Singapore, 2017), 7–29.

8. Wasana Wongsurawat, *The Crown and the Capitalists: The Ethnic Chinese and the Founding of the Thai Nation* (Seattle: University of Washington Press, 2019), 156–60.

9. Immigration from China to Thailand has a long history, and this chapter focuses on the period from late World War II to the early Cold War. The informants are mainly Chinese who immigrated to Thailand during this period and their descendants.

10. For the Chinese role in Thai nation-building, see Wongsurawat, *Crown and the Capitalists*.

11. Sawitree Thapphasut, "Khwam samphanth rahwang chumchn chaw thiy cin læa tawantkni krungthephmhankhr pheesho 2398–2453" [The relationship between Thai, Chinese, and Western communities in Bangkok 1855–1953] (Master's thesis, Chulalongkorn University, 1984), 28.

12. S. Wattanaset, *Keiyrtikhun phra mngkud kela* [The honor of King Rama VI] (Bangkok: Vatanapani Press, 1957), 127. Cited by Suthasinee Phonsakunphaisan, "Marshal Phibun Government's Policy on the Assimilation of Chinese in Thailand" (Master's thesis, Zhejiang University, 2014), 18.

13. Ganpelong Suwannai, *Rama VI and the Kingdom of Thailand* (Bangkok: Chulalongkorn University Publishing House, 1980), 221.

14. Ruizhen Huang, "Lama liushi de minzu zhuyi yu paihua sixiang jiqi yingxiang" [Rama VI's nationalism and anti-Chinese thought and its influence], *Nanyang wenti yanjiu* [*Southeast Asian Affairs*], no. 2 (2008): 74.

15. No. (L) 63.6.(G)/5, National Archives of Thailand, Bangkok. Cited by Huang, "Lama liushi," 76.

16. Suthasinee Phonsakunphaisan, "Marshal Phibun Government's Policy on the Assimilation of Chinese in Thailand" (Master's thesis, Zhejiang University, 2014), 19.

17. Ruheng He, "Zhongguo zhanqu de weilai zhanchang: Yuenan he taiguo" [Future battlefields in the Chinese war zone: Vietnam and Thailand], *Zhandi dangzheng yuekan* [*Monthly for Party Politics in Battlefields*] 1, no. 6 (1941).

18. "Yazhou de dier riben taiguo" [The second Japan in Asia: Thailand], *Bianyi yuebao* [*Editing and Translation Monthly*], no. 2 (1941): 1-2.

19. "Yazhou de dier riben taiguo," 1-2.

20. "Jiang weiyuanzhang dianqing taiguo dangju baohu huaqiao" [Chairman Chiang Kai-shek sent the telegram to Thailand authority to protect the overseas Chinese], *Guoji laogong tongxun* [*International Labor Information*] 7, no. 1 (1940): 33.

21. Eiji Murashima, *Karmeuxng cin syam* [Chinese Siamese Politics] (Bangkok: Institute of Asian Studies, 1996), 184.

22. Thongchai Winichakul, *Siam Mapped: A History of the Geo-Body of a Nation* (Honolulu: University of Hawai'i Press, 1994).

23. Thongchai, *Siam Mapped*, 165-67.

24. Zigu Chen, "Jinri huaqiao zai taiguo" [The current situation of Chinese in Thailand], *Shiri Huicui* 2, no. 12 (1940): 12-20.

25. Chen, "Jinri huaqiao zai taiguo," 12-20.

26. "Xianluo feihuan chuangjue" [The rapid deterioration of public order in Siam], *Xinwen Bao*, March 10, 1947.

27. "Xianluo feihuan chuangjue."

28. "Xianluo feihuan chuangjue."

29. "Xianluo zhengfu weifan xieyi paiji huaqiao midian" [Siam government's violation of the agreement to exclude overseas Chinese rice shops], Central News Agency (CNA) Bangkok (January 1947), 10.

30. It should be noted that the Phibun government's anticommunist sentiment was not ideological. Internally, opposing communism was complicated in the 1950s because it involved power struggles among Pridi's supporters, Phibun, and the Phin-Phao clique. See Anuson Chinvanno, *Thailand's Policies Towards China, 1949-54* (Basingstoke, UK: Macmillan Press, 1992), 80-84, 89-90. At the same time, Phibun's strategy of dealing with Communist China stemmed more from concerns for national security, internal power struggles, and geopolitical considerations. See

Tēchaphīra Kasīan, *Commodifying Marxism: The Formation of Modern Thai Radical Culture, 1927-1958* (Kyoto: Kyoto University Press, 2001), 125-28. During the first few years of Phibun's second term (1948-51), he did not take a strong anticommunist stance toward Communist China. See Daniel Fineman, *A Special Relationship: The United States and Military Government in Thailand,1947-1958* (Honolulu: University of Hawai'i Press, 1997), 54-63. In Phibun's later years in power (1955-58), he secretly improved relations with China and sent secret envoys to Beijing. See Kasīan, *Commodifying Marxism*, 66-67.

31. Zhifang Sun, "The Cold War Factor and the Transformation of Overseas Chinese Society in Thailand" (Master's thesis, Hunan Normal University, 2016).

32. Yuangrat Wedel, "The Communist Party of Thailand and Thai Radical Thought," *Southeast Asian Affairs* 1 (1981): 325-39. Also see Thomas A. Marks, *Making Revolution: The Insurgency of the Communist Party of Thailand in Structural Perspective* (Bangkok: White Lotus, 1994), 31.

33. *Renmin ribao* [People's Daily], "Meidi yu luanpiwen qianding xieding yinmou ba taiguo zuowei junshi jidi" [American imperialist signed the agreement with Phibun to use Thailand as a military base], November 21, 1951.

34. "The Road to Victory: Documents from the Communist Party of Thailand" (CPT official document, access from Thailand Information Center; n.d.), 6, https://archive.org/details/TheRoadToVictoryDocumentsFromTheCommunistPartyOfThailand/page/n3/mode/2up.

35. Kobkua Suwannathat-Pian, *Thailand's Durable Premier: Phibun through Three Decades, 1932-1957* (Kuala Lumpur: Oxford University Press, 1995), 228.

36. FO 371/129615, Chancery, Bangkok, to FO, the National Archives (UK), February 26, 1957. Cited by Suwannathat-Pian, *Thailand's Durable Premier*, 64.

37. Saiyud Kerdphol, *The Struggle for Thailand: CounterInsurgency, 1965-1985* (Bangkok: S. Research Center, 1986).

38. Jingxue Gu, *Gujun fengyun* [The story of stateless soldiers] (Bangkok: World Journal Press, 2019), 322-66.

39. Peter M. Lodge, "The United States' Role in the Creation and Development of the Association of Southeast Asian Nations" (PhD diss., University of Maine, 2008), 265.

40. Overseas Chinese Research Association, *Situation of Overseas Chinese in Asia and Africa* (Beijing: Overseas Chinese Publishing House, 1955), 113.

41. Overseas Chinese Research Association, *Situation of Overseas Chinese*, 113.

42. Central Overseas Chinese Investment Advisory Committee, *Overseas Chinese Economic Research Materials: Economic Situation of Chinese in Thailand* (Beijing: 1957), 21.

43. This decree itself was produced by Rama VI but was not implemented seriously until the time of Prime Minister Phibun Songgram in the 1950s.

44. Tonglaw, interview by the author, Bangkok, October 8, 2019.

45. Guangyi Wen, *Overseas Chinese History in Southeast Asia after World War II* (Guangzhou: Sun Yat-Sen University Press, 2000), 37.

46. *The History of Overseas Chinese in Thailand* (Bangkok: Huachiew Chalermprakiet University Chinese-Thai Study Center, 2004), 48.

47. Tonglaw, interview.

48. *History of Overseas Chinese*, 69.

49. Data collected by author from Bangkok Yaowarat China Town Heritage Center on October 11, 2019.

50. Data collected from Bangkok Yaowarat China Town Heritage Center.

51. Mr. Lee Yinwen, interview by the author, Singapore, November 2019.

52. Sun, "Cold War Factor," 2016.

53. "Taiguo duiwo shixing jinyun" [Thailand imposes an embargo on China], *Jingji daobao* [*China Economic Herald*] 225 (1951): 7.

54. Sun, "Cold War Factor," 2016.

55. Tonglaw, interview.

56. Sunil S. Amrith, *Migration and Diaspora in Modern Asia* (Cambridge: Cambridge University Press, 2011), 77–87.

57. Wongsurawat, *Crown and the Capitalists*, 140–41.

58. G. William Skinner, *Chinese Society in Thailand: An Analytical History* (Xiamen: Xiamen University Press, 2010), 314.

59. Wongsurawat, *Crown and the Capitalists*, 140–41.

60. *Taiguo guiqiao yinghun lu di qi juan* [The story of brave Chinese in Thailand returning to China], vol. 7 (Beijing: Zhongguo huaqiao, 2011), 39–45.

61. *Taiguo guiqiao*, 39–45.

62. "Xianluo qiaobao zao paichi" [The Chinese in Siam are suppressed] *Qiao Shen* 21 (1949): 21.

63. Institute of Asian Studies of Chulalongkorn University, *A Research Report on Teochew People and Their Hometown* (Bangkok: Chulalongkorn University, 1991), 90.

64. Hongbo Tian, Changlong Lan, and Keli Du, "Lun taiguo huaren shenfeng rentong chonggou jiqi zhengzhi suqiu" [The study of the changes of the Chinese identity and political demand in Thailand], *Shantou University Journal* (*Humanities and Social Science Monthly*) 34, no. 3 (2018): 89–93.

65. Tonglaw, interview.

66. Zhang Huatai, interview by the author, Chiang Rai, Thailand, February 12, 2018.

67. See chap. 4 in this volume: Prasit Leepreecha, "Voices of the Voiceless: The Cold War and the Hmong in Northern Thailand, 1965–82."

68. Sun, "Cold War Factor," 2016, 26–27.

69. Panuwat Chanasakun, "Double Identity Representation of Chinese Shrines in Phuket Muang District," *Journal of International Studies* (*Prince of Songkla University*) 7, no. 1 (January–June 2017): 179–96.

4 Voices of the Voiceless

The Cold War and the Hmong in Northern Thailand, 1965–82

PRASIT LEEPREECHA

> Mortars, paratroopers, and air support are being thrown into the growing battle between the Red Meos and Government forces in the North, a high-ranking police officer disclosed last night.
> —"Red Meos Use Modern Weapons," *Bangkok World* (December 9, 1968)

Today, the Hmong, one of the largest highland ethnic minorities in Thailand, might be looked on as an object of exotic tourism, evoking images of peaceful and smiling Hmong women wearing colorful dresses. In Cold War Thailand, from the late 1960s to the early 1980s, however, they were considered the most dangerous enemy—the "Red Meo" (Hmong)—that supposedly posed a serious threat to national security.[1] During this period, Cold War competition heated up in the region. The Communist Party of Thailand (CPT), which had chosen the strategy of *Pa lom muang* (Jungles surrounding the cities), continued their guerrilla warfare in the jungles and borderlands of northern and northeastern Thailand, while the Thai government was determined to smash all communist forces throughout the country. Both sides approached Hmong villages in the region and provided weapons, and, as a result, tens of thousands of Hmong in the conflict areas joined each side. Many Hmong were killed by either government or communist forces. Much worse, Hmong communities were divided into two camps that confronted each other. Fear and antagonism were imposed on Hmong people who joined either side. Relatives and family members killed one another, leaving painful memories that haunt the Hmong people even several decades after the end of the Cold War. How did the Hmong people interact with the Cold War world? Why did they join both sides of the conflict, and what happened to them?

The Hmong are one of the ten highland ethnic groups—or so-called hill tribes—along with others such as the Karen, Akha, and Lisu.[2] They are a transnational ethnic group, scattered throughout southwestern China, northern Vietnam, northern Laos, northeast Burma, and northern Thailand. With the end of the Vietnam War and the establishment of the Lao People's Democratic Republic in 1975, many Hmong refugees evacuated from Laos to Thailand and eventually settled down in western countries, including the United States, Australia, France, and Canada. In 2016, it was estimated that there were 207,000 Hmong people in Thailand, and approximately 10 million throughout the world, mostly in China, Vietnam, Laos, and the aforementioned western countries.[3]

The Hmong have a long history. Legends maintain that they originally resided in central China, along the Yellow River, thousands of years ago, though they eventually escaped to mountainous areas in southwestern China due to the expansion of the Han Chinese. In the first half of the eighteenth century, during the Qing dynasty, some Hmong further moved from southwestern China to mountainous villages in northern Vietnam, Laos, and Thailand due to the increase in conflicts between the Hmong and Han Chinese settlers, as well as repressive economic and cultural reforms imposed by the Qing government.[4] These Hmong ancestors eventually settled down in mountain villages of upper mainland Southeast Asia in the early nineteenth century, that is, long before the creation of the modern nation-states of Thailand and neighboring countries. According to Jean Mottin, a French Catholic priest, the Hmong started to migrate into the Tonkin area, which is at present northern Vietnam, in two waves from the 1800s to 1860s, and into the present northern Thailand areas from the 1830s to 1840s.[5]

In the colonial era, from the late nineteenth to the first half of the twentieth century, they became economically involved with two colonial powers, the British and French, the latter in Laos in particular, though the Hmong in Thailand were not subjugated by either. Around this time, the French colony and Thai government monopolized the opium trade, and the Hmong played a major role in cultivating and harvesting opium in order to sell it to both. That is why they preferred to live in high mountains with cold weather, areas that were suitable for opium cultivation, rather than lowland valleys.[6]

Then, in the 1940s, World War II broke out, though it did not affect Hmong people in Thailand in the way that it did the Hmong in French Laos.[7] This was because, in Thailand, which was not colonized by any European powers, there were no prominent local or national Hmong leaders who took particular sides in the war. Hmong who lived through this short period of war recalled that there was a "Japanese War," and that Japanese soldiers passed by their villages to the north. Some Hmong villagers remembered being forced to dig roads for them, while others were ordered to supply their horses to load Japanese soldiers' gear, though both of these lasted only for a few days. At the end of the war, when Japanese soldiers withdrew, some Hmong villagers bought their guns and bullets for hunting. In the early post–World War II era, anticolonial and independence movements spread like wildfire across many parts of Asia, but this did not impact the Hmong much either, largely because Thailand was not colonized by European powers or by the Japanese Empire.

Overall, prior to the escalation of the Vietnam War and Cold War politics, Hmong people in the mountainous areas of northern Thailand lived relatively quiet lives, isolated from the turbulence of global and national politics. In those days, they were mountain dwellers who were not controlled by the state government. Primarily due to low population density and the lack of state government regulation, Hmong people could move from mountain to mountain in order to find fertile lands for opium cultivation, remaining isolated in order to avoid disease contamination and keep themselves from being governed, as argued by James C. Scott.[8] However, with the escalation of the Vietnam War and Cold War politics, which eventually had huge impacts on Hmong communities in the mountainous villages of northern Thailand, they began seriously being affected by and, even more importantly, actively taking advantage of the Cold War world.

There has been some literature concerning the roles of the Hmong in the Vietnam War and Cold War, but the Hmong in Thailand have mostly been described simply as "victims" of the conflicts, or as "terrorists" (or CPT soldiers) who posed a threat to national security.[9] However, in this chapter, I would like to point out that the majority of the Hmong actually sided with the government and only one-third joined the communist side, many of whom joined the CPT to gain social justice and equal treatment. In short, Hmong experiences were much more diverse and ambivalent than is usually believed.

In a comparative dimension, as discussed by Masuda Hajimu, Native Americans and Chinese Americans made use of the Cold War to claim their civil rights and sovereignty and gain federal support.[10] Instead of viewing the ethnic Hmong in northern Thailand simply as "victims" or "terrorists," we will see them similarly as active agents who took advantage of the Cold War to achieve social justice, equal treatment, and economic development.

As we will see below, basic infrastructure and development projects were brought to Hmong people on both sides, due to their prominent military contributions during the Cold War. As a result, the Hmong in Thailand, whose population was around just 50,000 in the early 1960s, transformed themselves from a marginalized and discriminated "hill tribe" into one of the most prominent minorities in Thailand, though, to be sure, they have remained to some extent marginalized and underrepresented in Thai society in general.[11]

In addition to various primary and secondary sources, I have conducted and utilized oral history interviews with Hmong people on both sides of the conflict. An oral history approach is crucial for this research because the Hmong ethnic group did not have its own writing system until 1951, when the Romanized Popular Alphabet (RPA) system was introduced by missionaries who worked with the Hmong in Laos and Thailand.[12] While this has since become popular among the Hmong people, many older and non-Christian Hmong still cannot read and write. Thus, for the Hmong, oral transmission is the most important way to hand down stories from generation to generation.

Oral history can reveal Hmong villagers' direct experiences and points of view, which have been often obscured under the dominance of official records and existing documents that have tended to represent stories and perspectives of the mainstream—that is, in this case, the Thai government's—position. As Robert Perks and Alistair Thomson have explained, official narratives in written documents are more powerful and publicly accessible than narratives transmitted orally among villagers: "Through oral history interviews, working-class men and women, indigenous peoples or members of cultural minorities, amongst others, have inscribed their experiences on the historical record, and offered their own interpretations of history. More specifically, interviews have documented particular aspects of historical experience which tend to be missing from other sources."[13] Hence, conducting oral history can shed light on the experiences of people who have been hidden or misrepresented in mainstream narratives.

As stated above, under the influence of Cold War narratives, the Hmong people who sided with the CPT have been stereotyped as "terrorists" or "Red Meos," despite the fact that the majority of Thai people did not know why they took arms against the government from the beginning. Even though they were often labeled negatively as "separatists," what I have found is that they fought to protect themselves from being oppressed by state authorities. Furthermore, we know quite a lot about the Hmong who joined the CPT in the jungles, but, in reality, the majority of Hmong in Thailand sided with the state government as soldiers and village volunteers, though their stories have never been documented or publicized in mainstream Thai society. Below, we will see why the Hmong people decided to join the CPT or the government side, and what kinds of loss and gain they eventually experienced from fighting on both sides.

Southeast Asia and Thailand's Cold War

In Thailand, communist movements had their roots in the early 1930s. Following Ho Chi Minh from Vietnam, with the help of Vietnamese and Chinese immigrants in Thailand, the "Communist Party of Siam"—the predecessor of the CPT—was established in Bangkok in April 1930.[14] In response, in 1933, the Thai government declared an anticommunist act, arresting many communist members and sympathizers and deporting them to their homelands.[15] In the post–World War II period, such movements developed rapidly, mostly in urban areas, and thus the Thai government issued another anticommunist act in November 1952, banning the CPT and strictly controlling printing and other activities pertaining to communism.

Due to heavy suppression by the government, communist movements ceased operations in towns. Then, the CPT announced the strategy of "Jungles surrounding the cities"—*Pa lom muang,* in Thai—in 1958, emphasizing publicity campaigns toward the lower classes of people in both urban and rural areas who had been exploited and maltreated in Thai society. As a result, many villagers believed that they had hope for better lives, voluntarily joining the party and attending political and military trainings.[16] The first deadly armed battle between villagers and police—often called the "First Gunfire Day," or *Wan Siang Puen Taek* in Thai—occurred at Nabua village in Nakorn Phanom Province in northeastern Thailand on August 7, 1965. It marked the first day in Thai history in which deadly armed fighting between the CPT and the Thai government broke out. Following this incident, the CPT declared a militant strategy of armed struggle against the government.[17]

Following this battle, armed clashes spread throughout the country, especially in northern and northeastern Thailand, where the CPT had its greatest influence.[18] Meanwhile, on the opposite side, the Thai army set up the "Center for Subjugating Communists" for the purpose of getting rid of communists throughout the country.[19] Yet, the government could not eliminate communist movements in Thailand; rather, those movements intensified in the deep jungles of north and northeast Thailand, bordering with Laos, where they set up army bases and training centers, in areas that were inhabited by a number of ethnic groups, including the Hmong. One reason the CPT set up bases in these border areas was that they received significant support from China, Vietnam, and Laos, although later the Sino-Soviet conflict complicated this situation.

During the political turmoil in Thailand in the 1970s, not only farmers but also university students joined the CPT forces. This was particularly the case following the October 6, 1976, massacre at Thammasat University in Bangkok, when the lives of more than 2,000 university students were threatened, causing them to flee to northern Thailand's deep jungle area. This was because the CPT had established close relationships with the Hmong and other ethnic groups in mountain villages since the late 1960s. In this area, including Nan, Chiang Rai, Phayao, Petchabun, Phitsanuloke, and Loei provinces, the Hmong and other ethnic people became the CPT's core soldiers and civil supporters, accepting and taking care of newcomers from urban areas.[20] So, to begin with, why did the Hmong people decide to join CPT forces?

Hmong Fighting on the Communist Side

While only one-third of the Hmong in Thailand joined CPT forces, they played crucial roles in the CPT's armed fighting because of their high ability in jungle and guerrilla warfare, which was one reason that CPT leaders trusted Hmong soldiers and relied on them for protection. For the Thai government, on the other hand, the Hmong army—or "Red Meo army"—became an embodiment of fear. While Thai military officials generally did not fear any CPT forces if they were fighting in non-Hmong zones, the Hmong soldiers frightened them considerably and, in fact, caused much damage to Thai armies. News of the fighting was reported daily to the public; the headline of *Bangkok World* on February 13, 1968, for instance, stated, "Meo Blast Copter, Kill Six Soldiers, Chiengrai Northern Thailand," reporting that "an officer and five soldiers have been killed by Communist Meo tribesmen in remote village near the Laotian border."[21]

This is why images of "Hmong Communists" or "Red Meo soldiers" evolved into representative images of CPT forces that became widely known among the Thai public. In such imaginings, the Hmong people were even vilified as "separatists," secretly maneuvering to establish their own country. However, through detailed examination of the experiences of these Hmong soldiers, we can see that their fierce fighting derived from their oppression by the government, and that they joined the CPT forces not for the creation of their own country, but to defend and demand basic rights and dignity.

Although there has been some research on why many Hmong joined the CPT since the late 1960s, none has deeply investigated the direct experiences of those affected at the grass roots of conflict and warfare in mountainous villages. In the late 1980s, a prominent scholar in Hmong studies, Nicholas Tapp, attempted to link the Hmong uprising against the state government to the myth of the return of a legendary Hmong king, with an emphasis on the contemporary political context of the state government's habitual oppression. The problem with this argument, however, is that he did not carry out a firsthand survey among Hmong soldiers who had joined the CPT.[22] Thus, based on my oral history interviews with such former Hmong soldiers, I would point out more practical and personal factors: that is, Hmong villagers' negative and often miserable experiences with government authorities.

The dominant exercise of power among state authorities who reached mountain peoples in the mid-1960s and the simultaneous propaganda of the CPT resulted in the Hmong retreating to the jungle in northern Thailand. For instance, Bua Haw Yang, a former key Hmong leader who joined the CPT forces and now lives in Maneepruek village, Nan Province, recalled his experience and motivation as follows. After the clash between the CPT and Thai government forces in neighboring Nasa and Pha Daeng villages in 1966, Thai soldiers came to his village as the government had supposedly received information about communist activities there. Two Hmong men in the village were arrested, interrogated, tortured, and taken to Nan city for further investigation. This caused other Hmong villagers to fear similar raids and leave for the jungle to hide. Meanwhile, a few Thai people, who later turned out to be communists who had been trained in China, showed up in the village. They pointed out that the only way to avoid such cruel acts by Thai soldiers was to get out from under their rule, and that the CPT and communist doctrine would offer an opportunity to achieve such justice and freedom.

According to Bua Haw Yang, these communists told villagers that the only way to react to such brutal domination was to take arms to fight state authorities. After a while, the situation got even worse. The Thai government learned about communist activity in this jungle area and sent Thai soldiers to subdue it. Due to general hatred of communism and a common misunderstanding of all Hmong people being "Red Meos," Thai soldiers burned all of the Hmong villagers' houses in Pang Nong village in December 1967. Worse still, two nephews of a Chinese Hmong leader, who had been trained by the Thai Border Patrol Police and who worked on the government side, were killed by communists. Amid the confusion and chaos, Hmong villagers in seven neighboring villages dispersed; some joined CPT forces in the jungle, while others decided to move closer to the Thai government in the lowlands.

Government authorities' immoderate behaviors concerning local civilians were another main reason for ethnic Hmong to flee and join the CPT in the jungle. Such officers' attitudes were described in a common Hmong proverb as follows: "Facing tiger one will die, facing officer one will be deprived" (*ntsib tsov ces yuav tuag, ntsib nom ces yuav pluag*). For example, in the neighboring village of Kang Haw, just a few hours' walk from Maneepruek, a young Hmong, La Yi Lee, who was recruited by Border Patrol Police for training at that time, recalls the following:

> Around 1964, some government officers came to our village, though some were just traveling and passing by our village. Hmong villagers faced negative experiences with these officers. Whatever group of officers visited our village, they asked for taxes to be paid to the government. A leader of each group always claimed that they were the official representative of the government agency in charge of tax collection. Even eggs in chicken coops were taken by these authorities. They even shot pigs raised by villagers. Hmong villagers, thus, compared such behaviors to those of the wolf. Whenever villagers saw state officers showing up, they informed other neighbors, "Wolves are coming, hurry up to hide your valuable items!"[23]

The government's forcible resettlement plan was another major cause for the Hmong people to join the CPT to protect their basic rights (see figure 4.1). In the Hmong village of Khao Kho, Petchabun Province, Va Long Lee, a former leader of CPT forces in the area, recalled the government's relocation program and government officials' arrogant attitudes:

> At the beginning we lived in Phu Hin Rongkla, part of the Phu Lomlo and Phu Khithao, of Phitsanuloke Province. In 1964, we moved to Khao Kho Mountain in Phetchabun Province. Then, two years later, in 1966, we were compelled to move back to Phu Lomlo because the government was planning to set up Phu Lomlo to be a "Hill-Tribe Resettlement Site"—or *Nikhom Songkroh Chaokhao* in Thai. Villagers pleaded with the government for transportation, but government

FIGURE 4.1 Hill-tribe resettlement site of Phu Lomlo in 1965.
Courtesy of the former Hill-Tribe Welfare Division.

officials refused. More pressures for resettlement were put on villagers; thus, fifty Hmong leaders traveled to Bangkok in order to appeal to high-ranking officials for help. In Bangkok, however, they were poisoned with dinner foods provided by government officials, though nobody died. They asked the officials of the Public Welfare Department to bring them back home. Then, soon after they arrived in their villages, all of them left for the jungles since no one trusted the government anymore. In this same year of 1966, all Hmong people in our village and other neighboring mountainous villages were forced to move out, leaving for the new settlement site in Phu Lomlo.[24]

Va Long Lee continued to explain about his villagers' miserable experiences and his difficult decision to join the CPT forces:

Thai soldiers were sent to every Hmong village in that area. They even dared to shoot to intimidate villagers to join the resettlement program. After that, only small numbers of Hmong villagers agreed to join the government's resettlement project and moved to the resettlement site. Most villagers decided to flee to the jungle since they were scared by soldiers' intimidating shooting. At that time, I was an assistant to our village headman. We, the four representatives of the villages, appealed to our villagers who were already hiding in the jungles to come out and surrender to the government's instructions for resettlement. By that time, many Hmong villagers didn't trust us and some even threatened to kill us because we had been discussing with the government. However, while negotiating with government officers, they [the officers] also suspected that we had told villagers to join the CPT in the jungle since by this time the communist movement had already been spreading in the Phu Hin Rongkla area, and some Hmong people had sought communist help. Eventually, in order to protect my life, I decided to join my people in the jungle in 1967.[25]

Another Hmong villager, Nao Bee Lao, who lived in a nearby village on Khao Kho Mountain at that time, likewise recollected what happened. He also remembered the event in which fifty Hmong leaders went to and returned from Bangkok. According to him, after that event, a group of lowland Thai people came to his village and asked to buy pigs. After having a conversation, they asked the villagers if they had any problems. The villagers said to them that they were now being forced by the government to move out and resettle in Phu Lomlo. The villagers explained that they had asked the government for help with transportation but in vain, and that the villagers would have to move to the new resettlement site all by themselves.

Then, according to Nao Bee Lao, those visitors told the villagers that the government would give them only three months, either to resettle into the project site or to escape to the jungle. The visitors further offered the Hmong people training programs and weapons if they did not want to go to the resettlement site and wanted to protect themselves. By that time, the villagers realized that these visitors were CPT members. Then, according to Nao Bee Lao, quite a few Hmong, including himself, joined the CPT and came to receive training in communist thought in the forest for three months; nine months later, they actually received weapons that had been brought from China. In late 1968, these Hmong people dispersed into the jungle and joined the CPT to fight against the Thai government (see figure 4.2).

In this way, during the turbulent years of the late 1960s—particularly from late 1967 to early 1968—more and more young Hmong men and women escaped to the jungles to join the CPT, and many were sent to China for further training as the CPT had been developing close relationships with the

FIGURE 4.2 Hmong soldiers of the CPT with a Thai student.
Courtesy of Comrade Chart Saelee.

Chinese Communist Party (CCP). One young Hmong who was recruited and trained in China was Nao Bee Lao, mentioned above. He said that he started paying attention to how to use both herbal and modern medicine after experiencing severe sickness due to malaria as well as chemical powder dropped on Hmong by government aircraft, circa 1968. Then, in 1975, he was sent to China to study medicine. He joined the CPT group and walked from Khao Kho to Phu Miang, Uttaradit Province, and then crossed the border into Laos. Under the leadership of Lao comrades, he walked further and eventually crossed the Laos-China border, arriving at Simao, the Chinese town at the border.

From Simao, they took an airplane to Kunming and connected to Wenshan County by helicopter. In Wenshan, Nao Bee Lao spent four years studying medicine, with a focus on surgery and anesthesiology. In addition to medicine, he studied political and military sciences. After completing all of the training programs, he was sent to several major cities in China on a number of inspection trips before eventually returning to work in Thailand in 1979. One year later, in 1980, the Thai government declared amnesty for those who had joined the CPT in the jungle, which resulted in the return of students, farmers, and Hmong people to their families and communities, thus ending Thailand's Cold War. Therefore, he and other relatives decided to settle down in Khek Noi village, Phetchabun Province, where they have remained to the present day.[26]

Former Hmong leaders on the communist side, such as Va Long Lee and Nao Bee Lao, had already begun sensing that their war would end sooner or later. Communist China had begun adopting a new line of reforms and open-door policies. New conflicts arose between China and Laos, which resulted in the cutting off of a supply route that had been used to bring many goods and weapons from China to northern Thailand. These Hmong leaders had been involved in various forums for discussion and political analysis at both local and regional levels, and thus they had been vaguely aware that it would be impossible to continue their fighting for long. Nevertheless, for rank-and-file Hmong soldiers and villagers who fought on the CPT side, the sudden end of the war was a bolt out of the blue. They were very upset when they were told by their leaders that the CPT leadership had made an announcement that soldiers should hand in their weapons and surrender to the Thai government. "They were angry that CPT leaders had betrayed the Hmong people by asking them to fight for fourteen years but eventually gave up in 1981. On that day, the CPT's Hmong soldiers shot toward the sky, shouting with anger," said Song Lo Lao.[27] Eventually, however, the Hmong who joined the CPT disarmed themselves, and most went back to the mountain villages where they had lived prior to fleeing to the jungle, while others agreed to join their relatives in the lowlands.

While their sense of loss was unmistakable, it is simplistic to view the Hmong who joined the CPT as mere "victims" whose lives were trifled with in the turbulent seas of the Cold War. Looking more closely, we can see that they experienced gains by taking advantage of this situation. First of all, they were able to use Cold War politics to protect themselves, rectify injustices, and improve their social status. Prior to the arrival of the communist movement in the mid-1960s, Hmong in northern Thailand, along with other highland ethnic groups, had been looked down upon, often being cheated, oppressed, and heavily taxed by local authorities. For example, when local officials visited Hmong villages, they usually identified themselves as *Pho Fa*, literally meaning "Lord of Sky" or "King from Above," regardless of what kinds of agencies they belonged to. They not only behaved in a high-handed manner in villages, but aggressively collected taxes in the forms of both money and opium. Worse still, villagers were often cheated. Khu Vang Yang, a senior Hmong leader in Nan Province, recalled, "More than one team visited our village every year, especially following opium-harvesting season in January and February. Each team claimed that they were the real government representative to collect taxes."[28] Thus, Hmong villagers had been suffering cruel treatment and heavy taxes on farm fields, livestock, children, and even women's breasts, as well as lightbulbs even though no villages had electricity in those days, according to Moh Daeng, a Hmong leader in Chiang Rai Province.[29] For those villagers, the communist movement was a powerful weapon—or even a sort of savior—to fight oppression and to bring justice.

Second, the Hmong could use the communist movement as a vehicle to get opportunities for education and practical training. In fact, many young male and female Hmong were recruited and sent to study in China and Vietnam. For those people, including Nao Bee Lao, discussed above, as well as Moh Daeng and Phukong Laoyee, two prominent medical and military leaders in Hmong communities in Chiang Rai Province, there was little hesitation to accept communists' offers to study in China, as the Thai government and society at large at that time did not offer such opportunities to the Hmong and other highland ethnic groups. They walked for months through northern Thailand to Laos, to Vietnam, and to China, where they met Hmong people from other areas. Such medical and political trainings were conducted in China, while military trainings were carried out in both Vietnam and China. After being trained for a few years, they were sent back to their own villages. In some cases, even their children's generation was sent to China in the late 1970s. For those who did not go to China or Vietnam, other kinds of opportunities were provided to take courses and learn military activities in the jungles of northern Thailand. It should be noted that Hmong women were trained for gender equality and played much larger roles in various activities than those who sided with the state government.

Third, the Hmong could use the Cold War world as a way to improve their social status and, eventually, gain more recognition among the Thai public. Due to their prominent roles in armed fighting in the jungles, "Hmong" came to be synonymous with CPT soldiers causing serious damage to the Thai military. Because of that, the Thai government and public came to detest Hmong communists, but at the same time such impressions caused a sort of respect among Thai soldiers and society. For instance, there were some people in Thailand who were not Hmong but fled to the jungle because of their negative experiences with government authorities. While staying in the jungle, these people came to understand why Hmong people had fled to the jungle and taken arms to fight against the state government. They learned from the Hmong people while, in return, teaching and training them. Then, gradually, the Hmong's fame rose, which can be seen in a surge of publications in the twenty-first century. There have been many accounts, for example, of the lives of Hmong in the jungle, personal experiences of Thai comrades with the Hmong, and so forth.[30]

Thus, by now, stories of the Hmong who fought on the side of CPT forces have become relatively well known. Yet, that is only one side of the coin, as the majority of Hmong villagers actually did not join the CPT. Much less known are the stories of Hmong who sided with the Thai government. How did they choose to join the Thai government side, and why?

Hmong Fighting on the Government Side

In the conflict zones, such as Chiang Rai, Phayao, Nan, Loei, Phitsanuloke, and Phetchabun provinces, some Hmong people who disapproved of communists joined the Thai government side, although many of them had had unpleasant experiences with local authorities. Looking back, their choices seemed to be personal and even coincidental, rather than ideological or predetermined. Generally speaking, these Hmong tended to have close relationships with relatively nicer and more trustworthy local officials. Some had been recruited and trained by those authorities when they were younger. Khu Vang Yang, a senior clan leader in Nan Province, for example, recalled that Thai Border Patrol Police often visited his mountain village, Kang Haw, circa 1962, recruiting four young men from each village in the region and sending them to their training base in Chiang Mai Province. After being trained, these young men were sent back to their villages to teach and lead various development projects, and to gather information about communist movements.[31]

La Yi Lee was one such representative. He was recruited to join the "Hill Tribe Development Team" at the Thai Border Patrol Police Base in Chiang Mai Province in 1965. After being trained there for two and a half months, he and the other three were sent back to their village to teach villagers how to use modern medicines, how to cultivate and raise livestock, and how to identify and monitor communist activities. Their new roles, with their close relationships with Border Patrol Police, naturally caused tensions with those who had been sympathetic to the CPT or those who detested government authorities. Clashes among these opposing villagers eventually broke out in neighboring villages in 1967. Two of La Yi Lee's relatives in a nearby village were murdered by CPT soldiers. Then, rumors spread, maintaining that La Yi Lee and the other three would sooner or later be killed by communists. By the end of 1967, they, along with their families, had decided to leave their village, moving to the safe zone in lowland areas, where American missionaries had set up a mission station and where some Hmong students had already been staying in a Christian hostel. Eventually, their relatives and other villagers decided to follow these four families, moving to the lowland and settling in the Paklang Resettlement Village in early January 1968.[32] This was how Hmong people in Kang Haw and other villages "chose" their sides, while Hmong in many other villages dispersed into the deep jungle and joined the CPT.

By the same token, some Hmong leaders in Phetchabun Province had close relationships with local authorities and Christian missionaries who had been expelled from China and took the government's side after coming to Thailand. Chertua Lee, a former village headman, recalled becoming Christian and choosing the government side. His father was also a village headman, and thus he was in a position to get to know local officials, soldiers, and American missionaries in the early 1950s. Then, in the mid-1950s, his family became one of the first pioneer families to convert to Christianity. After that, they came to have a closer relationship with the missionaries.

A turning point arrived in the mid-1960s when communist activities in the region become conspicuous. The family consulted with missionaries and, as advised, joined the Thai government side. Chertua Lee was already an assistant to the village headman by that time, and thus he led a few other families down to the lowlands, while many other families decided to flee to the jungle. Four years later, he even became one of the leading Hmong figures who promoted the creation of a new resettlement site at Khek Noi. To protect this new village from communist attacks, he devoted himself to training and setting up a vigilance group, *Thaharn Chao Khao Arsa Samak* (Hill Tribe Volunteer Soldiers for Village Protection) and *Chao Khao Chaidaen* (Hill Tribe Border Police Force). Similar vigilance groups were set up in neighboring Hmong resettlement villages in Nan and Phayao provinces. Some of the major resettlement sites included Paklang and Songkwae in Nan Province, Prachapakdee in Phayao Province, Khek Noi and Lao Lue in Petchabun Province, and Chedi Koh in Tak Province.

In addition, as Thai authorities learned of the reputation of Hmong soldiers on the CPT side, the army and Border Patrol Police began training young Hmong men in the resettlement sites (see figure 4.3). Hmong soldiers became the majority of their volunteer forces, playing crucial roles in the

FIGURE 4.3 Young Hmong and Mien (Yao) Hill Tribe volunteer soldiers in Pratu Pha Training Camp, Lampang Province, 1971. Courtesy of Thawatchai Charuprapatsorn.

fighting. According to Chua Chai Yang, one of the pioneering Hmong volunteer soldiers, Hmong soldiers were no longer just guarding the village, but fighting side by side with Thai soldiers in mountain battlefields such as Khao Kho and Phu Hin Rong Kla, because they were accustomed to high mountain terrain.[33] "Skirmishes between Hmong soldiers on both sides occurred quite often. We had to fire at our enemies if we didn't know whether they were Hmong or not. If we saw and knew that they were Hmong, we just avoided firing," said Chua Chai Yang. Needless to say, quite a few Hmong volunteer soldiers were wounded and died in such battles. Many Hmong civilians who sided with the Thai government were also wounded and died because they stepped on land mines set up by communist soldiers.[34]

Hmong volunteer soldiers' monthly payments were much lower than those of official Thai soldiers, but they earned moral support and respect from Thai army officials and the general public, as well as benefiting from various kinds of developmental projects in the resettlement sites created to help new residents. Land was provided for each family, and new crops and cultivation techniques were introduced. Basic infrastructure, such as dirt roads, reservoirs, wells, water pipe systems, and even schools, was provided. Furthermore, "Hill Tribe Public Welfare Centers" were set up in each resettlement site to provide food, shelter, and healthcare services for the Hmong and other highland refugees soon after they arrived. Family and individual registration surveys were conducted, and citizenship was granted to these Hmong people. In addition, youth gained a chance to go to school;

some went to local village schools, while others were sent to towns for further study. Upon completion of certain levels of education, young Hmong and other ethnic people had opportunities to become public welfare workers, agricultural extension staff, local schoolteachers, soldiers, and members of the Border Patrol Police. Having grown up in such a village, the author of this chapter is, in a sense, one of the long-term products of the Thai government's development projects.

Ultimately, although the Cold War caused pain to the Hmong who decided to side with the government in the late 1960s, it also entailed opportunities for them to move down to lowland areas, where they shared in the benefits of various kinds of developmental projects. Hmong refugees, to be sure, faced many difficulties in adapting to lowland ways of life, and some had to struggle for survival. Yet, during half a century of living in lowland villages and towns, their offspring more radically changed their ways of life in comparison to the Hmong who sided with the CPT and were eventually exposed to modern life in the 1980s.

Conclusion

Prior to the 1960s, the Hmong people lived in remote and mountainous villages in northern Thailand. They rarely had contact with lowland Thai officials and villagers since there were no roads or transport vehicles. In the mid-1960s, with the escalation of the Vietnam War and with the dissemination of Cold War politics in Thailand, the Hmong first became a target of the communist movement due to their geographical position as well as their grievances with state authorities. By the late 1960s, government officials were being sent to Hmong villages in order to persuade villagers to side with the Thai government.

Such a dissemination of Cold War politics caused chaos for local Hmong people. Hmong leaders who had negative experiences with the state government tended to side with CPT forces, while those who maintained relatively more congenial relationships with local authorities tended to side with the government, thus opposing and fighting each other up until 1980. Because of such tensions among Hmong villagers, not only Hmong leaders but even close relatives were divided into two camps. Distrust among Hmong leaders and villagers on opposing sides caused the killings of many Hmong leaders and villagers on both sides. Many also lost their lives in battles against the government or CPT. Therefore, it is not surprising that, even four decades after the end of Thailand's Cold War, memories of the conflict still haunt the Hmong people regardless of whether they sided with the CPT or the Thai government.

In the Hmong language, an occurrence of disease contamination is described as *ib phaum mob*, literally meaning a "wave of disease," which spreads quickly and then disappears a while later. In this way, Hmong leaders who fought on both sides of Thailand's Cold War often use this metaphor of a "wave of disease" for the Cold War. According to this view, the Cold War was a political and ideological conflict that occurred far away in the global context but devastatingly affected the Hmong people in national and local contexts. It was a sort of "disease" that made the Hmong excited to take up arms but that left them blamed and stereotyped as "Red Miao"—the most dangerous tribes to national security—in the eyes of the state government and the general public. What was wrong, in this view, was the Cold War itself, which came and went. Thus, Hmong leaders and villagers' actions could be pardoned, making it possible for them to live together harmoniously. Indeed, the young Hmong people who grew up in the post–Cold War period have been harmoniously united, leaving memories of Cold War conflicts behind. Yet, in doing so, Hmong people's agency during the Cold War era has been rather obscured, making them appear mere victims.

Based on oral history interviews with Hmong leaders and villagers, I have, rather, explored the ways in which the Hmong people interacted with the Cold War world. Instead of looking merely at its impact on them, I have taken the other way around and investigated how they took advantage of the Cold War. What we have seen is that, although the Cold War did have a devastating impact on the Hmong, it was more ambivalent and complicated for them than is usually believed. We have seen that they could take advantage of their situation. Whether belonging to the government or the CPT side, they could rectify injustice to some extent. On either side, they could find opportunities for education and development. More importantly, the Hmong—a small ethnic group in Thailand with a population of 50,000 prior to the 1960s—became one of the most prominent ethnic groups in Thailand, with a population of 207,000 as of 2016, and well known nationally and internationally. In a sense, it could be said that the Hmong were able to open doors for broader sociopolitical and economic opportunities thanks to the Cold War.

During the national election campaigns in May 2019, Phukong Laoyee, one of the most prominent former communist Hmong leaders, and his Hmong team shed new light on their battles during the Cold War. According to him, he began fighting for social justice at an early age by leaving to join the CPT in the jungle for almost two decades. He emphasized that, although the Hmong people have attained a certain level of justice and recognition, new problems have emerged, such as cases of being toyed with in competition for natural resources, or of being scapegoated for drug smuggling. While his team did not gain any seats in the House of Representatives, his movement had a big impact. In fact, another Hmong politician, who is a son of former Hmong CPT soldiers in Tak Province and a member of the *Anakhod Mai* (New Future) party, did win in a national election and became a member of the House of Representatives. Moreover, not only these Hmong politicians, but younger Hmong generations in general, have been playing essential roles in local politics and civil movements. While the battleground has changed from the jungles to the legislative assembly, the Hmong's fight for justice and recognition has been continuing.

Notes

1. "Hmong" is the term that the Hmong people in Thailand use for themselves, while they consider "Meo" and "Miao" derogatory terms used by non-Hmong people. However, in China, the term "Miao" is a broader category that includes the Hmong and other groups, without any negative connotation.

2. Other hill tribes include the Karen, Akha, Lisu, Lahu, Yao, Khamu, H'tin, Lua, and Mlabri. Thai government officially categorized them as "hill tribes" from the late 1950s to the mid-2000s. Presently, these peoples prefer the term "Indigenous people" to refer to themselves.

3. Kong Nikhom Sang Ton Eng Lae Patthana Chaokhao [Division of Self-Help Settlement and Hill Tribe Development], *Thamniab chumchon bon phuenthisung, krobkrum phuenthi 20 changwat khong prathet Thai, prachampi 2559* [Directory of highland communities, in 20 provinces of Thailand in 2016] (Bangkok: Department of Social Development and Welfare, Ministry of Social Development and Human Security, 2016).

4. Robert D. Jenks, *Insurgency and Social Disorder in Guizhou: The "Miao" Rebellion 1854–1873* (Honolulu: University of Hawai'i Press, 1994).

5. Jean Mottin, *History of the Hmong* (Bangkok: Odeon Store, 1980). Also, see Christian Culas and Jean Michaud, "A Contribution to the Study of Hmong (Miao) Migrations and History," in *Hmong/Miao in Asia*, eds. Nicholas Tapp, Jean Michuad, Christian Culas, and GarYia Lee (Chiang Mai: Silkworm Books, 2004), 61–96.

6. William R. Geddes, *Migrants of the Mountains: The Cultural Ecology of the Blue Miao of Thailand* (Oxford: Clarendon Press, 1976).

7. In Laos, the Hmong people were divided into two opposing camps, one on the French and the other on the Japanese side, fighting each other. Due to this background, a civil war occurred in Laos when the French left in 1953. See, for example, Keith Quincy, *Hmong: History of a People* (Cheney: Eastern Washington University Press, 1988); Mai Na M Lee, *Dream of the Hmong Kingdom: The Quest for*

Legitimation in French Indochina, 1850–1960 (Madison: University of Wisconsin Press, 2015); and Touxa Lyfoung, *Tub Npis Lisfoom tej lus tseg cia* [The remnant words of Touby Lyfoung] (St. Paul, MN: Touby Lyfoung Foundation, 1996).

8. James Scott, *The Art of Not Being Governed: An Anarchist History of Upland Southeast Asia* (New Haven, CT: Yale University Press, 2009).

9. See, for instance, Jane Hamilton-Merritt, *Tragic Mountains: The Hmong, the Americans, and the Secret Wars for Laos, 1942–1992* (Bloomington: Indiana University Press, 1993); Chia Youyee Vang, *Fly Until You Die: An Oral History of Hmong Pilots in the Vietnam War* (Oxford: Oxford University Press, 2019); and Prasit Leepreecha, "Heroes of the Plain of Jars: Hmong Monuments and Social Memory in Laos and America," *Journal of Mekong Societies* 16, no. 3 (2020): 44–78.

10. Masuda Hajimu, "The Early Cold War: Studies of Cold War America in the Twenty-First Century," in *A Companion to US Foreign Relations: Colonial Era to the Present*, ed. Christopher R. W. Dietrich (Hoboken, NJ: Wiley Blackwell, 2020), 2:632–51.

11. For the population in the early 1960s, see Oliver Gordon Young, *The Hill Tribes of Northern Thailand: A Socio-ethnological Report* (Bangkok: Thai-American Audiovisual Service, 1961). For the population in 2016, see *Thamniab chumchon bon phuenthisung*, 8.

12. Yves Bertrais, *How the Hmong R.P.A. Was Created and Had Spread from 1953 to 1991* (Guyana: OMI, 1991).

13. Robert Perks and Alistair Thomson, *The Oral History Reader* (New York: Routledge, 1998), ix.

14. Eiji Murashima, *Kamnoerd Phak Communist Sayam (Pho So 2473–2479)* [Birth of Communist Siam Party, 1930–36] (Bangkok: Matichon, 2012).

15. Suthachai Yimprasert, *Phaen ching chart thai: Wa doy rat lae kan totan rat samai chomphon Poh Phiboonsongkram khrang thi song (Pho So 2491–2500)* [On the state and the resistance to the state during the reign of Marshal Poh Phibunsongkhram, the second time, 1948–57] (Bangkok: P. Press, 2007).

16. Ninlawadee Promphakping, Maniemai Thongyou, and Viyouth Chamruspanth, "The Extension of State Power and Negotiations of the Villagers in Northeast Thailand," *Southeast Asian Studies* 6, no. 3 (December 2017): 415–16.

17. Promphakping, Thongyou, and Chamruspanth, "Extension of State Power," 415–16.

18. Thikarn Srinara, *Lang 6 Tula: Wadui Khwamkhatyaeng thang khwamkhid Rawang Khabuankarn Naksuksa Kap Phak Communist Haeng Prathetthai* [Post 6 October: On ideological conflict between students and Communist Party of Thailand] (Bangkok: 6 Tula Ramluek, 2009).

19. Saiyud Kerdphol, *Pho Kho Tho Hai Pai Nai?* [Where does the CPT disappear?] (Bangkok: Aksorn Samphan, 2011).

20. Klum Phoen Nan, *Tamnan Dao Phraophrai Thi Phuwae Phuphayak* [Bright star legend on Phuwae and Phuphayak] (Bangkok: Art Edge Graphic, 2009); Chanthana Fongthale, *Chak Doiyao Thuong Phuphaji: Buntuk Pravattisart Kandoenthang Khong Numsao Haeng Duantula* [From Doiyao to Phuphaji: Historical records on journey of Young People of October] (Bangkok: Praew Printing, 2013); Mai Lee, *Phayu Fon*

Bon Phuphaji-Phachang [Rain storm on Phaji-Phachang mountains] (Pathumthani, Thailand: Rangsit University Press, 2016); and Thikarn, *Lang 6 Tula*.

21. *Bangkok World*, February 13, 1968.

22. Nicholas Tapp, *Sovereignty and Rebellion: The White Hmong of Northern Thailand* (Oxford: Oxford University Press, 1989). More recently, Ian G. Baird has studied the transnational, transcultural, and gender-relation–transforming experiences of the CPT Hmong people, but has not looked at how and why the Hmong got involved in Cold War politics. See Baird, "The Hmong and the Communist Party of Thailand: A Transnational, Transcultural and Gender-Relations–Transforming Experience," *TRaNS: Trans-Regional and -National Studies of Southeast Asia* 9, no. 2 (2021): 167–84.

23. La Yi Lee, interview with the author, August 2007.

24. Va Long Lee, interview with the author, July 2019.

25. Va Long Lee, interview.

26. Nao Bee Lao, interview with the author, June 2019.

27. Song Lo Lao, interview with the author, August 2019.

28. Khu Vang Yang, interview with the author, July 2016.

29. Moh Daeng Lee, interview with the author, March 2015.

30. See for instance, Chanthana, *Chak Doiyao Thuong Phuphaji*; Khana Tham Ngan Anusorn Phuphayak Changwat Nan, *Tamnandao Praoprai Thi Phuwae Phuphayak* [Brighten stars legend at Phuwae Phuphayak] (Bangkok: Art Edge Graphics, 2006); Mueanfun, *Lang Mai Daodaeng* [Red star behind the microphone] (Bangkok: 6 Tula Ramluk, 2005); Mueanfun, *Su Samoraphum Naewna* [Heading for forefront battle field] (Bangkok: 6 Tula Ramluk, 2008); and Siriluk Chanthavong, *Khoun Su Phuphayak* [Claiming to Phuphayak] (Bangkok: Sukhaphap Jai, 2006).

31. Khu Vang Yang, interview.

32. Prasit Leepreecha et al., *50 Pee Paklang: Chak Yoddoi Su Phuenrarp* [50 years Paklang: from mountain to lowland] (Nan, Thailand: Chomrom 50 Pee Paklang, 2018).

33. Chua Chai Yang, interview with the author, June 2008.

34. Chua Chai Yang, interview.

Part II **Local Imaginings and Identity Politics**

5 Reconsidering the Naxalite Movement
Local and Social Experiences of the Cold War in Kerala, India, in the 1960s

MUHAMMED KUNHI MAHIN UDMA

While there has been a surge in scholarly literature that explores India's Cold War experiences, there remains a general tendency to assume that the Cold War did not significantly affect India.[1] Such a view is generally supported by an understanding that India remained outside of the Cold War's bipolarity with its particular nonalignment and neutrality policy, and thus never became a venue for the serious Cold War violence that created bloodshed and traumatic memories in East and Southeast Asian, as well as Latin American, countries. However, careful analysis reveals that such a view ignores the significance of popular sentiments and public discourses among ordinary people, which create social reality on an everyday basis. Irrespective of the government's ostensibly neutral policy, popular attitudes in India were heavily predisposed toward Cold War logic. To begin with, both mainstream and leftist parties were actively employing Cold War rhetoric in everyday discourse. Such discursive engagements greatly helped the construction of Cold War reality in Indian public discourse, even though the Indian government supposedly pursued a non-aligned and neutralist foreign policy.

The Sino-Indian Border Conflict of 1962, concerning the Himalayan frontier, further consolidated such Cold War reality in Indian public discourse. Due to India's humiliating defeat, anticommunist sentiments became increasingly prevalent through the evolution of narratives that demonized Communist China. After the war, anticommunist sentiments began manifesting in violence as Indian communists and their sympathizers became targets of outrage across the country.[2] In other words, while the government distanced itself from Cold War politics, public discourses and their carriers—the people—were actively creating images of communist "enemies" within, thus incorporating themselves into the Cold War world.[3]

Such a discursive creation of communist "enemies" had significant meanings in India in the 1960s. This was because, with its large population struggling under poverty, as well as caste-based feudal oppression and exploitation, India was one of the most fertile lands for the growth of communist movements. Containing the growth of popular affinity toward communism and its promise of an egalitarian future, mainstream factions needed discourses that would depict communism as a force destructive toward India's traditions, religion, and wealth. In fact, there were carefully drafted discursive interventions, mostly adopting Western Cold War narratives, to create anticommunist sentiments in India and to limit the influence of communist parties among peasants and workers. Undoubtedly, such attempts were extremely successful, as far as India's mainstream discourses were concerned.

Nevertheless, a significant number of peasants and workers remained uninfluenced by such discourses, mostly because of their social and economic backwardness. They found a sort of hope in the communist-led social revolution since their long-standing resistance to feudal exploitation was becoming hopeless due to the nexus between the government and the feudal landed gentry in the countryside. These peasants and workers, mostly belonging to lower-caste communities, perceived communism as the vehicle of social change that could shatter the prevalent system of oppression and exploitation. They extended their support to radical communist groups that were willing to lead their fight against feudal exploitation and caste-based oppression. It was such grassroots-level support of struggling people that boosted development of the radical communist Naxalite (Naxal) movements in various parts of the country beginning in the late 1960s.

As we will see below, the spirit of the communist revolution, ignited by Cold War politics, significantly influenced the Naxalite incarnation of Indian radical communism in the 1960s. However, it is important to note that the history of communist violence in India is much longer than the Cold War tension between the United States and the Soviet Union in the post–World War II period.[4] In fact, Indian communists had created many violent struggles in the country since the inception of the movement in the 1920s, even though they had been unsuccessful in establishing a communist state in the Indian subcontinent.[5] The early radical activism had not adequately addressed the problems of the caste-based feudal system that denied the dignity of lower-caste people across the country. In other words, early Indian communism failed to navigate the complex structure of India's centuries-old caste system because it limited its scope to a conventional Marxist understanding of class struggle.[6]

The state of Kerala, located at the southwestern edge of the Indian subcontinent, was the site for the earliest radical communist struggles. This was particularly the case in Kerala's tribal-dominated districts where, as we will see below, Naxalite activism gained a foothold in the late 1960s. However, as in other regions in India, the early struggles in these districts were largely ineffective. This was because mainstream Indian communist parties failed to understand the problems in Kerala's tribal-dominated areas, where the upper-caste landed gentry, *Janmis*, had been exploiting the lower-caste Indigenous tribal people, *Adivasis*, by all possible means.[7] Placed at the bottom of the hierarchy in the Indian caste system, these Indigenous tribal people were helpless against the exploitation of Janmis, who controlled the largest share of Kerala's agricultural lands with their caste-based privileges. It was such a continuous failure of early communist struggles—and more specifically the mainstream communist parties' inability to address questions of caste and feudal exploitation—that prepared fertile ground for the evolution of the Naxalite movements in these areas in the late 1960s.[8]

Focusing on such social, cultural, and economic conditions that fostered radical communist politics in Kerala, this chapter traces the development of the Naxalite movement in the region since the late 1960s. It utilizes extensive oral history interviews conducted in the local language, Malayalam, and explores the ways in which Naxalite members adopted communist logic in their struggles against the feudal exploitation of tribal communities. In doing so, it demonstrates that the early history of the Naxalite movement in Kerala is, to a large extent, the history of Adivasi communities' resistance to Janmis' exploitation and discrimination. To be sure, Naxal violence in India's tribal heartlands has been a favorite subject of study ever since the Indian government began considering it a major challenge to national security. Title after title has appeared in Indian bookstalls every year, addressing questions of Naxal violence in states such as West Bengal, Jharkhand, Chhattisgarh, Orissa, Bihar, and Andhra Pradesh, where it has been particularly fierce and wide in scale. Most of these titles, however, end up describing such events in an overly sensational, journalistic, or heroic manner, without a more rigorous analysis of the social experiences of Naxalites and historical backgrounds of Naxalite violence.

Among the plethora of titles, sociologist Nandini Sundar's *The Burning Forest: India's War against the Maoists* stands out as an exceptional work in terms of academic quality as it presents an unbiased picture of struggles in the social lives of India's tribal regions.[9] Focusing on the Indigenous tribe living in Bastar, the southern part of Chhattisgarh, Sundar's study problematizes the mainstream depiction of the Naxalite movement as merely a militaristic challenge that needs to be dealt with by the firepower of the state. Instead, the book reveals the ongoing socioeconomic injustice toward helpless tribal people, presenting Naxalite violence as political resistance against various forms of exploitation. Likewise, anthropologist George Kunnath's *From the Mud Houses: Dalits and the Making of the Maoist Revolution in Bihar* is a credible academic exercise, exploring the socioeconomic conditions that have supported the evolution of Naxalite violence across the country.[10]

Scholarly attention to the social and local backgrounds of the Naxalite movement in India's tribal heartlands has begun to grow in recent years, alongside growing academic interest in Indigenous people, as well as their social lives, struggles, and resistance. Scholars using "history from below" approaches, including subaltern studies scholars, have explored tribal struggles against exploitation and caste-based oppression in attempts to problematize the elitist history of India.[11] Furthermore, with the surge of new academic interest, anthropologists, sociologists, and cultural studies and development studies scholars have conducted some highly interesting interdisciplinary research to explore various questions related to tribal life in India.[12]

However, most of the existing literature focuses on the central and eastern states where the majority of India's Indigenous population resides. There is little credible academic analysis that explores the socioeconomic and historical conditions that fostered the evolution of Naxalite movements in Kerala's tribal-dominated regions. In the very few studies that focus on Kerala's tribal population, attention is paid only to issues of land reform and the so-called Kerala model of development. Thus, there is a clear lack of scholarly work that examines the caste-based feudal exploitation of tribal communities in the southern part of India, on the one hand, and the role of radical communist movements in transforming such a traditional system, on the other.[13] Furthermore, Kerala's regional-language literature, written in Malayalam, has tended to either overly romanticize or vilify Naxalite politics, with little serious consideration of the historical and social conditions that nurtured Naxalite movements in the region.[14]

Last but not least, the existing literature discussed above has paid little or no attention to another significant element: the Cold War. Local and social experiences of the Cold War, let alone Indigenous tribal people's use of Cold War politics in their struggles, have not been adequately explored. This is largely because of the common presumption that India remained outside of the Cold War's bipolarity with its government's nonalignment and neutrality policy. In addition, the Cold War has tended to continue to be narrowly treated as a subject of diplomacy and international politics. Thus, recent studies, such as Zorawar Daulet Singh's *Power and Diplomacy* and Paul M. McGarr's *The Cold War in South Asia*, have begun shedding light on India's roles in Cold War politics, but these works have rarely broken beyond the boundaries of foreign policy studies.[15]

Nevertheless, in the field of Cold War studies, there has been an attempt to challenge such a traditional framework and to reconceptualize the Cold War in a way that could absorb its diverse manifestations beyond conventional grand narratives. Such intellectual pursuits, notably Heonik Kwon's *The Other Cold War* (2010) and Masuda Hajimu's *Cold War Crucible* (2015), have aimed not only to explain the discursive production and consolidation of the Cold War "reality" but to highlight grassroots experiences of this "imagined" war in different parts of the world.[16] Appending such scholarly efforts, this study attempts to examine how the "reality" of the Cold War was appropriated and functioned in India's tribal-dominated areas where movements against feudal exploitation took a violent turn. It shows that the discourse of the Cold War was not a mere influence but an active participant in shaping local struggles against various kinds of exploitation in the region. Focusing on the global-local relationship in the Cold War discourse, this chapter rightly belongs to part II, "Local Imaginings and Identity Politics," in this volume.

Though the primary purpose of this study was, initially, an exploration of the significance of discursively constructed Cold War reality in India's radical communist-led movement against feudal exploitation of marginalized communities, in the course of its development, this chapter also emerged as a study of the emotions involved in a fight against centuries-old caste-based social and economic exploitations. It demonstrates the importance of the social construction of emotions related to the Cold War, whether upholding the *hope* of a communist-led social revolution or fabricating the *fear* of communist-led destruction of traditional values, in an Indian context. Thus, though not particularly aimed at it, this study also joins the "emotional turn" in the discipline of history.

The Road to Radical Communist Politics

The history of Naxalite movements in India cannot be separated from that of communist parties in India. As we will see below, the Communist Party of India (CPI), the oldest communist party in India, went through split after split, producing several factions. While supposedly sharing the same goal—that is, to establish a communist state in India—eventually, all mainstream communist parties in the post–World War II period abandoned the strategy of revolutionary armed struggle, adopting a moderate line and joining in electoral politics.[17] However, many ardent supporters and sympathizers were not satisfied with such a compromising attitude. Many had taken inspiration from communist struggles in other parts of the world, particularly China. Some tried to keep alive the idea of communist revolution in India, even though the mainstream communist parties had begun preferring electoral victories. In this attempt, they received strong support from a section of workers, lower castes, and Indigenous tribal people, who had been suffering and struggling due to diverse kinds of exploitation. It was not surprising that, under the moderate, mainstream leadership, isolated radicals mushroomed one after another in different parts of India.

Tribal-dominated regions of Kerala had witnessed the eruption of such radical communist activities even before the beginning of the Naxalite movements in the late 1960s. To explore the links and antagonisms between mainstream communist parties and radical communist movements in this region, let us look into the life of Ayinnor Vasu, a man who traveled various paths of communist politics in Kerala (figure 5.1). At the time of India's independence from the British Empire in 1947, Vasu—also known as "GROW Vasu" because of his association with the Gwalior Rayons Workers' Organization (GROW) in Kozhikode—was eighteen years old. A year before India's independence, he began working as a weaver in the Commonwealth Weaving Mill in Kozhikode to support his struggling family. Born as the eldest son of an agricultural laborer, in a period of global depression and famine in India, he learned the lessons of poverty in his early years. According to him, in a family of eleven, eating even two full meals in a day was nothing less than luxurious at that time. Having grown up in such an economically impoverished family, he had to stop formal education in the fifth grade. However, he recalled almost eight decades later that the socioeconomic conditions in which he grew up had taught him many valuable lessons and gave a leftist orientation to his thoughts and views.[18]

A voracious reader, Vasu spent much of his early youth in local libraries and developed a good understanding of the sociopolitical realities within and outside the country. He recollected that the communist movements that were redrawing the political map of the world had given him new hope for the future. Indeed, with its large numbers of socially and

FIGURE 5.1 Mr. Ayinnor Vasu. Photo by the author.

economically oppressed peasants and working-class populations, India at that time seemed to be one of the most fertile lands for the growth of such movements.[19] In fact, in some states, such as Andhra Pradesh, West Bengal, and Kerala, communist movements had already established strong footholds in local politics. By this time, Indian leftist authors' writings, as well as various books and journals subsidized by the USSR, were widely available in Kerala, and these helped the young Vasu to adopt a Marxist theoretical framework for his understanding of caste and class exploitation in India. At that time, he was deeply influenced by prominent communist leaders such as Ayillyath Kuttiari Gopalan—famously known as AKG—and made a great effort to understand the ideas of the proletarian revolution and communist state. Eventually, he became convinced that communist revolution would be the only way to eliminate caste and class exploitation in India.[20]

It was his cousin, Krishanan, who introduced Vasu to the CPI, then the largest communist party in India. Since Vasu had already worked in a weaving mill in Kozhikode, he began to be active in the All India Trade Union Congress (AITUC), which was affiliated with the CPI. His vast reading and oratorical skills helped him to distinguish himself in the ranks of the union, and, in 1947, he became a full-fledged member of the CPI. In this crucial period, he believed that a CPI-led communist revolution was inevitable in India, as the vast majority of the population was facing various kinds of feudalistic exploitation. This was particularly the case in Kerala, where more than 50 percent of households owned no land, even though it was predominantly an agrarian state, causing various problems, most notably, extreme poverty among the majority and a severe food shortage.[21]

Thus, the moment immediately following independence appeared to be the best possible time, in Vasu's view, to start a communist revolution, with a large number of workers and farmers, as well as lower-caste Indigenous people, all suffering from and struggling with poverty and exploitation. However, the CPI made little effort to take advantage of such situations. Rather, it was beginning to transform itself into a regular parliamentary party, amending its revolutionary strategy and pursuing electoral success as its fundamental goal. Nevertheless, Vasu maintained high hopes for revolution. Like many of his fellow communists, he was unconvinced by the party's rationale for prioritizing electoral success and unwilling to accept the party's new moderate strategy, particularly with the escalation of the Sino-Soviet split in the 1960s. Vasu recalled that, in this period, he tried to associate with several radical leaders within the party and carefully observed growing ideological tension within the communist world.[22]

As the CPI headed toward a split in the early 1960s, particularly following the Indo-China War of 1962, due to mounting disputes between supporters of Soviet revisionism and Mao's traditionalism, Vasu joined with the latter, pro-China faction, which later became the Communist Party of India (Marxist) or CPI (M).[23] He believed that the new party, which was formed in 1964 by reinvigorating the revolutionary spirit of the Indian working class and peasants, would help to bring about a Chinese-model communist revolution. He put great effort into strengthening this new revolutionary faction by organizing his local working-class community and leading many workers' movements under its flag. However, to his disappointment, before long, the CPI (M) also abandoned its revolutionary strategy and began prioritizing electoral success, completely shattering his hope for a peasants' and workers' revolution, again.[24]

The turning point came in mid-1966 when a group of party members from Kozhikode, led by Kunnikkal Narayanan, approached the leadership of the CPI (M), seeking permission to publish a Malayalam translation of several pamphlets issued by the Chinese Communist Party (CCP). The party leadership discouraged their enthusiasm for popularizing anti-USSR and pro-China discourse in Kerala. Yet, ignoring the party leadership, they moved ahead with their plan and opened Marxist Publications (which later became Rebel Publications) in Kozhikode, making a crucial intervention in Kerala by publishing Maoist literature that criticized the revisionism of the USSR. While this hardened the leadership's attitude against them, the radical communist ideas they promoted began spreading and becoming popular in Kerala, particularly attracting many youths.[25] In late 1966, Vasu also started to mingle with a group of radical members in a secretive way.[26] Soon, the CPI (M) expelled many who were associated with Marxist Publications, including Kunnikkal Narayanan, from its primary membership by accusing them of secret involvement with the Central Intelligence Agency (CIA) of the United States.[27]

Once kicked out of the party, the radical faction led by Kunnikkal Narayanan intensified their activities popularizing Mao's revolutionary literature—and Maoism—in Kerala. They easily attracted many like-minded people, even though they had no materials or organizational capabilities to implement their activism. Still, many people from the CPI (M), either by resigning from the party or in a more secretive way, began joining this radical faction. Yet, while attracting many enthusiastic youths, the group could not develop a proper plan for action, as they failed to form a consensus on an appropriate strategy for a communist revolution in

India and were incapable of managing ideological disputes among their members.

While they were struggling to build solidarity within the faction, however, in May 1967, the first Maoist armed action in India broke out in Naxalbari village in the northern part of West Bengal.[28] The Naxalbari Uprising generated a great sense of exuberance among radical communists across India. Kunnikkal Narayanan and his faction started preparing for a similar kind of armed uprising in Kerala, although many faction members remained skeptical about whether such an action would be successful. Still, in the second half of 1967, many members, including Vasu, dedicated themselves completely to the cause of the communist revolution in India.[29]

During this period, Kunnikkal Narayanan's adolescent daughter Kunnikkal Ajitha, who later became one of the first female Naxalites of Kerala, began to associate with her father's radical faction by discontinuing her pre-degree course at the Providence Women's College in Kozhikode.[30] Her mother, Mandakini Narayanan, a teacher at Shri Gujarathi Vidyalaya Higher Secondary School in Kozhikode, who later resigned in order to join the revolution, was also part of this faction. As a daughter of communist parents, Ajitha had evidenced a leftist orientation in her thoughts from an early age. Though she was a voracious reader, according to her, it was the political life of her father that shaped her approach to radical communism and the Naxalite movements. Unlike most members, she never experienced extreme poverty or caste discrimination in her childhood.[31] But, as she recalled several decades later, her spirit for revolution was stronger than that of most members, and, in fact, she became one of the most important figures in the first Naxalite violence in Kerala.[32]

The Beginning of Naxalite Violence in Kerala

The faction led by Kunnikkal Narayan declared complete support for the peasant uprising in Naxalbari and actively campaigned against the CPI (M) leadership that was part of the ruling coalition in West Bengal, the United Front, which was trying to suppress the peasant revolt. The United Front government's decision to suppress the Naxalbari Uprising provoked sharp criticism from various corners, even within the cadres of the CPI (M). After this incident, many members decided to resign from the CPI (M) as a sign of protest against the party's stance against a genuine peasant movement. In Kerala, most of those who left the CPI (M) had continued their communist politics by forming a number of small rebel groups. Eventually, however, many such groups began associating with Kunnikkal Narayanan's faction. This newfound support from different parts of the state was one of the major factors that pushed the radical faction to prepare for immediate action in Kerala after the Naxalbari incident.[33]

As the Naxalbari Uprising had received wide attention from China, Kunnikkal Narayanan and his team decided to adopt the uprising as the model to be followed in their future revolution in Kerala. This stance received an official endorsement from China. After the Naxalbari Uprising, the CCP's organ *Renmin Ribao* (People's Daily) published an article titled "Red Guard," calling for a "relentless armed struggle" to overthrow the Indian government and to "forcibly seize power."[34] Its editorial declared on July 5, 1967:

> A peal of spring thunder has crashed over the land of India. Revolutionary peasants in the Darjeeling area have risen in rebellion. Under the leadership of a revolutionary group of the Indian Communist Party, a red area of rural revolutionary armed struggle has been established in India. This is a development of tremendous significance for the Indian people's revolutionary struggle. . . . India is a vast semi-colonial and semi-feudal country with a population of 500 million, the absolute majority of which, the peasantry, once aroused, will become the invincible force of the Indian revolution. By integrating itself with peasants, the Indian proletariat will be able to bring about earth-shaking changes in the vast countryside of India and defeat any powerful enemy in a soul-stirring people's war.[35]

In order to assert their ideological commitment to Maoism, the radical faction of Kerala agreed to follow Mao's strategy, as suggested by the CCP after the Naxalbari Uprising.[36] Such a strategy required the movement to begin from a rural area by first liberating peasants from feudal landlords' exploitation and then recruiting them for the revolutionary army. To implement this strategy, Kunnikkal and his team decided to start their revolutionary movement from a rural area where, they thought, they could easily mobilize public support for the revolution. They selected two regions, Thalassery and Pulpally in the Kannur district of Kerala, as starting points.[37]

Thalassery, a small coastal town in northern Kerala, was thought to be an ideal place to gather a large mass of workers from the cigarette and weaving industries in surrounding areas.[38] In these labor-intensive industries, exploitation, such as long work hours and low wages, was extreme, and workers had very difficult lives. While they too were making efforts to fight against injustice, their demands for fair wages and decent benefits remained unheard as mainstream political parties, including communist parties, largely ignored them. Therefore, Kunnikkal's faction expected them to rise up naturally and join the revolution, once the revolutionary movement made an initiative.[39]

Pulpally, a small town surrounded by thick rainforest, about 100 kilometers east of Thalassery, was thought to be another ideal place for beginning a peasant revolt in Kerala, as it was one of the major centers of agricultural migration. When the food crisis became severe after independence in 1947, the government of Kerala decided to promote agricultural migration to largely unoccupied hilly forest areas on the eastern side of the state.[40] In response to this policy, a large number of people from different parts of Kerala moved to the Pulpally region, which was mainly an unoccupied forest area, though there were some powerful landlords, Janmis, and many indigenous Adivasi settlements. Most Janmis in the area had been exploiting Adivasi people in an extreme manner, using them, for example, as unpaid labor on their large estates. An Adivasi male worker received only 2.3 kilograms of rough rice, while female workers received merely 1.4 kilograms as wages for a day's work.[41]

Though communist party units in this region had been fighting this exploitation, they could do nothing against exploitative Janmis, who were powerful and enjoyed significant influence over all existing political parties, including communist parties. The poor migrant settlers who arrived in this region were largely sympathetic toward the even more miserable Adivasis, and they started paying wages in money for Adivasi workers, which helped to establish a good relationship between the two groups. This new relationship, however, led the Janmis to turn against migrant settlers, as the settlers' approach was affecting the supply of unpaid laborers on their estates. The tension between migrant settlers and Janmis began to erupt in violence by the 1960s.[42] Thus, Kunnikkal's faction anticipated that such a volatile socioeconomic situation in the region would help a communist revolution.[43]

After finalizing Pulpally and Thalassery as starting points, they began mobilizing essential resources, namely recruiting revolutionaries and collecting essential weapons. However, in such a short period of time, they could mobilize neither a mass of enthusiastic and disciplined revolutionaries nor a large number of effective modern weapons. Their inefficiency in leadership and lack of organizational discipline, as well as lack of knowledge about revolution in general, were obvious from the beginning and severely affected their preparations. Being part of this attempt, Vasu recalled that he himself experienced such problems.[44]

Once the radical faction had decided to create two separate revolutionary units for Pulpally and Thalassery, Vasu became part of the Thalassery unit. The only female in the group, Ajitha, was placed in the Pulpally unit. The plan was that the first unit, led by Kunnikkal, would attack Thalassery Police Station and steal all available firearms. After the attack, with the stolen weapons, they would steal food grains from the government's storehouses and private grocery stores. Once these actions were accomplished, they would move on to Pulpally, where the second unit, led by revolutionary comrades such as Varghese, who was one of the most prominent communist revolutionaries in Kerala, were waiting to start their action following a report of the successful first attack in Thalassery. They also decided that, on their way to Pulpally, they would destroy all major bridges to hinder the police pursuit that would definitely be coming. According to a blueprint for this plan, once reports of the Thalassery attack spread, the second unit, which was supposed to be camping in Pulpally forest, would attack Pulpally Police Camp and Police Station. Following these two successful operations, both units would camp inside the deep forest and start recruiting the revolutionary army. The radical faction's leadership expected that, once the news of these revolts spread, struggling peasants and workers all over the state would stand up and come out in support of their revolution.

The choice of the Thalassery Police Station as their first target had both practical and symbolic rationales. On the practical level, as they had neither the resources nor the capability to procure any firearms from other sources, stealing police weapons was their only immediate option. On a symbolic level, they saw attacking the police station as representing an attack on state power. Moreover, the selection of their second target had another crucial purpose. The Pulpally Police Camp for the Malabar Special Police had been established in early 1968 after a dispute between migrant settlers and the Pulpally Temple authority turned into a violent clash. The background for this clash involved the temple authority's claim to about 27,000 acres of land, on which roughly 1,000 migrant farmers' families were settled. During the dispute, the police camp served not only as a base for the police that smashed settlers' resistance against the powerful temple authority supported by Janmis but also as a notorious site for torturing resisting farmers and Adivasi people. This was the most important reason for their selection of it as a target.[45]

In their blueprint, the leaders of the first unit expected that at least a thousand volunteers from different parts of the state would join by the scheduled date of the revolt in Thalassery. However, to their deep disappointment, they managed to mobilize just roughly 300 volunteers. As the faction's leadership remained incapable of providing any training to these volunteers, they were nothing more than an unprepared, undisciplined crowd. Their weapons were mostly wooden spears, machetes, and locally prepared low-quality bombs. The second unit, which was preparing an attack on the Pulpally Police Camp and Police Station, faced a similar situation. This unit gathered together only 100 revolutionaries, who also lacked training and discipline.

Still, the biggest problem was that there was no equipment for communication between these two units. While there was just a 100-kilometer distance between Thalassery and Pulpally, travel and communication between the two locations were extremely difficult. First, there was no proper road between them; hilly terrain and thick rainforest hindered any easy connection by land. Second, the Pulpally unit was camping inside the deep forest, making communication even more difficult. Thus, the second unit had to depend solely on the transmissions of All India Radio for information regarding the status of the Thalassery revolt. Eventually, this lack of communication led to the tragic result of the first Naxalite armed action in Kerala.[46]

The Moment of Uprising and Its Repercussions

Ignoring all such limitations, the first unit continued its preparations for attacking the Thalassery Police Station and directed the second unit to stay inside the deep forest until the news of the revolt in Thalassery reached it. As the revolutionaries were getting ready for the attack, a rumor spread that the police had already gotten wind of the uprising and were well prepared for it. For the group of unprepared volunteers, such a rumor was devastating enough to dampen their revolutionary spirits, as it sounded like a warning that the police would use firearms against them. Nevertheless, they marched to the Thalassery Police Station holding weapons and torches in the early hours of November 22, 1968.[47]

What actually happened is not entirely clear. However, local popular narratives maintain that, while preparing to attack the station, the revolutionaries mistook the sound of a darting cattle herd for a police charge against them, causing them to disperse from the station compound, leaving all of their weapons behind.[48] Yet, Vasu, who claimed to have been on the front lines of the march, refuted such stories, arguing that they were manufactured by the police to conceal their own embarrassing failure. According to him, the revolutionaries dispersed from the station compound for a totally different reason: when they entered the compound and threw bombs at the station building, there was no sign of police preparation for their attack. However, to the revolutionaries' disappointment, their locally made bombs did not explode, even though those were supposed to be the most important weapons they had.

This failure created a moment of bewilderment among revolutionary volunteers. While they were at a loss, about five policemen came running out, screaming, "Kollan Varunne!" (They are coming to kill us!). Hearing this, some perplexed revolutionary volunteers began running out of the compound. Seeing these volunteers charging off, others assumed that police units were coming to attack them, and thus they dispersed from the station area immediately. Vasu insisted that the well-known story of revolutionaries dispersing in all directions at the sound of cattle herds was merely a police fabrication in order to hide the fact that some policemen were screaming for help.[49]

Thus, the first unit's attack on the Thalassery Police Station embarrassingly failed. Nonetheless, it attracted enormous media attention, which might have been due to prevalent fears of a communist revolution. Because of the rising influence of Maoist thought and the escalation of the Vietnam War, many expected that radical communist movements might become a major threat in India, as, after all, it had quite suitable socioeconomic conditions for a communist revolution. The Naxalbari Uprising in 1967 further solidified such fears and concerns.[50] Thus, even though the first unit's attack ended in utter failure, it ignited a spread of anticommunist sentiments, on the one side, and an upsurge of revolutionary enthusiasm, on the other.

The second unit, which had been waiting deep inside the forest near Pulpally, listened to a report on their comrades' attack on the Thalassery Police Station via All India Radio, assuming that the revolt had begun successfully. Though they could not get further details, they decided to go ahead with their original plan, believing that they should start an immediate surprise attack before the Pulpally police prepared to meet the threat of revolutionary forces marching from Thalassery.[51] Therefore, just two days after the failed revolt in Thalassery, in the early hours of November 24,

1968, they attacked the police camp with their wooden spears, machetes, and locally prepared bombs.

First, they killed radio operators in the police camp in order to prevent the spread of the news. Then, they threw bombs and severely thrashed every officer they found in the camp, some of whom were badly injured, while others managed to hide and escape. As the second unit's mission progressed violently, one revolutionary volunteer was critically injured due to an accidental bomb explosion, seriously undermining other members' morale. Therefore, they decided to abandon the rest of their plan and take wounded revolutionaries to the hospital.[52]

Leaving the police camp behind, they had another thing to do, however: search for notorious Janmis who had been exploiting Adivasis and migrant settlers in the area. Eventually, they brought many Adivasis along with them on their way, raiding Janmis' houses to seize valuables, including money and jewelry, which they distributed to people in the local neighborhoods. In addition, they burned Janmis' property documents, including those collected from poor Adivasis as security for loans. Further, revolutionary volunteers opened Janmis' storehouses and distributed food grains to Adivasis and collected firearms from these raids. As such, the second unit's mission achieved a measure of success, yet still far from enough to bring about a successful revolution.[53]

While the Naxal raids in Pulpally indeed were helpful for Adivasis and migrant settlers in the area, they were simply not enough to mobilize large-scale public support for communist revolution. On the contrary, news reports on Thalassery and Pulpally attacks created extremely negative images of Naxalites (Naxals) and radical communism—or Maoism—throughout Kerala. Mainstream communist parties, and particularly the CPI (M), harshly criticized the Naxal violence. With the spread of these negative images of Naxals, it was easy for the police to mobilize public support for successfully arresting most revolutionary members who had been active in the Pulpally and Thalassery incidents.

In no time, the police arrested many revolutionaries, including Kunnikkal Ajitha, who had joined the police camp attack in Pulpally. In the following days, some revolutionaries, including Kunnikkal Narayan himself, surrendered to the authorities and accepted the failure of their attacks. Then, the captured and surrendered revolutionaries had to undergo one of the most inhuman and heinous kinds of police torture in history as the price for their attacks on the police. The following is a portion of Ajitha's memoir, in which she describes the brutal torture they faced:

> The interrogation began at the moment we reached the police station. Four or five policemen gathered around each comrade. They aimed severe blows at the comrade's back, stomach and chest with the clear intention of injuring the internal organs. One of them would hit with a clenched fist, while another would use his elbow to strike. The next would kick him with his boots. When one policeman pushed him backwards hitting at his chest, another would thrust him forward punching his back. After 10–15 minutes of such torture, the comrade would be a broken man, in body and spirit. . . . That night I was stunned by the way my dear comrades were being kicked about like a football, or rather like mad dogs![54]

Ajitha continues:

> In between, they aimed some blows at my stomach and poked me with their lathis [. . .]. A policeman pressed down the pointed end of his lathi with both his hands on my big toe, as ordered by the inspector. I didn't cry out though the pain travelled from my toes to the top of my head. Some of the policemen didn't miss the opportunity to molest me. . . . I was in a sari. I was asked to take it off. Under it, I was wearing trousers. The officer allowed me to keep them on. I didn't understand his intent. They made me remove the woolen jacket too that I was wearing over the blouse. Then, I was asked to walk out of the station in trousers and a blouse. Even as I walked, they were hitting me on the back and stomach. They made me stand on the platform of the flagstaff in the police station courtyard and paraded me to thousands of people who had thronged around. I trembled with humiliation and helplessness.[55]

Nevertheless, such police brutality against captured revolutionaries did not stop the spread of the Naxalite violence in Kerala.[56] Rather, it added fuel to the disturbances.

The year 1968 marked only the beginning of a bloody history of Naxalite violence, which evolved in Kerala in the following years. Many spirited revolutionaries, including Vasu, were not included in the first list of revolutionaries arrested by the police. Escaping from the police traps, Vasu joined the group of Varghese, to become part of other crucial Naxal operations in the region. Among the many operations he joined, one of the most noteworthy was the Thirunelli-Thrissileri revolt in 1969, in which the Naxals killed two Janmis, and ultimately put an end to the slave labor system in practice in the remote villages of Wayanad. This was an action against Brahmin Janmis who had been ruling neighboring villages, like Thirunelli and Thrissileri, with their muscle and political power. They had ignored all government regulations concerning minimum wages, forcing indigenous Adivasi people to work on their estates without any cash payment.[57]

As these Janmis had enjoyed the support of many mainstream parties, including even the CPI and CPI (M), the Adivasi people were left completely helpless against the Janmis. By raising and leading a rebellion against them, Varghese became a savior to these struggling Adivasi communities. Yet, in February 1970 following the Thirunelli-Thrissileri revolt, the police arrested Varghese with the help of local Janmis and killed him without a trial. A few days later, the police arrested Vasu, who had become Varghese's right-hand man during the Thirunelli-Thrissileri rebellion. He was captured when he finally came out of the deep forest to get some food. Eventually, he had to spend almost eight years in jail without a single day of parole, ending in 1977, when the Morarji Desai government decided to release all political prisoners, after putting an end to India's two years of National Emergency declared by the previous prime minister Indira Gandhi.[58]

Over the years, images of Naxalites in Kerala gradually transformed from completely negative to sympathetic and even positive. This was because, as stories of police brutality toward the Naxals and their sympathizers spread, many people grew sympathetic toward them and their causes. They denounced the police's brutal acts in many Adivasi villages in the name of searching for Naxalites and their supporters. It should be noted that there were many heart-breaking incidents of police torture and exploitation, as well as rape and sexual abuse, all conducted in the name of police campaigns against radical communist movements. Such police brutality was a major factor that pushed local people to embrace the Naxalite movement and intensified Naxals' outrage toward the police. And that was the major reason that the first targets of Naxal violence were police stations in the region. Following the spread of stories about police brutality, diverse social movements concerning human rights, as well as Janmi and police brutality in Adivasi villages, began evolving in the state.

Then, along with the transformation of previously negative images, the Naxalite movement in Kerala began attracting another mass of people, particularly students, and entered its second stage of activism in the 1970s, largely based in urban areas.[59] While this chapter does not cover the entire history of the movement, before finishing, let us think about the essence of their activism, ostensibly merely a manifestation of radical communist movements—or Maoism—in Kerala.

The Essence of Naxal Violence in Kerala

While both "communists" and "anticommunists" relied heavily on Cold War discourses, the Naxalite movement in Kerala evolved largely as resistance against the various feudal exploitations and oppressions. In a sense, viewed from Kerala, it was a fight to protect the fundamental human rights of the most marginalized people, such as those who had suffered centuries-long Janmi violence, those who had suffered labor exploitation and sexual exploitation, and those who had suffered from the illegal occupation of forest land and the destruction of nature.

Most central of all was the issue of Janmis' violence toward indigenous Adivasi people. In fact, every Adivasi village in Kerala has numerous stories of the cruelty, exploitation, and wickedness of Janmis. Women often were the most affected, as they were helpless against the sexual exploitation of Janmis and their friends. In some villages, every groom had to share his bride with a Janmi on the first night of his marriage. The powerful Janmis had a team of goons to punish anyone who challenged their orders, and to physically and mentally harass any workers who demanded fair wages. They promoted toddy—a type of local alcoholic beverage made from the sap of various types of palm trees in Adivasi villages—to weaken any resistance movement and to sexually exploit Adivasi women and girls. The cruel hobbies of Janmis included chopping off women's breasts, cutting off the noses and ears of workers who broke or challenged their code of discipline, and killing those who resisted their sexual fantasies.[60]

The story of Narayan Kutti Nayar, a Janmi from Palakkad, reveals Janmis' brutality in Kerala, at least to some extent. He was infamous for ignoring workers' demands for fair wages and employing goons to thrash and kill those who made such demands. His brutality against women included chopping off the breasts of a woman who demanded a fair wage for her work. His goons helped him to get any woman and girl he wanted to satisfy his sexual fantasies. He even killed one of his wives for resisting such a fantasy, as well as one of his own sons who demanded a share of the family property. Worse still, this kind of insane brutality was not exceptional in Kerala. It was the Naxalites who finally put an end to his brutal hobbies, alleviating villagers' sufferings, by attacking his house and decapitating him on July 30, 1970.[61]

It was such fierce resentment on the side of Adivasis and migrant settlers against Janmis that pushed them to join the communist parties. However, their problems with Janmis had to do with more than matters of economic and sexual exploitation and an individual Janmi's personality; deep down, the crux of the issue for lower-caste individuals was the Brahmanical social system itself, which treated lower-caste people, such as Adivasis, as evil, denying them any social space or meaning in public life, treating them as if they were unhygienic detritus. They had to hide away from upper-caste communities in public spaces and were not allowed to eat in restaurants where upper castes dined. They were even denied entry to temples where upper castes worshipped. Therefore, their struggles were, in essence, against the entire social system of discrimination and exploitation.

These people who were literally insulted and injured due to such a social order at first sought help from the CPI, as it seemed to be the most promising revolutionary party at that time. When the CPI abandoned its revolutionary strategy, these people joined the CPI (M). When they realized the CPI (M)'s inability to confront Janmis, they joined the Naxalites. Throughout this process, what these supporters followed was not really the party's guidance or ideology; they sought to follow energetic leadership that could help them in their situations. In other words, the large majority of Naxals in Kerala had no concerns with ideological debates within the communist camp, nor did they show much interest in revolutionary movements in other parts of India. They were concerned with their immediate enemies, the Janmis, who had been insulting and injuring them both physically and psychologically.

Kunnel Krishnan of Wayanad, who traveled India's many paths of communism, is a good example for thinking about the meanings and functions of "Cold War" politics in India (figure 5.2).[62] For him, what was central from beginning to end was Janmis' exploitation of Adivasis and migrant settlers. His first encounter with this issue occurred when he was just seven years old. His parents, along with his four siblings, migrated to the Manathavadi region in the thick hilly rain forest in 1949. As a child of migrant farmers, he learned the lessons of life through extreme poverty and became sympathetic to the life of Adivasis who were similarly suffering under Janmis' rule. Young Krishnan started his political life by associating with the leftist Kerala Student Federation (KSF) in his high school years. Since he had to support his struggling family, he could not continue with higher education at a university. However, he remained involved in left politics and helped the CPI to build a party unit in his village.[63]

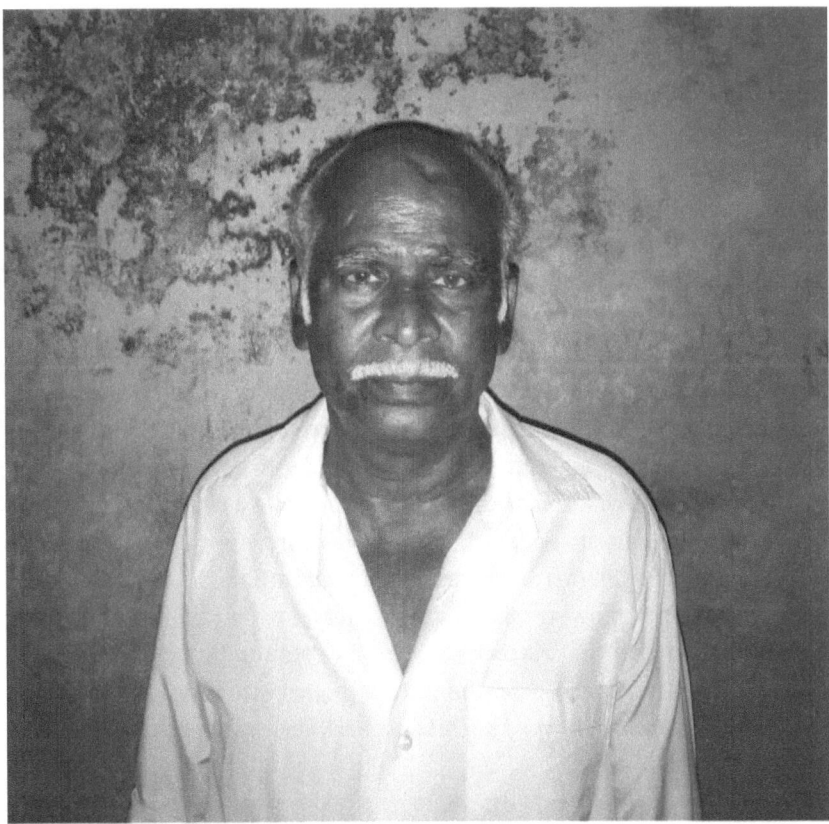

FIGURE 5.2 Mr. Kunnel Krishnan. Photo by the author.

The turning point came when his respected leader, Ayillyath Kuttiari Gopalan, or AKG, left the CPI to join the CPI (M) in 1964. Krishnan, with no hesitation, shifted his allegiance to the new party. He then committed to a number of movements that demanded land for Adivasis, challenging atrocious Janmi exploitation. However, he became deeply disappointed with left politics when he learned that many leftist leaders had developed good relationships with Janmis, ignoring their brutality and exploitation. In 1968, while he was disgruntled with the work of his party, he obtained an employment opportunity in Delhi. Accepting the offer, he left Kerala, though he recalled that he was not really happy about it.[64]

In the later months of 1968, his revolutionary spirit was reinvigorated by news of the Naxal attacks in Thalassery and Pulpally, regardless of the outcomes. He began learning more about the growing Naxal activism in Kerala through letters from his family and friends. Another turning point came at the beginning of 1970 when he received two letters from Kerala, one from his friend Varghese, who was already known for his energetic activities for Adivasi communities, and the other from Velappan Mash, who had been Krishnan's political guru. Both recommended that he return to Kerala to join the new revolutionary movement. After reading these letters, he did not have a second thought about resigning from his job in Delhi; he immediately headed back home in order to participate in the new communist movement and become a member of the Naxal group.[65]

When he got home, however, the Thirunelli-Thrissileri revolt was over, and his friend Varghese had already been murdered. As the police search for Naxal members intensified, he remained with the CPI (M), while secretly working to build a Naxal unit in his area. During this time, he began communicating with revolutionaries such as K. Venu and became part of a number of Naxal operations against Janmis. It was only in 1975 that he formally resigned from the CPI (M) and revealed his Naxal affiliation. Several months later, in June 1976, however, he was arrested and jailed, along with K. Venu and others, for the Naxal attack on the police station in Kayanna. Following his arrest, he experienced the taste of police brutality for a month in Maloorkunnu Police Camp in Kozhikode, and, thereafter, he served almost five years in prison.[66]

In this way, while utilizing the logic of communism, Krishnan's fight was always centered on Janmis' exploitation of Adivasis and migrant settlers in the rural areas of Kerala. This was also why many other social movements began to be sympathetic to Naxals. Indeed, by this time, several prominent social activists, such as those in the Dalit movement, as well as human rights activists such as Mani Parempett, had begun joining the struggle to build a dignified living space for Adivasi communities. Most were sympathetic toward Naxal violence because many accepted that the brutal Janmis knew only the language of violence.[67] That said, Naxals shifted their stance as well. While the early Naxals preferred violent tactics to put an end to the violence and exploitation of Janmis, later Naxals came to prefer attracting mass support for their cause to bring about the ultimate changes. In short, it was these Naxals who brought the real picture of human rights violations in Adivasi villages to public attention, so that even mainstream political parties, including the major communist parties, had to react and intervene. Such public interventions eventually put an end to Janmis' exploitation of Adivasis in the state of Kerala.[68]

Conclusion

Analyzing the accounts of various people associated with the Naxalite movement, we can see that India's "Cold War" was not simply an extension of the rivalry between the two superpowers, nor were India's "communists" and "anticommunists" merely pawns of each camp. It was, to be sure, the revolutionary spirit of communism that attracted many Indians, particularly in Kerala, because of the highly exploitative social conditions in the country. Deep down, however, many Indians were fighting their own battles, which were to transform the centuries-long caste-based system of exploitation. It was such relentless struggles that helped the Naxalite movement find many supporters and sympathizers among struggling populations. In short, their fight was basically against various injustices at home, even though they adopted a global ideology and claimed themselves as part of the global communist movement.

Whatever its objective, there is no justification for the Naxalite violence that claimed the lives of many innocent people. That said, the roles of the Naxalite movement should not be simply erased or denied due to its violent approach, without which the caste-based system of exploitation in Kerala could not have been transformed forever. The instrumental role of the Naxalite movement in breaking through the caste-based feudal system essentially reveals not only the significance of Cold War international politics in galvanizing local populations into action against various kinds of exploitation at home, but also the active participation of Indian people and society in driving India to embrace the Cold War reality even when the government tried to remain relatively outside the framework of Cold War politics.

Notes

1. For such recent work, see, for instance, Manu Bhagavan, *India and the Cold War* (Chapel Hill: University of North Carolina Press, 2019); Zorawar Daulet Singh, *Power and Diplomacy: India's Foreign Policies during the Cold War* (New Delhi: Oxford University Press, 2019); David C. Engerman, *The Price of Aid: The Economic Cold War in India* (Cambridge, MA: Harvard University Press, 2018); and Paul M. McGarr, *The Cold War in South Asia: Britain, the United States and the Indian Subcontinent, 1945–1965* (Cambridge: Cambridge University Press, 2013).

2. See Subho Basu, "Manufacturing Radicals: The Sino–Indian War and the Repression of Communists in India," in *The Sino-Indian War of 1962: New Perspectives*, ed. Amit R. Das Gupta and Lorenz M. Luthi (Abingdon, UK: Routledge, 2017), 197–214.

3. For making sense of Indian understanding of China in the context of the 1962 war, see Frank Moraes, "India and China," *The American Scholar* 32 (1963): 445–50.

4. For making sense of radical communist movements in India, see Bidyut Chakrabarty, *Left Radicalism in India* (New York: Routledge, 2015).

5. Victor M. Fic, *Peaceful Transition to Communism in India: Strategy of the Communist Party* (Bombay: Nachiketa Publications, 1969).

6. For making sense of the Indian mainstream left's approach toward the Indian caste system, see E. M. S. Namboodiripad, "Castes Classes and Parties in Modern Political Development," *Social Scientist* 6 (1977): 3–25. For making sense of the Indian caste system, see Gail Omvedt, *Understanding Caste: From Buddha to Ambedkar and Beyond* (New Delhi: Orient BlackSwan, 2011); and A. P. Barnabas and Subhash C. Mehta, *Caste in Changing India* (New Delhi: The Indian Institute of Public Administration, 1965).

7. The *Janmi* system in Kerala was largely a caste-based system. Janmis (feudal landlords or local chieftains) controlled a large share of agricultural land in Kerala even after independence. They were both politically and economically powerful and they highly exploited lower-caste communities and *Adivasis*. The term "Adivasi" denotes Indigenous tribal people in India and, to a large extent, South Asians in general. Literally, it is a combination of two words, *Adi* (earliest time) and *Vasi* (resident). The Adivasi community makes up about 9 percent of India's population. The major Adivasi groups in Kerala are Adiyanmar, Kurumar, Kurichias Ooralikal, Naikkar, Kattunaikkar, and Paniyar.

8. The practice of caste was much more heinous and inhuman than its theory. It provided a worthless and miserable life for social groups falling within the lowest layer of the hierarchy of purity. They were not only denied the use of public roads, public wells, and so forth, but also, in most cases, forbidden from entering the mere sight of upper-caste communities. In many senses, they had to live a life worse than that of an African slave. For making sense of the practice of caste in colonial Malabar, see William Logan, *Malabar*, vol. 1 (Madras: The Superintendent Government Press, 1951); and K. Saradamoni, "Agrestic Slavery in Kerala in the Nineteenth Century," *Indian Economic and Social History Review* 10 (1973): 371–85. For making sense of the caste-based system of exploitation that prevailed in the region, see K. Ravi Raman, "Bondage in Freedom: Colonial Plantations in Southern India c. 1797–1947" (Centre for Development Studies Trivandrum Working Papers 327, CDS Trivandrum, India, 2002).

9. Nandini Sundar, *The Burning Forest: India's War Against the Maoists* (London: Verso, 2019).

10. George J. Kunnath, *Rebels from the Mud Houses: Dalits and the Making of the Maoist Revolution in Bihar* (Abingdon, UK: Routledge, 2018).

11. For instance, Gyan Prakash, *Bonded Histories: Genealogies of Labor and Servitude in Colonial India* (Cambridge: Cambridge University Press, 1990).

12. For instance, Alpa Shah, *In the Shadows of the State: Indigenous Politics, Environmentalism, and Insurgency in Jharkhand, India* (Durham, NC: Duke University Press, 2010); Daniel J. Roycroft and Sangeeta Dasgupta, *The Politics of Belonging in India: Becoming Adivasi* (Abingdon, UK: Routledge, 2011); Ashok Kumar Sen, *Indigeneity, Landscape and History: Adivasi Self-Fashioning in India* (Abingdon, UK:

Routledge, 2018); and Alf Gunvald Nilsen, *Dispossession and Resistance in India: The River and the Rage* (Abingdon, UK: Routledge, 2010).

13. For instance, Darley Jose Kjosavik and Nadarajah Shanmugaratnam, *Political Economy of Development in India: Indigeneity in Transition in the State of Kerala* (Abingdon, UK: Routledge, 2015); and Luisa Steur, *Indigenist Mobilization: Confronting Electoral Communism and Precarious Livelihoods in Post-Reform Kerala* (New York: Berghahn, 2017).

14. For instance, R. K. Bijuraj, *Naxal Dinangal: Keralathile Naxalite/Maoist Prasthanathinte Samagra Charithram* [Naxal days: A holistic history of Naxalite-Maoist problems in Kerala] (Kottayam: DC Books, 2015); and T. Ajeesh, *Naxal Charitam Adiyantharavasthakku Shesham* [Naxal history after emergency] (Thrissur: Green Books, 2016).

15. Singh, *Power and Diplomacy*; and McGarr, *The Cold War in South Asia*.

16. Masuda Hajimu, *Cold War Crucible: The Korean Conflict and the Postwar World* (Cambridge, MA: Harvard University Press, 2015); and Heonik Kwon, *The Other Cold War* (New York: Columbia University Press, 2010).

17. See Fic, *Peaceful Transition*; and Chakrabarty, *Left Radicalism in India*.

18. Ayinoor Vasu, interview by the author, April 9, 2019.

19. In a recently declassified document of 1965, explaining the communist threat in India, the CIA observed that "India offers a uniquely favorable environment for Communist-front organizations. Its cultural, linguistic, racial and religious heterogeneity presents an ideal breeding-ground in which various dissident groups prosper and agitate for a wide variety of general as well as special political interests. A high degree of public interest—especially within the middle class—in political and social matters, combined with a considerable amount of emotionalism, a lack of sufficient knowledge about general and political matters, and frequently an anti-Western and vacillating bias have made it possible for the Communists to organize some 50 active fronts in India, 10 of which are affiliated to international communist front organizations. . . . The communist movement in India is not considered a foreign-dominated group by the great mass of the Indian electorate." See "Study in Ambivalence: Communist Front Organizations in India," May 24, 1965, CIA Online Archive, https://www.cia.gov/readingroom/document/cia-rdp78-03061a000300030004-3.

20. Vasu, interview.

21. John S. Moolakkattu, "Land Reform and Peaceful Change in Kerala," *Peace Review: A Journal of Social Justice* 19 (2007): 87–94.

22. For the ideological tension within the communist world during the Cold War period, see Lorenz M. Luthi, *The Sino-Soviet Split: Cold War in the Communist World* (Princeton, NJ: Princeton University Press, 2008).

23. For the split in the Communist Party of India, see Bidyut Chakrabarty, *Communism in India: Events, Processes and Ideologies* (New York: Oxford University Press, 2014).

24. Vasu, interview. For the similarities between the CPI and the CPI (M), see Philip G. Altbach, "The Two Indian Communist Parties," *Government and Opposition* 2 (1967): 289–95.

25. Ajitha, *Kerala's Naxalbari: Ajitha, Memoirs of a Young Revolutionary* (New Delhi: Srishti Publishers and Distributers, 2008); and Bijuraj, *Naxal Dinangal*.

26. Vasu, interview.

27. The party leadership of the CPI (M) expressed displeasure toward the activities of Kunnikkal Narayan by various means. Defining his activities as antiparty, they tried to alienate him from the party, presenting him as an agent of the CIA and arguing that his intention was to destroy communist movements in India by working within the party. Disappointed by the party's approach, Kunnikkal began to openly challenge party leadership. As a result of this, in January 1967, he was expelled from the party. See Ajitha Kunnikkal, interview by the author, April 9, 2019; and Bijuraj, *Naxal Dinangal*.

28. It was militant members of the CPI (M) who led the armed peasant uprising in Naxalbari. Following the uprising, CPI (M) expelled them from its primary membership. Later they formed a new party called the Communist Party of India (Marxist-Leninist) or CPI (ML). The term "Naxalite" evolved from the name of the village, Naxalbari. See Bappaditya Paul, *The First Naxal: An Authorized Biography of Kanu Sanyal* (New Delhi: Sage Publications, 2014).

29. Vasu, interview. For the beginning of Naxalite movements in India, see Biplab Dasgupta, *The Naxalite Movement* (New Delhi: Allied Publishers, 1974); and Mohan Ram, *Maoism in India* (New York: Barnes and Noble, 1971).

30. Ajitha, interview.

31. With a good amount of inherited property, the Kunnikkal family followed a middle-class lifestyle in this period. Though Kunnikkal Narayanan had faced a lot of setbacks in his business during these years because of his communist politics, the income of Mandakini Narayanan ensured the family's financial security. Ajitha, interview.

32. Ajitha, interview.

33. After the Naxalbari Uprising Kunnikkal Narayanan tried to associate with a Charu Majumdar–led Maoist group in West Bengal. However, he was unable to develop a good relationship with this group because of ideological and personal differences. See Bijuraj, *Naxal Dinangal*.

34. Ram, *Maoism in India*, 7.

35. Marxists Internet Archive, "Spring Thunder over India," *Renmin Ribao* [People's Daily], July 5, 1967, https://www.marxists.org/subject/china/documents/peoples-daily/1967/07/05.htm.

36. Welcoming these developments in Naxalbari, *Renmin Ribao* wrote in its editorial that "India is a country with vast territory; its countryside, where reactionary rule is weak, provides broad areas in which revolutionaries can maneuver freely. So long as the Indian proletarian revolutionaries adhere to the revolutionary line of Marxism-Leninism, Mao Tse-tung's thought and rely on their great ally, the peasants, it is entirely possible for them to establish one advanced revolutionary rural base area after another in the broad backward rural areas and build a people's army of a new type. Whatever difficulties and twists and turns the Indian revolutionaries may experience in the course of building such revolutionary base areas, they will eventually develop such areas from isolated points into a vast expanse,

from small areas into extensive ones, an expansion in a series of waves. Thus, a situation in which the cities are encircled from the countryside will gradually be brought about in the Indian revolution to pave the way for the final seizure of towns and cities and winning nation-wide victory." See "Spring Thunder over India," *Renmin Ribao*, July 5, 1967.

37. It was definitely not a unanimous decision. Many in the group believed that attacking the police station in Thalassery town was not a good idea. They wanted to start the revolt from a rural area as directed by Mao's theory. However, many revolutionaries, including Kunnikkal Narayanan, believed that the Thalassery attack was essential to attract public attention. Vasu, interview; and Bijuraj, *Naxal Dinangal*.

38. A bidi is a popular inexpensive minicigar of India. The bidi industry was the largest sector of employment after agriculture in Kerala during this period. For making sense of labor exploitation in the bidi industry, see M. Mohandas, "Beedi Workers in Kerala: Conditions of Life and Work," *Economic and Political Weekly* 15 (1980): 1517–23.

39. Bijuraj, *Naxal Dinangal*.

40. John S. Moolakkattu, "Land Reform and Peaceful Change in Kerala," *Peace Review: A Journal of Social Justice* 19 (2007): 87–94.

41. Kunnel Krishnan, interview by the author, April 7, 2019.

42. Krishnan, interview.

43. Vasu, interview.

44. Vasu, interview.

45. Bijuraj, *Naxal Dinangal*; Ajitha, *Kerala's Naxalbari*.

46. Vasu, interview; Bijuraj, *Naxal Dinangal*.

47. Vasu, interview.

48. Vasu, interview.

49. Vasu, interview.

50. Civic Chandran, interview by the author, April 16, 2019; Vasu, interview.

51. Ajitha, *Kerala's Naxalbari*.

52. Bijuraj, *Naxal Dinangal*.

53. Bijuraj, *Naxal Dinangal*.

54. Ajitha, *Kerala's Naxalbari*, 100.

55. Ajitha, *Kerala's Naxalbari*, 101.

56. For the punitive measures that Kerala police used against Naxalites, see Anonymous, "Life and Death in Kerala's Torture Camps," *Economic and Political Weekly* 12 (1977): 747–48.

57. Vasu, Author's interview.

58. Vasu, Author's interview.

59. Shivadasan Attappadi, interview by the author, April 12, 2019; Shilaja Attappadi, interview by the author, April 12, 2019.

60. Haridas Kozhikode, interview by the author, April 14, 2019; Mani Parempett, interview by the author, April 11, 2019.

61. Kozhikode, interview. Parempett, interview.

62. Krishnan, interview.

63. Krishnan, interview.
64. Krishnan, interview.
65. Krishnan, interview.
66. Krishnan, interview.
67. Parempett, Author's interview.
68. Baburaj T., interview by the author, April 13, 2019; Chandran, interview.

6 Theorizing Southeast Asia's ~~Cold~~ War

Timor in 1974–75

....

KISHO TSUCHIYA

In August 1975, a civil war suddenly broke out in Portuguese Timor. Legally still a Portuguese colony, East Timor, located on the eastern half of Timor Island on the southern edge of Southeast Asia, had been in turmoil following the Carnation Revolution in Lisbon in the previous year that brought about a decolonization proposal for all Portuguese colonies. On the island, many parties popped up all at once. Three were the most prominent, each with a different geopolitical inclination: one advocating a federation with Portugal, another favoring integration with Indonesia, and yet another campaigning for independence for East Timor. Amid rising tension, the initial attack was launched by pro-Portuguese conservative forces, led by Francisco Lopes da Cruz. They called their attempt an "Anticommunist revolutionary movement," demanding the complete elimination of "communists" from the territory, and attacked an opposing party that was championing the immediate and total independence of East Timor.

Surprisingly, however, the latter, which came to be known as the Revolutionary Front for an Independent East Timor (FRETILIN), was joined by the mass of Timorese soldiers in the Portuguese military force. They retaliated and eventually chased Lopes da Cruz's forces to West Timor in Indonesian territory. FRETILIN then unilaterally declared the independence of the Democratic Republic of Timor-Leste on November 28, 1975. As we will see below, during this turbulent period, supporters of both sides unleashed ancestral, communal, and personal grudges in the names of "anticommunism" on the one hand, and "nationalism" on the other. Still, further tragedy awaited East Timor; anticommunist president Suharto's Indonesia decided to "integrate" Portuguese Timor by force, and a full-fledged Indonesian invasion commenced on December 7, 1975, with an estimated death toll of 18,600 Timorese who were either killed or disappeared, and 84,200 Timorese who died due to hunger and illness.[1] Thereafter, until August 1999, eastern Timor was harshly ruled by the anticommunist Indonesian army as if it were a bastion of communist revolutionaries threatening Indonesia.

However, while all parties concerned—pro-Portuguese conservatives, FRETILIN, and Indonesia—utilized Cold War discourses, Portuguese Timor had never actually been a stronghold of a communist party, nor was it a place of strong Soviet, American, or Communist Chinese presence before 1974. The territory was inhabited by dozens of sociolinguistic groups, and they were divided into districts, subdistricts, and villages, within which the majority were prohibited by Portuguese policy from moving beyond their districts. At that time, Portuguese Timor was described as a "sleepy outpost of the Portuguese empire."[2] The Cold War might have been relevant to Portugal's more turbulent overseas provinces in Africa, but not to East Timor before 1974. Then, why did East Timorese people end up killing each other under the binary logic of communists vs. anticommunists? Why did Suharto's Indonesia decide to invade such an unprofitable "sleepy" outpost? How did the island come to be termed the "Cuba of Southeast Asia"?

In response to these questions, this chapter intends to make two types of conceptual contributions. First, it suggests a reading strategy for interpreting Southeast Asian experiences of the so-called Cold War. Second, it attempts to reinterpret the origin of the Indonesian occupation of East Timor by applying this reading strategy. Both reflect my thoughts about the current status of Cold War studies as a Southeast Asian historian and area specialist. In this chapter, I propose to use the term "~~Cold~~ War"—crossing out the word "Cold" but leaving it there—to clarify the local and actual (hot) nature of warfare on the ground, while, at the same time, highlighting the unerasable traces of the global conflict within local conflicts. Then, I approach it as a simulacrum, a product of what Plato called the "art of appearance-making."[3] I use "simulacrum" as a representation or image that appears as a perfect reproduction when looked at from a certain spot, but different from other angles. As I read through my primary sources and scholarly works on "the Cold War in Southeast Asia," it emerged to me as a group of simulacra, or many wars and conflicts of diverse nature that appear similarly as one global confrontation when looked at through the Cold War lens. Such an approach overlaps with Heonik Kwon's "the Other Cold War" and Masuda Hajimu's "the Cold War as an imagined reality," but this chapter intends to highlight slightly different dynamics.[4]

I use the concepts of the "~~Cold~~ War" and "simulacra" for three reasons. To begin with, empirical studies have shown that "the Cold War in Asia" was not cold at all, but characterized by "hot" wars, mass mobilizations, and social warfare. Thus, the term "Cold" should be crossed out. That said, second, a total erasure of the term "Cold War" would prevent us from contemplating important questions as to why and how this particular civil war and Indonesian invasion happened at this particular time. Thus, the term "Cold War" should be kept. Furthermore, the term "~~Cold~~ War" is useful to go beyond Odd Arne Westad's conceptualization of a "Global Cold War," which tends to see almost all kinds of conflicts in the period as parts of a single global confrontation.

As we will see below, as well as in other chapters in this volume, some local hot wars and social warfare, to be sure, were performed in the likeness of the Cold War. These, however, should not be seen as mere extensions or end results of the superpower confrontation, but would be better described as simulations of the Cold War by local and regional actors. Here again, there are reasons for both keeping and erasing the word "Cold" in "Cold War." Thus, using the term "~~Cold~~ War"—crossing out the Cold War but keeping its trace—is appropriate.[5] Altogether, this chapter approaches the ~~Cold~~ War(s) in Asia as simulacra of the Cold War and, in doing so, intends to overcome the current theoretical impasse in Cold War studies, characterized by the narrowly defined notion of the Cold War as a US-centric diplomatic experience, as well as conventional studies of "the Cold War in Asia."[6]

Recent studies of the Cold War, particularly following Odd Arne Westad's pioneering work on the "Global Cold War," have surely expanded its scope from a narrow US–Soviet rivalry to a confrontation between communism and capitalism almost everywhere in the world.[7] In doing so, this school of writing has revealed a massive amount of violence committed under the rhetoric of the Global Cold War, but has tended to present the Cold War as a single confrontation between communism and capitalism, as if a third world war happened without people noticing it. Yet, recent studies and discussions among scholars of Asia have exposed significant differences from such conventional views. First, Asians tended to be oblivious to the superpowers' "mutually assured destruction" strategy and the nuclear threats of the era. And more importantly, the "war" they talk about does not appear to have been "cold" at all. Instead, it was characterized by massive violence, as recent studies have emphasized. It was literally a hot war, not a cold one, nor a "long peace" at all.[8] Therefore, it would be utterly misleading to view such complex and often violent confrontations and vernacular variations as parts of one global war; it should better be understood as many wars that were imagined as one.

Being a Southeast Asianist, I cannot help recalling eminent Southeast Asia scholar John R. W. Smail's classic work, "On the Possibility of an Autonomous History of Modern Southeast Asia," published in 1961, in which he critiqued the colonial and nationalist historiography that had dominated Southeast Asian history, arguing that there should a social history of Southeast Asia—or an "autonomous history of Southeast Asia"—in which the main characters are Southeast Asians and the main stories are of local competition.[9] Along the lines of Smail, I would ask, "Could there be autonomous Cold War history writing in the rest of the world?" In fact, there have been warnings against an uncritical application of the Cold War as an analytical category, such as Matthew Connelly's call in 2000 for "taking off the Cold War lens" with regard to the Algerian War for Independence.[10] That said, I am not in complete agreement with Smail's and Connelly's proposals. As for Smail, we cannot totally do away with the categories of "colonial" and "national" when discussing the modern history of Southeast Asia. Studying the histories of Manila, Cebu, Singapore, East Timor, and so on is simply unthinkable without considering how the presence of outsiders influenced their courses of history.

By the same token, Connelly's call for "taking off the Cold War lens" is not enough to study certain aspects of Asian and global history in the latter half of the twentieth century. There is abundant evidence of selective Southeast Asian borrowings from American, Soviet, and Maoist rhetoric of "the Cold War." Also, there were hardcore Southeast Asian "C̶o̶l̶d̶ warriors" who dedicated their lives to the ideological struggle. Looking at these aspects, what happened during the Cold War era can be seen as a continuation of *longue durée* Southeast Asian dynamics of localization and adaptation of external ideas, cultures, and political thought.[11] In addition, during the Cold War era and since, observers have tended to interpret diverse dynamics of this region through "the Cold War lens," and such observers themselves have been important historical forces as well. Finally, a crude taking-off-the-Cold-War lens does not automatically lead to a creative interpretation by itself. If we unconsciously wear a nation-centric lens, for example, we will simply go back to each country's national history. Thus, instead of simply taking off the Cold War lens, we should try creating a new useful conceptual tool, based on studies of the C̶o̶l̶d̶ War, through which we can discuss transnational connections of ideas and senses of modernity, as well as important differences between Asian (and possibly Latin American, African, etc.) "Cold Wars" and the US-USSR Cold War.

A unique aspect of the "Reconceptualizing the Cold War: On-the-Ground Experiences in Asia" project is its positionality at multiple locations in Asia, as this opens up an opportunity to reconceptualize "the Cold War" using examples from Asian locales. This point is important because the positionality of the very concept of "the Cold War" is based on particularly US-centric or, to be more specific, diplomatic experiences characterized by a lack of actual war, sustained by imminent nuclear threats. That is why I decided to use the spelling of the ~~Cold~~ War, with a sign of erasure on the word "Cold," as an attempt to deconstruct the US-centric Cold War narrative. This is an intentional choice for a conceptual experiment, a deliberate provocation, and an argument to raise awareness that, for Asians, the Cold War was imagined, but real. I have developed this idea through taking part in "Reconceptualizing the Cold War" workshops in May and June 2019, as well as September 2020, in which a number of participants raised arguments comparable to Connelly's "taking off the Cold War lens."[12] While acknowledging its merits, I still oppose total exclusion of "the Cold War" from the terminology of Asian history. This is because, without the phrase, we are unable to discuss Asian differentiation, traces, localization, appropriation, dedication, and vernacularization of the Cold War in the latter half of the twentieth century.

The ~~Cold~~ War was neither a mere extension of the Cold War (i.e., proxy wars)—a nonevent—nor a lesser copy. Crossing "Cold" out does not mean that "the Cold War" is simply a false concept. On the contrary, the term "~~Cold~~ War" contains both "the Cold War" and its deletion. This chapter acknowledges the Cold War as a part of the US-centric diplomatic discourse and of ordinary people's imaginations. However, I would argue that Asian peoples' ~~Cold~~ War(s) should not be treated as a phenomenon exactly identical to the Cold War; ~~Cold~~ War(s) manifested as real war or as social warfare that simulated the Cold War. They were not merely the results of Asian peoples' art of appearance-making that includes conscious and unconscious imitation, selective appropriation, and vernacularization of the supposedly global confrontation, but also reflections of preceding experiences, emotions, and preexisting beliefs among particular groups and locales.[13]

There are plenty of examples in this volume of such simulations: namely, Indonesian Muslims' "anticommunism" that took the form of "holy war" (chapter 2); the Naxals' "class struggle" that challenged the abusive caste system (chapter 5); and Lao people's historically generated anti-Vietnamese sentiment that expressed itself through "anticommunist" rhetoric (chapter 7). Likewise, East Timorese and Indonesians in my case study reflected their social relations, generational tensions, recent local history, and suppressed emotions when they simulated the ~~Cold~~ War. Through this chapter, I would like to encourage readers to see local agency and creativity in such slight differences and derivatives, instead of easily dismissing them as mere obedience, distortion, or crude copies.

~~Cold~~ War simulacra are comparable to our recent experience of a "new normal" during the COVID-19 pandemic. In the West, ethnic Chinese and Asians were imagined as the early transmitters, just like the preexisting idea of the Yellow Peril. Japanese newspapers quickly identified the "youth" as a potential risk, reflecting the "silver democracy," or gerontocracy, of the country. South Korean fundamentalists bashed cult religious organizations for the spread of the virus, while in Mindanao (where I was) people started bashing gambling, street kids, delinquency, new family norms, and people from Luzon. While all of these imaginings were done under the name of epidemic prevention and adapting to the "new normal," a close look at these collective behaviors reveals that ethnonationalism, generational tensions, religious competition, family and gender relations, and tensions between urban and rural areas were at play. People are good at this art of appearance-making when an officially sanctioned ideology provides opportunities.

The concept of the ~~Cold~~ War(s) as simulacra is intended to challenge and overturn the conventional Cold War narrative of global history that was supposedly "the original."[14] Arguably, Cold War diplomacy was often framed by the ~~Cold~~ War, and, possibly, the American Cold War was a genre of Cold War imaginings and simulacra. The "global confrontation" in which Asians participated (i.e., the ~~Cold~~ War) was significantly different from the conventional notion of "the Cold War" and was embedded with many transnational and local meanings and aims.[15] The rest of this chapter, thus, is a conceptual experiment involving the ~~Cold~~ War and a case study from East Timor. The theoretical formulation of this chapter has been inspired by my case studies of maritime Southeast Asia, such as the discourses of anticommunism and practices of "red-tagging" in the Philippines (from the late 1940s to today), and the Indonesian Red Purge (1965–68), as well as primary sources collected for my PhD thesis on Timor Island history. In the sections below, I return to sources on the "East Timor Problem" in 1974–75, with the theoretical stance explained above.

・・・・・・

From 1974 to 1988, FRETILIN was, arguably, the most important East Timorese political organization, one often associated with—as well as sometimes consciously dissociated from—Marxism and Maoism. FRETILIN's public image is strongly associated with massive and enthusiastic social mobilization. Reportedly, it gathered the greatest number of committed members and followers among the Timorese during the decolonization process from 1974 to 1975. In 1977, it officially became a Marxist party, though now it is remembered more as the major "nationalist" force that resisted the Indonesian Occupation from 1975 to 1999.[16] This chapter emphasizes FRETILIN's simulation of leftist tenets, as well as interlocutors' reactions to (and also simulations of) that from 1974 to 1975. Thereby, I trace how diverse actors in the East Timor Problem socially constructed a Cold War world at a certain period in a certain locale.

Conventionally, scholars of East Timor studies have collectively treated the Cold War as a "weather," or a given international condition.[17] As a result, scholars and activists in the 1970s ended up reinforcing Cold War imaginings, while their successors in the post-Perestroika generations viewed Cold War rhetoric as merely an Indonesian pretext to justify illegal occupation.[18] This "Cold War as weather" approach has blinded us to important riddles concerning East Timor from 1974 to 1976. Namely, these works have tended to be preoccupied with political debates either justifying Indonesian actions or sanitizing FRETILIN's negative "communist" image and have not attempted to explain why various Timorese groups had to end up killing each other under Cold War rhetoric, even though there were no powerful communist forces nor superpower interventions in the region.

They have not explained why Indonesia invaded East Timor either. Even though the majority of the East Timorese were not communists and East Timor was not a place of strong Soviet, American, or Communist Chinese presence, the Timorese civil war in August 1975 and subsequent Indonesian invasion would have been unthinkable without the notion of the Cold War. Therefore, to understand the origin of these events, we must comprehend what exactly the "Cold War" was for Timorese people and for the Indonesian government. As such, this chapter emphasizes the performative effects of FRETILIN's movement, its interlocutors, and rivals' simulations of the Cold War, and how the global confrontation and the regional "threat" were perceived as real. As the narrative proceeds, this chapter suggests that their predominantly violent simulation of the Cold War was aimed at other purposes, such as creating the appearance of democratic support through mass mobilization and concealing personal motivations.

Below, I will reconstruct how particular components of US–USSR rhetoric, such as the ideas of world revolution, social revolution, and containment, appeared in vernacular forms. After explaining the background to the decolonization in 1974 and 1975, I will pick up relevant themes from FRETILIN's political campaigns in the Portuguese and Tetun languages. Then, in the latter part, I will discuss some responses from their interlocutors and those whom FRETILIN labeled "enemies of the people." Thereby, this chapter explores how the Cold War world was socially constructed by East Timorese leaders and ordinary people, as well as Indonesian and Australian stakeholders.

Historical Context: A Making of a Cold War Simulacrum

Although Portuguese Timor was described as tranquil and sleepy by some, the first half of the twentieth century was characterized by massive population loss and changes due to the colonial wars (estimated population loss of 32.5 to 44.8 percent between 1911 and 1913) and World War II (estimated population loss of roughly 10 percent between 1942 and 1945). After these chaotic experiences, Portuguese forces reoccupied the eastern part of Timor and ruled it for another three decades. As former European colonies in Asia proceeded along the path of decolonization and nation-building in the post–World War II era, the continuation of Portuguese colonialism was exposed to international criticism. Against this backdrop, beginning in 1951, a series of Salazar-Caetano dictatorships conceptually transformed Portugal from a vast colonial empire to a "multi-racial, multi-continental nation" in order to dodge criticism from international anti–colonialist activists. The Portuguese government in the 1950 and 1960s, then, emphasized the creation of the "new Portuguese," which included not just Portugal but Angola, Mozambique, and Timor, as if all made up one inseparable body, with notions of equal citizenship, multiculturalism, and multiracialism for all.[19] This tendency was further strengthened when later challenged by left-oriented revolutionaries in Portuguese "overseas provinces" in Africa in the 1960s. In this way, the post–World War II Portuguese corporatist system developed as a conservative version of "reform," as it needed "reform" that was neither "colonial," "anti–colonial," nor "communist."

Using the concept of the Cold War as an analytical category, the situations in Portuguese Timor from 1974 to 1975 can be periodized into three phases. The first covers April to August 1974, when the process of decolonization started but references to the Cold War dispensation remained marginal. The second, from September 1974 to August 1975, marked the entry of Cold War logic into the decolonization processes. This phase was characterized by a confrontation of ideas. Finally, the third phase refers to the time from the outbreak of the civil war to the beginning of the Indonesian Occupation, that is from August to December 1975, which observed a transformation of a cold war into a hot one.

The First Phase

"Decolonization" arrived suddenly in Portuguese Timor in April 1974 when military forces overthrew the Caetano dictatorship in Lisbon. The military junta then announced a decolonization proposal for Portuguese colonies. Although there was no highly active anti-colonial movement in Portuguese Timor, Timor was included in this plan, which legalized Timorese political parties for the first time. Many parties appeared in the following months, though only three were recognized by the Portuguese administration: the Timorese Democratic Union (UDT), the Timorese Popular Democratic Union (APODETI), and the Timorese Social-Democratic Association (ASDT)—the predecessor to FRETILIN. The three parties differed in their geopolitical designs: the UDT favored a federation with Portugal, APODETI favored integration with Indonesia, and ASDT favored an independent East Timor. Their platforms for social welfare, economics, and religion had more commonalities than differences.[20] ASDT's vision was rather simple, advocating for implementation of progressive autonomy toward independence, rejection of colonialism and racism, fighting corruption, and friendship with neighboring countries.

The Second Phase

September 1974 marked a change in the nature of the debate, as some Cold War themes (international solidarity, armed conflict, Maoism, anticommunism) entered Timorese political terminology. This was a time of massive mobilization and rising excitement for ordinary people. We can see such tendencies, for example, in ASDT/FRETILIN's warm reception of radical returnees from Lisbon, including members of the clandestine Maoist movement in Portugal.[21] In addition, the ASDT changed its name to FRETILIN, with an adoption of Cold War themes by naming itself the "Revolutionary Front for an Independent East Timor." Now, FRETILIN demanded recognition as the only representative of the people and insisted that it would overturn everything that had the flavor of colonialism, including class division, traditional authority, and exploitation.[22]

Another clear example of local actors' adoption of ~~Cold~~ War themes can be seen in a letter written by Jose Ramos-Horta, who had been FRETILIN's overseas representative, a self-claimed "moderate," and later a co-awardee of the Nobel Peace Prize in 1996. The letter was sent to the Chinese Embassy in Australia and was noticed by Australian intelligence. In the letter, he directly addressed "the Great President Mao," and described the possibility of an Australian and Indonesian invasion of East Timor.[23] He requested full support from China, including military aid and training, as well as international advocacy and propaganda campaigns.[24] He claimed that FRETILIN and himself were the "only legitimate representative of the people of East Timor," and declared their intention to "love our friends and kill our enemies." Australian intelligence shared parts of this letter with Indonesia.

Meanwhile, in September 1974, APODETI's representatives visited the Indonesian government in Jakarta, which had proclaimed itself an anticommunist regime, and asserted that the majority of the Timorese desired freedom from Portuguese colonialism and integration into Indonesia.[25] Following this month, the Indonesian military, as well as the public in general, began to view FRETILIN as a "left-leaning party." Indonesian newspapers such as *Sinar Harapan*, *Berita Yudha*, and *Kompass* labelled FRETILIN a "communist" party, urging an extension of the New Order regime's anticommunism to Timor. In these papers, the instability of the political situation, FRETILIN's affiliation with Maoism, and the Timorese people's support for integration were emphasized.[26] Similarly, Australian writers projected their ~~Cold~~ War worldview onto Timor, labeling the territory the "Cuba of Southeast Asia."[27] Such frantic reactions should be seen against the backdrop of the Vietnam War, particularly the victory of North Vietnam.

In the same month, in September 1974, FRETILIN reorganized itself in imitation of preceding leftist parties not directly from the USSR or China, but rather from the Lusophone world, such as Portugal's Maoist party MRPP, Guinea-Bissau's PAIGC, Mozambique's FRELIMO, and Angola's MPLA.[28] Its general decision-making body was the Central Committee. Below it, the party created three wings, which were the women's organization, the youth organization, and the labor organization. Returnees from Lisbon were instrumental in the establishment of these wings. FRETILIN also created a regional committee in each district to promote its political ideas, along with the party's anthem, political manual, literary texts, and regularly organized demonstrations, throughout the entire territory.

The generation gap, more than ideological differences, was an important factor that divided the political parties. FRETILIN Central Committee members' average age was estimated at twenty-two, and some youth propagandists were as young as thirteen.[29] In contrast, core members of the pro-Portuguese conservative party, UDT, were Eurasian elites (*letrados* and *mestizos*) in their thirties.[30] In the initial few months, ASDT/FRETILIN faced difficulty in gaining followers compared to the UDT, and its leaders found that their youth could be disadvantageous. Thus, they invited an already-respected local intellectual, Xavier do Amaral, who was thirty-seven, to be their president. Therefore, FRETILIN had to follow the social norm of seniority at its onset. Nonetheless, it began to adopt the idea of class struggle in September 1974, which it found useful for young intellectuals who were not yet established in society.

By this time, not only domestic actors but international observers, particularly those in Australia and Indonesia, on both right and left, connected the territory to "Cold War" discourses and events elsewhere (e.g., Vietnam and Cuba), conceptualizing East Timor as a potential communist country and a security threat for the region.[31] Meanwhile, Indonesian military mass media and a West Timorese radio station, Radio Kupang, began engaging in destabilizing activities in East Timor, labeling FRETILIN cadres "communists" and "followers of Mao," while advising UDT and APODETI leaders to eliminate them.[32] In response, FRETILIN labeled its rivals "fascists," "reactionaries," "traitors," "enemies of the people," and so forth. This list of FRETILIN's labels against its enemies is an interesting mixture of phrases used by Japanese occupiers and the Salazar regime's rhetoric and resistance against them. By the time just before the civil war in August 1975, FRETILIN's rhetoric included more threatening content, such as graffiti that read "death to traitors" and "burn the traitors."[33] In this period, all three Timorese parties actively organized demonstrations and used violent anti–colonial and ~~Cold~~ War rhetoric. According to some testimonies, it was during this period that an atmosphere of intense excitement, anger, and fear spread among the inhabitants. And all of these were associated with the parties' respective claims to be the "only representative of the people," "popular support," or "democratic support." Arguably, legitimacy was what was mainly at stake in their ~~Cold~~ War simulation.

The Third Phase

When the civil war between UDT and FRETILIN erupted on August 11, 1975, it was not clear which side had initiated the attack. It was later confirmed that the UDT started the coup, renaming itself the "Anti-Communist

Revolutionary Movement." The UDT's operation plan included "elimination of the FRETILIN Marxists from the political scene of Timor" and "withdrawal of all Portuguese communists in Timor."[34] However, FRETILIN's counterattacks had resulted in its temporary victory by September. FRETILIN became de facto ruler of the territory, and massive numbers of refugees entered Indonesian territory.

Suharto's view of these events is important to understand the Indonesian context of the invasion, and we can get a glimpse of it from a series of conversations between him and US president Gerald Ford and secretary of state Henry Kissinger. Since the beginning of his reign, Suharto's New Order regime had been based on anticommunism, and his concern about the spread of communism in Southeast Asia heightened following the victory of North Vietnam earlier in 1975.[35] He expressed his "fear" to the US leadership, stating that China and Vietnam could send reinforcements to leftist forces in the region to overturn noncommunist governments, a fear that Kissinger considered "exaggerated."[36] Suharto saw Portuguese Timor from this angle and said, "The problem is that those who want independence [of East Timor] are those who are Communist influenced. Those wanting Indonesian integration are being subjected to heavy pressure by those who are almost Communist."[37]

A textual reading of Suharto's language gives us an interesting insight. Unlike Indonesian military newspapers, Suharto never referred to FRETILIN simply as "communists"; he described them more carefully as "soldiers" who were "communist influenced," "almost communist," and "infected with communism."[38] In other words, he was astutely aware that FRETILIN was another kind of ~~Cold~~ War simulator that manipulated ~~Cold~~ War rhetoric from the opposite side.

A significant amount of evidence has suggested that Suharto, the Indonesian army, and strategic advisors had contemplated incorporation of Portuguese Timor into Indonesia as early as May 1974, but decided to intervene by force at the time of the civil war.[39] The ~~Cold~~ War perspective continued to frame their understandings and representations of the issue. The military newspaper, *Angkatan Bersenjata*, reported that the UDT had joined anticommunist forces, while depicting FRETILIN as left-leaning "terrorists" who massacred even small children. Referring to the refugee problem, the newspaper reported as follows: "Mistakes of the civil war in the Portuguese colony developed into an international conflict between the anticommunist forces and the communists." In this way, the paper described the situation through manipulating Cold War rhetoric, instead of representing it as a local conflict at Indonesia's periphery.[40]

This was followed by the notorious Indonesian invasion that began on December 7, 1975. Since then, mass media have discussed issues in Timor in terms of communism, anticommunism, regional security, and self-determination. The Indonesian Occupation of East Timor continued for twenty-four years. Such an unfolding of Timor's political changes reveals that it was constructed as a second-, third-, and even fourth-order simulacrum of Southeast Asian, Australian, and African simulacra of the Cold War.

FRETILIN's Cold War: Containment and World Revolution

How did FRETILIN perceive notions of "containment" and "world revolution"? Analysis of FRETILIN cadres' vernacular Marxism reveals both connectedness to and differences from these notions in Timorese imaginings of the Cold War. In this section, we examine a speech made in the period between the Civil War and the Indonesian invasion. To begin with, let us take a look at FRETILIN president Xavier do Amaral's Tetun-language speech on November 11, 1975, to think about how FRETILIN understood the global confrontation and its place in it. On that day, he celebrated the independence of Angola, a former Portuguese colony in Africa.[41] Angola had been devastated by a prolonged civil war among competing groups that was exacerbated by the military involvement of NATO, the USSR, and Cuba.[42] Amaral listed the peoples of Angola and other Portuguese colonies, as well as North and South Vietnam, as FRETILIN's "comrades" and "brothers and sisters" who were fighting against colonialism and imperialism. He referred to Portugal and the United States (in his word, "America") as examples of imperialists. He added, "When the Vietnamese people engage in war, they are not alone in their fight. . . . This is called INTERNATIONAL SOLIDARITY."[43]

In the period that followed, Amaral made a dangerous connection, calling the Indonesian government "a big fascist." Then, he expressed solidarity with liberation movements in Sulawesi, Sumatra, Kalimantan, and the Moluccas, arguing, "If Indonesia notices that we have already gained independence, it will awaken the eyes and ears of many Indonesian children." These regional liberation movements were not necessarily associated with the socialist bloc. However, the Indonesian government was afraid of territorial disintegration, and such a comment by a president

FIGURE 6.1 FRETILIN pamphlet's cartoon, "UDT and APODETI are agents of imperialism." Courtesy of the Timorese Resistance Archives and Museum.

within the Indonesian archipelago was simply unforgivable.[44] Then, Amaral contextualized such international issues within Timorese domestic politics. "You must have heard," he continued, "in Angola, MPLA, who defended the people, is not the only [party]; there are also traitors such as UNITA and FNLA." He went on to bring his party's local competitors into the analogy, stating that the UDT and APODETI were "traitors" in Timor, and that they were giving away the *maubere* people to the imperialists (see figure 6.1).

"Maubere" is a much-discussed, but controversial term. It is a common name for a man in the Mambae region, as FRETILIN leaders explained. The equivalent for a woman is *buibere*. Portuguese and lowland Tetuns had previously viewed Mambae uplanders as "uncivilized" and "ignorant." Thus, in the late Portuguese period, "maubere" came to mean Timorese who were not sophisticated (in the European sense) and ignorant. However, FRETILIN activists, who were inspired by Sukarno's idea of "Marhaenism," began to use "maubere" positively in order to signify unprivileged genuine Timorese who were unaffected by the decadence of European cultures.⁴⁵ Thus, "maubere" came to connote an attractive self-identification that attempted to unite previously separated populations, while at the same time estranging educated Timorese who considered themselves "civilized."⁴⁶

Amaral's speech summarily explained FRETILIN leaders' cosmology in terms of various "isms." On the one hand, they aligned themselves with *mauberism*, global anti–colonialism, separatism in Indonesia, and socialism. On the other, they denounced fascists, colonialists, and capitalists. Here, the Cold War binary division of the world appears as a global confrontation between the powerless poor majority and the rich powerful minority. It was a simulation of the Cold War binary, borrowing from the Lusophone world (e.g., the writings of Amilcar Cabral, Agostinho Neto, and Paulo Freire) and, to a lesser degree, Asian and Latin American equivalents (e.g., Sukarno, Ho Chi Minh, and Che Guevara). Amaral and other FRETILIN Central Committee members depicted other Timorese parties as "agents of imperialism." Although the UDT and APODETI had different visions for their future, their collaboration with Portugal and Indonesia was presented also as serving the United States, "the big imperialist." Amaral's Cold War involved a Manichean world like that of the Cold War but was composed of more diverse "isms" beyond communism and capitalism. Furthermore, his appearance-making disproportionately simulated the violent aspects of the confrontation rather than the "cold" ones, depicting it more as the Cold War than the Cold War.

Mobilization Campaigns

Although ideology has been an important thread in Cold War studies, the FRETILIN movement was a social revolution without ideological consistency as it was supposed to be an all-inclusive "revolutionary front" for all disgruntled Timorese people. For example, some cadres criticized colonialism for transforming the Timorese way of life, while others targeted traditional local authorities for being exploitative and backward.⁴⁷ In East Timor, the most commonly used languages were Tetun and Portuguese. To a certain degree, campaigns in these two languages were analytically distinguishable. Portuguese was a tool to communicate among the *letrados*, as well as to the international audience. On the other hand, Tetun was a tool to mobilize the rural population. For the most part, FRETILIN cadres utilized

Radio Dili, mural paintings, newspapers, political workshops, and literacy campaigns.

Another topic FRETILIN took up was gender. While other parties did not discuss the issue, FRETILIN's women's organization (OPMT; Organização Popular das Mulheres Timorenses) played a lively part in political campaigns. One of the most well-known figures was Muki Bonaparte, the founder of the organization and one of the few female FRETILIN Central Committee members, who often contributed articles to the party newspaper. She framed her organizations' struggles not just in ideological terms, but against both traditional and colonial social systems.[48] Her criticism, for instance, covered a wide range from the Indigenous marriage custom of *barlaque* to polygamy, prostitution, economic exploitation, and the lack of female participation in politics.[49] Then, she described her organization's mission as the "total destruction of all forms of exploitation of men and women." As such, despite unmistakable ideological language, FRETILIN's programs were more local and diverse.

A similar tendency toward localization can be found in various FRETILIN campaigns that were observed and recorded by a number of anthropologists and political scientists in rural areas of East Timor at the time.[50] Here, I limit my discussion to party songs, literacy campaigns, and the agricultural cooperative cultivation scheme. One of FRETILIN's party anthems, "Foho Ramelau" (Mt. Ramelau), became a hit song even outside of originally Tetun-speaking areas. It is a song about Timorese subordination and exploitation, which is framed within a worldview of ancestor and mountain worship. The title refers to Mt. Ramelau (2,986 m)—the highest holy mountain on Timor Island—to which the song is dedicated. The Mambai name of the mountain, Tatamailau, means "grandfather of all," and it is believed that ancestral spirits reside there. The lyrics read as follows:

Eh, Foho Ramelau, Foho Ramelau eh!
Sa be as liu o tutun,
Sabe bein liu o lolon eh!
Tansa Timur ulun sudur wain wain?
Tansa Timur oan atan wain wain?
Tansa Timur oan hakruk beibeik?
Tansa Timur oan atan beibeik?
Loke matan! Loro foun too iha o knua
Loke matan! Loro foun iha ita rain.
Hader Rai hun mutin ona la!

Hader loro foun sa'e ona la!
Hader kaer rasik kuda talin eh!
Hader ukun rasik ita rain eh!

[Hey, Mt. Ramelau, Mt. Ramelau!
Do you know anything higher than your peak?
Do you know anything greater than your body?
Why is Timor's head forever bowed down?
Why are Timorese children forever enslaved?
Why do Timorese children always bend over?
Why are Timorese children always enslaved?
Open your eyes! A new sun is above your hamlet.
Open your eyes! A new sun is above your (our) land.
Awake! The foot of the mountain is already white.
Awake! A new sun has already risen!
Awake! Take the reins of your own [*rasik*] horse! Awake! Govern [*ukun*] your land by yourself [*rasik*]!]

Note that the lyrics point out problems ("Why are Timorese children always enslaved?"), and then appeal to the Timorese to stand up ("Awake! Govern [*ukun*] your land by yourself [*rasik*]!"). As I have discussed elsewhere, the phrase *ukun rasik* is usually translated as "to govern oneself," "self-determination," or "independence," but the word *rasik* also refers to consanguinity.[51] Thus, "ukun rasik" could mean rule by kinship groups, excluding outsiders. Adding on yet another thing, "ukun rasik" was also explained by FRETILIN as the state in which "everyone can seek what they want."[52] What is interesting is that, while the song raises the higher purpose of class struggle and freedom, it utilizes kinship terms rather than standard Marxist terms such as capitalist exploitation and dictatorship of the proletariat. The song's structure, tone, and lyrics, in effect, appealed to Timorese "children" to have self-respect by mentioning the holy mountain and its majestic nature, to stand up by referring to social contradictions, and to unite by alluding to Timorese blood-ties and ancestral spirits.

Such campaigns were intended not only to enable rural populations to read and write, but also to "politicize" them. In FRETILIN's words, the purpose of its literacy project was to let the "maubere people" participate in "our liberation" from "colonialists, exploiters, enemies infiltrated into our movement, opportunists, ideas of petty bourgeoisie, and our own vices."[53] Here, we can see that FRETILIN borrowed Paolo Freire's method from his *Pedagogy of the Oppressed*.[54] Originally, this method of pedagogy was intended to blur the division between the teacher and the student, making both aware of power relations and political oppression in their particular environments, including those of schools. FRETILIN, however, dogmatically utilized Freire's pedagogy to mobilize the rural population against their competitors.

Let us take an example on the word *kuda* (horse) from the Central Committee's instructions for the literacy campaign:

> Before writing the word on the blackboard, we invite the learners to talk about "kuda." For example, what is it for? Who is on the horseback? (. . .). Why don't *maubere* have a car? Talk about cavalry. Was there any army before Portuguese colonization? Did the army serve the people during the Manufahi War? Also, the criminal coup of the reactionary UDT on August 11, did they defend the people? What was the purpose of the creation of the Maubere People's Defense Command? What is FALINTIL [Armed Force for National Liberation of Timor-Leste]? Why did the Timor People take up arms against the reactionaries and traitors of our Fatherland?[55]

As this pamphlet was distributed in November 1975, the context is the period soon after the party conflict between FRETILIN and UDT. This shows that political labels such as "reactionaries" and "traitors" were utilized even in district- and village-level basic education campaigns.

What was unpopular about FRETILIN is equally as interesting as what was popular about the party. One project that was opposed by farmers was FRETILIN's cooperative cultivation program in rural areas. Farmers resented it partly due to the ignorance of FRETILIN's young and urbanized leaders about Timorese agricultural practices, but mostly because of the party's proposal that half of the produce of a family's gardens and fields be expropriated by the state.[56] FRETILIN insisted on liberating the land from "colonial domination and the feudal system." However, rural populations in Timor already owned their own land by that time, so that FRETILIN's proposal was viewed as a new sort of taxation. Moreover, the farmers' dominant moral value had already been based on the practice of mutual help, so they had nothing new to learn from the moralistic lessons of FRETILIN's cooperatives scheme. As such, FRETILIN's regional committees often had to compromise with existing customary laws, traditional social structures, and the local interests of those they labeled "maubere" people. The people's simulation of FRETILIN's rhetoric on gender relations and its antagonistic view of society, on the one hand, and their rejection of the party's agricultural policy, on the other, indicate the utility of FRETILIN's rhetoric and moral politics rather than its actual policy enforcement.

Rural Utilization of the Cross-Party Rivalry

If the ~~Cold~~ War in the Timorese capital, Dili, was characterized by derogatory labeling, situations in rural areas were much more diverse and complex. Some general statements can be made. First, in the beginning, most of the deadly violence happened in the areas of Dili, Aileu, Maubisse, and Same.[57] Except for Same, these places were in or close to the capital city. In other districts, close family relationships and kinship deterred party members from resorting to harsh measures against members of competing parties, at least until August 11, 1975. FRETILIN's revolutionary ideas often collided with such sociocultural customs on the ground. Second, traditional authorities, especially those in "Portuguese loyalist" subdistricts, tended to support the UDT, which was considered the party in favor of the status quo. Their children, however, tended to join FRETILIN, the party in which young intellectuals could take initiative toward diverse ends.[58] Those who had records of resisting the Portuguese were likely to join either FRETILIN or APODETI, the anti-Portuguese parties. Below are examples of what happened in some relatively remote villages.

Let us, first, look at the village of Gari-Wai, located on the border between the subdistricts of Baucau and Venilale. This village included a hamlet called Mau-Kali whose inhabitants had grievances against neighboring villagers. When other hamlets of Gari-Wai decided to support the UDT, Mau-Kali swore allegiance to FRETILIN and advanced an argument to secede from the village. This angered other Gari-Wai villagers, who then trespassed on Mau-Kai land, impelling Gari-Wai villagers to vandalize Mau-Kali property, though they did not resort to violence against the villagers themselves.[59] Still, such an incident was previously almost unheard of, because politics was not a priority for villagers at all until August 1975.

A similar case can be seen in the village of Maubara, where national politics was not an issue before the outbreak of the civil war between UDT and FRETILIN, following which it, too, was suddenly politicized radically and many villagers began to be arrested for possessing either party's membership cards. In this village, at the time of FRETILIN's counterattack, a local FRETILIN-supporting militia murdered three sons of a local magnate, Jose Martinho Sanches, in an incident that was not important strategically. In terms of the ~~Cold~~ War, the FRETILIN militias killed them for being "reactionaries." In the national narrative, it was for their UDT membership. However, Southeast Asia scholar Douglas Kammen provides an alternative narrative based on interviews with the villagers of Maubara, emphasizing local and personal factors. According to his study, the Sanches family was connected to hated governor Calestino da Silva (who seized land and abducted people as slaves) by marriage alliance. Furthermore, the Sanches's large coffee plantation had been relying on villagers' forced labor. Worse still, the three sons were alleged to have sexually abused village girls. Kammen argues that these cumulative factors, rather than strategic needs or ideological reasonings, resulted in the murder of the three when FRETILIN supporters had the opportunity.[60]

Another case, involving Isabel Maria Marcal Sequeira's life story, captures similar local dynamics during the civil war period. From 1974 to 1975, her father, the *liurai* (translated as "king" or "chief") of Samalai did not join any party. However, all of the liurais of the area held a meeting with the deputy administrator of Baucau, who happened to be a UDT leader. Later, FRETILIN arrested all of these liurais. Subsequently, grudges within the family surfaced. The liurai's cousin, a member of FRETILIN, took part in the operation and threatened the liurai's family, saying, "Before it was your time, now it's MY time. You are going to be punished."[61] This cousin and FRETILIN members hit the liurai and shouted that he had stolen their land. Then, they ordered the liurais to clean the place, and said, "Liurai like telling the people what to do, now it's YOUR turn to do the cleaning."[62]

These episodes demonstrate that the master narratives of the Cold War and national liberation were often intertwined with preexisting personal and communal tensions and suppressed emotions (e.g., hatred, anger, jealousy, and fear) on the ground. Gari-Wai people saw political party membership as a new sense of belonging that could replace the preexisting divisions of villages enforced by the Portuguese. The cases from Maubara and Samalai imply that the Cold War and national rhetoric were utilized to justify perpetrators' personal revenge. It is important to note that even such pretended Cold War rhetoric constructed the Cold War simulacrum in Timor through reinforcing the notions of binary politics, the communist threat, and class struggle.

Politics of Labeling: Who Were "Reactionaries," "Traitors," and "Enemies"?

Social construction of "traitors" and "enemies" was a conspicuous aspect of the Cold War in Timor, as in other Southeast Asian cases such as the Indonesian Red Purge and the Malayan Emergency. These labels were loose and arbitrary and, thus, often convenient. Even FRETILIN president Xavier do Amaral was arrested in 1977 by militant FRETILIN members as a "traitor" for alluding to the possibility of negotiations with the Indonesian military. Then, who were those labeled "traitors" and "enemies"? They tended to include leaders and supporters of the UDT and APODETI, traditional authorities, coffee plantation owners, *mestizos*, and Timorese Catholic priests, as well as even "moderates" within FRETILIN's leadership.[63] Some ethnic Chinese who did not conform to FRETILIN were targeted as well. FRETILIN members accused them of various pretexts, from collaboration with colonizers and betrayal of their own country to excessive liberalism, opportunism, exploitation, and so forth.

The most easily recognizable "reactionaries" were local traditional authorities. Even before European colonization, Timorese societies were stratified into three classes: nobles (*datu*), commoners (*ema*), and slaves (*atan*). Nobles could sell their subjects to foreigners as slaves. Such local relationships between nobles and slaves were easily translated into FRETILIN's distinction between enemies and the people. However, other types of social elites, such as *letrados* (the educated), *civilizados* (the civilized), and *assimilados* (the assimilated), were exempted from such categorical accusations, largely because these were the classes from which all FRETILIN leaders came. The category of "mestizo" presented a more complicated issue because of their liminal status of (not) being Timorese.

However, those who were labeled "enemies of the people" were not necessarily "reactionaries," "fascists," or "sellers of our own country," as they were often labeled. Their position often reflected the Portuguese policy of the preceding period. To provide a context for mestizos and traditional authorities, as well as supporters of "Timor as Portugal," they were not "East Timorese" at the time, but already Portuguese citizens. The Portuguese post–World War II policy equalized the metropole and so-called overseas provinces, while permitting letrados and civilizados to apply for Portuguese citizenship, for which they were usually accepted. Of course, those who were labeled "uncivilized" were excluded from such fruits of "equal citizenship." Because the Carnation Revolution in Lisbon had overthrown the Caetano dictatorship, Portugal was heading toward democratization. Thus, those who were optimistic about the change in Lisbon tended to support the UDT, instead of choosing a potentially precarious independence of East Timor under FRETILIN.

Timorese Catholic priests were also labeled "reactionaries" for not supporting FRETILIN. In fact, most priests in 1974 and 1975 tended to support the APODETI and UDT. However, the priests' reasoning for such political thought varied. Some regarded FRETILIN as communists who tended to be atheists, although many Central Committee members were Catholics. Thus, the magazine *Cruzada Eucaristica* in Timor published an article on liberty and communism, and stressed that Catholics were prohibited from being involved in any activities for "the Communist party."[64] Other APODETI-supporting priests presented a view that Catholic theology students could get the same quality of education at Flores in Eastern Indonesia and in Lisbon, and the nearer the better.[65] They assumed that integration into Indonesia would accelerate the Christianization of Timor, which was, ironically, a historically correct prediction, though such an antagonistic relationship between the Church and the East Timorese nationalist guerrillas would change in the 1980s.

Contexts outside of the Cold War?

While the politics of labeling became rampant and Cold War vocabularies prevailed in East Timor in the mid-1970s, there were important underlying currents outside the Cold War world. For an examination of such historical and personal contexts, let us look at a man named Joaquim da Costa Guterres Junior, who lived in several villages, including Ossu, Uato-Lari, and Venilale—all rather remote villages in the eastern part of Timor Island. He did not leave written expressions of his thoughts, but even such a silent individual could not escape the politics of labeling. During the Indonesian invasion, he joined a pro-Indonesian militia and was thus considered an enemy of FRETILIN. Yet, a document from 1987 tells us that he was arrested by the Indonesian military for helping FRETILIN guerrillas. Though contradictory, at least at a glance, close examination of his life suggests that a person's political affiliation in certain moments and everyday deeds have deeper contexts than the Cold War.

His early records are found in Japanese sources. He was born in 1925 as the eldest son of Dom Joaquim da Costa Guterres, one of three "big men" of Ossu in Viqueque district. Joaquim Elder's traditional authority was broadly acknowledged by local villagers, but not by the Portuguese colonial administration.[66] The apparent reason for this was that he was not educated at Catholic missionary schools or able to build strong connections with the colonial administration. During World War II, Japanese agents took advantage of this situation. The Da Costa Guterres family collaborated with the Japanese, whereas the family patriarch's local competitors aided Australian guerrillas. Around the first half of 1945, Maeda Toru, a celebrated Japanese poet who served as an intelligence agent in Timor, brought Joaquim Junior and his friends to Japanese-occupied Dutch West Timor under the pretext of "uniting the East and West of the island." Then, something happened. Maeda wrote in his memoir that Joaquim Junior fell in love with a noble girl in West Timor. Then, other Japanese sources recorded a "wedding ceremony" between eastern and western noble families, in which Maeda acted as a matchmaker. After the war, Joaquim Elder was jailed by Portuguese forces and died the next year. Maeda, on his return trip to Timor in the 1970s, noted that Joaquim Junior had been exiled from Ossu to Uato-Lari, a more remote village. The traditional authority of the Da Costa Guterres family had already been handed over to his cousin.[67]

In 1959, an event in Uato-Lari caused a panic. The only Timorese rebellion in the years after World War II—the Viqueque Rebellion—erupted from this small village. The police reported that it was planned by the Indonesian consul, twelve Indonesian asylum seekers in Uato-Lari, disgruntled civil servants of Dili, and the villagers of Uato-Lari.[68] On the other hand, anthropologists emphasized the significance of the ethnolinguistic division between Naueti and Makasai in Uato-Lari village.[69] Interestingly, Joaquim Junior's name was never mentioned by either the police or anthropologists, although he lived in Uato-Lari and had a connection to some powerful men in Indonesian West Timor. His personal information was left by the Portuguese Public Institution for Education.[70] By the 1960s, he was legitimately married to a woman from Dili. He and his family sincerely returned to the church in Ossu to baptize his three children. He was a village council member of Uato-Lari and enrolled his children in the best missionary schools in Timor. There is no semblance of rebellious activities in these files.

Finally, his name is mentioned in a FRETILIN document dated 1987, titled "Prisons for APODETI and UDT Members." According to this document, "Joaquim Guterres" took part in the Indonesian capture of Baucau in 1975 and was decorated for this service in 1979. He became a commander of *Hansip* (a pro-Indonesian militia group) and a village head during the Indonesian Occupation. Venilale is located 15 kilometers north of Ossu and belongs to a region where his father and ancestors claimed their authority. But he was accused of giving medicine to FALINTIL guerrillas and hiding some of them. He was beaten by Indonesian commanders and arrested. Later he was released after paying Indonesian officers in buffaloes.⁷¹ So far, I have been unable to learn his fate after this.

What is implied in Joaquim Junior's silence and the records of his deeds? Looked at through a "Global Cold War" perspective, his status as a pro-Indonesian militia leader could be regarded as a typical feature of a "cold warrior." However, from his teenage years, he had intimate relations with Indonesia. His experience with Indonesia was entangled with the Japanese occupation, his father's legacy, his youthful love affair (possibly with an officially erased record of marriage), resistance against European rule, and so forth. He lived with secrets, joined pro-Indonesian forces, remained in East Timor, and carefully observed requirements to be a faithful Catholic, unlike his father. Such a life defies the ready-made categories of the Cold War, politicized ethnicity, decolonization, and Indonesian Occupation in East Timor.

Theorizing Disproportionate Simulations of the Cold War in Southeast Asia

Taken as a whole, what was the Cold War, particularly in the case of the East Timor Problem? First, I would argue that it was a simulacrum, imagined as part of a single global confrontation. Yet, it was a simulacrum of the Cold War minus the nuclear threat. An important absence in this chapter and contemporary sources is the idea of the "nuclear bomb." At the centers of the Cold War, the superpowers had a common fear of what was called "mutually assured destruction." However, an imminent threat of a nuclear war was largely absent in peripheral zones such as maritime Southeast Asia. This difference made Cold War discourse manipulable. In this area, the United States and USSR were largely absent, as they had little interest in the fate of Portuguese Timor in the mid-1970s. It was Timorese and Indonesian leaders who simulated the "Global Cold War." FRETILIN presented global socialist movements as on the side of East Timor's poor marginalized majority, while identifying the capitalist world with remnants of imperialism, fascism, and colonialism on the island. Suharto viewed FRETILIN as "communist" simulators, reacting against them as part of his regime's "struggles for independence against Communism."⁷²

The years of 1974 to 1976 in Timor were characterized by excessive energies and massive mobilization in comparison to the preceding "sleepy" years. Everything seemed to be moving. FRETILIN's campaign led the Timorese people to identify social problems in new ways. Colonial exploitation, traditional class divisions, and gender roles were suddenly taken up for discussion and criticized in public. Such political conscientization went hand in hand with social construction of "reactionaries," "traitors," and "enemies of the people." In return, competitors labeled FRETILIN as "communists" and "atheists." Rural communities also utilized party divisions to pursue local priorities and were affected by the expansion of conflicts. Seen in this way, it is clear that it was simulations of the Cold War, rather than actual deeds and real motivations, that determined the historical course of Timor in the years that followed. FRETILIN's imitation of leftist rhetoric and self-association with irredentism in Indonesia made it appear an existential threat for the Suharto regime and Timorese conservatives. In the view of FRETILIN's audience, simulators and "real communists" were equally dangerous. The FRETILIN leadership was fatally unaware of their performative effect in relation to Southeast Asian regional contexts.

To approach the Cold War as simulacra is to pay microscopic attention to the slightest differences at the exact moments when people were apparently doing the same thing. Through this approach, we can avoid the danger of reifying the Cold War as an unquestionable fact (Cold War studies within the Cold War perspective) or dismissing it as a mere Indonesian pretext to gain new territory (the post–Cold War interpretation). Also, it should not be reduced to nationalism, the concept of the Cold War as a "long peace," or proxy wars. As the word "Cold War" was transmitted, simulated, and materialized in various places, it was also transmuted into something else. As scholars of religion have found local agency in syncretism, historians should read the simulators' "agency" in such transmutation.[73] Exactly in this context, it is important to note that various "Cold wars" in different places were perceived, simulated, and experienced as if they were one real war. Simultaneously, the Timorese and Indonesians were not much interested in the "Cold" part of the "Cold War," and they did not simulate that part. Indeed, they disproportionately simulated the "hot" aspects of international affairs in a time full of fear, excitement, and violence.

One can think of both top-down and bottom-up explanations for their disproportionate art of appearance-making. A top-down explanation would maintain that the dualism of the Cold War and social construction of an existential threat were highly useful for national mass mobilization, whereas the "long peace" narrative was not. Fear of the Cold War was useful in local propaganda, just as the binary oppositions of Christianity/Islam and colonizer/colonized were in certain places and times. In the age of democracy and socialism, political leaders were required to create a semblance of democratic support in the view of domestic and international audiences. Notably, mass mobilization was among the few ways to create a semblance of democratic support in countries where institutionalized voting did not take place.

Likewise, the differences between the local leaders' and commoners' simulations give us a chance to glance at what was going on at the village level. A bottom-up explanation would maintain that an emphasis on violent ~~Cold~~ War was useful to conceal ordinary people's personal motivations in their political actions and violence. Although cultural anthropologist David Hicks has separated "tradition" from urban rhetoric in East Timor, political participation on the side of rural peoples was entangled with both, as we have seen above. The recent history of colonial wars and World War II, and the new political orders they consolidated, also generated suppressed but intense emotions among the people such as fear of war, jealousy, humiliation, and anger. Such emotions were often expressed along the lines of the ~~Cold~~ War rhetoric.[74] In conclusion, this chapter has demonstrated that various stakeholders in the East Timor Problem believed in, or consciously constructed, one global confrontation. As one looks into microscopic differences at different levels and in different places, it also reveals that they were fighting many different wars framed in many ways. In an interesting way, the superpowers, local leaders, and ordinary people on different sides were all accomplices in this global industry of constructing the Cold War world.

Notes

1. Commission for Reception, Truth and Reconciliation in Timor-Leste (CAVR), *Chega! The Final Report of the Timor-Leste Commission for Reception, Truth and Reconciliation,* vol. 1 (Jakarta: KPG in cooperation with STP-CAVR, 2013): 493–502, http://www.chegareport.org/.

2. Helen Hill, *The Timor Story* (Victoria: Timor Information Service, 1976), 1.

3. My usage of the word "simulacrum" is informed by Plato, *The Dialogues of Plato: Translated into English, with Analyses and Introductions,* trans. Benjamin Jowett (London: Clarendon Press, 1883), 1523; Gilles Deleuze, *Difference and Repetition,* trans. Paul Patton (New York: Columbia University Press, 1994), 66–69; Jean Baudrillard, *Simulacra and Simulation,* trans. Sheila Faria Glaser (Ann Arbor: University of Michigan Press, 1995), 1–42; and Ariel Heryanto, *State Terrorism and Political Identity in Indonesia: Fatally Belonging* (London: Routledge, 2006).

4. Heonik Kwon, *The Other Cold War* (New York: Columbia University Press, 2010); and Masuda Hajimu, *Cold War Crucible: The Korean Conflict and the Postwar Period* (Cambridge, MA: Harvard University Press, 2015), 1–9.

5. For the terms "writing under erasure," "traces," and "difference," please refer to Jacques Derrida, *Of Grammatology*, trans. Gayatri Chakravorty Spivak (Baltimore: Johns Hopkins University Press, 1976).

6. For the former, see, for example, Frederico Romero, "Cold War Historiography at the Crossroads," *Cold War History* 14, no. 4 (2014): 685–703. For the latter, see, for example, Ang Cheng Guan, *Southeast Asia's Cold War: An Interpretive History* (Honolulu: University of Hawai'i Press, 2018).

7. Odd Arne Westad, *Global Cold War: Third World Interventions and the Making of Our Times* (Cambridge: Cambridge University Press, 2005); also see Bradley Simpson, "Southeast Asia in the Cold War" in *The Cold War in the Third World*, ed. Robert J. McMahon (New York: Oxford University Press, 2013), 48–66; and Paul Thomas Chamberlin, *The Cold War's Killing Fields: Rethinking the Long Peace* (New York: HarperCollins, 2019).

8. These points are raised in the first and second workshops of the National University of Singapore's "Reconceptualizing the Cold War: On-the-Ground Experience in Asia" project. Please refer to Kisho Tsuchiya, "Workshop Report: Reconceptualizing the Cold War: On-the-Ground Experiences in Asia May 21–22, 2019, and June 22–23, 2019," H-Diplo Conference Report (CR-2019-1).

9. John R. W. Smail, "On the Possibility of an Autonomous History of Modern Southeast Asia," *Journal of Southeast Asian History* 2, no. 2 (1961): 72–102.

10. Matthew Connelly, "Taking Off the Cold War Lens: Visions of North-South Conflict during the Algerian War for Independence," *American Historical Review* 105, no. 3 (2000): 739–69.

11. Read, for example, Oliver W. Walters, *History, Culture, and Region in Southeast Asian Perspectives* (Ithaca, NY: Cornell Southeast Asia Program Publications, 1999), 27–40.

12. For more detailed discussion of these workshops, see Tsuchiya, "Workshop Report."

13. Plato, *Dialogues of Plato*, 1523. Plato separates "simple imitators of appearance" into two categories as follows: "One of the two classes of imitators is a simple creature, who thinks that he knows that which he only fancies; the other sort has knocked about among arguments, until he suspects and fears that he is ignorant of that which to the many he pretends to know."

14. Deleuze, *Difference and Repetition*, 69.

15. As for the phrase "global confrontation," I got it from Odd Arne Westad's book where he emphasized the importance of "the confrontation between the two worlds" and "global confrontation" and attributes such a worldview to Mao and General Orlando Agosti. See Odd Arne Westad, *The Cold War: A World History* (New York: Basic Books, 2017), 17–19, 163, 331.

16. Regular references to East Timorese nationalism and FRETILIN include Jill Jolliffe, *East Timor: Nationalism and Colonialism* (St. Lucia: University of Queensland Press, 1978); Bill Nicol, *Timor, The Stillborn Nation* (Camberwell, Victoria: Widescope, 1978): Jose Ramos-Horta, *Funu: The Unfinished Saga of East Timor* (Lawrenceville, NJ: Red Sea Press, 1986); Helen Hill, *Stirrings of Nationalism in East Timor: FRETILIN 1974-1978* (Sydney: Otford Press, 2002); David Hicks,

Rhetoric and the Decolonization and Recolonization of East Timor (New York: Routledge, 2015); and Michael Leach, *Nation-Building and National Identity in Timor-Leste* (New York: Routledge, 2017).

17. For critique of the "Cold War as weather" approach, see Masuda Hajimu, "The Early Cold War: Studies of the Cold War in the Twenty-First Century," in *A Companion to U.S. Foreign Relations: Colonial Era to The Present*, ed. Christopher R. W. Dietrich (Hoboken, NJ: Wiley Blackwell, 2020), 2:632–51.

18. For the former, see Jolliffe, *East Timor*; Nicol, *Timor, The Stillborn Nation*; and Hill, *Stirrings of Nationalism*; and, for the latter, see Geoffrey Gunn, *A Critical View of Western Journalism and Scholarship on East Timor* (Manila: Journal of Contemporary Asia Publishers, 1994), 1–18; and Sonny Ibaraj, *East Timor: Blood and Tears in ASEAN* (Chiang Mai, Thailand: Silkworm Press, 1997), 10.

19. Kisho Tsuchiya, "Awkwardly Included: Portugal and Indonesia's Politics of Multi-Culturalism in East Timor, 1942–1990s," *Asian Review* 30, no. 2 (2017): 79–102; and *Emplacing East Timor: Regime Change and Knowledge Production, 1850–2010* (Honolulu: University of Hawai'i Press, 2024), chap. 1, 3, and 5.

20. Jill Jolliffe, *East Timor; Nationalism and Colonialism* (St. Lucia: University of Queensland Press, 1978), 325–38.

21. The Portuguese Maoist movement was highly active in the early 1970s. Unlike the Portuguese Socialist Party and the Portuguese Communist Party, it never gained a seat in the national parliament. But FRETILIN's phrase *luta popular* (people's struggle), use of mural paintings (or graffiti) for propaganda, and Maoist orientation were primarily inspired by this group.

22. FRETILIN, *FRETILIN/Manual e Programa Políticos* [FRETILIN/Manual and Political Program], Lisbon, December 1974, pasta: 05005.002, Arquivo and Museu da Resistência Timorense (AMRT).

23. In the Timorese perspective, they experienced not only Japanese occupation, but Australian and Indonesian invasions during the Pacific War. Refer to Kisho Tsuchiya, "Indigenization of the Pacific War in Timor Island: A Multi-language Study of its Contexts and Impact," *War and Society* 38, no. 1 (2019): 19–40.

24. "Carta de José Manuel Ramos-Horta, presidente do Comité Político da FRETILIN, ao embaixador da República popular da China, solicitando a ajuda daquele país, que sempre prestou apoio às nações oprimidas e sob o jugo do colonialismo, por suspeitar que a Indonésia prepara uma invasão" [Letter from José Manuel Ramos-Horta, president of FRETILIN's political committee, to the ambassador of the People's Republic of China, requesting assistance from that country, which has always supported oppressed nations under the yoke of colonialism, due to suspicions that Indonesia is preparing an invasion], September 28, 1974, pasta 05000.274, AMRT.

25. "Menteri Sosial janjikan bantuan pangan utk Timor Portugis" [The Minister of Social Affairs promises food aid for Portuguese Timor], *Harian Umum Pagi Angkatan Senjata Edisi Nusa Tenggara*, September 7, 1974.

26. *Berita Yudha*, December 2, 1974; *Indonesian Observer*, December 6, 1974; *Kompas*, October 4, 1975; *Sinar Harapan*, July 2, 1974.

27. Denis Freney, *Timor: Freedom Caught between the Powers* (Nottingham, UK: Spokesman Books, 1975), 9.

28. Hill, *Stirrings of Nationalism*, 92–95.

29. Hill, *Stirrings of Nationalism*, 61–70; Hicks, *Rhetoric*, 46–55; and Jude Conway, ed., *Step by Step: Women of East Timor: Stories of Resistance and Survival* (Darwin: CDU Press, 2010), 26–27.

30. The phrase "Timorese elite" requires some explanation. The traditional ruling class has the titles of *liurai* (prince) and *datu* (noble). In this chapter, I decided to use "the traditional authority" to refer to this group of people. The educated (in the Western mode) are called *letrados* (the literate). The traditional authority and *letrados* overlap, but the terms refer to different types of authentication. The privileged mixed-blood population is called *mestizos*. The "native Timorese" who were assimilated into Portuguese culture are called either *civilizados* (the civilized) or *assimilados* (assimilated).

31. For instance, one of the most widely known Australian left-wing journalists, Denis Freney, wrote, "These events in Timor deserve close examination for there are similarities in the Timorese situation to past events elsewhere in the Third World, particularly in Vietnam, Cuba and Chile." Freney, *Timor*, 9.

32. Stephen J. Headley, "The Future of Portuguese Timor: Dilemmas and Opportunities," Occasional Paper 27, Singapore: Institute of Southeast Asian Studies, 1975; and Hicks, *Rhetoric*, 137–59.

33. Hicks, *Rhetoric*, 100.

34. Mario Lemos Pires, *Descolonização de Timor: Missão Imppóssivel?* [Decolonization of Timor: mission impossible?], 3rd ed. (Lisbon: Publicações Dom Quixote, 1991).

35. Regarding the social construction of Indonesian anticommunism since 1965, Heryanto, *State Terrorism*, is so far the most nuanced work.

36. See the two following documents on the National Security Archives: "Document 1: Memorandum of Conversation between Presidents Ford and Suharto, 5 July 1975, 12:40 p.m.–2:00 p.m.," https://nsarchive2.gwu.edu/NSAEBB/NSAEBB62/doc1.pdf; and "Document 3: Your Visit to Indonesia, Memorandum to President Ford from Henry A. Kissinger, ca. November 21, 1975," available at https://nsarchive2.gwu.edu/NSAEBB/NSAEBB62/doc3.pdf.

37. "Memorandum of Conversation between Presidents Ford and Suharto, 5 July 1975," 6.

38. "Embassy Jakarta Telegram 1579 to Secretary State, 6 December 1975 (Text of Ford-Kissinger-Suharto Discussion)," Secret/Nodis (24), 1. A scanned file is available at the National Security Archive website, https://nsarchive2.gwu.edu/NSAEBB/NSAEBB62/doc4.pdf.

39. See, for instance, Mattias Fibiger, "A Diplomatic Counter-Revolution: Indonesian Diplomacy and the Invasion of East Timor," *Modern Asian Studies* 55, no. 2 (2021): 587–628. The Center for Strategic and International Studies had already had a discussion about "Steps to Prevent Communist Agitator to Escape" and drawn up a list of "suspected communist agitators" among the FRETILIN leadership in August

or September. See also Sue Lannin, "Australia Received East Timor 'Hit List' before Indonesian Invasion," RN Breakfast, November 27, 2015.

40. "UDT jadi Gerakan Anti Komunis–FRETILIN Bakar Anak-anak" [UDT becomes an anti-communist movement–FRETILIN burns children], *Harian Umum Angkatan Bersenjata* (Nusa Tenggara edition), September 20–24, 1975.

41. Xavier do Amaral, "Discurso do Camarada Presidente" [Speech of comrade president], *Journal do Povo Maubere*, no. 8, November 15, 1975.

42. Westad, *Global Cold War*, 207–49.

43. Amaral, "Discurso do Camarada Presidente."

44. On Indonesian fear of geographic fragmentation, refer to Michael Leifer, "Indonesia and the Incorporation of East Timor," *The World Today* 32, no. 9 (1976): 347–54, at 349.

45. Supposedly Marhae is the name of a peasant whom Sukarno met, a peasant who is innocent, unpretentious and hardworking but struggling to survive because of the exploitation by the colonizers and the capitalists.

46. A balanced commentary on this phrase is in Hicks, *Rhetoric*, 191–95.

47. Hicks, *Rhetoric*, 195.

48. Muki Bonaparte, "Organização Popular da Mulher Timor: Texto de análise da situação da mulher timor" [Popular organization of Timorese women: Text analysis of the situation of Timorese women], *O Journal do Povo Maubere*, September 27, 1975.

49. Under the traditional custom of *barlaque* marriage, the family of the groom sends the family of the bride a significant dowry, including, for example, gems, swords, and 30 to 100 water buffalo if they are nobles (alternatively pigs or chickens, if they are poor). This can be understood as the purchasing of women, but many anthropologists have argued that it might have involved more practical meanings, such as providing support for the bride's family that loses its daughter and labor force.

50. Masao Yamaguchi, "Jiyuresuru henkyou kara-chimoru karano tegami," Chuo-koron 90, no. 11 (November 1975): 58–77; Elizabeth G. Traube, *Cosmology and Social Life: Ritual Exchange among the Mambai of East Timor* (Chicago: University of Chicago Press, 1986); Hill, *Stirrings of Nationalism*; and Hicks, *Rhetoric*.

51. Kisho Tsuchiya, "Southeast Asian Cultural Landscape, Resistance, and Belonging in East Timor's FRETILIN Movement (1974–75)," *Journal of Southeast Asian Studies* 52, no. 3 (2021): 515–38.

52. In Tetun, *"Povo ida bele hetan deit buat ne be nia hakarak bainhira nia rasik mak ukun an"* [People can just find what they want when they rule on their own], FRETILIN Manual and Program, 1974, 7.

53. "Como vamos alfabetizar o nosso povo Mau Bere de Timor Leste" [How are we going to make our Mau Bere people of East Timor literate?] in "Sumlemento no. 1," *Journal do Povo Mau Bere*, November 1, 1975, 2.

54. An English version is available as Paulo Freire, *Pedagogy of the Oppressed*, trans. Myra Bergman Ramos (New York: Seabury Press, 1970).

55. "Sumlemento no. 1," 2. FALINTIL was established on August 20, 1975, in response to the party conflict against UDT the same month. During the Indonesian Occupation (1975–1999), it became the main body of armed resistance.

56. Hicks, *Rhetoric*, 97.
57. Hicks, *Rhetoric*, 173.
58. Hicks, *Rhetoric*, 175.
59. Hicks, *Rhetoric*, 176.
60. Douglas Kammen, *Three Centuries of Violence in East Timor* (Singapore: NUS Press, 2016), 127.
61. Conway, *Step by Step*, 152.
62. Conway, *Step by Step*, 152.
63. The next two paragraphs are based on my analysis of how these words appear in issues 1–10 of *Jornal do Povo Maubere* (September–December 1975).
64. "Perguntas com Respostas: O que e a Liberdade? O que e Comunismo?" [Questions and answers: What is freedom? What is communism?] *Cruzada Eucarística*, December 3, 1974. Such a sentiment was expressed by Catholic priests who were both UDT and APODETI sympathizers. See Jorge Barros Duarte, *Timor Jeremiada* (Odivelas: Pentaedro, 1988), 27.
65. Yunus Adicondro, "Revolusi Di Bar & Biara," *Tempo*, June 15, 1974, 10–11.
66. For this paragraph, refer to Tsuchiya, *Emplacing East Timor*, 114–16.
67. Tōru Maeda, *Chimōru-Ki* [Record of Timor] (Tokyo: Soudosha, 1982), 162.
68. Refer to Janet Gunter, "Violence and 'Being in History' in East Timor: Local Articulation of Colonial Rebellion" (MA thesis, Instituto Superior de Ciências do Trabalho e da Empresa, 2008).
69. Janet Gunter, "Violence."
70. "Boletim de Abono de Familia, Certificate of School Attendance, Certificate of Baptism, etc. Foun" [Family Allowance Bulletin, Certificate of School Attendance, Certificate of Baptism, etc. new] box 1307, National Archives of Timor-Leste, Dili.
71. FRETILIN, "Prisões de Membros da APODETI e UDT" [Prisons of APODETI and UDT Members] press release, June 22, 1987.
72. "Memorandum of Conversation between Presidents Ford and Suharto, 5 July 1975," 2.
73. David Mosse, "The Politics of Religious Synthesis: Roman Catholicism and Hindu Village Society in Tamil Nadu India," in *Syncretism/Anti-Syncretism: The Politics of Religious Synthesis*, ed. Rosalind Shaw and Charles Stewart (London: Routledge, 1994), 108–26; and Julius Bautista, *Figuring Catholicism: An Ethnohistory of the Santo Niño de Cebu* (Quezon City: Ateneo de Manila University Press, 2010), 97–122.
74. Regarding the legacy and memory of World War II in the construction of the Cold War reality, refer to Masuda, *Cold War Crucible*, 4–5.

7 Anti-Vietnamese Xenophobia as the Vernacular Expression of Anticommunism in 1950s Laos

Rethinking (Not Removing) Our Cold War Lens

SIMON CREAK

Laos was synonymous with the Cold War through much of the 1950s. But this was because, just as the "Cold War" referred, unproblematically, to the confrontation between the US- and Soviet-led blocs, foreign observers tended to view the country's politics through the prism of American intervention, the conflict in neighboring Vietnam, and superpower geopolitics.[1] More recently, scholars using local sources and oral history have highlighted the local and regional roots of political ideas and ideology in post–Second World War Laos. While much of this work has focused on the communist Pathet Lao (lit. "Lao Country") movement, including its relationship with the Vietnamese communist movement, and life in the Pathet Lao zone, scholars have also started to reexamine anticommunist nationalism in the noncommunist Kingdom of Laos.[2] Building on this work and bringing royalist Laos into conversation with Cold War studies, this chapter considers how popular anti-Vietnamese attitudes contributed to on-the-ground perceptions of the Cold War in Laos.

Ryan Wolfson-Ford, author of the most comprehensive reappraisal of royalist Laos, argues that local understandings of nationalism, anticommunism, democracy, and modernity—not elite patron-client relations and US interference—underpinned local political debates and developments after the fracturing of the Lao Issara (Free Laos) independence movement in 1949.[3] Wolfson-Ford argues that Lao anticommunism drew on fears of Vietnamese and Chinese invasion, rooted in the past but revived with the communist victory in China and the Vietminh's war against the French. As in other contexts wherein communist activism was conflated with "red" or communist imperialism, anticommunist sentiments in the Kingdom of Laos were expressed in the vernacular terms of a reflexive nativism, which viewed communism as an imported, foreign ideology inherently opposed to Lao nationalism.[4] While capturing the ethnic and racial dimensions of Cold

War "social warfare," ethnosocial conflict in Laos differed from elsewhere in Southeast Asia. Although communist China was sometimes portrayed as an imperialist threat, as was the case elsewhere in the region, communist Vietnam represented the most direct source of fear in Laos. Besides the war raging there and the close cooperation between the Vietminh and the Pathet Lao, this heightened alarm emanated from the dense histories of conflict and population movement between the two countries. Anticommunists argued above all that the Lao race, culture, and Theravada Buddhist religion had to be protected from Vietnamese culture, which was not only Confucian, non-Theravadan, and non-Tai (the wider ethnolinguistic group of which the Lao were a part), but now also communist, making it even more irredeemably foreign and anathema to Lao culture and society.[5]

On one level, this fear was obviously xenophobic in the sense that the Vietminh represented an external threat. Crucially, however, anti-Vietnamese xenophobia was also based on the perceived internal threat of "others within": the Vietnamese-Lao already living (and often born) in Laos.[6] Disparaged as "Lao-Viets," these people were ostracized by anticommunist Lao for allegedly being loyal not to Laos but communist Vietnam. Anticommunists reserved their greatest contempt for Pathet Lao resistance leaders with natal and matrimonial links to Vietnam, who worked closely with the Vietminh to form the Lao resistance movement. Anticommunists saw "Lao-Viets" and the entire Pathet Lao as naive dupes of the Vietnamese communists, fooled into serving their masters' real objectives of invasion and colonization.

Both the external "Vietminh Vietnamese" and internal "Lao-Viets" were racialized by anticommunists through the use of offensive terminology and representations. While racism and xenophobia are separate phenomena, the use of racist terms and images reminds us that xenophobia refers not simply to the fear of outsiders (its etymological meaning) but to a broader "civic ostracism" incorporating resentment, disgust, feelings of incongruity, and other forceful emotions.[7] Like fear and vulnerability, these emotions can often fuel racialized ethnonationalism, the emergence of which in Cold War Laos was closely related to anticommunism.[8] In these ways, the Vietnamese (including Vietnamese-Lao) were seen to represent an existential threat to the Lao nation and race, from both without and within, according to a racial/national binary of "us" and "them" that neatly mirrored the Cold War polarity of noncommunist (us) and communist (them).

The visceral politics of fear and xenophobia in Laos highlights the importance of emotions in constructing and communicating Cold War bipolarities. Fear can be a deceptively complex emotion. One need not succumb to crude biological determinism to appreciate that fear of an invading force represents a natural or "basic" emotional response—as well as a rational one—even as such a reaction is acculturated through "beliefs, thoughts, imagination, [and] memories."[9] This "double-faced" character means that fear and xenophobia may simultaneously represent a universal response to a real threat, and a political affect that is "especially vulnerable to rhetorical manipulation."[10] To consider this dualism in relation to Cold War Laos, civic ostracism of the Vietnamese can be viewed on one level as a natural response to Laos's susceptibility to foreign incursion during a time of war. On another level, however, the sources examined in this chapter suggest that responses by anticommunist partisans were fueled by existing anti-Vietnamese sentiments—"emotional residues from the past"—which they readily stoked for contemporary political expediency.[11]

Although anti-Vietnamese sentiments were palpable from 1950, they did not simply appear with the onset of the Cold War. Rather, they built on an existing strand of nationalism defining the Lao nation in racialized terms, stimulated by French colonial policies favoring immigrant Vietnamese over local Lao and narratives recounting precolonial Vietnamese invasions of Laos. In other words, anti-Vietnamese xenophobia emerged as a Cold War issue from the 1950s but was not solely a Cold War issue; the ethnosocial warfare of Cold War Laos built on and exacerbated existing social cleavages. It is true, nevertheless, that these cleavages took on a distinct character during the Cold War, as they were drawn into the global dynamics of "the bipolar era," thus connecting domestic conflicts with global bipolarity.

To understand these dynamics, the chapter proceeds in three main sections. First, it presents a brief history of anti-Vietnamese sentiments in Laos between the late nineteenth century and the immediate post–World War II period. Second, the main section examines anti-Vietnamese sentiments during the 1950s as a "vernacular ideology" that viewed communism and anticommunism through the prism of local ethnic divisions. This section presents several examples of visual culture, particularly political cartoons. The racialized humor embedded within these sources captures the visceral and emotional resonance of anti-Vietnamese sentiments and is suggestive of more widely held beliefs. Finally, the paper concludes by considering implications for how we define and study the Cold War. Resisting Matthew Connelly's influential notion of removing the "Cold War lens," I argue that we should instead rethink our Cold War lens in a manner that highlights the global south's experiences of the Cold War, unsettles hierarchies between the so-called Cold War core and periphery, and helps understand how vernacular ideological forms comprised essential elements of the global bipolarity. In this way, the chapter develops an inclusive definition of the Cold War, but also calls for conceptual specificity in defining and reconceptualizing the Cold War in Laos, Southeast Asia, and beyond, based on the basic antagonism of the bipolar era.

Race and Nationalism before the Cold War

The anti-Vietnamese xenophobia of the 1950s built upon preexisting foundations. Although Lao kingdoms had always been crossroads for ethnically diverse populations on the move, particularly in the north of the country, new ideas of national territory and identity in mainland Southeast Asia encouraged nascent nationalists to reinterpret existing migrations in terms of "invasions." Preceding the French-sponsored cultural nationalism of the 1930s and 1940s, the first instances of racial nationalism emerged in the northern Luang Prabang Kingdom in the late nineteenth and early twentieth centuries. These ideas conceived of the Lao nation and race (Lao: *xat, xeua xat, xeua naeo*) in contradistinction to immigrant populations from neighboring countries. Most notable among the latter were the highly mobile "Ho" (Sino-Tibetan) and "Meo" (Hmong-Mien) ethnic groups fleeing the Taiping Rebellion in southern China. Later, Vietnamese settlers from the eastern territories of French Indochina became another foil for Lao racial identity.[12]

The perceived threat of invading "others" intensified in the first half of the twentieth century, as the French delineated and solidified Laos as a discrete territorial space within Indochina. After World War I, a Franco-Vietnamese "alliance" of colonial officials and local elites collaborated on a shared vision of "French Indochina," an unprecedented territorial creation attaching Laos and Cambodia to the eastern territories of Cochinchina, Annam, and Tonkin—formerly unified under the Nguyen dynasty and later comprising Vietnam.[13] Viewed from Laos, this project to create Indochina as a political and cultural reality implied a kind of double subjugation under both the French *and* Vietnamese. By the 1920s and 1930s, the Vietnamese represented the greatest external threat, in Lao eyes.

Seeking to develop the sparsely populated territory of Laos as a resource frontier, the French and Vietnamese produced plans to "repopulate" the territory with mass migration from the Vietnamese territories of Indochina. At the same time, the French built roads across the Annamese Cordillera, which they hoped would link Laos to eastern Indochina and sever traditional connections to Siam across the Mekong River and the Khorat Plateau. Although the migration scheme was shelved and the population of Vietnamese remained relatively small overall, the major towns of Laos along the Mekong filled disproportionately with Vietnamese, who dominated the colonial civil service, commerce, and wage labor. This predominance was due largely to racial stereotyping by the French, who viewed the Lao as a lazy and heedless race on the verge of extinction, in contrast to the more dynamic and intelligent Vietnamese, who also developed a superior and condescending view of the Lao. Hence, the two groups moved in separate social circles, sports clubs, and artistic societies in urban Laos.[14]

These developments fueled the first signs of what might be considered xenophobic nationalism in Laos. The most prominent local figure in these developments was Prince Phetsarath Ratthanavongsa, a highly ranked civil servant from a rival branch of the royal family to the king. Interviewed by the Hanoi press, Phetsarath declared that he did not oppose immigration outright, but emphasized that it should be controlled. The Vietnamese should observe local customs and laws, he argued, so they did not become "a state within a state."[15] The journalist paraphrased Phetsarath's concerns as follows: "The Indochinese Federation appears, to the weakest nations making it up [Laos and Cambodia], like an eye wash designed to allow the Annamese [Vietnamese] to rule over the others, under the protection of the French flag."[16] If Phetsarath's protests were restrained, wider enmity toward Vietnamese was apparent in a 1936 brawl at a soccer match in Vientiane between Lao and Vietnamese teams, which involved princes and other elites in the crowd, and in the racial undertones of an ensuing debate in the Hanoi press.[17] Meanwhile, young Lao elites engaged in cultural projects aiming to develop a distinctive Lao identity within French Indochina. Colonial officials with a fondness for the Lao also supported the notion of "Laos for the Laotians."[18]

This Franco-Lao project to protect and revive Lao culture received additional backing during World War II, when the colonial regime reproduced the nativist National Revolution of Vichy France throughout Indochina. Charles Rochet, the director of public education in Laos, collaborated with key members of the local elite on the Lao component, known as the Lao Nhay (Great Laos) renovation movement, which promoted Lao history, culture, and language, as well as sport and youth activities. The French viewed this contradictory project as a means of turning the Lao away from pan-Tai irredentism emanating from Bangkok. Just as important for participants, however, was the motivation of carving out a Lao cultural space in Indochina protected from the overbearing Vietnamese. As Rochet declared, "Lao people were being steadily turned into aborigines in their own land."[19] By the end of the war, participants believed that "[the] Lao can rule themselves rather than the French or Vietnamese. . . . The Lao knew that [historically] the Vietnamese and the Cambodians tried to absorb the Lao nation into their own nations as the whites used to do."[20]

This was not, however, the only Lao experience of the Vietnamese during the 1930s and 1940s. Other Lao figures spent these decades studying, working, and living in Vietnam, developing connections that would be critical in the years that followed. Foremost among these were the future leaders of the Pathet Lao, including Prince Souphanouvong (a half-brother of Phetsarath), Kaysone Phomvihane, and Nouhak Phoumsavanh, each of whom had ties to Vietnam through parentage or marriage. Within Laos itself, some urban Lao sympathized with the outspoken anticolonial sentiments of Vietnamese communities and sought to collaborate with the Vietnamese based on shared hatred of the French.

Attitudes toward the Vietnamese remained a key factor in the divisions that emerged after the Japanese *coup de force* of March 1945, which upended French rule before French forces reconquered Laos the following year and sent the incipient Lao Issara government into exile. As prime minister under the Japanese, Phetsarath replaced Vietnamese civil servants with Lao officials and relocated the Vietnamese officials and their families to the southern towns of Thakaek and Savannakhet. Meanwhile, conservative forces, including the king of Luang Prabang and the southern royal family of Champasak, remained loyal to the French. This was due in part to their preference for French rule over Vietnamese domination.[21] On the other hand, Lao nationalists in the south formed loose alliances with nationalist Vietnamese youth groups, who by then were under Vietminh influence. Souphanouvong consulted with Ho Chi Minh in Hanoi before he was made foreign minister of the Lao Issara government and signed a defense agreement with the Vietminh.

The Vietminh alliance remained a source of sensitivity, particularly among the Lao Issara moderates who staunchly opposed the Vietminh's communism. In 1949, moderate members of the Lao Issara accepted the terms of the Franco-Lao Convention, which granted limited internal powers to the Kingdom of Laos as an associated state of the French Union, and joined the loyalists in an expanded Royal Lao Government (RLG). In response, pro-Vietnamese radicals, including many located in eastern Laos and Vietnam, itself, reaffirmed their alliance with the Vietminh and continued their fight against the French and their Lao allies. Sidelining non-Vietminh-aligned members from their ranks, resistance leaders collaborated with the Vietminh in creating the Free Lao Front (Neo Lao Issara) and Pathet Lao in August 1950, and some joined the Indochinese Communist Party.

Thus were the battle lines drawn for the Lao civil war—and Cold War Laos. As with other insurgencies in Southeast Asia, the political cleavages in Laos could be understood as struggles over the future shape of the nation. These highly polarized battles pitted one group of nationalists against another, each with dramatically different views of what constituted national sovereignty, loyalty, and authenticity. In the eyes of the communist Pathet Lao, loyalists and moderates in the Associated State of Laos were traitors due to their ongoing links with France and, later, the United States. The "cosmology of socialist Laos"—and the "binary socialist mentality" that underpinned it—was based on a fundamental distinction between the virtuous Pathet Lao and the naive "lackeys" of the French colonizers and "American imperialists."[22] For noncommunist forces, however, the Pathet Lao had irredeemably betrayed the nation (*khai xat*, lit. "sold the nation") to the Vietnamese and communism, more generally, through its alliance with the Vietminh, a far greater threat to Laos than France. For committed anti-Vietnamese and anticommunist Lao, the perception of these two threats represented nothing less than an existential threat to the Lao nation and race itself.[23] Such opposing emotional extremes help to reveal the level of hostility and violence, including civil violence, with which Cold War battles were waged in Laos.

Anti-Vietnamese Nationalism and/as Anticommunism

Anticommunism in Laos was not static or one-dimensional but varied over time and among different proponents. Context was critical. One of the earliest statements of anticommunist ideology, a pamphlet titled *Le Laos, pivot idéal de la lutte contre le Communisme dans le Sud-Est Asiatique* (Laos: Ideal hub in the struggle against communism in Southeast Asia), was published by the Lao Issara's finance minister and chief propagandist, Katay Don Sasorith, in 1949. As Wolfson-Ford stresses, this was before US involvement in the country. Informed by francophone anticommunism, Katay highlighted the failure of the Soviet Union to deliver on its utopian promises, painted communism as antihuman and "un-Lao," and stressed the threat it posed to traditional institutions, including the family, Buddhism, and social hierarchy. He condemned "communist expansion, so dreadful and dreaded," in Central Europe, Greece, and China, and lamented that "communist movements are emerging everywhere, [including] in almost all the countries of Southeast Asia. In Indonesia, British Malaysia, Siam, Burma, Korea, [and] Japan, in particular, the red peril poses an increasingly distressing problem."[24]

Intriguingly, Katay did not believe that the countries of Indochina (Vietnam, Laos, and Cambodia) faced the same threat. Indeed, he argued that Laos would be resistant to any form of materialism thanks to Buddhism, which possessed a special "immunity to the communist virus." For this reason, he argued, Laos could serve as the United States' "ideal hub against communism in Southeast Asia."[25] Nor did Katay conflate the threat of communism with the threat of the Vietnamese; in fact, his tract did not discuss the Vietnamese or Vietnamese-Lao in any detail. While Katay was making a case for Laos to become an anticommunist hub in Southeast Asia, his perspective was framed by major Cold War confrontations further afield, particularly in Central Europe, Greece, and China, which then filled the international pages of newspapers in Bangkok, the base of the exiled Lao Issara. This was prior to the communist victory in China, the Korean War, the US pronouncement of the domino theory, and, most crucially, prior to the emergence of a Vietminh-allied revolutionary movement in Laos.

Elsewhere, however, Katay revealed his suspicions toward the Vietnamese in Vietnam and Laos, despite being part Vietnamese himself. In a heated exchange of letters with Souphanouvong upon the latter's resignation from the Lao Issara in 1949, he argued that Souphanouvong's "personal situation [was] very delicate because of his wife (who meddles openly and actively in political affairs)." The problems, he added, were her "national origins"—she was Vietnamese—and "political attitudes." Souphanouvong's "compromised position" made the Issara susceptible to French propaganda, he argued, as did the use in Laos of "guerilla troops more Viet than Lao, if not entirely Viet."[26] Souphanouvong countered simply that Katay was "anti-Vietnamese by principle or by prejudice," and that Katay's attitude toward his wife could "be true only under French domination that tried by any means to rouse among all Lao feelings of antipathy towards the Vietnamese."[27] Even in 1949, before the formation of the Pathet Lao in 1950, both sides understood how race could be weaponized in the brewing civil conflict in Laos.

Vernacular Ideology in Early-1950s Visual Culture

According to Wolfson-Ford, fear of the Vietnamese became a widespread Cold War issue with the Vietminh's invasions of Laos in 1953, which precipitated large public demonstrations in Vientiane. However, fear of Vietnamese invasion had already emerged as a key trope by the second half of 1950. Much had taken place in the short time since Katay's treatise and his exchange with Souphanouvong the previous year. Regionally, the Chinese Communist revolution (October 1949) had been followed by the outbreak of the Korean War (June 1950). Locally, the year had witnessed the creation of the Associated State of Laos (July 1949); the dissolution of the Lao Issara (October 1949); the formation of the royalist Lao National Army (March 1950); and the formation of the Vietminh-allied Free Lao Front and Pathet Lao (August 1950). These events dramatically polarized Lao politics and society. Given the Vietminh's key role in several of them, and especially the ongoing war, anti-Vietnamese xenophobia emerged as a key trope in local social conflicts.

Representing a powerful and evocative form of visual culture, cartoons produced during this period provide vivid and arresting representations of anti-Vietnamese ideology. These images undoubtedly served a propaganda function, and many were produced by and for the consumption of Lao soldiers fighting the Vietminh.[28] Nevertheless, the use of culturally embedded humor and stereotyping suggests that the cultural references embedded in the images were shared not just by the artists and editors who produced and published them, but also by the intended audience—or at least that there was reason to assume this to be the case.[29] Moreover, visual representations could communicate to an audience with mixed levels of literacy, an important consideration in a country where literacy rates remained low in the 1950s and 1960s.[30]

In one common representation, the Vietminh were portrayed as common criminals. In a captioned cartoon image of 1950, possibly intended for use as a propaganda poster, a Lao soldier beats a Vietminh cadre grasping a stolen chicken to the ground. The cadre is marked as Vietminh by his black clothing and Vietnamese-style skullcap with a communist star. Addressed to "Lao brothers and sisters," the caption urges villagers to immediately report Vietminh fighters to civil or military authorities so that Lao soldiers could "kill all the Vietminh thieves." Reinforcing the racial terms under which national "self" and foreign "other" were defined, the poster is signed "Blood of a Lao Soldier." According to the caption, the Vietminh are a potential "danger to your home." Here, the "home" (*ban*, also "village") can be interpreted as a metaphor for Laos as a whole, the home of the Lao, and the Vietminh as a foreign plunderer—a portrayal that relies on the racial stereotype of the Vietnamese as a criminal menace.[31]

An important outlet for the expression of anti-Vietminh xenophobia was *Nak Rop Lao* ("The Lao Soldier," also known by its French name, *Le Combattant Lao*), a bimonthly newssheet for Lao members of France's Forces du Laos. This newssheet was founded in 1947 to publicize the lives, exploits, and battles of Lao soldiers among their comrades and countrymen. The tone was light and polemical, moving between hagiographic accounts of battlefield conquests, reviews of Lao history, and humorous exchanges between fictional characters.[32] A common theme in the newssheet was the dyad of Vietnamese-as-invader and Lao soldier-as-protector. In the New Year issue in January 1948, a roughly drawn Lao soldier was superimposed over a map of Laos, its protector in perpetuity. The accompanying article explained that in 1947 the "Lao-Viets [Vietnamese-Lao] of Siam" had tried to conquer Laos, destroying bridges and laying ambushes near Vientiane and towns in the south, but were repulsed.[33] In October 1950, with considerably improved production values, *Nak Rop Lao* reported on an "enemy invasion" the previous August by around 1,000 Vietminh troops in Sam Neua, again withstood by Lao troops under French command. An accompanying cartoon showed a Lao soldier viciously bayonetting a hapless Vietminh combatant, arms raised in surrender, blood oozing from his torso. "They're going to invade. . . . Absolutely not!" reads the caption to this emotionally charged image.[34]

Cartoons by Riem Eng

In August and October 1950, *Nak Rop Lao* featured six cartoons by a certain Riem Eng, a talented and "mischievous" Lao artist, under the heading "Lao humor." Despite the title, these images encapsulated fear and hatred of Vietnamese, including both the Vietminh Vietnamese and their "Lao-Viet" comrades in Laos. That these cartoons did so in a humorous way suggests that racialized anti-Vietnamese nationalism was shared among the artist and his intended audience. Riem Eng's cartoons included three kinds of characters: Vietminh soldiers referred to as *Kaeo Vietminh* (lit. "Vietminh Vietnamese"), a compound including the pejorative term *Kaeo* for Vietnam/Vietnamese; Lao people of Vietnamese background (*Lao-Viet*), whose loyalty was to the Vietminh rather than Laos; and ordinary people or citizens

FIGURE 7.1 "Ha, ha, ha! Come and die for no reason!" *Nak Rop Lao*, 1950. Courtesy of Mémorial de Caen.

of Laos (*rasadon Lao*). Whereas the Kaeo Vietminh and Lao-Viet were cast, respectively, as enemy invaders and turncoat collaborators, the Lao people were their victims and heroic resisters.

In the first of Riem Eng's cartoons in August (figure 7.1), a Kaeo Vietminh officer, a Lao-Viet, and the "Lao people" stand atop a cliff. The officer and Lao-Viet gesture to the Lao to march forwards with promises of progress/prosperity (*khwam charoen*), independence, and paradise, but they are in fact walking off the edge of the cliff into an abyss and certain death. The Lao cry that the Vietnamese have tricked them into dying. A caption on the menacing, anthropomorphized cliff, representing the Vietminh, states, "Ha, ha, ha! Come and die for no reason!" In short, the Vietminh were deceiving the Lao people with false promises of liberation and prosperity.[35]

In the second cartoon (figure 7.2) there are two paths: a smooth one labeled "peace," leading to a rising sun; and a rocky one labeled "death," leading to a cave mouth labeled "Vietminh." Standing at the junction of the two paths, different leaders pull the "naive Lao people" in the two directions: royal attendants carrying the Kingdom of Laos's national flag invite them down the "peace" path, while Ong Lao-Viet—or Mr. Lao-Viet, using a

FIGURE 7.2 "Peace" path or "death" path? *Nak Rop Lao*, 1950.
Courtesy of Mémorial de Caen.

respectful Vietnamese kinship term for "Mr."—is about to drag the others down the "death" path using a rope. The captions tell us that there are two types of Lao leaders: those choosing independence and the "Vietnamese headed" (*mi hua kaeo*). While the former lead the Lao people voluntarily toward "the shining light of progress/prosperity," the latter drag them to "the mouth of the Vietminh."[36] The choice for the Lao is stark and, again, the treachery of the Lao-Viet is clear.

The third cartoon (figure 7.3) revolves around a gigantic image of Ho Chi Minh, gesturing forwards while sitting on a palanquin carried by "Lao stooges." More Lao stooges make up a band leading the procession, again fronted by Ong Lao-Viet. Banging cymbals and gongs, the party advances in a raucous procession. "March, march, march! Take him to our country!" (i.e., Laos), cry the stooges (using a respectful pronoun). Asked where they are taking Ho, Ong Lao-Viet replies, "To be the leader of Laos." "What about our own leader?" the Lao onlookers ask. "He's not capable!" comes the retort (using a common pronoun). In this way, the cartoon stokes the sensitive trope of Lao inferiority to the Vietnamese to inflame local fear and hatred. Why, the main caption asks, would the Lao wish for a Vietnamese leader when they have their own king and nobility?[37]

Anti-Vietnamese Xenophobia in 1950s Laos 185

FIGURE 7.3 "Take him to our country." *Nak Rop Lao*, 1950. Courtesy of Mémorial de Caen.

In the fourth cartoon (figure 7.4), size is again used to effect with a giant governor of Vietnamese background leading a band of Lao-Viet underlings dressed in Vietnamese style. When the Vietnamese take over Laos, says the governor, the people of "Lao-Viet country" (*meuang Lao-Viet*) will dress in this style. Aghast Lao onlookers exclaim, "What *is* that style? Whoa! The Lao will turn completely Vietnamese!" The caption below explains that if the Vietminh take Laos, they will change the country's customs, manners, and dress to become Vietnamese, as in this image.[38] Here the primary theme is the fear of losing the culture and traditions that set the Lao apart from the Vietnamese, whose Confucian culture is foreign to the Theravada Buddhist Lao.

Two months later, two more of Riem Eng's cartoons appeared in *Nak Rop Lao*. In the first (figure 7.5), a "Kaeo Vietminh" soldier barks at a group of Lao people sitting on the ground in fear. "We're brothers. We must help each other achieve independence," he cries. Standing behind the Lao, two sycophantic Lao-Viet agree, but the ordinary Lao people are not convinced. How can the Lao get independence, they cry, when the Vietminh "come and kill Lao like that!" referring to two more Kaeo Vietminh soldiers torturing another Lao person behind the first Kaeo Vietminh. The theme of this cartoon

186   Simon Creak

FIGURE 7.4 "Whoa! The Lao will turn completely Vietnamese!" *Nak Rop Lao*, 1950. Courtesy of Mémorial de Caen.

FIGURE 7.5 "We must help each other achieve independence." *Nak Rop Lao*, 1950. Courtesy of Mémorial de Caen.

FIGURE 7.6 Vietminh arsonists. *Nak Rop Lao*, 1950. Courtesy of Mémorial de Caen.

is Vietnamese oppression. The caption reads, "The Kaeo Vietminh beat and kill Lao people. They oppress and screw down on the Lao until they die."[39]

In the final cartoon (figure 7.6), more Kaeo Vietminh soldiers are torching a bridge. A Lao schoolchild cries as a schoolhouse across the river also burns. Pulling up in his car across the river, a trader asks what started the fire. How will they make a living now, he asks. The Kaeo Vietminh set the fire, cries a passenger. "It's completely ruined." The child wails because he cannot go to school. Kaeo Vietminh officers tell them all to relax. They will build a new bridge and, besides, they would not want the French to be able to cross.[40] Here the Vietminh are represented as vandals with callous disregard for the Lao people, happy to sabotage livelihoods, schools, and businesses for their own agenda.

Although the editors of *Nak Rop Lao* lauded Riem Eng for his humor and artistic proficiency, the cartoons contained dark and serious themes relating to the Vietnamese and Vietnamese-Lao in Laos, including invasion, domination, crime, destructiveness, and disloyalty. The images were racially charged. In addition to drawing Vietnamese as bulbous and deformed monkey-like figures, with oversized hands, feet, and heads, Riem Eng referred to the Vietminh as "Kaeo"—an ambiguous word historically that was used pejoratively in this context. It appears that, before the emergence of the name "Vietnam" and associated terms such as "Viet," "Kaeo" was a simple descriptive term in the Lao language for Vietnam and the Vietnamese.[41] However, it took on a pejorative tone in the postwar period, precisely when it was compounded in phrases such as "Kaeo Vietminh" (meaning the Vietminh as opposed to other Vietnamese) and "Kaeo-headed Lao leaders." By the time the Pathet Lao seized power in 1975, the term was not just offensive but politically incorrect as the Vietnamese were the senior partner in the *ai-nong* (older brother-younger brother) forces that had defeated the United States, and the most important of Laos's "fraternal socialist countries." After the revolution, therefore, the word "Kaeo" was effectively proscribed in official speech (though it continued to be used in slang). Another cutting term used throughout Riem Eng's drawings was "Lao-Viet." Referring to ethnic Vietnamese in Laos, the "Viet" portion of the phrase implied "not real" Lao: in effect, disloyal or treasonous.

Vernacular Expression of Anticommunism in the Late 1950s

The Lao fear of Vietnamese invasion reached a crescendo in April 1953, when Vietminh–Pathet Lao forces thrust deep into Lao territory and threatened to take Luang Prabang in northern Laos and, later in the year, Thakhek in the south. Mass demonstrations in Vientiane sparked by the Vietminh invasion suggested that fear of Vietnamese invasion was palpable and widespread. In the event, both towns were spared, and the immediate threat receded. The Geneva Accords of 1954 required Vietminh forces to leave Lao territory, and the Pathet Lao's public political wing, the Lao Patriotic Front, joined the first coalition government in 1957. But the respite was short lived. The failed integration of Pathet Lao units into the Lao National Army sparked a new political crisis and military conflict, as well as the return of Vietnamese troops to Laos in 1959. With the global Cold War reaching a crescendo on other fronts, anti-Vietnamese xenophobia re-emerged as a renewed force in Laos.

During this late-1950s period, the perspective of anticommunist warriors in Laos was more internationalized than in 1950. Employing tropes recognizable throughout the anticommunist world, they painted communism as a global scourge, condemning the "communist imperialism" of the Soviet Union and Communist China. Writers emphasized the totalitarian nature of communist rule and the oppressive impact this would have on ordinary Lao people's lives: forced labor, elimination of private property, compulsory military service, and so on. They also stressed the danger communism posed to Buddhism and the monarchy—the most cherished cultural institutions of Laos—and caricatured life in the USSR, the People's Republic of China (PRC), and the Democratic Republic of Vietnam (DRV) as harsh and oppressive.[42] Within this increasingly international outlook, however, the fear of invasion and oppression by the Vietnamese—and, increasingly, the Chinese to the north—remained palpable. To integrate the two perspectives, the Vietnamese and Chinese communists—and their Pathet Lao "lackeys"—were increasingly portrayed as branches of an international movement.

The most important anticommunist organization during this period was the military-dominated Committee for the Defense of National Interests (CDIN). Formed in mid-1958, the CDIN declared it was a civic movement rather than a political party, but it assumed cabinet posts later that year, declared a state of emergency in late 1959, and dominated politics for several years through both constitutional and extraconstitutional means. Preaching a "new breed of anti-communism" that was more militant than earlier expressions, the CDIN launched a cultural crusade in defense of the Lao nation and race.[43] Cartoons in the CDIN newspaper, *Lao Hakxa Sat* (Lao Protect the Nation), portrayed Khrushchev and Mao as untrustworthy, duplicitous, and hungry for expansion, and dismissed the neutralism of Nehru and others as dangerous and naive.[44] For Wolfson-Ford, the CDIN represented "the high-water mark of RLG anti-communism."[45]

Despite funding the CDIN received from the US Central Intelligence Agency, Wolfson-Ford stresses the local roots of its anticommunism, particularly "ethnic tensions." As we have seen, this ethnic dimension was not new to the late 1950s; rather, the CDIN combined existing anti-Vietnamese ethnonationalism with growing fears of communist imperialism, particularly Chinese expansion. As Wolfson-Ford explains:

> The CDIN saw the Cold War as a struggle for survival of the tiny Lao state against a mighty Red Sino-Vietnamese tide. For the CDIN, the Cold War in Laos was not a clash of capitalism and Marxism, neither of which was well-established in the country itself, but was in fact a much older conflict in which the Lao fought against the Sino-Vietnamese under the guise of a global Cold War, which was merely a pretext. Marxism served to mask the old idea of Sino-Viet conquest of the Lao.[46]

Images of Vietnamese invasion and domination thus figured prominently in representations of the perceived communist threat. The CDIN viewed Vietnamese military action in Lao territory in the late 1950s, particularly communist efforts to develop what would become the Ho Chi Minh Trail into southern Vietnam, as an effort to restore colonialism in Laos under the Vietnamese. "Colonialism is not dead!" declared a front-page story in *Lao Hakxa Sat*: "It seeks to return to Laos under another form . . . colonialism by the settling of other peoples formerly colonized [i.e., the Vietnamese]. . . . Laos has just freed itself from foreign domination! It does not want to submit to a new [domination] under any form whatsoever. No to the return of colonialism!"[47]

As during the First Indochina War, cartoons provided an effective and emotive means of communicating the perceived threat. Many emphasized the threat posed by "Red China" (Lao: *chin daeng*), as the PRC was dubbed in RLG publications, and communist imperialism in general. Among several cartoons appearing in *Lao Hakxa Sat* in 1959, two examples in June encapsulated this theme. The first image, "New Flowers of Tibet," shows a Buddhist monk, with Lhasa's Potala Palace in the background, watering a grave adorned with a headstone reading "Here lies Tibetan independence," a reference to the Chinese suppression of the Tibetan uprising. With a smiling Mao standing back holding a plough and appraising his handywork, an overweight European—presumably Khrushchev—offers a flower adorned with a small hammer and sickle.[48] The second, "The Order of Hungary Awarded after the Exploits of Tibet," connected events in Tibet to Soviet suppression of the Hungarian revolution in 1956 and, implicitly, to Laos. With armed soldiers and a burning Potala Palace in the background, Khrushchev pins the Order of Hungary medal on Mao's lapel.[49] These cartoons warned not only that Laos might be the next victim of a communist invasion, but that communism represented a grave threat to Buddhism, the religion shared by Tibet and Laos.

These images portraying Chinese designs on neighboring countries came together in a powerful cartoon of September 1959, captioned "Pancha-Shila or Coexistence: 'Translated into Vietnamese or Chinese'" (figure 7.7). In this image, a repulsive-looking, hairy-legged Sino-Vietnamese figure, a communist star and hammer and sickle positioned over his shoulder, crouches on a map of Asia. With his left leg planted in northern Vietnam, his toes seemingly clawing across the unmarked border into Laos, he stretches his enormous and hairy right leg across the Asian continent to India, via Tibet.[50] This cartoon not only raised the specter of Sino-Vietnamese expansionism in Asia, but ridiculed Nehru's misguided neutralism—referenced by the mention of Pancha-Shila, the Five Principles of Peaceful Coexistence, which he had developed in 1954 with Zhou Enlai—in light of China's actions in Tibet. For an informed Lao audience, the cartoon would have evoked expansionist

FIGURE 7.7 "Pancha-Shila or coexistence: 'translated into Vietnamese and Chinese.'" *Lao Hakxa Sat*, 1959.

Sino-Vietnamese designs on Lao territory, the specter of invasion, and the risks of neutralism.

Lao Hakxa Sat was not the only outlet for such views. A mid-1961 cartoon in *Echo de la liberté* (figure 7.8), a small newspaper published by the CDIN's religion minister, Prince Sopsaisana, returned to the more proximate theme of Vietnamese invasion through its Pathet Lao proxies. This simply drawn cartoon of four panels starts with the Pathet Lao's Souphanouvong sitting on a throne, the Kingdom of Laos's coat of arms behind him, and a bowing Ho Chi Minh offering a small missile or bomb. "The Vietminh are at your disposal," says Ho in the first panel (still using the term "Vietminh" to invoke invading Vietnamese). In the next two panels, as he stands up and places his arm around Souphanouvong, Ho adds, "They aid you in the struggle . . . against imperialism. . . ." In the final panel, however, Ho pushes Souphanouvong down and replaces him on the throne, as he adds, ". . . in order to ensure order, peace, and neutrality."[51] As in the earlier works of Riem Eng, this cartoon contains multiple negative images of the Vietnamese—invasion, domination, and duplicitousness—and condemns Souphanouvong and the Pathet Lao for their collaboration. In addition, it ridicules "neutralists"—

FIGURE 7.8 "The Vietminh are at your disposal." *Echo de la liberté*, 1961.

probably the Committee Supporting Policy for Peace and Neutrality—as naive fools for believing the Vietnamese–Pathet Lao alliance could result in anything but a Vietnamese takeover.[52]

Anti-Vietnamese fear and xenophobia reached their zenith between the mid-1960s and early 1970s, as the conflict in Vietnam and Laos escalated to all-out industrial war. As the war intensified and communist forces reinforced the Ho Chi Minh Trail through southeastern Laos, the fear of invasion again appeared to have become a nightmare reality. The anticommunist press in Vientiane blamed the DRV—and its Pathet Lao lackeys—for the war, violence, and destitution that resulted. During this period, the specter of Chinese expansionism retreated as communism became indivisible from "Vietnamese aggression."[53] According to prominent Lao historians Mayoury and Pheuiphanh Ngaosyvathn, a visceral strand of anti-Vietnamese racism emerged for the first time during this period; however, such sentiments had been intensifying since at least 1950.[54]

As noted above, the triumph of the Pathet Lao in 1975 subsequently made anti-Vietnamese racism and xenophobia unutterable at an official level in Laos.[55] Anti-Vietnamese sentiments can still be heard in private, including pejorative use of the offensive term "Kaeo," but these have no obvious connection to the vernacular ideology of the Cold War era. This can be contrasted with members of the Lao diaspora formed through the exodus of RLG officials, soldiers, and teachers. After 1975, these opponents of the Lao People's Revolutionary Party (LPRP), which emerged after the war as the political force behind the Pathet Lao, despaired at the stationing of some 50,000 Vietnamese troops in Laos—officially to pacify anticommunist resistance movements—as evidence that their fear of invasion had come true. With the LPRP and the Communist Party of Vietnam (CPV) remaining each other's closest allies even today, long after the troops' withdrawal in 1990, diasporic communities post amateur historical maps on Facebook representing "Red Laos" as a "colony of Red Vietnam." Such assertions—worthy of a separate study—suggest that for some on the losing side, the Cold War has never really ended, and the contest between communist and anticommunist nationalism will continue for as long as the LPRP retains power and its alliance with the CPV.

Rethinking (Not Removing) Our "Cold War Lens"

It has become a commonplace that local experiences and iterations of the Cold War were imbricated in longer histories of colonialism, decolonization and post-colonial nation building.⁵⁶ Anti-Vietnamese xenophobia born of fear of invasion and colonization certainly made this true of Cold War Laos. In this perspective, it may be tempting to "take off the Cold War lens," in Connelly's influential phrase, and to consider this period of history in Laos in anticolonial terms.⁵⁷ This indeed is the approach of revolutionary historiography, in which the "National Liberation Struggle" or "Thirty-Year Struggle"—as the LPRP calls the three-decade (1945–75) fight against French colonialism and American imperialism—represents a classical narrative of national becoming.⁵⁸ Yet, adopting a narrow nationalist lens has its own problems, since in this narrative, the "Cold War" (Lao: *songkham yen*) refers in an orthodox manner to the Soviet-American confrontation of 1945–91. Even if LPRP historiography links this global confrontation to the American intervention in Indochina, this has the unfortunate effect of making Laos—when considered in a Cold War studies framework—a mere recipient of the global Cold War, albeit in a nationalist rather than orientalist frame.

Rather than taking off the Cold War lens altogether, then, we should rethink which Cold War lens we apply. We gain important insights into local, regional, and global history by considering ethnosocial warfare in Laos as a Cold War struggle rather than as a separate, predominantly national phenomenon. This local social conflict was also intimately connected to the global Cold War in the sense that rival nationalists tended to see themselves as being allied to communist movements elsewhere, or as staunchly opposed to socialist principles and alliances on ideological or nationalist grounds.⁵⁹ In this sense, Cold War Laos was defined by a primary antagonism reflecting the global communist-anticommunist divide—what anthropologist Heonik Kwon refers to as the "bipolar era"—even while it was fundamentally about how these groups viewed the place of the Vietnamese in the Lao nation.

The fact that these ideologies were often expressed in vernacular form does not mean that ideology was not present or that they did not relate to the Cold War. Rather, Vietnamese and communist expansion were conflated as a single threat, with the fear of Vietnamese invasion serving as the most immediate, concrete, familiar, and relatable aspect of communist expansion. While it may be possible to see these events principally in nationalist terms, doing so would sever Laos's domestic links to the global Cold War antagonism—the unifying feature of the global bipolar era—consigning the "real" Cold War to the global north. In this well-rehearsed view, the Cold War (singular) was genetically external to Asia or Southeast Asia, a foreign set of meanings imported through "interventions," such as the US aid program and military operations in Laos. This is deeply misleading. As Kwon emphasizes, "The reality of the global conflict consisted of many locally variant, sometimes mutually contradictory realities."[60] Masuda Hajimu makes a similar point in the introduction to this volume.[61] The challenge for scholars of the Cold War's global south, especially Asia and other locations where the Cold War was violent and deadly, is "revitalizing the semantic struggle against the dominant meaning of the cold war, and beginning to think of it in an alternative, more modern way, free from the hierarchical composition of center and periphery."[62]

To rephrase Connelly's felicitous metaphor, then, our challenge is not so much to take off the Cold War lens, but to ensure we apply a Cold War lens that sharpens and illuminates—and does not obscure or dim—a global south perspective.[63] Implicit in this statement is the existence not only of many Cold Wars, but of multiple Cold War lenses. With many Cold Wars—or experiences of the Cold War—one's conceptualization (or lens) will inevitably vary, too, in a manner that reflects one's concerns or values. To be sure, this makes inevitable a certain relativism and circularity in defining and studying the Cold War. This is unavoidable since the "Cold War" as a label—unlike the bloody conflicts that largely comprised it in Asia and elsewhere—was not an actual war but a metaphor.[64] The metaphorical nature of the Cold War label poses problems in terms of periodization, specificity, and even basic definition, given the violent "hot" wars that killed millions in Cold War Asia and elsewhere.[65] The most basic elements of a metaphorical "war"—its key protagonists, periodization, and ultimately its meaning—are open to interpretation and contestation in a way that those of actual wars are not.

This is not to suggest, however, that all social conflicts that took place during the period of the Cold War should be considered parts of it. Orthodox Cold War scholars such as Federico Romero and Holger Nehring are right to insist that a meaningful definition of the Cold War must be cognizant of its fundamentally antagonistic quality—a point that Kwon echoes despite his vastly different approach.[66] The problem with the orthodox analysis is its insistence that the antagonisms that mattered hierarchically were those that occurred in the North Atlantic "core" of the conflict. On the contrary, the truly global dimension of the Cold War was the way that these antagonisms reproduced themselves throughout the world—as a "global civil war."[67] This does not mean that these fundamental antagonisms were always expressed in the same way, however, or that expressions in the Cold War "periphery" followed those in the "center." Rather, they took on localized or vernacular characteristics, which differed throughout the world. In Laos, anti-Vietnamese xenophobia was a key means through which this antagonism was created and expressed.

Conclusion

This chapter has made two connected arguments. The first is that anti-Vietnamese xenophobia and racism functioned as a vernacular form of anticommunism in Laos. These beliefs can be considered a kind of "vernacular ideology" in the sense that proponents employed locally and historically rooted language and ideas to convey a sense of existential threat to the Lao race and nation. Debates over the true nature of the Vietnamese in Vietnam and Laos—"brothers" in revolution versus grave threat to national territory and patrimony—represented an example of social warfare in Cold War Laos. This preexisting social divide, inflamed by and conflated with the bipolar divisions of the Cold War, helps us to understand a key aspect of the Cold War in Laos: the clash between two irreconcilable views of the nation. The fact that these ideas were expressed in vernacular form does not mean they did not relate to the Cold War; rather, Vietnamese expansion was conflated with communist expansion, the fear of Vietnamese invasion serving as the most immediate, concrete, familiar, and relatable threat of communist expansion.

The second argument, stemming from the first, is broader and more conceptual. While it may be possible to take off the Cold War lens to escape the orientalism of orthodox Cold War narratives, this can have the paradoxical consequence of leaving the Cold War to the global north and again consigning the global south to the Cold War periphery. In this view, Asia and other "peripheries" did not produce the Cold War in any substantial sense but received it through military and other "interventions." Instead, we should carefully rethink our Cold War lens in a way that illuminates the experiences and productions of the Cold War in global south contexts and recognizes their essential function for many people in the world in defining the bipolar era. Implicit in this approach are the recognition that the global Cold War comprised many Cold Wars and the insistence that we continue to unsettle traditional hierarchies between Cold War "core" and "periphery." As a metaphor rather than an actual war—notwithstanding the existence of many "Cold War" real wars—the Cold War label has always lent itself to interpretation. Granted, the recognition of multiple Cold Wars and its corollary, the existence of multiple Cold War lenses varying with one's values, exposes the field to an inherent relativism and circularity. If we cannot avoid this relativism and circularity, we can recognize and embrace it, while also insisting on conceptual specificity that recognizes the fundamentally antagonistic quality of the bipolar era.

Notes

1. For example, Arthur Dommen, *Conflict in Laos: The Politics of Neutralization* (London: Pall Mall Press, 1964); Hugh Toye, *Laos: Buffer State or Battleground* (London: Oxford University Press, 1968); and Arthur Dommen, *The Indochinese Experience of the French and the Americans: Nationalism and Communism in Cambodia, Laos, and Vietnam* (Bloomington: Indiana University Press, 2001). This tendency was—and still is—especially pronounced in studies of US foreign policy in Cold War Laos. See Seth Jacobs, *The Universe Unraveling: American Foreign Policy in Cold War Laos* (Ithaca, NY: Cornell University Press, 2012); and William J. Rust, *Before the Quagmire: American Intervention in Laos, 1954-1961* (Lexington: University Press of Kentucky, 2012).

2. For the Pathet Lao movement, see Christopher Goscha, "Vietnam and the World Outside: The Case of the Vietnamese Communist Advisers in Laos (1948-62)," *South East Asia Research* 12, no. 2 (2004): 141-85; Vatthana Pholsena, "The (Transformative) Impacts of the Vietnam War and the Communist Revolution in a Border Region in Southeastern Laos," *War & Society* 31, no. 2 (2012): 163-83; Martin Rathie, "History and Evolution of the Lao People's Revolutionary Party," in *Changing Lives in Laos: Society, Politics and Culture in a Post-Socialist State*, ed. Vanina Bouté and Vatthana Pholsena (Singapore: NUS Press, 2017), 19-55; Vatthana Pholsena, "War Generation: Youth Mobilization and Socialization in Revolutionary Laos," in *Changing Lives in Laos: Society, Politics and Culture in a Post-Socialist State*, ed. Vanina Bouté and Vatthana Pholsena (Singapore: NUS Press, 2017), 109-34; and Patrice Ladwig, "'Special Operation Pagoda': Buddhism, Covert Operations and the Politics of Religious Subversion in Cold War Laos," in *Changing Lives in Laos: Society, Politics and Culture in a Post-Socialist State*, ed. Vanina Bouté and Vatthana Pholsena (Singapore: NUS Press, 2017), 81-108. In my own work, I have examined the significance of revolutionary rhetoric in producing the "cosmology of socialist Laos" and particularly the communist regime's "binary socialist mentality"—its ironclad distinction between the "American imperialists" and their Lao "lackeys," on the one hand, and the virtuous new society created by the Pathet Lao, on the other. Simon Creak, "Abolishing Illiteracy and Upgrading Culture: Adult Education and Revolutionary Hegemony in Socialist Laos," *Journal of Contemporary Asia* 48, no. 5 (2018): 761-82; and *Embodied Nation: Sport, Masculinity, and the Making of Modern Laos* (Honolulu: University of Hawai'i Press, 2015), 190. For the Kingdom of Laos, see Ryan Wolfson-Ford, "Ideology in the Royal Lao Government-Era (1945-75): A Thematic Approach" (PhD diss., University of Wisconsin–Madison, 2018), published in revised form as Ryan Wolfson-Ford, *Forsaken Causes: Liberal Democracy and Anticommunism in Cold War Laos* (Madison: University of Wisconsin Press, 2024). Parts of Wolfson-Ford's thesis and

especially his book explore similar terrain to this chapter. The current chapter, which was drafted in early 2019 and revised in mid-2021, draws mostly on Wolfson-Ford's thesis. For additional reappraisals of the RLG era, see Sophie Sidwell, "A New Interpretation of Kong Le's Neutralist Coup in Laos," *Sojourn: Journal of Social Issues in Southeast Asia* 35, no. 1 (2020): 1–30; Creak, *Embodied Nation*, chap. 4–5; and Simon Creak, "Sport and the Theatrics of Power in a Postcolonial State: The National Games of 1960s Laos," *Asian Studies Review* 34, no. 2 (2010): 191–210.

3. Wolfson-Ford, "Ideology."

4. On race and ethnicity as "social warfare," see Masuda Hajimu, *Cold War Crucible: The Korean Conflict and the Postwar World* (Cambridge, MA: Harvard University Press, 2015), chap. 7, esp. 206–8. On the transnational Cold War politics of race, ethnicity, and loyalty among Chinese overseas in Southeast Asia, see Taomo Zhou, *Migration in the Time of Revolution China, Indonesia, and the Cold War* (Ithaca, NY: Cornell University Press, 2019); Chien Wen Kung, *Diasporic Cold Warriors: Nationalist China, Anticommunism, and the Philippine Chinese, 1930s–1970s* (Ithaca, NY: Cornell University Press, 2022); Nu Anh Tran, "Denouncing the 'Việt Cộng': Tales of Revolution and Betrayal in the Republic of Vietnam," *Journal of Southeast Asian Studies* 53, no. 4 (2022): 686–708; and Wen-Qing Ngoei, *Arc of Containment: Britain, the United States, and Anticommunism in Southeast Asia* (Ithaca, NY: Cornell University Press, 2019).

5. Ryan Wolfson-Ford, "Nativism and Nationalism in the Remaking of Lao Anticommunism," Paper presented at the Society for Historians of American Foreign Relations Annual Meeting, New Orleans, Louisiana, June 18, 2020; see also Wolfson-Ford, "Ideology."

6. For the term "others within," used in a different way, see Thongchai Winichakul, "The Others Within: Travel and Ethno-Spatial Differentiation of Siamese Subjects 1885–1910," in *Civility and Savagery: Social Identity in Tai States*, ed. Andrew Turton (Richmond, UK: Curzon, 2000), 38–62.

7. Donald Haekwon and Ronald R. Sundstrom, "Xenophobia and Race," *Critical Philosophy of Race* 2, no. 1 (2014): 23.

8. Wolfson-Ford, *Forsaken Causes*, chap. 5.

9. See Marta Gil, "Emotions and Political Rhetoric: Perception of Danger, Group Conflict and the Biopolitics of Fear," *Human Affairs* 26, no. 2 (2016): 212–26; see also Barbara H. Rosenwein, "Worrying about Emotions in History," *American Historical Review* 107, no. 3 (2002): 836, on "basic emotions" like fear and anger, and the cultural factors that shape them.

10. Gil, "Emotions and Political Rhetoric," 213.

11. Barbara Keys, "Emotions in Intercultural Relations," in *Asia Pacific in the Age of Globalization*, ed. Robert David Johnson (London: Palgrave Macmillan), 215.

12. Ryan Wolfson-Ford, "Strangers in the Hills: Social Disruption and the Origins of Lao Nationalism (1873–1911)," *South East Asia Research* 25, no. 4 (2017): 412–30. Following Goscha, it would be more accurate to use "Annamese" for the period before 1945, but I use "Vietnamese" for consistency and clarity. Christopher E. Goscha, *Going Indochinese: Contesting Concepts of Space and Place in French Indochina* (Copenhagen: NIAS Press, 2012).

13. Goscha, *Going Indochinese*, 13.
14. Soren Ivarsson, *Creating Laos: The Making of a Lao Space Between Indochina and Siam, 1860-1945* (Copenhagen: NIAS Press, 2008).
15. Ivarsson, *Creating Laos*, 107.
16. Goscha, *Going Indochinese*, 68.
17. Creak, *Embodied Nation*, 1-3.
18. Ivarsson, *Creating Laos*, 109.
19. Vatthana Pholsena, *Post-war Laos: The Politics of Culture, History and Identity* (Singapore: ISEAS Publishing, 2006), 87.
20. Anonymous, "Memoirs of a Young Official (Official M)," in Joel Halpern, "Laos Profiles," Laos Project Paper 19, June 19, 1961.
21. See, for example, "Prince Boun Oum of Champassak," in Halpern, "Laos Profiles," 10.
22. Creak, "Abolishing Illiteracy"; Creak, *Embodied Nation*, 190.
23. Wolfson-Ford, "Ideology," 181.
24. Katay Sasorith, ed., *Le Laos, pivot idéal de la lutte contre le Communisme dans le Sud-Est Asiatique* [Laos: Ideal hub in the struggle against communism in Southeast Asia] (Bangkok: Editions Lao-Issara, 1949), 16. See also Wolfson-Ford, "Ideology," 136.
25. Katay, *Laos, pivot idéal*.
26. Note on the subject of the resignation of Prince Souphanouvong by Katay Don Sasorith, minister of finance, May 12, 1949. Reproduced in MacAlister Brown and Joseph Zasloff, *Apprentice Revolutionaries: The Communist Movement in Laos, 1939-1985* (Stanford, CA: Hoover Institution Press, 1986), 347.
27. Letter to Katay Don Sasorith from Prince Souphanouvong, May 13, 1949. Reproduced in Brown and Zasloff, *Apprentice Revolutionaries*, 356-57.
28. The images and publications discussed in this section were located in the records of Jean Deuve, a French military advisor to the RLG who worked in the counterintelligence and information services and later published books on the war in Laos. See Fonds Deuve, Mémorial de Caen, Caen, France.
29. For elaboration on this point, see Creak, *Embodied Nation*, 100-101.
30. See Bruce Lockhart, "Education in Laos in Historical Perspective," unpublished manuscript, National University of Singapore, 2001; and Creak, "Abolishing Illiteracy."
31. This image is reproduced and discussed in Creak, *Embodied Nation*, 108-9. It can be accessed at Fonds Deuve, dossier 27, Éphémérides et presse local de 1950 (originaux), Mémorial de Caen. It is possible the label "thief" (*chon*) was aimed at denying the Vietminh's political motives, as in Malaya where the British initially labeled Malaya Communist Party guerillas as "bandits." See Philip Deery, "Malaya, 1948: Britain's Asian Cold War?" *Journal of Cold War Studies* 9, no. 1 (2007): 29-54.
32. See also Creak, *Embodied Nation*, chap. 3.
33. *Nak Rop Lao*, no. 6, January 8, 1948, 1-2.
34. *Nak Rop Lao*, no. 39, October 1, 1950, 1. Also see Creak, *Embodied Nation*, 109.
35. *Nak Rop Lao*, no. 37, August 1, 1950, 6.

36. *Nak Rop Lao*, no. 37, August 1, 1950, 6.

37. *Nak Rop Lao*, no. 37, August 1, 1950, 7.

38. *Nak Rop Lao*, no. 37, August 1, 1950, 7.

39. *Nak Rop Lao*, no. 39, October 1, 1950, 6.

40. *Nak Rop Lao*, no. 39, October 1, 1950, 6.

41. The term "Kaeo" may derive from Giao Chi, the former Chinese commandery near Hanoi. I thank Nathan Badenoch, Saowapha Viravong, and Ryan Wolfson-Ford for helpful discussions of this term. See Wolfson-Ford, "Prelude to the Fall: The Monarchy and Three Factions in Seventeenth-Century Laos," paper presented at the Association for Asian Studies (AAS) Annual Conference, Toronto, March 16–19, 2017, 15n48, for an example of "Kaeo" being used in the late nineteenth century.

42. See, for example, "Defense de la civilization lao," *La Tribune des Jeunes* 1, no. 1 (April 15, 1957): 3.

43. Wolfson-Ford, "Ideology," 208–16.

44. See various issues of *Lao Hakxa Sat* in 1959, which featured cartoons with these messages, two of which are referred to below.

45. Ryan Wolfson-Ford, "The Committee for Defense of National Interests: An Anti-communist, Buddhist Nationalist Movement (1958–1960) in Post-colonial Laos," unpublished paper presented at the Interrogating Buddhism and Nationalism workshop, January 28, 2018, Asian Studies Center, University of Oxford.

46. Wolfson-Ford, "Ideology," 208–9.

47. *Lao Hakxa Sat*, no. 28, October 19, 1958, 1, cited in Ryan Wolfson-Ford, "Phoumi Nosavan, the Royal Lao Army, and the Limits of Dictatorship in Democratic Laos, 1958–1964," paper presented at the Association for Asian Studies (AAS) Annual Conference, Denver, March 2019, 10.

48. *Lao Hakxa Sat*, no. 16, June 1–15, 1959, 1.

49. *Lao Hakxa Sat*, no. 17, June 16–30, 1959, 1.

50. *Lao Hakxa Sat*, no. 25, September 28, 1959, 1. See also Wolfson-Ford, "Phoumi Nosavan," 10. I thank Ryan Wolfson-Ford for sharing this source.

51. *Echo de la liberté*, July 26, 1961, 13. See also Wolfson-Ford, "Ideology," 178. I thank Ryan Wolfson-Ford for sharing this source.

52. See Sidwell, "New Interpretation," for discussion of this group.

53. Wolfson-Ford, "Ideology," 416.

54. Mayoury Ngaosyvathn and Pheuiphanh Ngaosyvathn, *Paths to Conflagration: Fifty Years of Diplomacy and Warfare in Laos, Thailand, and Vietnam, 1778–1828* (Ithaca, NY: Cornell University SEAP Publications, 1998), 30.

55. For a discussion of related issues at the 2009 SEA Games in Laos, see Simon Creak, "Sport as Politics and History: The 25th SEA Games in Laos," *Anthropology Today* 27, no. 1 (2011): 14–19.

56. See, for example, Prasenjit Duara, "The Cold War as a Historical Period: An Interpretive Essay," *Journal of Global History* 6 (2011): 457–80; Tuong Vu, "Cold War Studies and the Cultural Cold War in Asia," in *Dynamics of the Cold War in Asia*, ed. Tuong Vu and Wasana Wongsurawat (New York: Palgrave Macmillan, 2009), 1–16; Odd Arne Westad, *The Cold War: A World History* (New York: Basic Books, 2017);

and Christopher E. Goscha and Christian Osterman, *Connecting Histories: Decolonization and the Cold War in Southeast Asia* (Washington, DC: Wilson Center Press, 2009).

57. Matthew Connelly, "Taking Off the Cold War Lens: Visions of North-South Conflict during the Algerian War for Independence," *American Historical Review* 105, no. 3 (2000): 739–69.

58. Oliver Tappe, "Faces and Facets of the *Kantosou Kou Xat*—The Lao 'National Liberation Struggle' in State Commemoration and Historiography," *Asian Studies Review* 37, no. 4 (2013): 433–50.

59. As Wolfson-Ford argues, virtually all political figures and groups in Laos—besides the Pathet Lao—were explicitly anticommunist, including so-called neutralists. Wolfson-Ford, "Ideology," 179.

60. Heonik Kwon, "Experiencing the Cold War," in *Experiencing War*, ed. Christine Sylvester (London: Routledge, 2010), 91. For elaboration, see Kwon, *The Other Cold War* (New York: Columbia University Press, 2010).

61. See Masuda's introduction to this edited volume, "Reconceptualizing the Cold War: On-the-Ground Experiences in Asia."

62. Kwon, "Experiencing the Cold War," 91. Kwon writes "cold war" in lowercase.

63. For all the impact of Connelly's article, he still writes about US foreign policy from an American perspective. Connelly, "Cold War Lens."

64. Kwon, *Experiencing the Cold War*, makes a similar point about the difference between a real war and the Cold War as an "imaginary war," though he does not call it a metaphor.

65. Kwon, "Experiencing the Cold War"; see also Kwon, *The Other Cold War*.

66. Federico Romero, "Cold War Historiography at the Crossroads," *Cold War History* 14, no. 4 (2014): 690; and Holger Nehring, "What Was the Cold War?" *English Historical Review* 127, no. 527 (2012): 923.

67. Heonik Kwon, *After the Korean War: An Intimate History* (Cambridge: Cambridge University Press, 2020), 57–58.

Part III **Individual Hope, Negotiation, and Trauma**

8 Bodyguards of the US Military?
The Voices of US-Educated Okinawans, 1949–72

KINUKO MAEHARA-YAMAZATO

During the US military occupation of Okinawa (1945–72), the US government was involved in a wide range of educational and cultural activities in the occupied islands. The US military scholarship program to send students to the United States for higher education was one such activity. Between 1949 and 1972, more than a thousand Okinawans were given the opportunity to study at American higher education institutions. Most Okinawans on US military scholarships studied in the fields of social sciences, humanities, and education; the top three majors were business administration, teaching English as a second language, and economics. Under the US occupation, having a degree from the United States was highly regarded and gave these Okinawans an employment advantage. Upon returning from the United States, many US-educated Okinawans worked in the fields of higher education, business, and politics. In general, they held higher status and had privileges that distinguished them from other Okinawans. They became collectively known as the *beiryu-gumi* (US student group).

This study analyzes the life stories of Okinawans who received US military scholarships to study in the United States during the occupation. The US military used this study-abroad program with the explicit intention of educating future Okinawan leaders who could understand and support the US administration of Okinawa, creating a leadership amenable to control by the occupying military government. This chapter, however, focuses not on such intentions but on the experiences and perspectives of the Okinawans. It provides an understanding of how Okinawans experienced the study-abroad program. While acknowledging that the scholarship program was an integral part of US Cold War strategy, I present the experiences and emotions of those who participated in their own words and show how they express their perceptions of the program, as well as their views of their own lives under the US military occupation. This paper attempts to show how documenting and analyzing the study-abroad participants' narratives allows them to be understood not as passive actors of Cold War cultural propaganda, but as active agents who took advantage of the opportunities available for their own purposes to live in US-occupied Okinawa during the Cold War.

The US study-abroad program was not unique to postwar Okinawa. As noted in previous studies, cultural and educational exchange programs were a significant US Cold War strategy in Asia.[1] In what Christina Klein called a "global imaginary of integration" among allied societies, these programs worked to represent idealized images of the United States and to "win the hearts and minds" of people.[2] Studies on US-Japan cultural diplomacy have also revealed how information and education policies initiated by the US government were designed to reeducate Japanese, mainly targeting intellectuals and educators, which led to the construction of a pro-US Japan.[3] Shibusawa showed further that, to foster American public support for policies regarding postwar Japan, government-sponsored study-abroad programs, such as Government Aid and Relief in Occupied Areas (GARIOA) scholarships, represented Japanese students as "junior allies in the Far East" and "students of democracy needing US guidance and mentoring."[4]

This chapter first shows how the US study-abroad program in Okinawa was part of the US project to rehabilitate the educational system in the war-devastated islands while also working as a US Cold War strategy to develop leaders who would support the US administration in occupied Okinawa. Based on my analysis of official documents concerning the program, I illuminate how the US government used the program to educate Okinawan youth, promote the American way of life, and foster the ideology of democracy in Okinawa. The program was important for the United States' continued occupation of Okinawa to secure the territory as a base for its military presence in Asia during the Cold War. In addition, based on my analysis of practices of recruitment, scrutiny, and patronization of Okinawans who studied in the United States, this chapter shows how the occupation operated as a continuation of colonialism. The US military viewed Okinawans as inferior, dependent, and indecisive people who needed US guidance to achieve civilized status. Such Orientalist views were evident in the practices of the study-abroad program and worked to justify the occupation.

The second part of this chapter focuses on the experiences and emotions of the beiryu-gumi. While the US-centered Cold War framework is helpful in understanding the US military's intentions in establishing the program and its views of Okinawans, it does not capture the complexity of the views of Okinawans toward the program. The US-centered Cold War approach sees the US military as the key actor in the creation of the Cold War order in occupied Okinawa, while the beiryu-gumi are seen as simple tools—nothing more than people manipulated by US interests. However, the study-abroad program created a relatively high level of interest and competition among Okinawan youth. It received approximately 200 applications each year, with less than a quarter successfully gaining places. For example, for the 1962–63 program, there were 207 applicants, of whom 35 were selected to study abroad; for the 1963–64 program, there were 197 applicants and 42 were selected.[5] What were their emotions and motivations as they pursued US higher education, particularly those who had been indoctrinated in anti-Americanism and fought in the war as Japanese soldiers? How did they experience their US studies? Were they simply "pro-Americans" or "bodyguards of the US military," as often described to the public? What were their social roles after returning from the United States, and what feelings did they have toward Americans, Japanese, other local Okinawans, and other beiryu-gumi?

Reexamining Cold War Okinawa from the perspective of individuals rather than that of the US government or military authority is worthwhile because it helps us to achieve a better understanding and reconceptualization of the Cold War on the basis of individuals' interpretations of the postwar world, as well as the choices they made, which were situated in their own social dynamics.[6] As Masuda Hajimu has argued, taking a biographical approach to the Cold War shows that it was a "social construction of an imagined reality, in which many people participated in restoring order and harmony through marginalizing disagreements at home."[7] This chapter attempts to illustrate this through the eyes of US-educated Okinawans to reveal their desires, feelings, and choices, and to show how the beiryu-gumi came to participate in and shape the Cold War in Okinawa.

The life-story method is crucial to this research. As defined by Daniel Bertaux, it is an approach to studying a life, or a life as told.[8] Analyzing people's life stories illuminates the intersections between individuals and society. It allows us to understand how the Okinawans' stories of their lives under the occupation reflect their views of themselves, America, and Okinawa. As Okinawan Americanist Miyagi Etsujiro has emphasized, postwar Okinawa was not merely a site where Americans viewed Okinawans, but a site where Americans, Japanese, and Okinawans viewed each other and built their self-images based on the gazes of the others.[9] An analysis of this tripartite relationship has importance in the study of postwar Okinawa.

This study also contributes to postwar Okinawa studies. Previous research has focused on Okinawans' struggles against and resistance to Japanese and American power, and on various cultural and social movements in which the people of Okinawa challenged colonization and militarization.[10] Annmaria Shimabuku showed the interdependence of US-Japan colonialism in Okinawa and argued that Okinawans' resistance to the ongoing problem of US military bases should be understood as resistance toward this "mutual colonialism."[11] Yamazato Katsunori similarly claimed that postwar Okinawa can be better understood through the lens of cross-cultural contact, rather than a neat categorization of occupied versus occupier, to reveal the complex dynamics of cultural contacts and conflict, influence and confluence, fusion and confusion, and coercion and inequalities that postwar Okinawa experienced.[12] Through examining the life stories of Okinawans who received education in the United States, this chapter centers on the personal experiences and emotions that were shaped by the postwar social dynamics in Okinawa. The goal is to unravel the connections between these emotions and their alignment with occupation policies, with a specific focus on the United States' establishment and practice of the study-abroad program for Okinawan youth.

This chapter focuses on the early 1950s and examines how the beiryugumi students negotiated their social and political positions through study-abroad programs.[13] My analysis shows how they took advantage of study-abroad opportunities to address their own needs and to create strategies to live in US-occupied Okinawa. Their narratives of their motivations to study in the United States demonstrate their abhorrence of Japanese militarism, which had brought about the war, the devastation of Okinawa, and the loss of many lives. Their narratives also highlight their aspirations for higher education and career achievement, which had not been possible under Japanese administrative rule before the US occupation. They also reflect on their positive experiences in the United States and interactions with Americans, which they clearly separate from support for the US military occupation of Okinawa or anticommunism; the interviewees express a sense of appreciation for their encounters with American civilians in the United States, which were distinctly different from encounters with US military personnel in Okinawa. In fact, while studying abroad, they encountered others' understandings of the problems of the US occupation of their homeland such as human rights violations and gained knowledge and perspectives that led them to challenge the situation in postwar Okinawa.

Recruitment, Scrutiny, and Patronization of Cold War Leaders

Lasting from April to June 1945, the Battle of Okinawa was one of the bloodiest ground battles during the Pacific War, resulting in many deaths among the Japanese and American forces. During the battle, more civilians were killed than were soldiers on both sides combined. Okinawa was used as a strategic site for both the United States' and Japan's military operations during the war: for the United States, as a base to launch an invasion of Japan, and for Japan, as a place to take a stand to prevent it. When Japan surrendered at the end of the war in 1945, Okinawa was placed under US military occupation for twenty-seven years until 1972. It was governed first by the US Military Government of the Ryukyu Islands (1951) and then by the US Civil Administration of the Ryukyu Islands (1950–72). While the occupation of Japan ended in 1952, following the San Francisco Peace Treaty of 1951, Okinawa remained under US administration for another twenty years. Even after *Nihonn Fukki*, or Okinawa's reversion to Japanese administration in 1972, Okinawa was still the site of a large US military presence, which remains today, due to the US-Japan Status of Forces Agreement, despite many Okinawans' hopes.

The postwar educational rehabilitation of the Ryukyu Islands by the US military government began before 1948, when the US Navy administered the islands. The US Navy's report on military activities from April 1945 to July 1946 summarized the educational situation in Okinawa and noted that the educational system had been restored to its prewar level by July 1946 because of the Navy's efforts. This rehabilitation during the early years was intended to ensure that "all matters having [a] nationalistic or militaristic tendency were strictly forbidden."[14] The report also noted that "school texts were strictly censored to guard against any undesirable content prejudicial to American ideals and polities."[15]

The Navy listed four items in its report as tasks of great importance to turn over to the US Army, which administered the islands from July 1946 until the end of the US occupation in 1972. These tasks included determination of the future political status of the Ryukyus, finding a solution for their overpopulation, and the integration of the whole of the Ryukyus into a unified political entity. A fourth item was also listed: "provisions for educating young Ryukyuan men and women abroad to take the place of their elders engaged in the professions in the Ryukyus." However, the US government was not willing to fund a rehabilitation program until 1949 because of the Ryukyus' uncertain political status.

In 1949, the United States began underwriting rehabilitation projects to secure Okinawa as America's "keystone of the Pacific" and as a critical strategic site for US military expansion amid the Cold War in Asia and the Pacific. To avoid appearing to be colonizers, the US military's direct government rule was replaced by the US Civil Administration of the Ryukyus Islands (USCAR), and the Ryukyu government was also established. However, the USCAR was still a subordinate organization of the US armed forces and overall control by the US military government remained unchanged.

In the same year, the US military government began sending Okinawans to the United States for higher education. The Education Department of the Office of the High Commissioner of the USCAR later took over program administration. That year, two Okinawans were sent to the United States, supported by the GARIOA fund, which was mainly dedicated to the rehabilitation and economic development of the war-devastated islands. In 1950, the United States provided a larger amount of GARIOA funds to send approximately 53 students, followed by 53 and 76 in 1951 and 1952, respectively (figure 8.1). From 1949 to 1972, the Education Department of the Army sent approximately 1,045 Okinawan students to the United States.[16] Most were men, though approximately 10 percent were women. Under Japanese administrative rule, there was no postsecondary educational institution in Okinawa, except for a normal school (*shihan gakko*) for training teachers. Therefore, those who wanted to study at higher education institutions needed to go to mainland Japan, but opportunities were limited. Therefore, the US study-abroad program was met with a high level of interest and competition among Okinawans.

However, the first Okinawans to study abroad in the postwar period were those who received scholarships from the diasporic Okinawan community in Hawaiʻi. Okinawans in Hawaiʻi were the first to extend aid to war-devastated Okinawa after the end of the Asia-Pacific War and the devastation of the Battle of Okinawa. They established the Okinawa Relief and Rehabilitation Foundation to coordinate their relief efforts, collecting donations from Okinawans across the Hawaiian Islands—including pigs, goats, clothing, books, and school supplies—and sending them to Okinawa. The relief programs also included support for the establishment of a new university in Okinawa, although this was realized by the US military government in 1950. In addition, in 1948, the Okinawa Relief and Rehabilitation Foundation gave five Okinawans an opportunity to study at the University of Hawaiʻi for one year.

FIGURE 8.1 Okinawan students departing for the United States on July 15, 1952. In total, seventy-six students, including one of the interviewees, M. Y., departed for the United States from the White Beach Naval Base on Okinawa Island. Courtesy of Okinawa Prefectural Archives.

The US military scrutinized the activities of the Okinawan students sent to Hawai'i because the organization was "suspected of being controlled by persons of pro-Communist leanings."[17] A further investigation was called for, and the scholarship program only lasted for one year. Having established its own program to send Okinawan students to the United States, the US military continued to investigate communist tendencies among program applicants. Many interviewees recounted that they were fearful of the CIA investigating their political affiliations and those of their families and relatives. They knew that if they had participated in anti-US movement activities or expressed any communist ideas, they would not be able to go to the United States. A female interviewee who studied in the United States from 1967 to 1969 observed, "We can say that those who were educated in the United States during the US occupation of Okinawa were those who did not participate in the movement to claim Okinawa's human rights when others did."[18]

Program participants were aware of being situated within these political dynamics and had accordingly strategically chosen not to actively engage in the political movements of the time. Many interviewees recalled rumors of CIA spies among the university students; thus, being apolitical was an important strategy for their access to US higher education.

All applicants were required to take written exams and be interviewed. They were assessed by USCAR staff. A high degree of English proficiency was one of the most important requirements for success. Before leaving for the United States, selected students underwent intensive language and culture training, which involved around 150 hours of classes.[19] While 75 hours were spent on improving English skills, the remaining half of the time was divided between studying American history and learning about the American people, government, economics, culture, and the college system.[20]

If applicants passed the first screening, they underwent a second one, which was a strict physical checkup. Some male participants had bitter memories of their physical examinations. One, who studied abroad in 1970, described it as a "most humiliating experience."[21] He recalled being asked to disrobe so that his penis could be checked for evidence of venereal disease and being required to parade naked in front of several American doctors. Even when they passed the physical exams, final results would not be given to applicants. There were even some who passed all screenings, with passports to the United States ready, but, on the day of departure, were told, without any explanation, that they would not be able to leave the islands.

For those who were successful in being permitted to leave for the United States, another preparatory course at the Orientation Center at Mills College in Oakland, California, was mandatory on arrival in the United States, before they were sent to their assigned university or college. Mills College was exclusively used for Okinawan students. The six-week program was sponsored by the Department of Defense in cooperation with the Institute of International Education and designed to further improve students' English skills and expose them to American culture through several extracurricular activities, such as visiting the local city hall, factories, and supermarkets.

Reading a review of the 1954 orientation program for thirty-one Okinawan students at Mills College indicates how the American organizers of the program viewed the students. The orientation staff and professors commented on the "psychological barriers" between the Okinawan students and Americans and noted that they felt inferior to Americans in many ways.[22] Obvious examples were Okinawans who used "sir" to address all American men in any position, even those of "the most modest authority," and their insistence on standing when talking with Americans. "This group still suffers strongly from feelings of inferiority and certain underlying personality characteristics of a defensive nature resulting from their experiences in the isolated area from which they came. There is also a marked attitude of subservience toward authority. This last point is particularly noticeable with Ryukyuan students who come from a group that has now come of age under US military influences if not occupation per se. Such influences though strongly paternalistic are nevertheless inadvertently an inhibiting factor in encouraging individual personality development."[23] The report proposed that university professors invite Okinawan and American students to their homes for dinner and informal conversations to help the Okinawans build friendly relationships with their American peers. However, the Okinawans were observed to limit their activities to the campus. The report recommended hiring a junior counselor the same age as the Okinawans to help strengthen the program's aims and overcome the disadvantage of isolation from American students.[24] As the report indicated, the American staff made great efforts to build closer relationships between the Okinawan and American students to help the Okinawans overcome their sense of inferiority.

After Okinawan students returned home, their social roles and career paths were often determined by the USCAR. This was particularly the case for earlier participants. Their US academic accomplishments were valued in occupied Okinawa, especially by those who worked for American-affiliated companies, such as the Bank of the Ryukyus, and the civil government. Furthermore, US officials supported the activities of the Golden Gate Club, an alumni association established in 1952 by earlier returnees (figure 8.2). This club became a place for the US military personnel to meet and collaborate with returned students. Club members' gatherings were usually held at Harbor View, an exclusive officers' club belonging to the US military. The privilege of being able to enter Harbor View created a shared sense among returnees of their difference from other Okinawans.

Even High Commissioners often gave speeches at the Golden Gate Club and emphasized that beiryu-gumi were the leaders of Okinawa. On September 1, 1959, for example, High Commissioner General Donald Booth gave a speech on "The Future of the Ryukyu Islands," in which he referred to US-educated Okinawans as "the future leaders" of the Ryukyu Islands.[25]

FIGURE 8.2 Golden Gate Club members' meeting with General Paul Caraway, high commissioner of the USCAR, on March 11, 1961. The man shaking hands is one of the interviewees, M. Y., the former president of the Golden Gate Club. Courtesy of Okinawa Prefectural Archives.

The next high commissioner, General Paul Caraway, gave even stronger praise at the club's monthly meeting on March 5, 1963, though his speech backfired. This was because, while strongly commending club members as highly sophisticated and praiseworthy for their contributions to developing mutual understanding between people in Okinawa and the United States, he referred to ordinary Okinawans who worked for the Government of Ryukyu Islands as lacking efficiency and further belittled the "autonomy" of the Ryukyus under the occupation as a "myth."[26] The speech was strongly criticized by local newspapers. In the context of the occupation and the political tensions in Okinawa at the time, Caraway's speech worsened the public's perceptions of US-educated Okinawans, adding credence to the general public's view of them as "pro-American" or the "bodyguards of the US military."[27]

Early Participants' Life Stories

This section presents the life stories of three beiryu-gumi who studied in the United States in the 1950s. First, however, I would like to share my experience of collecting their life stories in order to discuss Okinawans' openness and hesitation in sharing their stories. For my oral history interviews, I located interviewees using a snowball sampling strategy. That is, I asked personal acquaintances who were US study-abroad program participants to refer me to other participants who might be interested in sharing their experiences with me. Because the US occupation is still a sensitive topic in Okinawa due to the continuing presence of US military bases and related social problems, this sampling method was the most appropriate for my research because an introduction from a previous interviewee allowed me to easily develop a rapport, and it was culturally appropriate.[28]

Despite using this method, developing a rapport with some interviewees remained challenging. During my initial contact, I noticed that some were sensitive about being interviewed about their experiences due to being investigated by the CIA previously. One was suspicious of my project and asked where I received my funding. He rejected my request by saying that it was a delicate subject and told me about his experiences of being interrogated by Americans about his US experience upon returning to Okinawa. To overcome these challenges, I shared my own study-abroad experiences, which allowed them to feel more comfortable when we started their interviews. I introduced myself by saying that I was born and raised in Okinawa and had attended a local university there, and that I had been a recipient of a US government scholarship to study in Hawai'i. I also told them about the scholarships that young Okinawan students receive today and some of the experiences that they have in their studies.

When conducting some initial interviews, I noticed that physical space was very important for the interviewees to be able to recount their memories. Therefore, I asked them to choose preferred times and places for interviews, which I conducted in both public and private places, such as hotel lounges, coffee shops, and the interviewees' houses. The public place most often chosen by interviewees was the lounge of the former Harbor View hotel where Golden Gate Club members used to meet. The other public place they chose was the Place House, where female interviewees used to go shopping during the occupation because it was the first American-style shopping mall. I was also often invited to interviewees' houses to conduct interviews. On the day of their interview, some male interviewees wore

T-shirts from their university alma maters. They told me about their visits as alumni to their universities after retirement, which became a good icebreaker.

The first interviewee was M. Y., who studied political science in Oregon from 1952 to 1955. Upon returning to Okinawa, he became president of the Golden Gate Club and worked closely with General Paul Caraway to improve the US study-abroad program by promoting it in Okinawa and improving returned students' career pathways.[29] The second interviewee was M. O., who participated in the program in 1951 after surviving the Battle of Okinawa as a student soldier. After the war, he studied in Tokyo for his bachelor's degree in 1950 and later received his study-abroad scholarship and studied journalism for his master's degree. He worked as a professor at the University of the Ryukyus and became a governor of Okinawa. He was devoted to the promotion of peace and later publicly opposed the continued presence of US military bases.[30] The final interviewee was Y. A., who participated in the US study-abroad program in 1950. He also survived the Battle of Okinawa as a student soldier. After the war, he received a scholarship to study psychology in the United States and worked as a professor at the University of the Ryukyus. Y. A. became an important figure in Okinawa, where he established a local university. Peace was included as one of the university's missions and he taught a class focused on it.[31]

M. Y.'s Life Story

My first meeting with M. Y. was on August 6, 2010. He was born in Ishigaki, one of the Yaeyama Islands, in 1928. His father passed away when he was seven years old, and his mother raised him alongside his two older sisters. He attended elementary school in Ishigaki and then moved to Okinawa Island to pursue further education at a junior high school in Naha. The Pacific arena of World War II had begun when he arrived in Naha. By his third year of high school, he and his classmates were seldom at school because they were helping construct roads and an airport for the Japanese Army. In September 1944, with the war looming closer to Japan, his mother encouraged him to evacuate to Taiwan to continue his education. Before he could evacuate, however, he visited Yaeyama and became stuck there because of the outbreak of the Battle of Okinawa in April 1945. Despite these setbacks, his aspirations toward higher education remained strong. He recalled that his experience of the war on Yaeyama was not as severe as those who experienced it on Okinawa, although many Yaeyama Islanders suffered from malaria and many died. He graduated from junior high school in Yaeyama in 1946 and worked on his mother's farm, but he studied every night after work because he wanted higher education. In those days under the US occupation, however, travel between islands was restricted and it was difficult to pursue higher education on the Japanese mainland.

In 1946, M. Y. heard about Chyogi Miyara, former head of the Yaeyama subprefecture office, who had resigned because of his difficult relationship with American officials. The mayor and many municipal staff members had also resigned; therefore, positions were suddenly available at the municipal office. M. Y. applied to work for the new mayor, Kozen Yoshino. Then, in 1948, he resigned his position to attend the Okinawa Foreign Language School in Gushikawa on Okinawa Island, which had been newly opened by the US military government for training translators and interpreters. During the immediate postwar period, before study-abroad programs for Japan and the United States were established, the only postsecondary school for young Okinawan elites was the Foreign Language School, where they could take part in an intensive training program to become interpreters. M. Y. spent two years there learning English. Afterwards, he returned to Yaeyama to work as an interpreter for the mayor, Yoshino. In the first elections held on the island in 1950, however, Yoshino lost the mayoral elections to the former mayor, Miyara. Subsequently, M. Y. resigned.

After working for two years as an interpreter for the Yaeyama civil government, M. Y. passed the exam for the US study-abroad program. He then studied political science in Oregon from 1952 to 1956. When asked why he chose to study in the United States, he observed that he wanted to study in mainland Japan but could not do so. Therefore, as an alternative, he studied in the United States: "I wanted to attend higher education in Japan but going to Tokyo required too much study. At the Foreign Language School, many other students studied hard so that they could go to the mainland. However, I served as a president of the student union and could not focus on my studies. After graduating from the Okinawa Foreign Language School, I returned to Yaeyama and worked as an interpreter. My English skills were much needed because of the US occupation. My senior peers from the Foreign Language School also encouraged me to study in the United States."[32] M. Y. remembered the day of his departure to the United States very well. He was about to board the ship for the United States, but was suddenly told by a US officer, without any reason, that he could not leave. To this day, he does not know the reason, but he assumed that it was because of his service as a student leader for the Foreign Language School, where he compiled all of the students' complaints in order to improve conditions at the school. For example, there was no electricity for a long period, and he worked very hard to secure an electricity supply. Deeply disappointed at not being able to leave for the United States, he returned to Yaeyama. At that time, he thought that he would never try again to study in the United States. In 1952, however, he was told that he could leave for the United States.

One of the highlights of his four years in Oregon was serving as a cast member in the USCAR's promotional propaganda film *Leader for Tomorrow* in 1959. The film mainly shows the activities of four Okinawan university students at their university, where they come to understand the importance of American democracy and learn about American culture. The film also promoted an idealized masculinity for male US study-abroad students. M. Y. knew that the film was propaganda but felt that showing the actual experiences of the program participants encouraged students to aspire to studying in the United States. Like him, other program participants enjoyed seeing themselves in the film.[33]

Upon returning to Okinawa, he was assigned to work for the USCAR. One of the tasks that he completed during his first two years was to translate the "Melvin Price Report" in 1956.[34] This report explained the importance of the position of Okinawa for US military strategies in Japan and the Philippines. Its release led to an island-wide demonstration because it indicated a permanent lease of land for military use, lump-sum rent payments, and new land acquisitions.

Then, from 1958 to 1965, M. Y. worked for the US Council in Okinawa, during which he also served as president of the Golden Gate Club for three terms, from 1960 to 1963. He was close to General Paul Caraway, high commissioner of the USCAR, and contributed to making the study-abroad programs work more efficiently by conducting surveys with all returning students and sending his recommendations to both the USCAR and the Ryukyu government. He shared an example, explaining that one returnee had worked for the Ryukyu government but had had to quit his job to study in the United States. He wrote recommendation letters to help beiryu-gumi obtain privileged positions. He explains, "Although we had returned from our study in the United States, we did not have any privileges. Now when you say that you have studied in the United States, people admire you, but in those days, American university education was not positively accepted compared to students returning with a university education from mainland Japan. I was the Golden Gate Club president at the time, so I was very close to General Caraway and helped to improve the program. Although General

Caraway received much criticism from the general public, he listened seriously to my requests and suggestions."[35] M. Y. also helped establish a program for younger Okinawans to study on military bases and initiated the establishment of the Ryukyu Foundation, which provided scholarships, promoted academic research for cultural advancement, and assisted in other culture-related projects. He felt a sense of responsibility as a scholarship recipient to contribute to Okinawa after returning home. Many program participants also said that they developed a feeling of obligation to "give back" to Okinawa what they learned in the United States.

After leaving the USCAR, M. Y. worked for the Ryukyu government from 1968 to 1972. After Okinawa was returned to Japan in 1972, he worked for the Esso oil company until his retirement in 1988. During the interview, he reflected on his relationship with US officials: "In looking at the ways in which the Japanese government deals with Okinawan issues, I feel that it was easier to deal with the United States. I guess I am favoring the United States because I worked closely with the Americans. I sometimes argued with some American officials, but we became good friends when the dispute was over. We could say to each other, 'Let's go for a drink.' But this cannot happen with the Japanese. Even if we ask, they will say, 'No, thank you.' It was better to negotiate with the Americans."[36] M. Y.'s narrative shows that he preferred the United States as a partner to work with. Toward the end of the interview, I asked him what the US occupation of Okinawa meant for Okinawans. He replied that although Okinawans had many limitations under the twenty-seven years of the occupation, they could be involved in the administration and gained political, administrative, and economic experience, which differed from the time before it.[37]

M. O.'s Life Story

I conducted my first interview with M. O. on July 28, 2011. M. O. was born on Kume Island in 1925. His father emigrated to Brazil to earn money to send home to raise his family. Growing up on a small island, M. O. always dreamed of leaving to see the outside world. He studied at an elementary school on Kume but, like other top students, soon left the island to attend school in Naha, where he entered the *shihan gakko* (a training school for teachers). He spent one year at this school but spent his weekends working on the Japanese military base. At the end of March 1945, he was drafted into the Japanese Imperial Army as a member of the Student Corps of Blood and Iron for Emperor (*Tekketsu Kinnotai*). Although he was badly injured in the Battle of Okinawa, he survived the war, while many of his classmates died. He felt that postwar life in Okinawa was as miserable for the survivors as the wartime period because of the trauma of war. Some of his classmates suffered mentally for the rest of their lives not just because they experienced the war, but because they survived while their family members died. Thousands of war victims could not be mourned because their bones were never found.

After the war, M. O. attended the Foreign Language School and took an exam to study in the United States and another to study in Japan. He passed the exam for the United States. Furthermore, despite severe local competition to study in Japan, he also passed the exam to study English at Waseda University from 1950 to 1954. He asked a much-respected teacher where he should go. The teacher's advice was to go to Japan first and then to the United States because if he went to the latter first, he might become pro-American. During the interview, he described the general difference between those who had studied in the United States only and those who had studied both in Japan and the United States: "Those of us who studied in Japan could see the United States objectively. However, those who went to the United States as an undergraduate, they became pro-American. They cannot be even critical about the problems of the US military bases."[38]

He recalled that the presence of American soldiers was much less obvious in mainland Japan. He felt that there was less tension on the mainland, and that people had freedom of movement. Although mainland Japan was also under Allied control, he saw Tokyo as being "a totally different place" and "a place of freedom." He could discuss political ideas more freely in Tokyo than on Okinawa, where there was great tension between the local population and US authorities. Under US policies designed to prevent the spread of communism, there were restrictions on Okinawan people's movements and information was censored.

While a sophomore at Waseda University, he and a friend worked together to create a peace memorial monument for survivors, to be sent to Okinawa. Yet, he faced opposition even from his professors because the word "peace" was viewed as associated with communism in postwar Japan. He was told that if he helped create the monument, he might not be able to go to the United States. Despite these warnings, however, he was able to send it to Okinawa in order to heal his homeland.

Although he had passed the US exam, the date of his departure was not given until the very last moment. He knew that the CIA was investigating him, so he was delighted when he heard that he had been accepted to study journalism at Syracuse University, where he studied from 1954 to 1956. He recalled that "studying in the United States allowed me to learn about American democracy and furthermore to learn what it means to be human. I was forced to learn these lessons thoroughly."[39] He came to think this way because he witnessed racial discrimination, as well as Americans' sincerity, during his stay in the United States.

> There was racial segregation. When my friends and I went to the "colored only" bathroom, a white man told us that we should use the ones for the whites. I had to face the issues of racial discrimination in the United States. One day, my Mexican classmate and I noticed that an article in the local newspaper about a crime specified the race of the criminal as being African American, although the newspaper usually did not indicate people's race when whites committed crimes. We brought up this issue to the class and discussed the topic until finally the professor agreed with us. We spoke to the newspaper to criticize their biased journalism. A couple of weeks later, this racial reference was removed from the article. Through this experience, I noticed this as a good aspect of the United States. Another good aspect of the US that I noticed was that Americans treated foreigners like us the same as Americans. Even though we did not pay taxes, we could visit public libraries. I experienced the American democracy; thus, studying in the US had a great impact upon me. Americans supported me during the term of my office. When the rape by military personnel occurred in 1995, it was Americans who compensated us for the trauma of the rape victim. I received several letters from American psychologists who wanted to offer counseling to the rape victim and who said that the scars of being raped may not be healed, but it could be worse. I did not receive any such letter from Japan.[40]

M. O. noted that his subsequent commitment to world peace came from his experiences in the United States, as well as Americans' sincerity regardless of nationality. Toward the end of the interview, he described the significance of the study-abroad programs:

> When America occupied Okinawa, as was normal, they tried to create leaders who would support the US policies. It is the same as any other occupying forces. When Japan occupied China, Japan invited Chinese students to Japan to be educated. When Vietnam

was occupied by France, Vietnamese students were sent to France to be educated and in India, Indian students were sent to England. But ironically, these students are the ones who usually stand up to resist the occupying forces. There used to be many professors from Michigan State University at the University of the Ryukyus who always told us not to see the Americans stationed in Okinawa as being the same as those who are in the US because they were different. These professors often said there was no true democracy in Okinawa, but there was true democracy in the states. We never knew what true democracy was in Okinawa, but going to the US helped me to realize what a true democracy is like.[41]

After returning from the United States, M. O. worked for the University of the Ryukyus from 1958 to 1990. In 1990, he became governor of Okinawa and served for eight years. During his governorship, he resisted the continued US military presence and refused to sign the renewal of the US military's lease. He used some of the networks that he had acquired during his US studies to try to achieve his goals. In contrast to the stereotypical representation of beiryu-gumi as simply pro-American, he publicly opposed the continued presence of Americans as military occupiers. He passed away in June 2017.

Y. A.'s Life Story

I conducted my first interview with Y. A. on July 27, 2010. Y. A. was born in the northern area of Okinawa Island in 1929 and attended elementary school in Nago. His parents emigrated to the United States and later returned to Okinawa. In 1937, when Y. A. was ten years old, his older brother, F. H., who had been born in the United States, left Nago for the states. Y. A. attended local elementary and junior high schools, but his graduation ceremony was canceled due to the war. In 1944, he was drafted into the Japanese Army as a sixteen-year-old student soldier. He fought US soldiers on the battlefield and his friends died near him. He said, "I felt nothing at that time just because I think I was too brainwashed." He was also injured severely but did not feel any sadness at being injured or losing his friends. After being discharged due to this injury, he fled with his family into the mountains to hide.[42]

While Y. A. fought for Japan, his brother F. H. grew up in San Francisco during the war and received training to become a US military intelligence agent. F. H. read reports of the Battle of Saipan in 1944 where many Japanese soldiers committed suicide. He felt that he wanted to help Okinawans to surrender by talking to them in the Okinawan language. Thus, he participated in the Battle of Okinawa as a military intelligence agent. When Y. A.'s father heard that his son F. H., was in Okinawa, he decided to come down from the mountains to see him despite his family's opposition. Although his American brother eventually came to rescue him, Y. A. initially wanted to stay in the mountains to complete his mission as a Japanese soldier.

Y. A. survived the war. Like M. O., all he wanted to do after the war was to attend school. He also attended the newly opened Foreign Language School and studied every night. When asked about his motivation to study in the United States, he stated that he and many other youths appreciated the opportunity granted to them to access US higher education. He described the US study-abroad program as being their "hope" for escaping their situation, emphasizing the limited opportunities available in postwar Okinawa:

> I was brainwashed to believe that Japan would win the war. However, when Okinawa was first bombed on October 10, I sensed Japan's defeat, but of course, I did not say this to anyone. When the war ended and Japan surrendered, I felt relieved and I believe many other Japanese felt the same. I felt relieved that I did not have to end my life on the battlefield. All the youth felt similarly, thinking that they did not have to be conscripted into the war anymore. I never considered the US as our former enemy nation when I decided to apply for the program. After the war, all I wanted to do was to go back to school. I felt that studying in the US was more a hopeful action that expressed our desire for continued survival.[43]

Instead of seeing the United States as a former enemy, Y. A. recalled that the youth regarded the program as offering them a way forward in creating an alternative future. He also mentioned that due to the outbreak of the Korean War, it was thought that Okinawa would become a new battlefield. He remembers that his friend envied him leaving the island because he did not have to face or worry about war again. His positive attitudes toward the United States before his departure can also be understood when he described his relatives who had migrated to the United States prior to the war.

Program participants who went to the United States between 1949 and 1960 traveled by US military ships to San Francisco, California, which was then a journey of at least twenty days. Many early participants reminisced that they would never forget the feeling they had when they saw the Golden Gate Bridge emerge from the fog as their first impression of the United States. Y. A. said San Francisco "appeared out of the fog and the scenery was just like a fairy tale." He studied psychology in the United States for four years. During the last two years of his studies, he worked as a dishwasher in a dormitory to earn money. He compared the United States with Okinawa's postwar conditions and felt there was a huge gap between the two countries. Nevertheless, his experience of being a student in the United States was positive: "I felt America was a generous country. Even though they won the war, they did not brag about it. They did not treat us discriminatorily. As America is referred to as a melting pot, the Americans did not mistreat the students from Japan because of their former enemy nation. My stay was comfortable. Maybe my experiences would have been different if I went to Europe."[44]

Y. A. shared his experience of returning to Okinawa after study in the United States, when he worked as a professor at the University of the Ryukyus. He felt that, as there were still few university graduates in Okinawa, the expectations toward those graduates were high. He also felt a sense of responsibility to contribute to postwar Okinawan society. At the end of the interview, I asked about his perceptions of the US occupation of Okinawa. He responded, "In a sense, the US occupation of Okinawa was a good one. Although Okinawa was a small island, people began to see the outside world. It was not like in the rules where the people in military uniforms were controlling the island. Americans also wear civilian clothes. After the war ended, we had to work together with the Americans to survive in our daily postwar life."[45]

Japanese militarism had brought about the war, the devastation of Okinawa, and the loss of many lives. Some of the early participants who served as student soldiers in the war, like Y. A., turned against any acts that might lead to war. After his retirement, he became an important figure in Okinawa and established a university in northern Okinawa, which focused on promoting peace. He served as the first president of the university. He passed away in April 2015.

Beiryu-gumis' Motivations to Study in the United States

The program participants' narratives about life during the US occupation show that they used the program for their own purposes. As seen above, the Battle of Okinawa survivors saw studying abroad as an opportunity to escape from the limited opportunities available in the devastation of postwar Okinawa. Rather than seeing the United States as a former enemy, they regarded the program as a way to create their own alternative futures.

A major motivation for earlier program participants was the lack of higher education facilities in Okinawa before 1950, when the USCAR established the University of the Ryukyus. Prior to the war, Okinawans went to mainland Japan to pursue higher education. Owing to the low standard of living of most Okinawan families, it was difficult for parents to send their children to mainland Japan. With the outbreak of the war, they stopped their studies and returned to Okinawa. During the US occupation, a study in Japan program was launched alongside the US study-abroad program. However, during the early postwar period, there was much more competition for study in Japan program and Okinawan participants could only access a limited range of fields, such as medicine. Thus, early program participants emphasized that they appreciated the opportunity granted to access higher education in the United States.

Early program participants saw America as a place of hope, which contrasted with the Japanese militarism that had brought about the war, the devastation of Okinawa, and the loss of many lives. Some of them had served as student soldiers in the war, believing that Japan would win. However, after witnessing the cruelty of the war and the inhuman acts that led to the deaths of many of their classmates and family members, they rebelled against Japanese militarism. Even participants who were too young to serve during the war witnessed many inhuman acts by Japanese soldiers. Many felt that Japanese soldiers had mistreated local civilians. They also remembered that Japanese soldiers came and took their food and even told them to leave their houses so that the soldiers themselves could stay there. Consequently, as interviewee K. M. said, "The United States as a study-abroad destination over Japan was a natural choice for me."[46]

In addition, frustration with their lack of freedom in postwar Okinawa under the occupation was a push factor for those who studied abroad. In Okinawa, under policies designed to prevent the spread of communism, there were restrictions on people's movements and information was censored. Okinawans could not travel outside the Ryukyus; thus, many felt that participating in the study-abroad programs was the only way they could regain freedom of movement. Furthermore, US censorship resulted in limited numbers of books being available to students.

Program participants were also motivated by other factors. Some had a positive image of the United States because of relatives and family members who had emigrated there prior to the war. After Okinawa was incorporated into Japan in 1879, a great number of Okinawans migrated to Hawai'i, the Americas, Asia, and elsewhere around the Pacific to find work. Remittances sent by these emigrants helped support Okinawa's economy. Thus, Okinawan emigrants' and returnees' narratives about the promise of the United States attracted the participants to the idea of studying there as a source of hope.

Studying in the United States was a means for participants who came from disadvantaged socioeconomic backgrounds to improve their economic and social status. For example, interviewee T. Y. studied in the United States from 1959 to 1963. He had lived in Taiwan until he was seven years old but, when the war ended with Japan's defeat, his family was made to return to Japan as repatriates from the colonies. They were very poor and did not have much food. They received rations from US soldiers in Okinawa, which created fewer negative images of Americans than were held by other Okinawans. T. Y. believed that studying abroad would enable him to obtain a better job.[47] Another interviewee, M. I., recalls that studying abroad was the sole opportunity for her to leave her house and escape from the societal norm to care for her elderly parents. She grew up in a single-mother household and was expected to get a job as soon as possible to take care of her mother. The only way out of their homes for young women at that time was through marriage. However, by studying abroad, she managed to emancipate herself from the constraints of societal expectations.[48]

In alignment with Luong Thi Hong's analysis in chapter 9 in this volume, which examines the cases of young Vietnamese women joining the Youth Volunteer Forces, the study-abroad program provided young Okinawans with the opportunity to attain personal liberation. Motivations to study in the United States narrated by the beiryu-gumi reflect the limited choices they had to negotiate in their situational environment, leading them to embrace the future-oriented emotion of hope that shaped their decision to study in the United States.

Conclusion

The establishment of the study-abroad program during the US occupation of Okinawa was a crucial strategy for the United States not just to provide local Okinawans with the opportunity to access higher education and rehabilitate the war-torn islands but also to foster Okinawan leaders who would support US policies. The program was significant in representing these US-educated Okinawans as students of democracy and as model products of US-occupation cultural programs. That is why their alumni association club, the Golden Gate Club, was valued highly by American officials and its members were often referred to as leaders of Okinawa. Due to limited opportunities for Okinawans to access higher education in mainland Japan under military rule, the US study-abroad program was met with a high level of interest and competition. The program, indeed, provided opportunities for upward social mobility and privilege for the returnees who would supposedly become US allies—Cold War partners—in occupied Okinawa.

Many returnees, in fact, lived up to American expectations very well. Their narratives of Americans as being better partners, compared to their earlier Japanese counterparts, as well as their views of the United States as a place of true democracy and a nation of racial tolerance, helped to reproduce, rather than challenge, the notion of American exceptionalism and that of the Cold War. In a sense, whether consciously or not, beiryu-gumi returnees indeed helped to shape and maintain the Cold War world. Furthermore, many Okinawans considered this program part of the US occupation strategy—or, more frankly, part of the colonization project of the islands carried out through the US-Japan collaboration, as typically seen in the practices of screening and censorship of program applicants. Local people thus perceived that being apolitical was an important strategy for being selected for the program.

That said, it is still too simplistic to view the returnees as "pro-American" or "bodyguards of the US military," as often described. Nor were they mere cold warriors or agents of colonization. To begin with, in contrast to the stereotypical representation of beiryu-gumi as "pro-American," one of my interviewees, M. O.—Mr. Ota Masahide, governor of Okinawa from 1990 to 1998—publicly opposed the continued presence of the Americans as military occupiers of his homeland. Others also promoted peace movements, as well as other social movements as educators and activists.

In addition, examined against the backdrop of personal experiences, as well as local and historical contexts, their stories might appear differently. For people who remembered Japanese colonization and militarism, and the Japanese soldiers' cruel treatment of Okinawans in wartime, US occupation, from the beginning, might not simply have appeared as the conduct of the former "enemy." For them, it was Japanese militarism that had brought the war to the islands, causing the devastation of Okinawa and the loss of many lives. Thus, for some early participants, the United States as a study destination, rather than Japan, was a natural choice. Moreover, for those who came from lower socioeconomic backgrounds, the US study-abroad program seemed to offer upward social mobility. For many others, too, the program seemed to provide opportunities to access higher education, to gain mobility beyond Okinawa, and to improve their lives within war-devastated Okinawa. In short, by shedding light on such personal and social backgrounds, this analysis intends to give a glimpse of how their individual lives did not necessarily reflect Cold War ideology, how they utilized the Cold War world for their own purposes in US-occupied Okinawa, and that they might have been fighting different kinds of struggles underneath the Cold War.

Notes

1. See, for instance, Catherine Ceniza Choy, *Empire of Care: Nursing and Migration in Filipino American History* (Durham, NC: Duke University Press, 2003); Colleen Woods, "Seditious Crimes and Rebellious Conspiracies: Anti-communism and US Empire in the Philippines," *Journal of Contemporary History* 53 (2018): 61–88; Naoko Shibusawa, *America's Geisha Ally: Reimagining the Japanese Enemy* (Cambridge, MA: Harvard University Press, 2006); and Donna Alvah, *Unofficial Ambassadors: American Military Families Overseas and the Cold War* (New York: New York University Press, 2007).

2. Christina Klein, *Cold War Orientalism: Asia in the Middlebrow Imagination* (Berkeley: University of California, 2003), 23.

3. See, for instance, Kishi Toshihiko and Tsuchiya Yuka, *Bunka Reisen no Jidai: Amerika to Ajia* [Culture in the age of the Cold War: America and Asia] (Tokyo: Kokusai Shoin, 2009); Tsuchiya Yuka, *Shinbei Nihon no kochiku: Amerika no tainichi joho* [Constructing a Pro-US Japan: US information and education policy and the occupation of Japan] (Tokyo: Akashi, 2009).

4. Shibusawa, *America's Geisha Ally*, 176. See also Kinuko Maehara-Yamazato, "'Studying in the US Was the Only Hope': Life Stories of GARIOA Students from Okinawa under US Military Occupation," *International Review of Ryukyuan and Okinawan Studies* 6 (2017): 21–36.

5. Golden Gate Club, "Aid to the Ryukyu Islands Student Exchange Program" (1963), 13.

6. Masuda Hajimu, *Cold War Crucible: The Korean Conflict and the Postwar World* (Cambridge, MA: Harvard University Press, 2015).

7. Masuda, *Cold War Crucible*, 286.

8. According to Daniel Bertaux, the life-story method examines a life, or a life as told. See Daniel Bertaux, ed., *Biography and Society: The Life History Approach in the Social Sciences* (Beverly Hills, CA: Sage, 1981), 7–9. In this volume, Isabelle Bertaux-Wiame points out that examining the ways in which people tell their life stories allows us to understand the ways storytellers attribute meaning to their own lives. See Bertaux-Wiame, "The Life-History Approach to the Study of International Migration," in Bertaux, *Biography and Society*, 249–65.

9. Miyagi Etsujiro, *Senryosha no me: Americkajin wa "Okinawa" wo do mitak ka* [The eyes of the occupiers: How did Americans view "Okinawa"?] (Naha, Okinawa: Naha shuppansha, 1982).

10. Laura Hein and Mark Selden, *Islands of Discontent: Okinawan Responses to Japanese and American Power* (Lanham, MD: Rowman and Littlefield, 2003).

11. Annmaria Shimabuku, "Transpacific Colonialism: An Intimate View of Transnational Activism in Okinawa," *New Centennial Review* 12, no. 1 (2012): 131–58.

12. Yamazato Katsunori, "The Birth of a University: The Background and Some Problems Concerning the Establishment of the University of the Ryukyus," *Okinawan Journal of American Studies* 1, no. 1 (2004): 10–18; and "Ibunkasesshoku no Seitaigaku: Sengo Okinawa no Ibunaka Sessyoku wo chushinni" [Postwar Okinawa and cross-cultural contact], *Southern Review* 30 (2015): 1–22.

13. Between 2010 and 2019, I conducted a series of interviews in Okinawa with thirty-eight US study-abroad program graduates, focusing on their study-abroad experiences between 1949 and 1972, but also touching on their lives after returning to Okinawa. See Kinuko Maehara-Yamazato, "Encountering Gendered and National Selves: Identity Formation of Okinawan Students in the United States during the US Occupation of Okinawa," in *Gender, Power, and Military Occupations: Asia Pacific and the Middle East since 1945*, ed. Christine de Matos and Rowena Ward (New York: Routledge, 2012), 43–59; and "'Studying in the US.'"

14. "Report of Military Government Activities for Period from 1 April 1945 to 1 July 1946." Series: Activity Reports of the US Naval Military Government of the Ryukyu Islands, April 1945–July 1946, record group (RG) 260, 000010453, USCAR, Okinawa Prefectural Archives, Haebaru, Okinawa.

15. "Report of Military Government Activities for Period from 1 April 1945 to 1 July 1946."

16. Golden Gate Club, "Aid."

17. "Ryukyu Students, 1949," 48, General Correspondence, 1949–1951, Series: Ryukyu Civil Affairs Files, RG 338, 0000112849, Okinawa Prefectural Archives.

18. M. H., interview by the author, June 27, 2011.

19. Golden Gate Club, "Aid."

20. Golden Gate Club, "Aid," 26.

21. R. M., interview by the author, June 13, 2010.

22. "Review and Evaluation 1954 Session of the English Language Institute and Orientation Center for International Students, Mills College, Oakland, California" (1953), 4, Ryukyuan GARIOA Student Program (1954–1955 Orientation), RG 319, Records of the Office of the Chief of Civil Affairs, box 33, US National Archives, College Park, Maryland.

23. "Review and Evaluation 1954 Session," 3.

24. "Review and Evaluation 1954 Session," 3.

25. "[Donald] Booth at Golden Gate Club" (1959), series: News Media Organization Articles and Release Files, 1959–1972, RG 260, 0000044937, USCAR, Okinawa Prefectural Archives. See also Kinuko Maehara-Yamazato, "Returning from US Study Abroad: Cold War Representation and Construction of Beiryu-Gumis'

Identity in the US Military Occupation of Okinawa," *Ryudai Review of Euro-American Studies* 63 (2019): 19–38.

26. "HICOM General Caraway Speech to Golden Gate Club (March 5, 1963) Autonomy," series: 1603–04, Chief Executive of GRI Internal Political Activity Files, 1955–1970, RG 260, U81100623B, USCAR, Okinawa Prefectural Archives.

27. GARIOA Fulbright Okinawa Chapter, *Shashin to Essei: Beiryu 50 nen* [50 years of photographs and essays of US study abroad] (Naha, Okinawa: Hirugisha, 2000), 16; also see Maehara-Yamazato, "Returning from US Study Abroad" and "'Studying in the US.'"

28. Theodore C. Bestor, Patricia G. Steinhoff, and Victoria Lyon Bestor, *Doing Fieldwork in Japan* (Honolulu: University of Hawai'i Press, 2003).

29. This first section is based on M. Y., interview by the author, August 6, 2010.

30. This second section is based on M. O., interview by the author, on July 28, 2011.

31. This third section is based on Y. A., interview by the author, on July 27, 2010.

32. M. Y., interview.

33. Maehara-Yamazato, "Encountering Gendered and National Selves," 43–59.

34. For the Melvin Price Report (8 June 1956), see the transcript of the report which is available in the Ryukyu-Okinawa History and Culture website, http://ryukyu-okinawa.net/pages/archive/price.html.

35. M. Y., interview.

36. M. Y., interview.

37. M. Y., interview.

38. M. O., interview.

39. M. O., interview.

40. M. O., interview.

41. M. O., interview.

42. Y. A., interview.

43. Y. A., interview.

44. Y. A., interview.

45. Y. A., interview.

46. K. M., interview by the author, July 15, 2011.

47. T. Y., interview by the author, July 13, 2011.

48. M. I., interview by the author, July 19, 2011.

9 The Voices of Young Vietnamese Women Volunteers during the Vietnam War

LUONG THI HONG

An image of Vietnamese women is well known to the world, perhaps largely through the experiences of the First Indochina War (1945–54) and the Vietnam War (1954–75).[1] During these Vietnamese resistance wars, women played crucial roles in gaining victory by joining the war effort in large numbers, as an ancient Vietnamese saying maintains: "When war comes, even the women must fight." Beginning in 1965—that is, with the full-scale escalation of the Vietnam War—there was a massive mobilization of men and resources for the war. Then, when all of the young men had gone to the battlefields, women were responsible for taking their husbands' places in the fields and maintaining agricultural production to ensure enough food for the front lines. They also needed to take care of their families and defend them from the American bombardment.

Many even went to the battlefields as members of women's volunteer forces; in fact, one of the most well-known images of young Vietnamese women might be the photograph of a captured American pilot, walking with his arms tied behind his back and his head bowed, under the guard of a young Vietnamese woman. During the war and since, the woman in this picture has been considered a symbol of Vietnamese patriotism. As such, it is not surprising that the most conventional narrative concerning Vietnamese women in the war has highlighted their participation in fighting for "their national liberation," with "the spirit of patriotism." As historian Sandra Taylor maintains, they were described as "heroines in the manner of the Trung sisters, and they were inspired not only by the love of country but by Communist ideology."[2] Such narratives have portrayed Vietnamese women taking part in the war with a spirit of patriotism, solidifying an image of national heroines.[3]

In addition, Vietnamese women have been often described as victims of the war—tragic heroines who suffered the consequences of the bloody conflict in their national struggles for independence. Young women in the volunteer forces had to face death and physical pain every single day. During their service, they had the duty of transporting ammunition, carrying loads on their backs of approximately twenty to thirty kilograms from one station to another all day long.[4] As one recollected, "Bodies were struck down by fever, hunger, and death. The hostile environment was infamous for its rain, mud, poisonous vines, and leeches. Daily life was a series of accidents, bombings, and chemical attacks. The most common feelings were pain, fear, and horror."[5] In fact, in one of the women's volunteer units, 60 percent of volunteers died or were injured due to an American bombardment.[6]

The junction called "Đồng Lộc," located at the beginning of the Hồ Chí Minh Trail, is well known for its deep association with the sacrifices and losses of young women volunteers. In late 1967, the US Air Force bombed the North with increasing ferocity. Strategic transport routes through Hà Tĩnh Province were destroyed. Among them, Đồng Lộc Junction was on the only road that connected the North to the South and, thus, was extensively bombed. In only eight months, from March to October 1968, 48,600 bombs of many kinds were dropped on Đồng Lộc Junction, making it known as the "bomb bag" or "death door." At this junction, the task of helping with logistics was handled by ten young women volunteers. They helped thousands of trucks go through, even when bombs hit there fiercely. Tragedy occurred on July 24, 1968, when a series of bombs struck the mouth of the shelter where they were hiding, killing them all. This famous episode gives us impressions of how their work took them to one of the most dangerous sites at that time, and "wherever there were danger and death, there were volunteer youth."[7] Therefore, in Vietnam and elsewhere, popular narratives have tended to cast women as pure tragic heroines.

Yet, the full story of these young women is largely untold, not only in English-language scholarship but even in northern Vietnam. Having enlisted in their units through local branches of the Hồ Chí Minh Youth Union after 1965, they were directly involved on the battlefield, transporting ammunition and weapons, paving and fixing roads, and taking care of wounded soldiers. Their lives were deeply hidden in the seemingly male domain of violence and death, but they had dreams. Many dreamed of love, beauty, and family lives with their children. How did they feel when they saw their faces had become pale, thin, and weak in mirrors in the shadows? What would their feelings be when they were still in their twenties with sexual urges while most men, including their loved ones, went to war? What would their feelings be after the war when they came back to their hometowns and when they found themselves getting older while their health got worse? These were women who had to choose nontraditional lives in their early twenties. These were women who went through lives that were completely different from a conventional sort of happy life, which could be characterized by sweet families with lovely children—lives they might have dreamed of if there were no war. Then, why did they enter into such strenuous lives? What were their motivations?

As we will see below, they tended to come from underprivileged classes and might were ethnic minorities in Vietnamese society. Most came from the countryside and had not had opportunities for education beyond secondary school. Most did not know anything about the Cold War, nor were they aspiring to defend socialism or hoping to play roles in a global political struggle. So again, what motivated them to participate in the war, devoting themselves to serve as members of volunteer forces under heavy bombardment along the Hồ Chí Minh Trail?

While Vietnamese women at war have tended to be described merely as tragic victims or patriotic heroines, this chapter, based on oral history interviews and various other materials, reveals far more complex and colorful accounts of why they joined the volunteer forces, and what kinds of personal feelings they had during and after the war. Along with the part III theme of exploring individual voices and emotions, this chapter investigates the personal emotions of Vietnamese women volunteers underneath a seemingly ideological confrontation between two opposing camps. It shows that it was their love, resentment, passion, and remorse—rather than ideological doctrines—that drove them to get involved. In exploring such an aspect, this chapter contributes to the reconsideration of the Cold War narratives, as well as national history narratives, through the perspective of young women's experiences in Vietnam.

Through a dozen interviews with women in Nam Định, Hà Nội, and Thanh Hoá provinces to analyze their motivations and roles, I came to sense that all they did might have been triggered by personal and emotional rather than ideological motivations. In order to examine this point, in addition to my oral history interviews, I have used a wide range of primary sources, including personal memoirs, wartime photographs in museums, and artifacts, as well as secondary sources such as books, journals, and monographs. While women in South Vietnam also had diverse experiences during the war, this chapter focuses on young women who participated in women's volunteer forces in the North.[8]

A History of Young Volunteer Forces

From the beginning of the First Indochina War (1945–54), the Communist Party of Vietnam (CPV),[9] led by Hồ Chí Minh, keenly recognized that its resistance war would be extremely arduous and prolonged. As early as December 12, 1946, the CPV pointed out in the directive titled "Resistance War of All People" that they would need to "mobilize all human and material resources" and "appeal to all citizens to participate in national, comprehensive, and long-term resistance war."[10] In response to this exigent situation, the strategies of "people's war" and "long-term resistance war" were quickly adopted, and, from that point on, the CPV encouraged the entire population to join in their struggle. To attract younger people, the first team of youth volunteers was established in 1950 under the direction of Hồ Chí Minh. It was set to serve *Chiến dịch Biên giới* (the Border Campaign) in 1950, consisting of 225 members in three divisions. The service period for these youth volunteers was six months, and they had the same level of benefits as soldiers.[11] Their tasks were to support soldiers, transport ammunition and weapons, bring wounded soldiers to the rear, and clean up battlefields. The first team was dissolved after completing its tasks and service period.

The contributions of this first team inspired the Central Youth Union to establish the second team in October 1950, which consisted of 1,737 members from Phú Thọ, Bắc Giang, and Bắc Ninh provinces.[12] The nature of the team changed as well. From this point on, it did not dissolve after each campaign, but became a permanent organization, continuously recruiting new members to replace those who had completed their service period.[13] Thus, the number of youth volunteers increased to approximately 3,000. In mid-1953, Hồ Chí Minh directly instructed his secretary, Vũ Kỳ, to organize another team, which would be composed of youth from eighteen to twenty-five years old in good health with good records, who would be able to serve as volunteers for a much longer time.[14] Within just a few months, the new team, with 850 members, mostly from underprivileged families, was established.[15] Furthermore, in the same period, the Ministry of Transportation set up another youth team, with the main tasks of constructing roads and repairing bridges in the northern provinces.

Thus, by the end of 1953, there were three youth volunteer teams in the North: one organized by the Central Youth Union, one led by Vũ Kỳ, and one set up by the Ministry of Transportation. Then, in December 1953, at a meeting among representatives of these organizations, they announced that they would integrate and establish one organization together, so that youth volunteer forces would be strengthened in both quantity and quality. In the well-known Điện Biên Phủ campaign in 1954, approximately 18,200 young volunteers joined the CPV forces; among them, 8,000 directly participated in battle, while the rest provided transport and medical support.[16] Within four months, another 6,000 were involved in battle.[17]

Addressing the roles of youth volunteers in fighting French forces, General Võ Nguyên Giáp stated, "Ensuring transport for food and ammunition supply was an extremely important task in the Điện Biên Phủ campaign. The enemy could not imagine that we were able to overcome such difficulties. Without the support of youth volunteers, the soldiers would have faced extreme difficulties. Volunteers contributed to the great victory of our nation. I always consider them to be soldiers."[18]

Having recognized youth volunteers' contributions, the leaders decided to further expand mobilization efforts. In the first phase of the Vietnam War (1954–64), which did not yet involve large-scale warfare, the volunteers were largely organized for various economic development duties. When North Vietnam came out of the First Indochina War in 1954, the socioeconomic sectors were severely deprived, and the people could have faced a famine.[19] To deal with such a situation, the North carried out an economic recovery and development project, implementing the first five-year plan in 1961, which required a large-scale mobilization of human resources. Some youth volunteers were mobilized to construct new roads and restore railway lines, while others undertook other tasks, such as fixing telephone lines, repairing irrigation facilities, and restoring agricultural production facilities.

With the massive engagement of US troops and escalation of the Vietnam War in 1965, the Central Committee of the Vietnam Youth Union launched campaigns that encouraged its members to take part in the national struggle for unification. During full-scale war, transportation of food, weapons, and ammunition became some of the most dangerous duties, which needed a significant amount of manpower. Furthermore, due to intensive US bombardment, many roads, ferries, and bridges were destroyed and, thus, needed to be repaired. Therefore, in May 1965, the Ninth Conference of the Central Committee Executive Committee decided to organize the teams of volunteer forces. Following this, on June 21, 1965, the Youth Volunteer Forces were officially established under a directive issued by the prime minister. They were modeled after regular military forces: Eleven to thirteen people composed each squad; three squads composed each platoon; and three platoons composed each company.[20]

The first recruitment campaign was carried out in twelve provinces in North Vietnam, gathering together 52,000 members (Thanh Hoá: 14,500; Nghệ An: 6,500; Hà Tĩnh: 6,500; Quảng Bình: 3,700; Hưng Yên: 2,500; Hà Nam: 3,200; Hà Nội: 3,000; Hải Phòng: 2,000; Ninh Bình: 1,800; Hà Đông: 1,200; Nam Định: 5,600; Hải Dương: 1,500).[21] Because of the urgency, volunteer teams were prearranged promptly. Even before stabilizing its organization, each unit had to march on long journeys immediately for hundreds of kilometers under bombardment. When they arrived at their destinations, no one was waiting or preparing for them; most squads had to organize camp sites, make tools, and dig wells to supply drinking water.

The more brutal the war became, the larger the numbers of volunteers became. It is interesting to note that, in almost all communities, the numbers of young volunteers who applied were larger than the numbers targeted. In Hoàn Kiếm quarter (Hanoi), for example, local governors requested 200 volunteers and, eventually, more than 1,000 young people registered.[22] A similar scene could be seen in Can Lộc district (Hà Tĩnh) where, with a target of recruiting 400 members, the number of applications reached 3,193. Similarly, the target for Thanh Hoá Province was 14,254 people, but the number of applications reached 65,000.[23] The total number of young volunteers reached 350,190, of whom 187,208 were women, accounting for 53.46 percent. Among them, 202,913 individuals, accounting for 57.94 percent, were directly involved in the war.[24] Usually, women made up more than half of youth volunteers, with a rate of around 53 percent.[25]

The Youth Volunteer Forces played important roles in the war. It has been recorded that these forces constructed 102 roads (approximately 4,130 km); transported 10,000 tons of weapons and food; repaired nearly 3,000 key traffic sites that were routinely destroyed by the US bombardment; flattened up to 100,000 bomb holes; shot down fifteen airplanes; captured thirteen pilots and nearly 1,000 enemy soldiers; destroyed twenty tanks and vehicles; and served in nearly 1,000 battles.[26] These numbers alone indicate the vital roles of young volunteers during the bloody war.

Social Composition and Motivations

In June 1965, the Youth Volunteer Forces officially began recruiting youth who were in good health and willing to participate. More than half, and in many cases the large majority, were female volunteers between sixteen and twenty years old when they joined; some were even younger. Members had diverse backgrounds. Most were from agricultural communities, whether coming from farmers' or former landlords' families. Also, there were students from middle and vocational schools, children of cadres, women belonging to ethnic minorities, and youth from overseas Vietnamese families returning home, as well as Christians, nuns, and monks.[27]

That said, most came from poor families in rural areas of northern Vietnam. For instance, the Youth Volunteer Force No. 51 of Hanoi was established on February 12, 1967, and had over 400 members, of whom 72 percent were female, over 80 percent were seventeen to twenty years old, and 78 percent came from rural or suburban regions.[28] Another example is group No. 609 of the General Department of Railways; this team consisted of 140 women and 3 men, most of whom were farmers between eighteen and twenty-two years old.[29]

Also, there were ethnic minorities in the volunteer forces, as well as those belonging to Christian communities. For instance, quite a few youth from the Hmông, Tày, and Thái ethnic minorities in Lạng Sơn, Lào Cai, Bắc Thái, and Thanh Hoá provinces, who usually remained within their communities, decided to join. Likewise, some young Christians in Nam Định, Ninh Bình, and Hà Đông provinces were willing to join. According to incomplete statistics, in the first recruitment, more than 1,000 members of ethnic minorities and 1,360 Christians joined.[30]

Indeed, there is no shortage of these sorts of stories concerning enthusiastic and patriotic participants. According to these narratives, the war attracted even nuns who, generally speaking, were not supposed to join in this sort of secular forces. One well-known case is that of Đàm Thị Dần, a twenty-six-year-old nun from Thanh Trì, Hà Nội Province, who wanted to join the Youth Volunteer Forces, even though the Youth Union was not planning to mobilize members from churches and pagodas.[31] Đàm Thị Dần wrote a letter to the Youth Union and asked her grandmother if she could become a member of a youth volunteer team. Despite her grandmother's initial hesitation, she wrote a second letter of application to the Youth Union, and her application was eventually accepted. In any case, whatever their motivations, as we will look into below, it is at least reasonable to say that North Vietnam's volunteer forces were composed of diverse groups of people, though most tended to come from underprivileged families in rural areas.

These young women's motivations, regardless of class or ethnicity, seemed simple and clear, at least at a glance. After all, they had witnessed murderous bombardment by US forces, which killed their families, relatives, and friends, and prompted them to change their lives. For example, one teenage girl, named Nguyễn Thị Thảo, was sixteen years old when her parents and brothers were killed before her own eyes in the Christmas bombing of Hanoi in 1972. These horrific images deepened her hatred of the US forces, prompting her to join the volunteer force within days afterward. She recollected later that she did so because, if she did not become involved in the military service, a lot of her friends and neighbors might be killed in the same way as her parents and brothers.[32] Thus, as emphasized in mainstream narratives, many women became involved in the war because of their anger, as well as their desire to protect their families and communities.

That said, beyond these conventional narratives, there were more complex and diverse factors involved. For young women belonging to ethnic minorities, participation in the war was a chance to get out from their underprivileged lives and, more specifically, to avoid being forced to marry at an early age those they did not love. Actually, similar dynamics could be found not just among ethnic-minority women, but women in general. As in other societies during World War II, many Vietnamese women recognized that the Vietnam War was a chance for them to gain more rights and opportunities and to improve their status in society. For them, the establishment of the volunteer forces appeared like a once-in-a-thousand-year opportunity because, unlike the army, in which only men could enlist, women were able to join the volunteer forces and demonstrate that they were worthy and able to do things just like men.[33] Thus, as in the case of ethnic minorities, for some women, joining volunteer forces was a chance to improve their position in their families, communities, and society.

In fact, quite a few women were able to find new lives after leaving their villages and joining the volunteer forces. For example, the Unit No. 551 volunteer force, which belonged to Hà Tĩnh Transport Company, was composed of 120 volunteers, with 82 women among them. When they joined, some of these women volunteers were still illiterate and had to ask someone else to write their names on their applications. Yet, after joining the team, they became able to write and continue their education depending on their needs. In fact, after three terms of service, five members enrolled in universities, twelve went abroad for study, nine continued learning at secondary schools, and fifteen studied at elementary schools.[34]

According to statistics of the former Youth Volunteer Union, roughly half of young volunteers in the period of 1965–68 were illiterate; in just a few years, however, the percentage of illiterate volunteers was said to have declined to only two percent. By the same token, after completing their tasks, more than 11,000 members gained access to higher education, among whom 650 studied overseas.[35] Therefore, it is reasonable to say that the war (and volunteer forces) created opportunities for young women to change their lives. If they had stayed at home in their villages, it would have been hard for them to have access to higher education, and they would not have been able to transform their social positions from farmers to workers or intellectuals.

Young women from landlord families and overseas Vietnamese also found opportunities to change their social status by enlisting in the Youth Volunteer Forces. Some girls applied so that they could follow or find their boyfriends on the battlefields. There was a case in which one girl who fell in love with a soldier was so worried about him that she eventually volunteered to join the volunteer forces to follow him.[36] In short, it is reasonable to say that Vietnamese women's motivations to go to the battlefields were not as simple as is commonly told. While often depicted as "national heroines" or "tragic victims," they were not merely passive figures but active ones, with much more diverse and colorful motivations. Below, based on my oral history interviews, we will look into other sorts of "ordinary reasons," such as economic, social, or personal factors, to go beyond the common perceptions of volunteers' motivations.[37]

The Story of Trần Thị Lan

Trần Thị Lan was born in a rural community in the Red River delta.[38] When she was three or four years old, her mother passed away. Growing up with faded images of her mother, she had to work as the only woman in her family. Her father was a boatman who shipped villagers across the river. Her family did not have land to cultivate, so they remained quite poor. Every day after school, she had to help her family cut grass for the cattle and submit it to the village's agricultural cooperative. After completing the primary level, she left school. At the age of fourteen, she witnessed intensive bombing because, beginning on June 13, 1965, the US Air Force began to attack Nam Định and Ninh Bình provinces, and the northwest region of Hà Nội Province where her hometown is located.[39]

This means that the bombardment extended over a wide area across the North, from the city to the countryside, and even to the mountainous areas. Trần Thị Lan's community suffered the same fate as other villages in the North; immediately following the escalation of the war, it underwent a baptism of fire and death. During Operation Rolling Thunder, which continued for three years from 1965 to 1968, the US Air Force used aircraft about 203,000 times to hit targets.[40] The number of bombs used in this operation increased dramatically: 30,000 tons in 1965; 255,000 in 1966; and 352,000 in 1967.[41]

Because of this, all resources were prioritized for the national struggle, with the slogan "all for the front lines." All foodstuffs were saved for the front lines, and thus the food shortage was extremely serious. Starvation was not common even during the war years, but the diet was very simple. The staple food was rice, but it was available only for seven to eight months in a year. Even in the countryside of Thái Bình Province, which was known as a rice-producing area, people were able to eat rice for nine months at most.

Because the shortage of rice, many families had to eat porridge with boiled corn, arrowroot, boiled potatoes, or tubers. The side dishes, if available at all, were water spinach, amaranth, or sweet potatoes. The sauce was usually soy sauce, shrimp paste, fiddler sauce, or crab sauce. Even coastal communities that produced fish sauce had to supply it to the state, and what was left was used sparingly for guests or on special occasions. Poultry, such as chickens, ducks, and geese, along with their eggs, had to be sold to buy pens, paper, and clothes for children to study. Pigs had to be sold to the state according to compulsory quotas assigned to each agricultural cooperative. Killing cattle was strictly forbidden.

Therefore, village life was miserable all year round. If farmers wanted a meal with meat, fish, and alcoholic drinks, they had to wait until special occasions, such as the Tết holidays, weddings, funerals, or other festivals. Popular dishes at that time were boiled pork, taro soup cooked with bones, and assorted vegetables fried with minced meat or pig heart. Chicken, bamboo shoots, or vermicelli were found only in the dishes of privileged families. In many villages, boiled pork was the most expensive dish. If there was an anniversary, none dared to eat any food provided; foods were divided equally for each person later to take home for their children.

According to official statistics, in Ninh Bình Province, where Trần Thị Lan lived, each person had only ten kilograms of rice per month.[42] Therefore, the life of a farmer was very difficult. Poverty was a common situation, and the life of Trần Thị Lan was not an exception. At that time, she was still a young teenager, and the teenagers' appetite for food was stronger than for other age groups. She always had to eat corn, potatoes, and tree bark owing to the food shortages. Meanwhile, according to the agricultural cooperative's regulations, all families without cultivated land, like hers, had to provide ten kilograms of grass to the cooperative every week to feed the cattle. Every day at the time for cutting the grass, she heard her older sisters talking about joining the youth volunteer force. If she became a volunteer, she could go to a new place and be well fed because the government would subsidize her.

The turning point came when the war escalated in the North. Large numbers of teenagers were joining the Youth Volunteer Forces, and Trần Thị Lan too decided to become a youth volunteer for a simple reason: she thought that she would be able to eat more and to have more clothes. She recalled that she was so happy on the day she was accepted. For a poor woman like her, it was a moment when she could find a way to be fed; actually, it was a good moment for her family too, as her enlistment meant one less member to be fed. Although, as a member of the volunteer force, she got enough rice to eat when her team was in the North, when they went deeper into the South, nearing the battlefields, food became less and less available. Thus again she had to endure being hungry as she had in her village.

Most young volunteer women had to live in critical conditions. The amount of rice supplied for them decreased month by month, from twenty-one kilograms per month to eighteen, then fifteen, twelve, and even only six kilograms.[43] In 1968, on the first day of the Lunar New Year, each woman was given only one piece of candy to celebrate the Tết holiday.[44] When the rice was out, they had to eat porridge and wild vegetables. One unit stationed in the Cô Tô mountain area did not have rice to eat for twenty-seven days and had to survive by eating only vegetables.[45]

Trần Thị Lan's team faced a similar critical situation when all roads in the region were badly ravaged and no goods could be transported to the front lines, making her unit suffer from a shortage of rice. She remembered a time when her unit was stationed in a mountainous area without anything to eat for several days. Much worse, it was the monsoon season, with lots of rain all day long. She had only two sets of clothes. Thus, in the evening, her team had to build a fire to dry their clothes, and, the next morning, they had to put them on again. However, luckily, such a tense situation happened only a few times. Aside from the fear of death, she still had a much happier and better life after joining the young volunteer force, as she was much more well fed than as a farmer in her home village.

Eventually, after two years of service, she returned to her hometown. She was allowed to study at a vocational school and had a better life; at least, she no longer had to suffer from hunger.

The Story of Ngô Thị Hoa

Ngô Thị Hoa's life is another untold story.[46] She was the first child in a poor family of four children in a rural area in Thanh Hóa Province in the North. At first, she had no intention of joining the Youth Volunteer Forces, but when she was sixteen years old, in 1969, her parents arranged a marriage for her with a man in the same village. While the young man also asked her to marry him, she did not like him because he was short and arrogant, with malformations in his legs. Still, it was considered a privilege at that time to have someone ask her for marriage, especially when almost all young men had gone to fight. This was particularly the case because he was the son of a cadre working in the cooperative, with considerable power in the village.

In traditional Vietnam, particularly in rural areas, women were expected to follow men's decisions. That was considered a virtue. The following was commonly believed: When young, women had to obey their fathers; after marriage, they had to obey their husbands; and, after their husbands' deaths, they had to obey their eldest sons. If any woman did not follow this custom, she would be ostracized. If a woman did not have a husband but got pregnant, she had to shave her hair and apply lime to her head so that it would not grow again. There was a social norm to view "unsound women" as harmful to the very roots of society. It maintained that, if she did not maintain her place well, her actions would harm not just her family, but the entire society. Therefore, the status of women was, generally speaking, very low, and women had no voice in family and society.

Meanwhile, Hoa's parents kept pressing her to marry the man they had chosen for her. If she would not obey, they might not consider her a member of the family anymore. Worse still, no one would marry her due to unpleasant rumors. The lives of rural women were still constrained by strict moral codes, and she could be ostracized and estranged in the village if she were to break such codes. A Vietnamese folk poem likened such women's fates and feelings of lamentation to a drop of rain as follows:

Thân em như hạt mưa sa
Hạt vào đài các, hạt ra cánh đồng.
Thân em như dải lụa đào
Phất phơ giữa chợ, biết vào tay ai.

[I am like a drop of rain
Dropping into the wells of pearl
dropping in the rice fields.

I am like a piece of silk
Flying in the wind,
not knowing who will grab it.]

This poem refers to the harsh and unpredictable fates of Vietnamese women who did not know where they would be brought to or who would take them. Then, where was the destination of the raindrop called Ngô Thị Hoa, and who "grabbed" her?

Actually, she chose her fate by herself. After several nights of thinking, she decided to write an application to join the volunteer forces. Her parents were only notified of her decision on the morning she left home. She was still sixteen, so too young to think about the consequences of her decision. She did not know or care about the nature of the Vietnamese War, nor did she know what the Cold War was. She just wanted to run away from the arranged marriage her parents had set up. It could be said that her desire for a new life inspired her to leave home and to join the volunteer service.

In a sense, the war allowed her to get out of various constraints in her family, community, and society. At the same time, however, it forced her to go through another kind of severe life that ordinary teenaged girls in her village did not need to experience. On the battlefield, she had to face death every single day. There was an occasion when a bomb hit and blew up a bridge where she was working, blowing her into the river. On another occasion, she was blown into a hole nearby. She remembered that, one such time, she woke up with a black face, with only her white eyes standing out. Such were common everyday experiences for her teammates.

One of her team's tasks was to bury dead soldiers. On one occasion, a bomb hit where her team stayed, killing a number of her comrades. She had to collect all of the corpses of her friends, none of whom had an intact body. After completing her task and returning to her tent, she could not eat anything that day. Another task she remembered well was bomb disposal. This was important to ensure continuous transportation of supplies, and it was the duty of young volunteer women to destroy unexploded shells. This was so dangerous that, before each time they engaged in bomb disposal, the volunteers held a celebration ceremony; everyone knew that they might die on that day. Fear, pain, and anger clung to her at all times.

Still, that was not all. Besides facing death, in their long struggles on the Hồ Chí Minh Trail, Ngô Thị Hoa and her teammates had to suffer from the harsh climates in the mountains and jungles, as well as a baptism of chemicals including Agent Orange, containing dioxin, which the US forces used during the Vietnam War. Many women were exposed to the herbicide and, as a result, suffered from various deadly diseases. It made many of them no longer able to be mothers. Hoa knew that several teammates suffered from the effects of Agent Orange. Still, she did not regret participating in the Youth Volunteer Forces, because it was one of the best times when she was able to make her own way in life.

Also, she was extremely lucky. She fell in love with a young male volunteer who worked in the same unit. Any love affair, let alone a sexual relationship, was forbidden in the volunteer forces. One teammate, in fact, advised her to give it up. Yet, there was another teammate who knew why Hoa had joined the team from the beginning and advised her not to give it up. At that time, there were many similar "couples"; they lay together in trenches, but still avoided sexual relationships. Because of the stern discipline and regulations in the army, soldiers as well as volunteer members were not allowed any intimacies.[47]

After four years of service as a young volunteer, she was discharged and returned home. By this time, her parents were no longer angry at her. They knew that their daughter had faced death many times, and that it was extremely lucky for her to return home. They no longer tried to force her to marry someone she did not like. Luckier still, when her boyfriend in the volunteer force completed his service, they got married. She moved to her husband's hometown, and they have lived together until now, with four children. Four years of military voluntary service served her well, liberating her from traditional social constraints.

The Story of Nguyễn Thị Mùi

Nguyễn Thị Mùi was born in 1942 to a landlord family in Thanh Hoá Province in the North.[48] She was the ninth of ten children in the family. Her father was a doctor, and her mother was a local trader who was, according to her, quite smart and put all of her efforts into the family. Compared to her neighboring families' children, Mùi was a rich child. Her family did not suffer from poverty even when most families in the village were out of rice. She was considered a little "princess" during her childhood. It seemed that her friends, as well as neighbors, were jealous of her family.

Then, a storm of land reform swept over the North from 1953 to 1956, hitting her family hard, as landlords' land was distributed to poor peasants. This resulted in clear distinctions between children of landlords and of peasants, and radical discrimination against the former. When labeled part of the "bourgeoisie," members of these families were ostracized and had no chance to access higher education. This happened to Mùi's family. All of their assets were confiscated, and they were suddenly in a painful and difficult situation. Her parents had nothing to feed ten children. Her father was so frustrated that he passed away shortly afterward.

In 1956, Hồ Chí Minh acknowledged serious errors in the land reform programs that had incorrectly classified small landlords and middle-class families, like hers, as "bourgeois." However, once labeled as coming from a "bourgeois" family, it was not easy for her to continue her studies. Yet, while being accused of being a landlord's daughter and ostracized by villagers, Mùi maintained her determination to continue her schooling. On going back to secondary school, she had to lie that she was born in 1944 to show that she was young enough. Luckily, she was able to complete secondary school. However, she was not allowed to get higher education because of her family background.

Mùi was told by a local committee official that she had only two choices if she wished to go to university in the future: one was to serve as a soldier and the other was to join a youth volunteer team—the predecessor of the Youth Volunteer Forces. She chose the latter because, unlike the army, the volunteer team did not require a strict check on family backgrounds. Mùi went to the local committee again and applied in 1963, when she was twenty-one years old. While it was a hard choice, the youth volunteer team provided an opportunity for her to change her family background, as well as her social status.

Before joining, Mùi could not imagine how hard it would be. Born into a wealthy family, she simply did not know what the life of a youth volunteer would look like. One task she remembered well was building a new road, from Quảng Xuân to Thọ Xuân, with a length of more than 100 kilometers in a mountainous region. She was still young and healthy, so she did not find the work hard. With her height at 170 centimeters (5'7"), she was assigned to drive bulldozers to smooth the road. The only thought in her mind at that time was that she had to try her best to be recognized.

After her family's status was finally restored, she returned home to her village. With her tasks in the volunteer force completed, she was now treated favorably, and she was offered a position with a cooperative store in Thanh Hoá Province. She was still determined to prove that she was not afraid of any hardship even though she came from an affluent family, so she expressed willingness to work in a mountainous region. The local authorities, thus, transferred her to a state-run general store in a mountainous district of Hồi Xuân near the border with Laos. After one year of work, she was permitted to return to her hometown and had permission to study at a university in Hanoi.

Examining her life story, we can tell that the Cold War logic had an ambivalent impact. After all, it was communist politics that shattered her peaceful, relatively privileged life in the village. Yet, she could also take advantage of Cold War politics by joining the youth volunteer team, wiping away the label of a "bourgeois" background and climbing up the social ladder. It is interesting to note that, while fully utilizing Cold War logic, she was not really motivated by ideology or political aspirations. For her, it was more like a practical tool to get rid of the "black mark" on the family's record and have access to higher education.

Conclusion

The Vietnam War—which is often called the "Anti-American Resistance War" in Vietnam—has been conventionally viewed through Cold War and national liberation narratives, with particular attention to political and military aspects. Therefore, when Vietnamese women become subjects for research and discussion, they have tended to be described as either "victims" of international politics or "heroines" of national liberation. However, behind such commonplace descriptions, there were much more complex and diverse stories of ordinary women on the ground. By exploring several individual life stories, this chapter scrutinizes the experiences of young Vietnamese women, arguing that they were not simply "victims" or "heroines" but had their own variety of struggles for personal liberation.

Oral histories of Vietnamese women volunteers reveal that most came from underprivileged families in rural areas or ethnic-minority communities in mountainous regions. Due to low levels of education, many had few concerns about the Cold War or national liberation, at least at the outset. Rather, they often had more practical and personal concerns. To be sure, many women must have participated in the war due to sheer anger, as well as desires to protect their families and communities—the motivations that go well with conventional national liberation narratives. Yet, quite a few women went to fight as volunteer force members for a variety of other reasons. This was particularly the case because when the Vietnam War evolved into full-scale warfare, it also provided a chance for many young women to get out of economic or social constraints and change their destinies by becoming members of the Youth Volunteer Forces.

As we have seen, some individuals engaged in the war for personal reasons, such as getting out from poverty and hunger, avoiding family and community pressures for marriage, wiping out disgrace and climbing up the social ladder, or even searching for future boyfriends and husbands. By participating in the war, these young women actively took these opportunities to find new social roles beyond traditional roles as mothers and wives, as well as new "selves" that could erase who they previously were. In a sense, while women in Western societies were fighting to liberate themselves by using condoms, burning bras, and championing new legislation, women in Vietnam were on the same page, pursuing personal liberation by joining the Youth Volunteer Forces and going to fight, though, for them, it was not metaphorical but literal war, with actual death and violence.

It could be said that the war provided opportunities for young women to ponder and search for their roles in society beyond their household and beyond their traditional roles as mothers and wives, but, once the war was over, most women were subsumed into conventional modes of social order, whether willingly or unwillingly. These women were now obliged to follow all kinds of traditional roles, which had not been available nor encouraged during wartime. Actually, most women willingly accepted going back to "normal" gender roles. Many were not really waiting to be promoted and assigned higher-paid jobs, nor did they wish for their husbands to take further responsibilities in terms of housework. Also, most young women who had escaped from villages by joining volunteer teams were pushed back to their villages and homes, as conventional gender norms and notions of womanliness were restored after the war.

Oral histories of these women could offer valuable insights, not just for adding information about diverse experiences of ordinary people during the Cold War, but for destabilizing conventional understandings of the Cold War as a confrontation between superpowers. As we have seen, for young women from rural areas with underprivileged backgrounds, the US-USSR rivalry, or even national liberation, was not really the central issue, as much as other individual concerns, family and community pressures, and gender and social norms and constraints. Many women, indeed, had a variety of motivations other than "communism" or "capitalism" when they acted in the ways they did.

Then, if we were to see the history of the twentieth century as characterized by struggles of daily life, such a framework could be used to rewrite the history of the Cold War. In other words, by looking closely at people's everyday lives, we can contribute to the reconceptualization of the Cold War narrative, moving beyond the concerns of political elites and state-to-state relations. When people and everyday lives are placed at the center of narratives, such approaches can relativize Cold War international politics, relegating it to the background and bringing to the fore broader and long-lasting concerns of societies. Hence, we will be able to reconceptualize the histories of the Cold War and the twentieth century.

Notes

* I would like to express my sincere thanks to Masuda Hajimu for allowing me to present the early version of this chapter at the NUS "Reconceptualizing the Cold War" workshop and helping me to develop this chapter. I am grateful to Kisho Tsuchiya and Joey Long for reading and commenting on a draft version. My special thanks go to the Harvard-Yenching Institute for providing me with a grant to conduct my research.

1. The period from 1954 to 1975 in Vietnamese history has been described in various terms by scholars. In Vietnam, the war has been called the "Anti-American Resistance War," the "Second Indochina War," the "Vietnamese Civil War," and "the Vietnam War." For this paper, I will simply use the term "Vietnam War."

2. Sandra Taylor, *Vietnamese Women at War: Fighting for Ho Chi Minh and the Revolution* (Lawrence: University Press of Kansas, 1999), 115. The Trung sisters (Hai Bà Trưng) mentioned in this quotation were military leaders who established and ruled the monarchy for three years after commanding a rebellion against the Han dynasty in AD 40. Although they were eventually suppressed by the Han army, they are regarded as national heroines of Vietnam.

3. A wide range of books and articles have been published in Vietnamese and English referring to the women's patriotism: for instance, Văn Tùng, *Lịch sử Đoàn Thanh niên Cộng sản Hồ Chí Minh và phong trào thanh niên Việt Nam, 1925–1999* [History of Ho Chi Minh Communist Youth Union and Vietnamese youth movement] (Hanoi: Thanh niên, 2001); Phương Trang et al., *40 năm Thanh niên xung phong 1950–1990* [40 years of Vietnamese youth volunteers] (Hanoi: Thanh niên, 1990); Văn Tùng, *Lịch sử Thanh niên xung phong Việt Nam, 1950–2001* [History of Vietnamese youth volunteers] (Hanoi: Thanh niên, 2002); *Sáng mãi phẩm chất nữ thanh niên xung phong Việt Nam* [Praising the characters of young Vietnamese volunteer women] (Hanoi: Thanh niên, 2013); Thu Hiền, *Những người phụ nữ nổi tiếng trong lịch sử Việt nam* [The famous women in Vietnamese history] (Hanoi: Văn hoá Thông tin, 2014); Thị Thu Trương et al., *Lịch sử phụ nữ Nam bộ kháng chiến* [History of southern women in Resistance War] (Hanoi: Chính trị Quốc gia, 2015); Bá Nam Lâm and Quang Hiền Vũ, *Lịch sử Hội Liên hiệp Phụ nữ Việt Nam, tập 1, 1930–1976* [History of Vietnamese Women's Union, vol. 1, 1930–1976] (Hanoi: Phụ nữ, 2017); and Taylor, *Vietnamese Women at War*.

4. Văn, *Lịch sử Đoàn Thanh*, 413.

5. François Guillemot, "Death and Suffering at First Hand: Youth Shock Brigades during the Vietnam War (1950–1975)," *Journal of Vietnamese Studies*, 4, no. 3 (Fall 2009): 17–60.

6. Nguyễn Hồng Thanh, *Thanh niên xung phong những trang oanh liệt* [The glorious time of youth volunteers] (Hanoi: Thanh niên, 1996), 247.

7. Karen Gottschang Turner with Phan Thanh Hao, *Even Women Must Fight: Memories of War from North Vietnam* (Hoboken, NJ: John Wiley, 1999), 74.

8. When discussing the voices of women in the war, mainstream literature in Vietnam has tended to focus on women in the North who were "politically enlightened" and who joined nationalist movements against the French and American forces. Other voices of women in the South, for instance, who did not participate in political activities, who shared the fate of the "enemies," or who escaped from their villages and became prostitutes serving soldiers in urban areas and foreign military bases in order to support their families, have not been adequately studied. Further research is needed on these topics because it could shed new light on more complex and diverse stories that could similarly contribute to the reconsideration of the Cold War narratives and national history narratives.

9. The Communist Party of Vietnam (Đảng cộng sản Việt Nam) was founded in February 1930. The party has been renamed several times, as the Communist Party of Indochina (Đảng Cộng sản Đông Dương, October 1930), the Workers Party of Vietnam (Đảng lao động Việt Nam, February 1951), and the Communist Party of Vietnam (Đảng Cộng sản Việt Nam, December 1976).

10. Đảng Cộng sản Việt Nam [Communist Party of Vietnam], *Văn kiện Đảng toàn tập, tập 8 (1945–1947)* [Collection of party's documents—Complete series, vol. 8 (1945–1947)] (Hanoi: Chính trị Quốc gia, 2000), 151.

11. Trương Thị Mai Hương, *Thanh niên xung phong miền Bắc trong kháng chiến chống Mỹ, cứu nước, 1965–1975* [Youth volunteers in the North during the Anti-American Resistance War, 1954–1975] (Hanoi: Quân đội Nhân dân, 2016), 13.

12. Trương, *Thanh niên xung phong*, 14.

13. Đoàn Thanh niên Cứu quốc Việt Nam [Youth Union for National Salvation of Vietnam], "Tổng kết thành tích công tác Đội Thanh niên xung phong công tác trung ương từ tháng 7/1950–2/1952" [Summary of the Central Youth Volunteers Team from July 1950 to January 1952], 34, folder 2, dossier 1256, Library of Ho Chi Minh Communist Youth Union Central Committee, Hanoi, Vietnam.

14. Hồ Chí Minh, *Toàn tập, tập 8 (1953–1954)* [Collected works, vol. 6 (1953–1954)] (Hanoi: Chính trị Quốc gia-Sự thật, 2011), 331–32.

15. Trương, *Thanh niên xung phong*, 20.

16. Văn, *Lịch sử Thanh*, 129.

17. Nguyễn, *Thanh niên xung phong*, 46.

18. Đặng Đình Chấn, *Huyền thoại thanh niên xung phong Việt Nam* [The legend of Vietnamese youth volunteers] (Hanoi: Thông tấn xã Việt Nam, 2009), 98.

19. Hồ Chí Minh, *Toàn tập, tập 14 (1963–1965)* [Collected works, vol. 14 (1963–1965)] (Hanoi: Chính trị Quốc gia-Sự thật, 2011), 273.

20. "Regulations and rules of volunteer youth," 8, folder 4, dossier 31, Library of Ho Chi Minh Communist Youth Union, Hanoi, Vietnam.

21. "Report on the Movement of Youth Volunteers Guaranteeing Transportation in the Anti-American Resistance War," 6, folder 4, dossier 93, Library of Ministry of Transportation, Hanoi, Vietnam.

22. Văn, *Lịch sử Đoàn Thanh*, 365.

23. Nguyễn, *Thanh niên xung phong*, 148.

24. The statistic from the Vietnamese Former Youth Volunteers' Association was provided to the author.

25. Trương, *Thanh niên xung phong*, 70.

26. Hội cựu thanh niên xung phong Việt Nam [The Vietnamese Former Youth Volunteers' Association], *Tư tưởng Hồ Chí Minh về trường học lớn thanh niên xung phong* [Hồ Chí Minh thought on a large school for young volunteers] (Hanoi: Chính trị quốc gia sự thật, 2017), 134.

27. Guillemot, "Death and Suffering," 17–60.

28. Nguyễn, *Thanh niên xung phong*, 131.

29. Lê Chân Phương, *Phong trào phụ nữ "ba đảm đang" trong cuộc kháng chiến chống Mỹ, cứu nước* [The "Three Responsibilities" Movement during the Anti-American Resistance War] (Hanoi: Phụ nữ, 2005), 87.

30. Trương, *Thanh niên xung phong*, 70.

31. Nguyễn, *Thanh niên xung phong*, 149.

32. Lại Văn Ly, *Hồi ký tuyến lửa những năm tháng sôi động* [Memorizing the fire routes in the exciting years] (Quảng Bình: Sở Giao thông vận tải Quảng Bình, 1993), 81.

33. Nguyễn, *Thanh niên xung phong*, 148.

34. Nguyễn, *Thanh niên xung phong*, 111.

35. Hội cựu thanh niên xung phong Việt Nam, *Tư tưởng Hồ Chí Minh*, 88.

36. Hội cựu thanh niên xung phong Việt Nam [The Vietnamese Former Youth Volunteers' Association], *Thanh niên xung phong Việt Nam 60 năm làm theo lời thơ Bác Hồ dạy* [The Vietnamese youth volunteers: 60 years of following Uncle Ho's teaching] (Hanoi: Quân đội nhân dân, 2010), 614.

37. In reproducing the life stories of the three individuals, I used pseudonyms in order to avoid situations in which anyone could be harmed by the information given to me. However, I tried my best to offer as much detail as possible while retaining the integrity of the voices and memories of all individuals who talked to me. I used Vietnamese name order, by which the family name precedes the middle name and then the given name.

38. This section is based on my interviews with Trần Thị Lan in April and July 2019, as well as February 2020.

39. "Report of Central Government Offices on the Air Defense in 3 Years (1965–1967)," Prime Minister Folder, no. 3, dossier 14731, Vietnam National Archive No. 3, Hanoi, Vietnam.

40. "Report of Central Government Offices."

41. "Report of Central Government Offices."

42. "The Report on Farmers' Lives in 9 Years (1961–69)," General Statistics Office Folder, Vietnam National Archive No. 3, Hanoi, Vietnam.

43. Nguyễn, *Thanh niên xung phong*, 121.

44. Văn, *Lịch sử Đoàn Thanh*, 401.

45. Văn, *Lịch sử Đoàn Thanh*, 413.

46. This section is based on my interviews with Ngô Thị Hoa in April and July 2019.

47. Lê, *Phong trào phụ nữ "ba đảm đang,"* 90; and Ban liên lạc toàn quốc nữ chiến sĩ Trường Sơn–Đường Hồ Chí Minh [The Nationwide Committee of Trường Sơn-Hồ Chí Minh Trail female soldiers], *Nữ chiến sĩ trường sơn ngày ấy-bây giờ* [Trường Sơn female soldiers: Then and now] (Hanoi: Chính trị-hành chính, 2012), 254.

48. This section is based on my interview with Nguyễn Thị Mùi on December 12, 2019.

10 The Red Guards in Burma, 1960s–80s
An Oral History

BIN YANG

As an unexpected result of my fieldwork on *zhiqing* (educated youth) in Yunnan, I have met dozens of former Red Guards and interviewed more than ten who were dispatched from urban cities to rural or frontier regions under orders of Mao Zedong during the Cultural Revolution (1966–76).[1] In Yunnan, local Red Guards were sent from city areas, such as Kunming, to rubber farms in southern ethnic-frontier regions, while some from Beijing and Shanghai also went voluntarily to this tropical frontier, with high revolutionary spirits. No sooner had they arrived in these regions, however, than many ran away from their assignments and joined the armed forces led by the Communist Party of Burma (hereafter CPB), which had just obtained renewed support from the Chinese Communist Party (hereafter CCP). These youths thus crossed the Sino-Burmese border, beginning legendary but tragic years in the jungles of the borderland. While this is often considered merely part of Mao's strategy of "exporting revolution," this chapter intends to complicate such a simplistic narrative, asking, How did these youths join in the CPB's campaigns, and why?

The chapter includes my oral history interviews with five former Red Guards, four men and one woman. They came from diverse family backgrounds: one whose father had joined the Chinese Revolution in Yan'an in 1934; one whose father studied at the University of Chicago after World War II; one whose father was labeled a rightist in 1957; one from a local cadre family in Yunnan; and one a returned overseas Chinese from Indonesia in the early 1960s. Their experiences in the CPB were diverse, as well: serving in a hospital, fighting on the front lines, taking over a middle-rank position, and so on. Some returned to China as early as 1974, while the last went back as late as 1993. They shared their own experiences and revealed many vivid details of daily life in Burma, touching on various issues, such as ethnicity, gender, and culture, as well as stories about their comrades and battle experiences. They also provided their views on the CPB, Sino-Burmese relations, and the Cold War.

As such, this chapter relates to the part III theme of examining individual life stories underneath what was seemingly Cold War politics. It reveals their personal motivations and emotions, instead of simply assuming that they were ideologically indoctrinated in Mao's China, showing that, contrary to common assumptions, most zhiqing joined the CPB not for the purposes of "exporting revolution" or achieving world revolution but to grab a chance to change their current, hopeless lives. It also shows that the fate of the CPB and its armed struggles was not simply conditioned by Cold War politics but was often swayed by other social and local conflicts, such as ethnic tensions.

Background: The CPB, the CCP, and the Burmese Government

The CPB was founded on August 15, 1939, with seven members, including Aung San, the father of modern-day Myanmar (Burma). In 1950, fearing the possible threat of Communist China, Burma became one of the first countries to acknowledge the People's Republic of China (PRC). During the honeymoon period of the early 1950s, these two countries raised the "Five Principles of Peaceful Coexistence" as their ideals and standards of international relationship. Therefore, Beijing not only greatly compromised in its border negotiations with Burma, but stopped aiding the CPB's armed struggles against Burmese government forces. The Burmese government, for its part, banned the CPB in 1953. As a result, throughout the 1950s and 1960s, the CPB remained an illegal entity in Burma, moving its revolutionary bases around southern and northern jungle areas.

Many CPB leaders and their soldiers who retreated to China circa 1950 were placed in Sichuan Province; they were later called *Sichuan laobing* (the Sichuan veterans). They were assigned to work in local mines, enterprises, and governmental posts in mountainous areas. Some married local Sichuanese women. Ethnically Burmese, many were senior officers of the CPB. As we will see below, almost seventeen years later, in late 1967, they were assigned a new mission of armed struggle in Burma and became the core of the reenergized CPB forces. These CPB leaders were called *Laomian* (old Burmese) by the younger zhiqing generation. Similarly, another group of CPB forces, led by famous general Luo Xian, retreated to China following their defeat in battle against the Burmese army circa 1949–50, and was placed in Guizhou Province. This group was largely made up of ethnic groups such as the Jingpo and the Wa, and they came to be called *Guizhou laobing* (the Guizhou veterans).² Both Sichuan laobing and Guizhou laobing were much older than all of the zhiqing, who were mostly under twenty years old. Thus, these two groups of veterans were usually addressed jointly as *laotouzi* (old men) by these youths. The nickname carried mixed messages of honor and respect, on the one hand, and complaint and contempt, on the other, depending on different contexts. These two groups of CPB remnants were locked up in Sichuan and Guizhou for more than a decade, as though completely forgotten.

The tide of change came in the 1960s. In March 1962, General Ne Win took control of Burma through a coup d'état and launched the so-called Burmese Way to Socialism. As a result, tensions rose between Burma and the PRC, and, as early as 1964, Beijing decided to rearm the CPB, whose leaders included Thakin Than Tun (brother-in-law of Aung San), Thakin Zin, and Thakin Ba Thein Tin. Other Burmese senior officers were also called back from CPB remnant forces across China and sent to Yunnan and then Burma to reenergize the CPB's armed struggle in Burma. In this way, Burma became one of the earliest test cases of Mao's strategy of "exporting revolution." The launch of the Cultural Revolution and its overseas developments further aggravated the hostility between the two countries, prompting Beijing to increase its aid to the CPB. Then, on the first day of 1968, the armed struggle led by the CPB was reignited in the Sino-Burmese border area.

By that point, Guizhou laobing had also been persuaded to join the CPB and to become its military backbone. In order to provide military, logistics, and medical support, Chinese military advisors and personnel were selected from the People's Liberation Army (PLA). Furthermore, following the conventional practices of the CCP in the 1950s, as seen in the cases of its aid to Vietnam and Laos, an advisory team was dispatched by the CCP and became (or at least was intended to become) a cornerstone of the CPB's armed struggle in Burma. Last but not least, Beijing allowed the CPB to recruit its soldiers from China, opening avenues for ethnic-minority peoples and zhiqing to join the CPB's armed struggles. The next section briefly describes the historical moment when CPB leaders were called to Beijing to meet Mao Zedong, immediately before they headed to Burma to reignite their armed struggles.³

Before Departure: Thakin Ba Thein Tin's Audience with Mao Zedong

On the afternoon of November 26, 1967, after taking a photo with the backbone of the CPB officers, Thakin Ba Thein Ti (Chinese name Ke Sheng) and other CPB leaders had an audience with Mao Zedong. In addition to Mao, sixteen other Chinese leaders were present, including Zhou Enlai, Kang Sheng, and other ministerial-level cadres. These names themselves illustrate the drastic changes in CCP leadership following the launch of the Cultural Revolution. On the CPB side, ten leaders, including Thakin Ba Thein Tin himself, as well as Ke Ming, He Gao, and Luo Xian, were present.

The eighty-five-minute meeting was practically a farewell, because these CPB cadres would immediately depart for Yunnan and then Burma. Hence the talk provides information key to understanding the CPB's planned armed struggle. Through the meeting, Mao deepened his understanding of the CPB. He learned that Sichuan laobing and Guizhou laobing had been "frozen" in China for seventeen years, having been placed in Sichuan and Guizhou, respectively. Over these years, Sichuan laobing had increased in population to over 480, largely because of marriages and births, while Guizhou laobing had declined in population from nearly 400 to 347, as some passed away and others returned home. Most Burmese were originally rural people, and it was in China that they began to study, including learning the Burmese and Jingpo languages, while their spouses and children studied medicine, radio, the use of dynamite, and the repairing of arms, preparing for armed struggle. By this time, most had already moved to Baoshan, Yunnan Province, and the first group of 330 soldiers were preparing to depart for Burma.

Thakin Ba Thein Tin was aware of the sudden change in CCP policy to rearm the CPB and resume its armed struggle. Thus, he announced that the CPB would be able to return to Burma precisely because of the victory of the Mao Zedong line in the Cultural Revolution, implicitly accusing Liu Shaoqi and Deng Xiaoping, who had "frozen" them in China for so long, of wasting their youth. Meanwhile, the general of the CPB's ethnic force, Luo Xian, who had originally been trained by the British early in his life, joined the meeting a bit late, and immediately caught Mao's attention. It was the first time that Mao met Luo, and Mao seemed to sense the profound roles that Luo would play in the coming armed struggle.

Luo, forty-five years old, had been in China for eighteen years and promised Mao that he could fight for another thirty years. He told Mao that most of his group's members had been working in factories in Huangping in Guizhou Province for a long time, and that many were not Burmese, but spoke the Burmese language. He further explained that his people had joined the Red Army under the leadership of the CPB, and that he had helped the CPB to make contact with the Kachin forces he had been overseeing.

Then, Mao highlighted the mass line, emphasizing that the CPB must rely on the masses, build its own revolutionary base, and study political, military, and other works. As for ethnic-minority peoples, such as the Jingpo and the Wa, Mao told him to mobilize Chinese Jingpo for the armed struggle. Luo Xian was very pleased, because this was what he had hoped to ask for. Mao stated, "You go look for them, take as many as you can, take the youth." This was the moment when the CPB was allowed to recruit its soldiers from China, opening the ways for ethnic-minority peoples and zhiqing to join its armed struggle.

CPB leaders' audience with Mao in November 1967, to be sure, suggests that the CPB's armed struggle from 1968 onward originated from Beijing's international strategy: namely, boosting the line of the Cultural Revolution in the short term, and exporting a wave of revolutions in the long run. Yet, for hundreds of zhiqing who joined in the CPB's armed struggles, their stories were not so neat and straightforward, as they did not necessarily do so because they were encouraged as such, nor did they simply follow Beijing's strategies.

From Red Guards to *Zhiqing*, and to *Dang Miangong*

Beginning in the 1950s, urban youth had been often mobilized to go to rural areas to help with agricultural production in the countryside and to solve unemployment problems in the cities. Then, with the official launch of the Cultural Revolution in May 1966, the Red Guards—namely, students who directly responded to Mao's call to overthrow all kinds of systems—ceased attending classes and joined in the new wave of "revolution." On the one hand, the Red Guards helped Mao to get rid of "conservative" remnants in the party and administrative systems, as represented by Liu Shaoqi and Deng Xiaoping. On the other hand, social chaos reigned on such a scale that even Mao found it hard to control. Thus, in December 1968, Mao issued a directive instructing that it would be extremely important for educated youth to experience life in the countryside, and to accept being reeducated by poor and lower-middle peasants.

Immediately, his words turned into another national campaign, famously known as the "Up-to-Mountain and Down-to-Countryside" movement, in which more than twenty million urban youths were sent to rural villages as well as state farms in remote, mountainous, and often frontier regions. In this way, the Red Guards turned themselves into zhiqing—educated youths who were sent to rural and frontier areas. Most zhiqing can be classified into two groups: *xiaxiang zhiqing* (countryside zhiqing), who were dispatched to rural villages and worked together with peasants in people's communes; and *nongchang zhiqing* (farm zhiqing), who were assigned to work in state farms that were also in remote areas. In Yunnan, countryside zhiqing were mostly local Red Guards from the provincial capital, Kunming, and farm zhiqing were those who came from other big cities, such as Beijing, Shanghai, Chongqing, and Chengdu. While both groups' zhiqing rushed to join the CPB's armed forces, the majority, relatively speaking, came from countryside zhiqing.

I got to know and began interacting with former Red Guards through *Yunann Zhiqing Lianyihui* (Yunnan Zhiqing Association), an organization established by a few zhiqing activists in Kunming.[4] With their support, I first attended their annual gathering in Anning County, a suburb of Kunming, in the winter of 2007, and, with much mutual understanding and agreement, I extended my invitation to some former zhiqing to be interviewed. These interviews were conducted one on one in a hotel and nearby restaurants in Kunming, mostly in the winter of 2007 and summer of 2008. Not surprisingly (in view of zhiqing's tragic and somewhat negative connotations), not all former Red Guards accepted my invitation for interviews. Only a few immediately expressed enthusiasm, while the majority kept silent. As for those who expressed initial interest, I contacted them, one by one. It is a pity that a woman, a daughter of a Burmese leader who initially agreed to an interview, changed her mind overnight and turned down my request after her husband, another former Red Guard, dissuaded her.

During my interviews, all zhiqing interviewees often used the phrase *dang Miangong*. *Dang* literally means "serve as" or "work as," and *Miangong* is the abbreviation of *Miandian Gongchandang*, that is, the Communist Party of Burma, the CPB. The frequent use of this term suggests that they assumed that they came to belong to the CPB, even though they were not members when they joined. Eventually, however, many were admitted into CPB membership.

The Story of Mr. Cao

Mr. Cao was born in Yan'an in 1948, into an elite and revolutionary family, with a father who had joined the CCP in 1938. His family followed the army southward, and, in 1950, they arrived in Yunnan. Compared to general conditions in China, his childhood was relatively better. The family certainly faced difficulties from time to time, but at least never suffered from hunger.

Thus, Mr. Cao even had trouble understanding when his classmates brought up issues of famine and starvation. His family had never perceived the dark side yet. "We thought that the CCP was all right, and that nothing was dark. We had never lived at the bottom rung of society," he said. To him, at least at that time, most CCP cadres seemed to be clean and disciplined, caring for the common people.[5]

Before the storm of the Cultural Revolution, his father was standing vice director of the Provincial Court, who was dispatched from Chongqing to Yunnan because Yunnan provincial courts did not have adequate cadres. There was a regulation that stipulated that the provincial director position must be assumed by a cadre at the "Red Army" level.[6] Mr. Cao's father was of the "Eighth Route" level and, thus, could take only the vice director position.[7] Yet, as the number-two in the Provincial Court, his father oversaw major affairs. In addition, his father served as standing vice-secretary of the Political and Legal Council in Yunnan Province. Mr. Cao clearly showed pride when he recalled his father, though his tone always remained calm.

However, the Cultural Revolution changed his family's fate. His father came under attack and was literally beaten by Red Guards. Mr. Cao also came under fire: "I was the first to be attacked when the Cultural Revolution began. The police, persecution squad, and court system were all remade anew, as if all of the previous system had been smashed. I was attacked in 1966 and was put into a study group in 1967 and 1968. Our family did not see each other, and we lost contact. My parents' salary became nonexistent; it was replaced by just a basic living subsidy, a dozen yuan. And, then, we were sent down to the countryside, forcibly."[8]

In February 1968, he was dispatched to a small village at the far western end of Yunnan province, near the Sino-Burmese border. The village was located more than thirty kilometers, or four to five hours' walk on mountain roads, from a regional town, Mangshi. It was an extremely small and remote village of Han people in a largely ethnic-minority people's district. His group was housed in an abandoned horse stable, sleeping all together on a big flat bed, with the intention of making them zhiqing. Then, did he become a model zhiqing, learning from the peasants and becoming a peasant himself? Not really. "I never went out to work and did literally nothing, so I had few impressions of the place. . . . We stayed in the village for about twenty days, until we could no longer bear it. While staying there, we did pay frequent visits to friends and classmates. We did not want to return to the village. Become peasants? [We] could not become peasants."[9]

In the end, Mr. Cao and his four friends—that is, five out of the ten zhiqing stationed there—left the village within a month and joined the CPB. Their departure was relatively soon, and it made quite a splash. As a result, the rest of the zhiqing were moved to the foothills of the mountains where living conditions were relatively better. "Then, I stayed in the CPB for eight years, which was neither a long nor a short time," he said.[10]

Why did he leave the village and decide on dang Miangong? "Many factors accounted for the departure of zhiqing to Burma. Our reasons were combined, not individual," he replied.[11] To begin with, they had been going through the turmoil of the Cultural Revolution, and their political position belonged to a comparatively radical group, called the *Paopai* (cannon faction), which held up high a revolutionary idealism, characterized by calls for continuous Chinese revolution and world revolution. Second, they were experiencing overwhelming disappointment through the "down-to-the-countryside" program. After all, they were the "educated youth" who were born, educated, and raised in the cities, and they were not used to rustic environments in remote corners of the country. In such deserted villages, nobody could care for them. He recalled their situation as follows: "The propaganda at that time maintained [that zhiqing should be] 'putting down roots in the frontier for [their] whole life.' It wasn't a training just for three or five years. Tell me, how could we live there for the rest of our whole lives? Doing the revolution there? Wasn't it bullshit? Those poor peasants were illiterate. How could we get educated by them?"[12]

It was a lie, he said, that "putting down roots in the frontier" could contribute to the revolution. Recalling his profound disillusionment, he said, "I felt lost because our stay there had nothing to do with the revolution. We would just remain there as peasants forever, and there was no way out."[13] At that time, the only way out was to join the liberation army. There was no other way. It was under such circumstances that they made a decision: "It must be better to join the revolution and die, so that we would not waste our lives. It must be better than just becoming peasants."[14] To be sure, not all zhiqing joined the CPB forces. Many simply did not dare to go. Even among those who joined the CPB, some escaped within a few days or a month. Yet, as Mr. Cao repeatedly used it in the interview, the term "no way out" (*mei chulu*) expressed their feelings at that time very well.

All zhiqing, in other words, were surely influenced by Maoist idealism and utopianism that called for sacrificing their lives for the world revolution. Nevertheless, the immediate stimulus was the disappointing contrast between their past urban lives and their present impoverished rural lives, and between their past glorious experiences and their present feelings of being useless, powerless, abandoned, and unfairly treated. In short, for many zhiqing, and at least for Mr. Cao, in particular, their decisions were not emotionally impulsive, nor did they obediently follow the party's instructions. Their choices were quite practical and rational in their own way, with calculations of seeking better and more exciting opportunities to leave their poor, dull, and harsh lives in the secluded villages. Essentially, it was their own initiative to change their lives.

The Story of Mr. Chang

Mr. Chang was one of the earliest zhiqing to decide to join the CPB. He was born in 1951 into a senior cadre family. His father had joined the Red Army in 1934 and worked in the Central Guard Regiment, protecting Mao Zedong and other high-ranking CCP leaders. When the CCP took over China, his father was the military representative of the Kunhua General Hospital in Kunming. Later, he worked in the Provincial Medical Department, Public Transportation Department, and Material Bureau. Once the Cultural Revolution was launched, however, Chang's father, who was then vice-director of the Material Bureau in Yunnan Province, was labeled as "antiparty, antisocialism, and anti-Mao," the so-called Three-Anti elements. Chang, of course, was unable to accept such a change, but he felt hopeless when he saw a photo of the CCP's Ninth National Congress.[15] In it, Lin Biao and other CCP latecomers were sitting on the left side of Mao Zedong, while Zhou Enlai and other senior cadres sat on the right side, signifying that Lin Biao occupied the top seat, having been appointed heir to Mao Zedong.

Meanwhile, his father was placed in the May 7 Party School to be reeducated. His mother was assigned to work in a small storehouse in the mountains. Mr. Chang himself was dispatched to a rural village, where he was bored and restless, thinking, "It should not be like this." Thus, he developed an idea for a way out: "These senior cadres and their children, like us, were all labeled 'children of antirevolutionaries,' and we would have no day of deliverance. We felt bored in the countryside. Thus, we went to dang Miangong, joining the Burmese Communist Revolution and fighting armed struggle led by the CPB, so as to prove whether we, the children of the revolution, were real revolutionaries or antirevolutionaries."[16]

Chang left the village in December 1969 to join the CPB. But, actually, he had become acquainted with the CPB almost six months earlier. At that time, he visited other zhiqing quite often, and, when he visited the border area, he met members of the People's Army on the Burmese side. They looked the same as the PLA soldiers, except for their uniforms. Chang had no idea who they were, so he asked. He was told that they were the People's Army led by the CPB. Then, he jokingly asked them whether he could join them. They said no but recommended that he go to the recruitment station in Menghai to join the No. 303 unit. This piece of information changed the course of his life. After returning to his village, he had further thoughts. Mao Zedong's words mandated "putting down roots in the countryside," which would last for one's whole life. But, in reality, it did not seem to work as such, especially for him, because of his parents' disgrace of being labeled "Three-Anti elements." The future seemed dim. Thus, he decided to join the CPB.[17]

Chang and his friend Zhang went together. The two walked about 200 kilometers, from Tengchong to Zhefang, which took several days, arriving on December 31, 1969. Then, they entered Burma and, via the recruitment station, joined the CPB forces. From the beginning, they demanded to be placed in the most capable unit, and, eventually, Chang was placed in the No. 1 Company of Guarding Battalion, which was known for its bravery. It was the unit that dared to take on any difficult tasks that other units were unable to complete. It was, in Chang's words, the "dare-to-die" corps. He recalled that they did not take on any easy battle, and the death rate was high: "Our company-level officials saw a low survival rate. Most died by the time I left, with a few being heavily wounded. As to the platoon- and squad-level officers and common soldiers, even more died."[18]

In its heyday, his company had nearly 170–80 members in total; among them, 70–80 were zhiqing, from Kunming and other provinces. However, by the time he was demobilized in June 1974, Chang and his friend Zhang were the only survivors of the Kunming zhiqing. Quite a few left after facing various difficulties. Some went to the Golden Triangle, joining Nationalist Party (Kuomintang; KMT) forces. But the majority sacrificed themselves in battle. During his time in Burma's jungles, Chang was gradually promoted. In China, he would not have had any chance to join the Communist League (due to his parents' "Three-Anti" label), but, in Burma, he was admitted to the Burmese Communist League, and then to membership in the CPB itself.[19]

At the beginning of the 1970s, particularly after the death of Lin Biao in 1971, the tide of politics changed again, and so did Chang's life. He recalled, "After the Lin Biao Incident, Old Zhou came back to be in charge. And both domestic and international policies changed, as well. Domestically, many senior cadres showed up, one by one. As for foreign policy, supporting the CPB became of secondary concern."[20] In fact, beginning in 1972, the Chinese advisory team began withdrawing, the military budget dropped, and ammunition and military material support was reduced. The CPB was, then, asked to be independent, and to take the initiative to solve its own problems by itself.

By that time, Chang's father had moved back to Kunming as well and was waiting for a new position. During his stay in Burma, Chang had stopped communicating with his father, but he had become increasingly concerned about him. Thus, with the change of the political tides, he decided to go back to China in 1974. For him, becoming part of the Miangong meant a way to prove that the children of "revolutionary cadres" were not like those of the "Three-Anti elements"; thus, after such a label had been taken off, or at least faded out, he did not need to fight anymore.[21]

The Story of Mrs. Wu

Mrs. Wu was the only woman who agreed to be interviewed. She was born in 1950 in Sichuan Province. Her parents moved from Chongqing to Yunnan's provincial capital Kunming and worked in the electronics industry. In 1957, however, her father was labeled a "rightist." Then, in 1969, during the Cultural Revolution, she was dispatched to Ruili, a town on the frontier bordering Burma, and became a zhiqing. Her village was very close to the border at Wanding, and thus she came to know a lot about the CPB. At Ruili, she met her future husband, Mr. Wang Yuankun, who had arrived there about a year earlier. Mr. Wang, however, soon left town and joined the CPB; he had been caught up in a factional struggle, which pushed him to join the Miangong.

Meanwhile, the Battle of Bangsai (Pang Hseng) broke out in 1969 between Burmese and CPB forces, and Wang joined the CPB. He continued to communicate with his schoolmates through letters, inviting them to join the CPB, which some did. Wu recalled, "A few classmates departed. At that moment, it seemed that zhiqing were not willing to become peasants because we had no idea about our future. We were simply unwilling to face the yellow earth with our back to the sun. So, we all hoped for some opportunity to come in order to do something, something meaningful."[22]

After the Bangsai Campaign, Wang and his friends occasionally visited Wu's group, although, at that time, they were still just schoolmates. At some point, they invited Wu and her schoolmates to pay them a visit, which they did, going from Wanding to Bangsai, bringing necessities, such as soap and toothpaste, as gifts. At Bangsai, they were shown around the area. Wu was very excited as she crossed the border river between China and Burma. Wang and his friends were also excited and proud to tell them about the Bangsai Campaign they had just participated in. Following this visit, these groups continued paying visits to each other, and Wu and Wang formed a love relationship.[23]

Wu, however, was hesitant at first because her mother had warned her not to think about personal affairs while she was in the countryside. If she were in a relationship, it would be difficult for her to go back to urban areas even if she were recruited there. However, she changed her mind. First of all, even though she had heard news of some zhiqing being recruited for urban jobs, she knew that such a thing would never happen to her due to her father's "negative" political background. Second, she thought that joining the CPB might not be a bad idea. There was a recruitment station on Chinese territory for the Miangong; and most Miangong soldiers were actually Chinese, whether ethnic minorities or zhiqing, who were mostly younger than or in their early twenties, and whose education had been disrupted due to the Cultural Revolution. While she was wavering, some zhiqing continued joining the CPB and Wu received more information about them.[24]

For her, the turning point came circa 1970, when divisions among local people in the frontier regions also began to depend on different class labels, following what had happened elsewhere in China. With the start of the class division, some frontier people began running away to Burma, and the zhiqing's situation worsened as well: "The situation we zhiqing were in seemed to be almost impossible to sustain. Our future was bleak. It was unlikely for us to have any urban job opportunity."[25] This was also the moment that Wu and Wang's relationship further developed. Wang once told Wu that she should leave Ruili if she could find any recruitment opportunity elsewhere. Yet, soon after he said this, he seemed to regret it. He seemed worried about losing her if she left for the big cities. Wang returned immediately and straightaway asked her to go with him. Wu recalled the situation as follows: "I gave another thought. Our relationship had been already confirmed at that time. Then, if he goes there, we'll go there together. I thought, let me work out for myself how to manage in that kind of environment. And I do not care whether I die or not. It is common to be killed on the battlefield. If I survive all kinds of difficulties and pains, I might have a bright future when the Burmese Revolution succeeds. So, I did not inform my family. This is because I was afraid that they might disagree."[26]

In May 1970, Wu left Ruili and went to Burma to join Wang and the CPB. Wang went straightaway to perform his military duties, while Wu stayed at the recruitment station for a while. She was soon assigned to work at the front hospital. Sometimes Wang paid visits to the headquarters as well as to the hospital. As newcomers, Wu and another Jingpo girl were assigned to cook, which was a kind of test for new members, replacing two other girls who had left to study medical services. After one year of cooking, Wu was also assigned to study medicine.[27] In the front hospital, all staff spoke Mandarin, including the director, who was ethnically Kayin (Karen), and could speak the Jingpo, Burmese, Chinese, and Kayin languages. The frontline hospital was politically tense, since a lot of family members of Guizhou laobing and Sichuan laobing, with various political views and backgrounds, gathered there.

Things began to be more complicated by 1973. First of all, Wang contracted a kidney disease, and also began to doubt the Miangong cause. Secondly, among zhiqing, another wave of factional struggles rekindled. Fed up with the recurrence of factional struggles and tired of being criticized, Wang asked Wu to return to China. She initially refused, thinking that, if he left, it would mean his accusation was confirmed. Yet, sooner or later, they became worried that they would be ill treated if they stayed. "We had seen enough of the internal factional struggles at the top of the CMB, the so-called Sichuan Gang, Guizhou Gang, all of which were unlikely in the early years," she recalled. Eventually, in early 1974, they went back to China, just before the Chinese New Year.[28]

The Story of Mr. Zhuang

Mr. Zhuang was born in Indonesia to a Hakka family that had been there for five or six generations. His paternal grandfather and maternal grandparents were all Hakka. His paternal grandfather had died young, and Zhuang never met him. His family returned to China in 1961 when he was eleven years old, following the rise of anti-Chinese movements in Indonesia, particularly after 1959. Amid such rising tensions, Beijing dispatched a ship, the *Guanghua*, to Indonesia to pick up the Chinese-Indonesians who hoped to leave. The ship traveled to Guangzhou, and then those families were sent to Kunming. That included his family, and thus Zhuang went to school there, until the storm of the Cultural Revolution disrupted his life when he was in the third year of middle school.[29] "My schooling ended in 1966. I didn't read a single book for three years until 1969," he recalled.

Then, in March 1969, he was sent to the countryside in Yingjiang County and worked at the Dehong Dai and Jingpo Autonomous Department. Within half a year, at the end of that September, he joined the CPB.[30]

When asked why he joined the CPB, Zhuang simply stated that there was a recruitment station at the border on the China side, adding, "It was a trend at that time. It didn't matter whether it was the best thing to do or not. We were young. Many classmates and friends were saying that they would go there. We were in the countryside. We were so young. What did we know? It was so boring working in the fields, but we could not think of any way out from there. So it was just a thing to do at that time. Everyone was doing it; just going there [to join the CPB]." For him, working in the countryside seemed to be truly meaningless. It felt like an endless repetition of working, eating, and sleeping. Thus, joining the CPB did not seem like a bad choice. Many zhiqing left one after the other. It was like a wave, he recalled; classmates left, and friends left. "It was pretty fashionable," he added.[31]

Going to the Burmese side and meeting some CPB members, Zhuang noticed that they were almost identical to PLA members; the only differences were uniforms and titles. "I was a scout [in the CPB army], and guarded captives. In the Battle of Mengbo and Battle of Bangsai, we took more than 200 or 300 captives from the Burmese forces," he recalled.[32] However, in August 1970, about a year after joining the CPB, he was injured. The unit had succeeded in launching a first and a second attack, but then it was ambushed. One squad leader died immediately. Zhuang and two other soldiers tried to find a place to set up a cannon to make a counterattack against the enemy, the Burmese No. 102 Battalion.

But it was Zhuang's turn to get injured. He lost a lot of blood, but still managed to run back fifty to sixty meters and cross over a slope where he knew there was a safe place, and there he lost consciousness. Medical staff gave him a lot of morphine. He was immediately taken to a village, where the military communication company used six soldiers working in shifts to carry him on a stretcher to the base hospital. "They walked for a whole day, from the first morning to the second before they reached the Banhou Hospital, situated along the border. It was August and raining, so I had to sit up to keep the wound from going bad. At the hospital, my wounds were taken care of, and, within a day or two, I was moved back to China, to the Zhefang Hospital, Mangshi—that is, No. 108 PLA Hospital. I was hospitalized for over a month."[33]

After a month in the hospital, Zhuang was discharged. He was told that he should take a rest and did not need to go back to the front line. Thus, he stayed in Menggu, where the Logistics Department and the Headquarters of the Miangong were initially located. He was in charge of guarding warehouses and captives. Meanwhile, he was admitted into membership of the CPB. In the second half of 1972, he became vice-secretary of the party branch in the Logistics Division of Menggu, supervising seven to eight members.

In the first quarter of 1973, Zhuang was dispatched to the Wa State, which is *Wabang* in Chinese and *Meung Vax* in the Wa language. He spent more than twenty days walking from Menggu to Wabang. "No sooner had I arrived there than I was ordered to go to Beiwa [Northern Wa] County, to conduct social investigations, organize peasant associations, and so on." However, this task did not include land reform. "There was no such thing [as land reform]. Burma was different from China. The hill people were very backward. They did not even have pants. Many went to work naked. A lot of men did not wear anything."[34]

At a glance, a pejorative tone is unmistakable in his first impression, but, from then on, he became deeply involved in ethnic issues in Burma. This was partly because, by this late period in 1973, approximately 70 percent of the CPB armed forces were composed of Wa people. Furthermore, most of the Wa people came from the Beiwa County area, which was the most populous county in the Wa State, with a population of 200,000. Beiwa County had 11 districts, 105 rural towns, and more than 2,000 villages.

With his understanding of ethnic issues and conflicts deepened, he came to be aware of how rigidly the CPB and its armed forces were ethnically stratified, with the mainstream Burmese at the top and ethnic minorities, like the Wa, at the bottom. Quite a few zhiqing recognized the ethnocentric attitude among Burmese leaders and complained about it. Like other zhiqing, Zhuang also came to view Burmese leaders as difficult to get along with. Later he even found at least one reason for the eventual collapse of the CPB in their attitudes and factionalism: "There were too many factions. All kinds of tensions, and all these broke out when they reached a certain point." Eventually, in 1983, he returned to China. However, his involvement with the Wa people was not severed; since 1992, he has returned to the Wa State quite often, as he became a representative of Doctors Without Borders (*Médecins Sans Frontières*) when it set up a hospital there.[35]

The Story of Mr. Zhu

Mr. Zhu was born into an intellectual family. His mother was a graduate of Shanghai Jiaotong University, where she studied economic management.

Later on, she worked at the headquarters of the Bank of Jiaotong. His father went to the National Southwestern Associated University, which was created during the Sino-Japanese War (1937–45) through a merger of Peking University, Tsinghua University, and Nankai University. After World War II, his father worked for the United Nations Relief and Rehabilitation Administration (UNRRA) and, later on, went to the United States to study at the University of Chicago, majoring in history and sociology. Zhu's father had an intimate relationship with the CCP. "In the early 1930s, he had frequent contacts with the CCP, and was once very close to them. However, he did not become a party member until his last years," Zhu recalled. According to him, his father was the eldest son and, thus, was not able to wholly devote himself to the CCP as he had to take care of his family. Yet, before leaving to study in the United States, he had opened a bookstore in Kunming, along with a CCP friend.[36]

Then came the communist victory in China in 1949. "The CCP needed people after the Liberation and groups of cadres were called back. My father was one of the earliest to return to Beijing."[37] At first, Zhu's father served as an associate research fellow at North China Revolutionary University. All local governments were busy establishing their own organs, and he was invited to work in Shenyang in northeast China. His mother was then working at the statistics bureau there. A few years later, in 1954, both were transferred to the State Statistics Bureau in Beijing. Yet, with the radicalization of Chinese politics in the 1950s, their backgrounds became counterproductive. His mother was moved to Yunnan in 1958, being assigned to work at the provincial statistics bureau in the name of "supporting the frontier." Likewise, his father was dispatched to Yunnan, assigned to work in the provincial department of coal. Zhu followed his parents to Kunming at the age of nine.

Still, Zhu's childhood was calm and happy. He had good memories of visiting Xiangshan, a former imperial garden at the foot of mountains in the northwestern suburbs of Beijing. Also, he attended a private school, which was probably the most expensive in China. His younger brother went to kindergarten under the auspices of the State Council. In short, his family could still enjoy lives relatively superior to those of common people. Not until the Cultural Revolution did their lives really change, and even then, not at first. Zhu was in his third year at the middle school in 1966, and did nothing in the first three years of the Cultural Revolution from 1966 to 1968. "I did not become a Red Guard at the beginning. We, the middle school students, were not allowed to join the Cultural Revolution. So, I ran away to Sichuan to play around. My eldest brother was there."[38]

In September 1968, the schools started implementing the "class line," and, in October, the class structure in China was reversed. Yet, even this did not affect Zhu's life yet. He recalled:

> We did not feel that we were under attack, but I returned from Sichuan to Chongqing, where a lot of [Red Guard] students from Beijing had arrived. They were really formidable, arresting people all around. I picked up a newspaper and found the words, "Down with Mao Zedong." I read it again carefully but found no facts. It was purely made up. I talked about this with my classmates when I returned, and my schoolteachers heard and scolded us. But we were still so young, so it was not serious. We were simply not allowed to attend [Red Guard] activities such as the national day parade.[39]

What really changed his life, then, was the beginning of the "Up-to-the-Mountain and Down-to-the-Countryside" program at the end of 1968. He signed up for it in school, and then was dispatched to Tengchong at the western edge of Yunnan Province, bordering with Burma. In the beginning, Zhu did nothing in particular but just played around. He and his friends did not care much about what they did. Then, they were further dispatched to a Wa-nationality autonomous village.

By that time, Zhu's father was under fire, criticized as a "special agent" and first, put in a study group under supervision, and then, eventually imprisoned for the rest of the Cultural Revolution, ten years. His mother was placed in the District Cadre School, staying with the youngest brother, while his elder sister was assigned to work in the Cultural Working Troupe. Another younger brother was dispatched to the same rural village as Zhu. Zhu himself stayed in the village for two to three months, during which he visited friends in many neighboring counties near and far. Thus, he spent only about thirty days working in the fields.

At that time, Zhu received a tiny amount of money for his activities, in addition to some remittances from his mother. Thus, economically speaking, his situation was not particularly terrible. "But I felt mentally desperate," he said. "And then, I heard that some zhiqing had gone to join the Miangong." It was the Red Guards' tradition to pay visits to their classmates and schoolmates and even to visit Beijing and many other revolutionary sites free of charge. It was during these visits and interactions that Zhu heard of the CPB, which was widely mentioned among his friends. As he recalled later, "Zhiqing were going everywhere, and they were like connecting doors."[40]

The talk about the CPB by word of mouth among his friends indeed opened a door for him. As a matter of fact, Zhu was feeling hopeless in the village. "It was not a matter of hardship or the fear of hardship. [But] I felt that the future there was too bleak," he said.[41] He decided to join the CPB, but he still did not know where he should go. Thus, he walked about fifty to sixty kilometers a day for several days, while staying in friends' and classmates' houses along the way. After he passed Mangshi and arrived at Zhefang, his direction became clear. He was told to follow a mountain path for a few more kilometers, and then he would see a village with a river reflecting golden sunshine. Following this direction, he continued to walk, and he finally found a few iron-sheet shacks. That was the recruitment station for the CPB.

In the CPB forces, he was placed in the No. 2 Yunnan Ethnic Unit, which was composed of members of many ethnic minorities such as the Jingpo, Dai, and Lisu people, who were all lower-ranking officers, commanding squads, platoons, companies, and battalions. A few years later, Zhu submitted his application for membership, and he was eventually admitted into the CPB. Compared to other zhiqing who returned to China in the early 1970s, he stayed for a relatively long time. For him, the change of tide came in the year of 1976, which observed the deaths of Zhou Enlai, Zhu De, and Mao Zedong. By that time, Beijing was appealing to former zhiqing to return in what amounted to a call for demobilization.

Zhu, however, was reluctant to return. Finally, in 1980, he went to study in the "foreign training" class at the military college in Kunming, which was set up to train midlevel "foreign" officers. Back in China he noticed that politics were more relaxed, and that his family's conditions had improved. After being trained in China, he returned to the CPB and stayed two more years before eventually leaving Burma. Yet, he did not return directly to China. Instead, in 1983, he went to Thailand. After ten years of studying again, going to college, and doing business, with considerable financial success, he eventually returned to Kunming in 1993.[42]

Reflections

My fieldwork and interviews themselves contained far more details and information than are transcribed above, and I must admit that I have missed many opportunities. In the following I would like to share some reflections.

First, unlike what has been claimed or commonly assumed, most zhiqing did not join the CPB for purposes of "exporting revolution" or achieving world revolution; they did so to grab a chance to change their current, seemingly hopeless lives. That said, as we have seen, many joined the CPB as a way to maintain their revolutionary enthusiasm and to live up to, rather than challenge, their Cold War worldview that was surely derived from Maoist political indoctrination from the 1950s onward. In a sense, these zhiqing were not mere pawns of Beijing's strategies, but, through their own personal and practical decisions and actions, contributed to the reproduction and maintenance of the Cold War world on the ground.

Therefore, second, these zhiqing's and the CPB's actions were significantly influenced by the tides of politics, particularly those of the Cultural Revolution, which shaped the course of the CPB's armed struggle, both directly and indirectly. Third, it is nonetheless interesting to note that the fate of the CPB and its armed struggles was not simply conditioned by Cold War politics, nor prescribed by a communist worldview; more often than not, it was swayed by hidden social and local conflicts, characterized by ethnic tensions as well as Burmese ethnocentrism, which remained persistent problems within the CPB and its armed struggle.

Most zhiqing who agreed to my interviews were, relatively speaking, from elite revolutionary families. Their parents tended to be high-ranking officials or intellectuals who had had close relationships with the CCP. Generally speaking, they had had many privileges, enjoying their relatively superior lives. However, the launch of the Cultural Revolution turned their fates upside down. Their parents came under fire and, consequently, they suffered as well. Such were the common experiences that provided a background for their future choices. These zhiqing joined the CPB largely, if not decisively, due to dramatic changes in the status of their families. By the same token, they returned to China largely because of the rehabilitation in status of their families.

They probably dared to accept my interview invitations because they felt safe in contemporary China, because of their relative success, and because of their social networks and economic wealth. In addition, they were better educated and had a sense of responsibility to share what happened. It was extremely unfortunate that more common, ordinary former Red Guards, who were not from elite families, were generally reluctant to agree to my interviews. Some showed interest in sharing their experiences and one actually accepted my invitations. But, in the end, none of them showed up. Therefore, narratives of grassroots Red Guards and zhiqing remain relatively fragmentary and less well known. I wish that I could have interviewed more ordinary former Red Guards to understand common people's experiences and feelings.

For the zhiqing I interviewed, the CPB's armed struggle provided a rare opportunity to escape from China, to pursue their own fates, and to realize their individual dreams, which turned out to be as important as their devotion to Maoism and world revolution. That said, while they escaped from China by their own choice, their frontier revolutionary experiences were not much different from their Red Guard experiences in China. Thus, it could be said that these Red Guards in Burma had been similarly shaped by the tides of domestic politics in China and the bilateral relationship between China and Burma, as well as the Cold War. Hence, my interviews have illustrated how Chinese politics shaped the lives of zhiqing, and how those changes in CCP policies accounted for the temporary success and eventual failure of the CPB and its armed struggle.

At the same time, my interviews show a glimpse of a hidden undercurrent of ethnic tensions, which also significantly conditioned the course of the CPB and its armed struggle. Ethnic tensions indeed were evident in the CPB. When discussing the problems and eventual failure of the CPB, all zhiqing listed such tensions as a key factor. In fact, the CPB and its armed forces were ethnically stratified. The top layer of the party was predominantly occupied by Burmese who were in charge of party politics and ideology. In contrast, the backbone of the armies, including key military leaders and soldiers, was predominately composed of ethnic Wa and Jingpo people, who were later joined by the zhiqing, who were predominantly Han Chinese. Many zhiqing sensed prevailing Burmese chauvinism, and they often complained about Burmese leaders' ethnocentrism, suggesting a possibility that those Burmese leaders and ethnic-minority soldiers might have been also utilizing Cold War logic to fight their own battles.

Regardless of their motivations or dreams, many died, and many more were injured, all of whom were marked by trauma. Those who survived recognized their failure, more or less, but continued asking, did they betray the revolution or did the revolution betray them? A few chose to stay on, but not for the reasons in their original revolutionary blueprint. A handful of returnees succeeded politically or economically, while most simply remained ordinary folks. The pervasion of Cold War politics, the end of the Cold War, and the coming of the post–Cold War era all occurred like waves in which these zhiqing swam, drowned, or survived. Only a very few managed to reach the shore safely, though none without trauma.

Notes

* I am grateful to those *zhiqing* who accepted and helped with my fieldwork and interviews. An early draft was presented at an international workshop, "Reconceptualizing the Cold War: On-the-Ground Experiences in Asia," held at the National University of Singapore on June 22–23, 2019. My thanks go to Masuda Hajimu and many other workshop participants for their support and comments.

1. Bin Yang, "'We Want to Go Home!'—The Great Petition in Xishuangbanna, Yunnan, 1978–1979," *China Quarterly* 198 (June 2009): 401–21; and Chinese translation with revisions, titled "'Ningke shatou, yeyao Huijia'—1978–1979 Xishuangbanna Zhiqing daqingyuan shuping," *Modern China Studies* 20, no. 1 (January 2013): 99–141.

2. The background of the CPB's armed struggle, including the alliance of ethnic forces and the arrival of the Red Guards, has been sketched by Tom Kramer in his studies of the United Wa State Party. This paper, nevertheless, provides much more detailed information on these matters. See Kramer, *The United Wa State Party: Narco-Army or Ethnic Nationalist Party?* (Washington, DC: East-West Center, 2007), 11–16.

3. Song Yongyi, ed., *Jimi dang'an zhong xin faxian de Mao Zedong Jianghua* [Talks by Mao Zedong recently discussed from classified archives] (Guoshi Chubanshe, 2018).

4. For the details of this association, see its website: http://www.cnzq.org/ynzq/INDEX016.HTM.

5. Mr. Cao, interview by the author, 2008.

6. Referring to the CCP cadres who joined the Chinese Revolution during the first Civil War period (1927–June 1937).

7. Referring to the CCP cadres who joined the Chinese Revolution during the Anti-Japanese War period (July 1937–1945).

8. Mr. Cao, interview.

9. In the early stages of the Cultural Revolution, one of the most common activities among Red Guards was called *cuanlian*, which meant frequent visits and discussions among friends and classmates.

10. Mr. Cao, interview.

11. Mr. Cao, interview.

12. Mr. Cao, interview.

13. Mr. Cao, interview.

14. Mr. Cao, interview.

15. Mr. Chang, interview by the author, 2008.

16. Mr. Chang, interview.

17. Mr. Chang, interview.

18. Mr. Chang, interview.

19. His admission to the CBP was as a frontline member (*huoxian rudang*), which meant that he was a member of the party only on the battlefields.

20. Mr. Chang, 2008. "Old Zhou" referred to Premier Zhou Enlai. While most people, out of respect, referred to him as "Premier" (*Zongli*) or "Premier Zhou"

(*Zhou Zongli*)," Chang and those from revolutionary cadre families called him "Old Zhou" (*Lao Zhou*), revealing a sense of intimacy and respect.

21. Mr. Chang, interview.
22. Mrs. Wu, interview by the author, 2008.
23. Mrs. Wu, interview.
24. Mrs. Wu, interview.
25. Mrs. Wu, interview.
26. Mrs. Wu, interview.
27. Mrs. Wu, interview.
28. Mrs. Wu, interview.
29. In China, a "middle school" signified a three-year school following five to six years of elementary school education.
30. Mr. Zhuang, interview by the author, 2008.
31. Mr. Zhuang, interview.
32. Mr. Zhuang, interview.
33. Mr. Zhuang, interview.
34. Mr. Zhuang, interview.
35. Mr. Zhuang, interview.
36. Mr. Zhu, interview by the author, 2008.
37. Mr. Zhu interview.
38. Mr. Zhu interview.
39. Mr. Zhu interview.
40. Mr. Zhu interview.
41. Mr. Zhu interview.
42. Mr. Zhu interview.

11 Afterlife of Cold War Memories
Familial Transmission of Martial Law–Era Memories in the Post–Cold War Philippines

MARY GRACE R. CONCEPCION

In 1961, the Philippine congress instigated anticommunist witch hunts through its Committee on Anti-Filipino Activities (CAFA), which was patterned after similar committees during the McCarthy era in the United States. The main targets of these witch hunts were professors and students who professed progressive ideas. However, they backfired, resulting only in the revitalization of Marxist study sessions and nationalist and liberal writings, as well as the rise of various student organizations and demonstrations against the CAFA. Thus, throughout the 1960s, youth and student movements were at the forefront of the anti-imperialist movement.[1] In 1964, the leftist youth organization *Kabataang Makabayan* (Patriotic Youth), or KM, was established. In 1968, university students led by Jose Maria Sison reorganized the Communist Party of the Philippines.[2] From January to March in 1970, youth and students also led what would be known later as the First Quarter Storm—a series of demonstrations and protests against the Ferdinand Marcos administration. Furthermore, students from the University of the Philippines barricaded the campus against encroaching police during the Diliman Commune in February 1971.

President Marcos signed Proclamation 1081, dated on September 21, 1972, on the pretext of controlling the communist insurgency.[3] The United States supported the Marcos dictatorship in suppressing what was considered "communism," based on its Cold War politics that had been kept up since the post–World War II era. Washington had, for instance, helped the earlier Roxas and Magsaysay administrations curb the Huk Rebellion through providing counterinsurgency measures in the late 1940s and 1950s.[4] Furthermore, the United States, together with the International Monetary Fund and World Bank, established economic ties with a series of dictatorships through an outpouring of aid for the anticommunist insurgency and the backing of free markets. It was the "'thawing' of the Cold War" that caused the United

States to withdraw its support for the Philippine dictatorship.[5] The Marcos dictatorship eventually ended in February 1986 through a people's uprising, later known as the EDSA Revolution or People Power Revolution.[6]

During his rule, Marcos tried to squelch any political opposition under the logics of Cold War politics and combating communism and did so through utilizing torture methods imported from the United States. The US Army developed these techniques in Vietnam and Central America and transmitted them to the Philippine Army through the Central Intelligence Agency (CIA). Lieutenant Colonel Rolando Abadilla and Lieutenant Rodolfo Aguinaldo—known as "Marcos's top torturers"—were reportedly trained by the CIA.[7] With the suspension of the writ of habeas corpus during Martial Law, the military could arrest dissenters on mere suspicion. After raiding their houses, the military would take these activists to "safehouses" for interrogation. There, they would be subjugated to torture techniques such as Russian roulette, the "water cure," burning and electrocution of the genitals, and injection of a "truth serum."[8] Historian Alfred McCoy further explains how the torturer exhibits power over the tortured: "Much of the pain from torture is psychological, not physical, and is based upon denying its victims any power over their lives."[9] This can cause life-long psychological damage. How have such cruel and tragic experiences of the Cold War Philippines been remembered (and not remembered)? How have such memories been transmitted from parents who had real-life experiences of the era to their children who did not? How have these children received such memories? What are the functions and implications of such Cold War memories in contemporary Philippine society?

These are not merely historical inquiries, because memories of the Martial Law era under the Marcos dictatorship have been vehemently contested in recent years, despite its human rights violations, with 3,257 dead, 35,000 tortured, and 70,000 imprisoned.[10] For instance, enthusiasm for strongman rule resurfaced with the vice-presidential campaign of the dictator's son and namesake Ferdinand "Bongbong" Marcos Jr. in the 2016 elections. Though the former senator lost by a margin of a fraction of a percentage point, his candidacy spurred heated debates about how to remember the Marcos dictatorship: Should we remember it as a dark time when the country was mired in debt and haunted by human rights abuses, or as a Golden Age of economic progress? A sense of "historical revisionism" has been popularized through social media, such as Facebook groups and YouTube videos that romanticize the dictatorship while distorting historical facts.[11]

The rise of such revisionism in recent years is not a coincidence, nor is it an isolated phenomenon. In fact, there has been a so-called memory boom in the past decade or so concerning the Martial Law era. Many scholars, writers, and artists have examined and discussed lived experiences of the so-called Marcos babies—the generation who spent their childhood under Martial Law. Notably, they have interrogated the lack of memories of the Marcos years among today's youth.[12] Therefore, it is timely to study the memories (and lack thereof) of the children of Martial Law martyrs and survivors. Such investigation is important because they have witnessed the aftereffects of their parents' physical and psychological torture. Since the Cold War has provided a "plethora of signs" marked by "anti-communist witch hunts, psy-war counter-insurgency tactics, glorification of patriarchal and militaristic principles, violent suppression of Othernesses," we can examine how the children view their parents, who have been "demonized" for their activism, and how this has affected parent-child relationships even after the end of the Cold War.[13]

While there are conventional vessels of memory transmission, such as mass media, museums, or other modes of cultural production, this chapter focuses on a more intimate venue of memory production: family. Using Marianne Hirsch's concept of the "generation of postmemory," I study how children of Martial Law activists situate themselves and their parents' struggle. "Postmemory," as defined by Marianne Hirsch, refers to how "powerful" and "often traumatic" incidents that happened before the birth of the succeeding generation are remembered vividly because of the profound and moving ways the previous generation has relayed such memories. For the "generation of postmemory," these traumatic events may not have happened directly to them and may be told to them through stories in their childhood. Nonetheless, such memories of the unexperienced past are appropriated as one's own and may have a lasting impact on the next generation. Parents' sufferings are often projected and recreated in the minds of their children, making them relive their parents' trauma.[14]

Through psychoanalysis, Nanette Auerhahn and Dori Laub have analyzed "intergenerational memory" and the transference of trauma to second-generation survivors of the Holocaust and argued that children have "become burdened by memories that are not their own."[15] Studies on postmemory show how children of survivors articulate their own parents' trauma through mediums such as photographs and artwork, digital storytelling, and group identification by organizing themselves as children of the dictatorship's victims.[16]

Along with the part III theme of individual life stories, in this study I focus on the transmission and reception of these memories. By *transmission*, I mean the ways in which stories are told—their spontaneity, rituals of remembrance, or life stories recounted in printed, oral, or artistic forms. By *reception*, I refer to how children negotiate with their parents' memories as they are growing up. Though I use the term "postmemory," I delve little into the ways that much of the parents' memories affect their children "deeply and affectively as to seem to constitute memories in their own right."[17] Instead I concentrate more on the parents' telling and the modes of delivery, and on how these children receive these stories. As will be discussed in a later section of this chapter, some of the parents' narratives are marked by gaps and silences, leading children to question these nontellings.

Though interviews suggest that these recollections are normalized since the children "grew up with these memories," their parents' memories form their own consciousness of Martial Law. This understanding of the Martial Law era also affects their understanding of the present regime. More importantly, the children have to live with the "afterlife" of their parents' struggle, as they witness their own parents confronting their own memories. Rather than "aftermath," the term "afterlife" best describes the "continuing and persistent symbolic and material effects of the original event of violence on people's daily lives, their social and psychic identities, and their ongoing wrestling with the past in the present."[18] In this sense, the "afterlife" of political violence resonates not only in terms of the harrowing ordeals experienced by the parents, but also in how the succeeding generation perceives them. As time passes, certain traumatic memories can be released that coincide with the child growing up and reaching a level of understanding and maturity.

・・・・・・

Using the ground-up approach used in area studies, I have interviewed five children of Martial Law survivors who were born during the later part of the dictatorship, or many years after. These "children" are currently adults aged from twenty-five to forty years old, having little to no memory of that period, but now old enough to have lived with their parents' recollections. Their parents joined the activist movement under Martial Law and are known ex–political prisoners. These children also take part in artistic and academic endeavors that are critical of both Martial Law under Ferdinand Marcos Sr. and the former Rodrigo Duterte administration.[19]

The first interviewee, Sally, was born in 1985 and is working for an alternative media company. Her father is a poet, literary critic, and professor who was detained in 1974 and released the same year. Her mother also taught at a university.[20] Another interviewee, Andrew, was born in 1981 and is a member of a progressive artists' organization. His mother was a beauty queen turned guerrilla fighter and detainee who passed away in the 2000s. As can be gleaned from their years of birth, Sally was one year old, and Andrew was not yet five years old when Martial Law ended in 1986. It is between the ages of two and a half and four years old when children start developing autobiographical memories.[21] Both have declared that they have no memories of that period.

The next two interviewees were born years after the dictatorship. Karlo was born in 1991 and teaches at a university. His father, who was part of the activist movement and was imprisoned under Martial Law, taught at the same university post Martial Law until his retirement. Karlo's mother was also part of the movement during the dictatorship and worked for a women's nongovernmental organization (NGO) after 1986. She passed away in the 2000s. Another interviewee, May, was born in 1995 and works in a protest theater company that has its roots in the Martial Law period. Her father is a theater and movie director and one of the well-known political prisoners who were heavily tortured under the dictatorship. Her mother was also a playwright and artist who died in the 2000s.

Beth represents an interesting case, as she was born in Beijing in 1979. She is a theater actress and teaches drama at a university. Her parents were sent by the Communist Party of the Philippines to establish political links with the Communist Party of China. The family returned shortly after the People Power Revolution in 1986 and her father has become a writer and academic. Thus, she has no memories of living in the Philippines during Martial Law as she spent her early childhood in China.

As the children grow up with stories of their parents' struggles in waging the antidictatorship fight, they negotiate the past narratives of their parents' sacrifices to their own relatively more comfortable lives. In their adult years, they have arrived at a more mature understanding and appreciation of their parents' political struggles and frame these as part of the nation's history. Though they are proud of their parents, they feel anger and pain when they witness them relive their own sufferings due to the popular clamor for authoritarian rule and the blatant disregard for human rights. The parents' past trauma lives in their children's imaginations and the adult children must deal with their parents' retraumatization, especially since

Duterte's election as president and the threatened return of the Marcoses to the highest public offices came just a few years before the fiftieth anniversary of the declaration of Martial Law in 2022. This public discourse makes them reflect on their own subject positions and their own forms of dissent against the return of a despotic government.

Growing Up with These Stories

From the point of view of the children, central to these narratives are the personal struggles of their parents under the Marcos dictatorship. These include how they met and raised families while in the underground activist movement: for example, how Karlo's mother and father were politicized as university students, how they went underground, how his father was arrested and tortured in prison, how they rebuilt their lives after release from prison by teaching at university and forming NGOs, and how they viewed the RA-RJ split in the 1990s.[22] The parents also narrate difficulties with their own parents. For instance, Beth's parents were suddenly exiled to China without their own families knowing where they were.

These accounts are also anchored in how a certain class fought against the dictatorship. Andrew remembers being told about his family's ancestry as landlords. The family patriarch disowned Andrew's mother because of her proletarian outlook and activities, such as organizing workers and the peasants, making them aware of the abuses of big landlords and capitalists, and advocating for land reform, which went against the family's class interests. Andrew is also interested in his mother's stories of how the "rich kids" became allies of the underground movement and mobilized against Marcos in their own capacity by driving cars and ferrying activists, as well as smuggling letters.

Memories relayed to the children can also be related to the depth of experience of the parents. May has listened to her father talking about how he lived underground in the countryside, how he suffered detention and torture, and how he wrote plays in prison. Her father has also talked about her aunt, who became a *desaparecido* during Martial Law.[23] On the other hand, some narratives focus on a singular event. Sally has repeatedly heard about how her father was captured and detained but knows few details of her parents' political involvement.

All of the interviewees recounted that, from their earliest recollections, they grew up with these stories. Often they were told spontaneously as dinner conversation or while the family was watching television news. There would be a trigger such as discussing current events, which would connect to the parents' experiences of Martial Law. These stories were framed more as opinions than emotions, which the parents would relate to their own lives.

Within the confines of the house, some rituals can become conversation starters for children to ask questions and follow-up questions. On May's aunt's birthday, her father would light a red candle, and May would ask, "Why light a red candle instead of a white candle?" Her father would answer that red is the color of the revolution.[24] These rituals can also be spontaneous. When Andrew massaged his mother's thick and calloused foot, she would narrate how she walked barefoot in the countryside for ten years because she could not master wearing slippers without splashing mud all over them. The narration would continue through follow-up questions asked by the children. Andrew says, "We'd ask, 'How did our uncle die?' My mom would reply, 'He was cornered in an ambush.' Then we'd ask 'Mom, what's an ambush?'"[25]

By their small and fleeting nature, children also weave in and out of crowds, and become unnoticed in the background, able to eavesdrop on surrounding conversations. Karlo recalls, "When they were talking about something serious [e.g., life under Martial Law], they didn't shoo me away. I was just there, listening." When his mother was still working for a women's NGO, he would wait for her in the office and talk to the grown-ups there.[26]

Sometimes adults would invite them to be active listeners. The life stories of parents are also told through the stories of their friends. Sally recounts that during parties, her parents and their contemporaries would talk about their experiences under Martial Law, and she would listen inconspicuously. A favorite anecdote was how Sally's father tried to escape the police by running until he was exhausted, and then was caught. His comrades who shared the same prison cell would attest to his humility despite being a distinguished professor in a well-known university and would marvel at how well he would clean the toilets in jail.

Small children are also captive audiences of the stories of their parents' contemporaries; as children, they are particularly amenable. Beth explains that when she was younger, a lot of her parents' friends would spend the night in their home and converse with her: "I was just there hanging around. When there were female visitors, I was the most *accessible* [emphasis mine] to them. For instance, they would braid my hair and tell stories. It was really very spontaneous."[27]

In other cases, the medium of narrating one's life story is through the lives of others. Andrew's mother would tell of her relationships with other people, and in the process, the experiences that they had together: "She would introduce us to her friends and tell us stories about them: We were together in this event. And then we fought the dictatorship. We were part of the same prison cell."[28] Similarly, May's father would talk about his experiences with her colleagues in the theater company, who were with him in the movement.

Though these children recount having knowledge of these stories growing up, they acknowledge that they do not have actual memories of Martial Law. However, they do have a consciousness of having known about the memories of their parents, which frame their understanding of Martial Law. May mentions that "I grew up with these stories. So, I've learned the memories since as far as I can recall. I don't ever recall a time that I didn't know about Martial Law. I grew up with the knowledge that what happened during this time was not good, that Marcos was the dictator. So I grew up with the activist worldview that my father has. Not the same level as Dad but we understand each other."[29]

Part of this "activist worldview" is the awareness of social issues and activities within the movement, which will be elaborated on below. Karlo is more precise, recalling that he would hear conversations about Martial Law when he was between four and eleven years old. At that age, he did not have the courage to show his interest and to ask for more information, although he would press for more details later, in his adolescence.

Awareness of their privileged or middle-class positions also affects the children's reception and remembrance of their parents' memories.[30] Andrew says that he had no memories of that period because "I was nearly five when it ended. I had no memories of my own. I did not feel the struggles of Martial Law." Moreover, his house offered a safe refuge, which shielded him from demonstrations outside: "I grew up in a family-owned apartment building. The streets really never came up to us in their raw form. But those who came to my house, they were activists. Ah, mommy's buddies. So it's just normal."[31]

Because of their comfortable upbringing, the children were not able to perceive the magnitude of their parents' narratives when they were younger. When Beth was born, the family had already adjusted culturally to their life in China. In addition, she did not have to experience life under Martial Law in the Philippines. It was only later on when she returned to the Philippines that she was able to imagine what her parents and their comrades had gone through: "When I was a kid, in China, I didn't experience what my parents experienced because I was a kid. I got everything that I needed.

If it was cold, we had gloves. If we were hungry, we had food. What they suffered when they were in China because of Martial Law, I didn't really experience that."[32]

The awareness of this privileged position also results in parents *not* telling much of their stories. Sally observes that there were few extensive conversations about her parents' Martial Law experiences when she was a child. She surmised that what her father went through did not compare with what others experienced. That is why he would not talk much about prison. Though Sally's father was imprisoned for eleven months, he did not undergo physical torture, unlike other detainees, since he was already a well-known professor during that time.

These children, *as children*, were constantly surrounded by these stories of their parents' lives. In the next section, the ways that the parents would tell their life stories will be investigated: how they relayed or withheld distressing details of their experiences that might be upsetting to their own children, and how they injected these accounts with political importance for their children who may have grown up in more comfortable circumstances.

Framing the Struggle

The form of the story depends on the storyteller, which affects the angle and the content of the narratives. Karlo notes this difference among his parents: "My father is more interested in the theoretical and intellectual stuff in the movement because he is a professor. My mother was more interested in the people." As a child, he was captivated by his mother's delivery: "The event was heavy, but her storytelling was funny." One memorable narrative for him involved Lean Alejandro's death.[33] "She was one of those who retrieved Lean's body after he was ambushed by the military. She said, 'Even if he was bloody, he was still handsome.'"[34] Even if the descriptions were replete with details, she often digressed to other anecdotes. Nonetheless, Karlo feels that his mother's narratives were interesting. On the other hand, he was able to appreciate his father's political musings later on when he studied at a university.

The framing of the story is evident in how Andrew views his mother's life story: "My own memories being largely absent, this mythical woman is the central figure." Andrew considers his mother a lead character in the "tale of the *buena familia* [good family] who had the privilege of having not to get involved." Her mother's circle of friends are "characters who are introduced to us" in this "backdrop epic tale" of their family's dispositions. Details of how his mother went to the mountains and faced malnutrition while pregnant, causing all her teeth to fall out, "filled in the landscape" of this narrative, along with vibrant descriptions of the flora and fauna of the countryside. The prison experience, often described by others as a tormenting ordeal, was also approached differently by his mother like a "a puzzle-solving activity, how to keep cool, how to investigate, and how not to let on that you have a plan." As far as Andrew knows, his mother was not tortured. Her incarceration became a narrative of how "an obstacle was placed in her way, and how she overcame it" instead of the usual "trials and tribulations."[35]

Sharing one's life stories can take the form of social praxis, such as going to political rallies. May explains that her father has two ways of teaching: "One way is really by talking to me through lecture-type stories and casual conversations. Another way is just by exposing me, letting me see."[36] Her father would talk about Martial Law like a history lesson, and would inject his personal experiences there. Because of the overtly political nature of the parents' lives, private personal experiences could act as a springboard for discussing the bigger political milieu, or vice versa. This appreciation for the seemingly mundane, or the vaguely theoretical, would shift as a child matured into adulthood.

Comprehension and Perception from Childhood to Adulthood

As children grow older, their understandings of their parents' stories change. For Beth, this gradual shift in perspective coincided with her family's return to the Philippines after the People Power Revolution in 1986, as she started elementary school. The physical distance, in a country where the culture and the political climate were worlds apart from those of China, led her to situate herself more within the context of her parents' narratives: "I know that when we were still in China, I guess that because of my age, I wouldn't be able to imagine the gravity of the situation whenever I hear these stories. It was only after coming back here, with a little bit more maturity, or with a bit of understanding of bigger words that I heard more often of things that happened to our family, and at the same time of things that happened to their friends who remained here."[37]

As noted above, these children interacted with their parents' contemporaries in the activist movement. A certain fondness developed among these surrounding adults. It was only later on as adults that these children realized the political importance of these figures in the struggle. For them, personal and political relations have become intertwined. As Karlo mentions, "I consider my mother's friends my uncles and godfathers. Later, I was surprised because when I was a kid, I didn't know that they were big figures in the anti–Martial Law movement."[38] Similarly, Andrew states, "I thought that my mother's bourgeois friends were just her bourgeois friends. However sympathetic they might have been, their involvement was just that. I didn't know that they were active in the struggle."[39]

In their young adult years, the children developed a more mature comprehension of their parents' actions in light of politics and ideology. They developed a more nuanced appreciation of their parents' answers to their questions that seemed inadequate to them when they were younger. May shares, "About the countryside, I remember asking my father 'What do you do there? You'll just wait for a fight?' He replied, 'No, of course not.' Then he explained that 'We teach the people.' So for a long time, I cannot understand. What they're doing is good, why are you being jailed and killed? And until now, actually there are a few aspects to that question. It's still difficult to explain. Although as I grow older, I understand more."[40]

As the child matures into adulthood, appreciation of the parent's story deepens. In the previous section, Karlo reflects that the narrative may be centered on a single political event, yet his father told his side differently from his mother. He elaborates further: "Let's say my parents talk about the *Kahos*, yet they have a different take. My mother is more interested in the outcome and the people involved. My father is more interested in probing the causes why it happened. When I was older, I became more interested in the root causes, but when I was a kid, I was interested in the story, because it's a story."[41] Later on, at university, he was able to relate to his father's theoretical analysis—the "intellectual stuff." He also learned to appreciate the intensity and implications of his mother's narrative, which on the surface seemed to be just an amusing story of ordinary people. As he grew older, he "revisited" his mother's stories by probing further. The story then grew and became more detailed compared to the earlier telling.[42]

While gaps in stories were filled in in subsequent retellings, narratives could also lose their details since storytellers are prone to forget as they age. May meditates on this process on both the effects of narration to the teller and to the listener: "Many times, the stories repeat but I still don't get tired of hearing those. As I grow older, my understanding differs. So the same story that my dad told me at five years old has a different meaning when I hear it again at fifteen years old. My dad also doesn't remember everything because of his age. He'll only remember it when there's a trigger."[43] Later on, there would be an understanding of how the parents would come to terms with their own experiences. The children, as adults, would eventually sense why their parents would convey or evade certain memories.

Confrontation and Evasion: The "Afterlives" of These Stories

Through time, the story changes along with the parent-child dynamics. Painful memories are now described to an adult who is deemed capable of handling them, while the parent has become capable of acknowledging the experiences and the emotions. Around this time, the parents are afforded distance to confront and process their own memories.[44] Sally, who earlier stated that her father did not talk much about his own personal life during Martial Law, recalls, "When I was in high school, we were having a light conversation about Martial Law. Then he talked about his life in prison. Suddenly, he cried. I was surprised."[45]

Evasion does not necessarily manifest through silence; it can also happen through selective retelling. Karlo's father used the "political" to evade the "personal." He was able to pause and reflect on his life when he distanced himself from the movement in the 1990s. As Karlo recollects, "Everything manifested when he left the movement. The '90s and the post–Martial Law period were more difficult than his life during Martial Law."[46] Later, Karlo took advantage of his father's manic phases, when he would incessantly talk about his private life, and his repressed memories of torture were finally released. The psychological effects on his father differed from those on his mother, who, through repeated storytelling, was able to release her emotions. Karlo contemplates this difference as follows: "My mother was more stable in terms of temperament because she had already talked about it. My father used the intellectual stuff, but he had a lot of baggage. I think that my mother could already live with that experience. My father was still carrying a lot of issues because he was tortured. Maybe that was his way of telling us that he had that experience, even if we were talking about intellectual stuff. There were times that if you'd ask him about personal stuff, he wouldn't be very detailed about it. Eventually, that would change."[47] The story changes also in the way that what was previously denied is now admitted. The sordid aspects of May's father's torture could now be depicted publicly in a television show, which he had previously hidden from his daughter. May analyzed that this "lie" was intended not only to protect her, but to allow him to eventually come to terms with his suffering:

> There were times that he had a hard time talking because it was still painful to remember. For instance, that part of torture, when a piece of broomstick [*walis tingting*] was inserted [in his genitals]. When he told me about it, his story was different. He told me that it didn't happen. So I believed it. And then there was a television show about his life. In that scene, it happened. So I asked my dad, "I thought that it didn't push through, but in the television show it happened?" Then he admitted, "Actually, it happened. I just denied it. I just denied it in my head, but it happened." He has a tendency of blocking those painful memories of torture. That's manifested by him denying that it happened, like that particular type of torture. Then lately, he will admit that he actually lied about it. Or one way that it manifests also is that he won't talk about it. But eventually, he will tell me, though it will take a few years and multiple times of me asking the same questions.[48]

Denial also occurs by not admitting the memory to the children. This was done by dismissing difficult questions, which could expose certain dilemmas the parents faced. Andrew reminisces, "I remember asking my mother, did [you] ever kill anyone? To which she told me to shut up. I think that was wise. On one hand you're gonna ask the question, so that it's cool, my mom is cool. But I think my mother was saying that if ever she did it, it wasn't something she was proud of. Perhaps that was what was implied."[49]

Postmemory, therefore, is not just having the parents' experiences live through the minds of the next generation who have no actual memories of that period, but having their offspring witness firsthand the psychological effects of torture and incarceration. The children would now have to deal with these memories, and how others perceive the political involvement of their parents.

Normalizing Stories, Normalizing Pain

Since these children have grown up with these stories, in a sense, they have become normalized and ordinary from their perspectives. Beth did not realize the extraordinariness of her family's life until other people reacted to her father's short stories: "When I read about it, *ay*! We have been talking about this over numerous dinners, but he just added a few details. But I never saw it that way. This is how it affects other people. So I guess, because it's your own family you don't realize the gravity or relevance of that in terms of other people."[50]

Andrew similarly observes, "Everyone seems so amazed and we were like a bit, okay."[51] However, some children would downplay these memories, to the point that they do not remember these stories as they take them for granted. They realize their familial and historical importance too late. Andrew admits:

> By the time we're talking about it in school, we [my siblings and I] were like, "Yeah, yeah." We know, you don't have to tell us more on Martial Law even if there were many gaps in our mental image of Martial Law. It's not really *umay* [tired], but "Been there, done that." We grew up with this, this legendary figure. So it was the same mistake to treat this as mundane. With your earlier question if I remembered any rallies or anything, no, nothing. Even after Martial Law, the activist activities going around the house were not remarkable. Looking back, I would say that we were nonchalant about it. We were blasé. We heard some of these stories before. My regret now is that we didn't pay enough attention, and we lost her journals. So now it's like, "What was her story? Who was that person again?" We are taking it for granted to a certain extent.[52]

Though Karlo enjoys listening to his mother's stories, he also discloses regret for not having the courage to ask for more details until after his mother died. Through hearing his father's stories repeatedly, he has become attuned to the pain, but he could not vocalize his feelings to his father: "Really, I don't know what to say because what can I say? Do I say, 'Oh, pity you?' It's difficult, right? It's difficult to listen even if he talked about it many times. The stories become more and more detailed in the long run."[53]

Living with these stories, May acknowledges that the emotions are harrowing to both the parent and child: "The stories have a certain pinch even if you hear about them many times. Same with my dad, even if he talked about it repeatedly, there are moments when it still gets to him." The parents' stories, as depicted by others in many artistic forms, portray a more vivid picture in the adult child's mind. Because May's father is a well-known Martial Law survivor, his story has been relayed in numerous television, movie, and theater shows. This affects May "emotionally, for I can imagine the stories vividly also because they're there in movie form."[54] May describes how she can visualize her father's life story—its milieu during the Marcos dictatorship, and the people surrounding them—and intertwine it with stories of the incidents that resonate up to the present:

> Yeah, I imagine vividly those stories, even stories of those who were activists during that time. He talks about iconic figures like Liliosa Hilao and Emmanuel Lacaba. They may not be close to my dad, but I can imagine these stories. He also tells the stories vividly. He's a very good storyteller. He should be, he is a writer. It doesn't really reach a point where I dream about it. But sometimes passively. For example, I see in the news or hear that somebody was shot. Like in Nueva Ecija, there was a priest who was killed. Yeah, I remember the stories again. Then I think, it's happening again. This is the now, but the stories that my dad has from the 1970s still happen today.[55]

For the generation of postmemory, the political is intimately lived through the personal; torture during the Marcos dictatorship is not something that happened in the abstract, but to their own parents. Such familial histories also have a bearing on the political stances of the children.

Political Decisions and Guardianship of Memories

From the adult children's perspective, the stories that their parents tell them affect both their personal lives and political outlooks. On one level, some feel that they are guardians of their families' stories.[56] Because of his interest in his parents' narratives at an early age, Karlo speculates that his parents were "deliberate" in passing these stories on to him. Thus, he describes these memories as "constitutive" of his person.[57]

The legacy of his mother as a legendary figure is also a major concern for Andrew. He is conscious of how the media would portray her as a beauty queen instead of an activist: "We were wary about the beauty queen angle. I thought that we already know feminism. It was never really a big deal for us kids. It was small, it was the least remarkable thing she ever did."[58]

The parents' experiences with the activist movement also made their children wary of certain factions of the left. Beth, whose parents defected from the movement, recounts that she did not join any activist organization when she entered university. Even if he is politically identified with the left, Karlo is also skeptical because of his father's experience of having gone through the RA-RJ split. However, his father reminds him of the inherent complexities within the movement: "My father says that he is a Marxist at heart and he believes that the movement is not monolithic. It doesn't destroy the whole theory just because he experienced this."[59]

The adult children were not forced to have the same political outlooks as their parents; rather, their parents have influenced their decisions. Though seeing herself as not at the same level as her father in terms of intellect and experience, May explains that she chose to be politically aligned with her parents "not because I just swallow everything he teaches. It's because he really makes me understand."[60]

Where the personal meets the political, these stories are important because certain values are transmitted. For Andrew, these are the following: "How to keep a brave front, to take a stand, to favor the marginalized. We weren't given EDs or educational discussions, but through those stories, there was a transfer of values that we apply in our bourgeois life, like how to have dignity. This was contextualized with what she did in her life."[61]

In the end, it is not just the stories that are transmitted but family history, values, and politics—along with skepticism, wariness, and jadedness. Though not being forced to take the same paths as their parents, the children do acknowledge that their influence is there.

Contextualizing the Personal and the Political

The previous sections have described personal reasons that activist memories of the parents were passed on to children: the natural curiosity of children, encounters with parents' former comrades with whom children are affectionate, and the fondness parents hold for these memories. Parents also narrate their experiences because they are still part of the activist movement or have scholarly and artistic productions tied to their involvement during Martial Law. This section discusses the historical circumstances that enabled generational transmission of activist memories in certain families. It will also elaborate on the functions of these memories and, specifically, how memories of political violence circulated within the family affect the political outlook of the children.

In other societies and contexts, activist memories tend to be untransmitted or altered due to absence in the state narrative. Only decades later will there be an opening of discourse, depending on political circumstances. For instance, the Indonesian killings of members of the PKI (Indonesian Communist Party) and its sympathizers in 1965–66 were excluded from the official state narrative under the Suharto regime. Children of political prisoners exiled in Buru recount that they learned about the true circumstances of their parents' absence in their lives only after the resignation of Suharto in 1998. Although some children negotiated these memories through silence, others would be empathic to their parents' causes and attempt to retrieve stories of the past.[62] Kar-Yen Leong concludes that amid the silencing of opposition during Suharto's New Order regime, the period after the *reformasi* allowed the political detainees and their children to share their harrowing experiences of the previous era. The family then acts as a conduit to counter the sanctioned state discourse, as seen in the biographies and oral histories of dissidents and their offspring about the New Order.[63] Such examination of the effects of government persecution on the family could be particularly relevant as we interrogate how the bigger public discourse shapes the private circulation of memories.

The emergence of a "democratic space" and the lifting of censorship immediately after the end of the Marcos dictatorship in 1986 resulted in a state of "euphoria," wherein print and broadcast media openly discussed topics such as the mass movement, human rights, and other national issues.[64] Former political detainees were able to recount their activism and torture through these forums.

However, in the immediate aftermath of Martial Law, the atrocities of that period were not yet fully embedded in the educational system. My interviewees would mention with regret that Martial Law was not taught about extensively in schools then because it was recent and not yet history. Yet within that democratic space, due to the opening up of media and proliferation of NGOs, activist memories could be shared. Karlo, who spent his childhood within a women's NGO where his mother worked in the 1990s, observes of the post–Martial Law milieu:

> In the 1990s, people who were involved in the movement did not appreciate the legacy of the struggle. So the memory is there, but it was not seen that these memories should be cared for and protected. During that time, everything was still new, and there was the optimism for democratic reconstruction. There was the proliferation of NGOs and cause-oriented organizations where a lot of the members were veterans, former activists, and party members. These NGOs tried to mimic the structure of these activist organizations. So in a way, the 1990s was a way to relive those years in a more permissible environment, because the social problems were still there.[65]

Activists continued to relay their memories to their offspring because parents saw continuing repression post Martial Law. May, who grew up during the 2000s, mentions that the corruption and the human rights violations during the Joseph Estrada and Gloria Macapagal-Arroyo presidencies could be linked to the authoritarianism during the Marcos dictatorship: "One thing my dad always tells me every time I say the word EDSA Revolution, he always says that it was not a revolution. He always would say that even when I was young. It was just an uprising because the horrors of Martial Law never ended. On paper, Martial Law ended, but the practices of impunity still continue."⁶⁶

Based on their parents' experiences during the Marcos dictatorship, the children understand that the Cold War practices of human rights violations continue in the Philippines, even today. Sally terms the period starting in the mid-2010s "de facto Martial Law" since there are parallels between the Marcos Sr. and Duterte administrations. She observes intensification of the Duterte's administration's red-tagging and anticommunist propaganda, and notes rising numbers of enforced disappearances and extrajudicial killings. Beth observes that activists today still chant "the same slogans" because "it's the same time exact things that you write down as in the 1970s," since there is no substantive difference in succeeding administrations, despite the change of presidencies.⁶⁷ Andrew laments that Martial Law is usually seen as an isolated event instead of as part of the social and political structure that ensures the continuation of despotic regimes: "There's a tendency to treat Martial Law as a catastrophe or an accident, as if we got sick all of a sudden. There are many symptoms, ingredients, and characteristics of our society that were carried over even after EDSA 1986. The democratic transformation did not take place. So there should be an attempt to break that complacency to say that we are already democratic. Especially now, it's getting obvious."⁶⁸

Activist memories of the previous generation also function as a way to make sense of these authoritarian practices despite their different forms. May articulates that the historical revisionism in social media during the last Duterte administration has made it difficult for her generation to discern "who the enemy is because they are disguised in many forms," as opposed to her father's time, under Martial Law, when "the enemy [was] clear." May makes the following distinction: "Before, there was media blackout. So, what people know is nothing has been reported. Now, it's not even a blackout. It's really revisionism." The "strong stories and strong knowledge" from her father equipped May to identify who the "enemy" is "in this very hazy political situation today."⁶⁹

The parents' memories also affected the children's ways of resisting the Duterte administration. Beth felt that the current milieu was scary but vacillated on how to fight the administration: "When Martial Law happened, my parents were young, they were in college, they were ready to fight. I have a kid now. I don't know if I will fight or not. Maybe if I fight, I will see where I am right now. But, at the same time, I feel like, am I a coward for not doing anything?"[70] This hesitancy about being an activist under the Duterte administration was linked to her parents' misgivings toward the activist movement under Martial Law. On the other hand, Sally perceived the structural problems of Philippine society along with May and Andrew. She directed her anger not only toward the Marcos family and ex-President Duterte, but toward the "state" and its machinery.[71] She felt that the recent times were scary, and that people should have fought by protesting the Duterte administration through street demonstrations. This would have made the opposition more visible, rather than limiting dissent to social media platforms.

The political climate immediately after Martial Law allowed for the dissemination of memories within both personal circles and popular media. However, because of the euphoria of democratic reconstruction, there was no conscious effort to guard these memories within the schools and disseminate these to the next generation of Filipinos. Within the families, activist memories have continued to be recounted, since the parents saw that the corruption and repressive practices of succeeding presidencies were no different than those of the Marcos dictatorship. This has affected the understanding of the children toward the Duterte administration and since.

Conclusion

Though the Cold War officially ended on the global scale in 1991, the aftereffects of the Marcos dictatorship and torture methods learned from the CIA and implemented by the military on dissenters have had profound effects. This affects intimate, familial relations, particularly those of parent and child. Through this study of postmemory, one analyzes the transmission and reception of memories that are passed to the second generation that has no actual recollections of that period. Among the strategies of narration are denial and evasion, or framing stories in ways that evade the personal. The children also live with the "afterlives" of their parents' memories. As the child transitions into adulthood, the parents also continue to process their own traumas, which leads to the opening up of certain aspects of their torture that were previously repressed. Hence, not only does the child's appreciation of the stories change, but so do the understanding and details of the parents' narration.

As children grow up, attitudes toward these memories also mature—what was vague before is now better understood, and what was unappreciated before is now valued. Though these stories have become "normalized," since the children "grew up with these stories," the parents' experiences frame their understanding of Martial Law. The children acknowledge that they make their own political decisions even if their parents' experiences influence their political outlooks. There exists also a guardianship of memory as they pursue intellectual and artistic activities that are critical of the Marcos dictatorship and of continuing despotic regimes and political repression.

The interviews suggest that the children see the continuities between the atrocities of the Marcos dictatorship and the last Duterte administration. This implies that they connect personal memories of their parents' torture and resistance under Martial Law to the bigger social and political structures that ensure the continuation of authoritarian rule. Despite the absence of personal memory of Martial Law, they pinpoint the generational differences in how these regimes manipulate information and memory: through censorship and media blackout during the Marcos dictatorship, and through historical revisionism through social media under the Duterte administration and since.

Interrogating the nature of transmission of familial memory is important socially, politically, and historically in both Philippine and Southeast Asian contexts. By contextualizing the effects of the Cold War within the region, one can glean the effects of state-sanctioned discourse on cultural particularities within the intimate and the familial. This reveals the complexities when the official discourse of the state differs from the memories of the family.

The psychological effects of Cold War tactics can explain why some families value their memories or treat them with indifference. The reasons behind these retellings/ nontellings can be linked to the effects of trauma, and to differing concepts of "closure" and "moving on." Hence, some activists sought to rebuild their lives after the end of the dictatorship, while others continued with their activist involvement with the view that the problems persist to this day. Likewise, they could attempt to confront the past or treat it with nostalgia. Though regimes attempt to silence or distort memory through state-sanctioned means, the circulation of memory through personal and familial networks can help challenge state narratives. Children can take on artistic and scholarly endeavors to ensure that the memories are kept alive, and, in their ways, their parents' stories continue to be told.

Notes

* The author acknowledges the Office of the Chancellor of the University of the Philippines Diliman, through the Office of the Vice Chancellor for Research and Development, for funding support through the PhD Incentive Award.

1. Jose Maria Sison, *The Philippine Revolution: The Leader's View* (New York: Crane Russak, 1989), 12.

2. Jose Maria Sison, founding chairperson of the reestablished Communist Party of the Philippines, notes that the growth of the youth and student movement affected the class composition of the party. See Sison, *Philippine Revolution*, 57.

3. Gene Segarra Navera, "Metaphorizing Martial Law: Constitutional Authoritarianism In Marcos' Rhetoric (1972–1985)," *Philippine Studies: Historical And Ethnographic Viewpoints* 66, no. 4 (2018): 421.

4. Navera, "Metaphorizing Martial Law," 424–25; and Eva Hansson, Kevin Hewison, and Jim Glassman, "Legacies of the Cold War in East and Southeast Asia: An Introduction," *Journal of Contemporary Asia* 50, no. 4 (2020): 496.

5. Teresa S. Encarnacion Tadem, "The Emergence of Filipino Technocrats as Cold War 'Pawns,'" *Journal of Contemporary Asia* 50, no. 4 (2020): 531.

6. Jocelyn Martin, "Martial Law as Philippine Trauma: Group Culture, the Sacred, and Impunity in Three Memoirs," *Philippine Studies: Historical and Ethnographic Viewpoints* 66, no. 4 (December 2018): 476.

7. Alfred McCoy, *Torture and Impunity* (Madison: University of Wisconsin Press, 2012), 117–18.

8. See Raissa Robles and Alan Robles, *Marcos Martial Law Never Again* (Quezon City: Filipinos for a Better Philippines, 2016).

9. McCoy, *Torture and Impunity*, 117.

10. McCoy, *Torture and Impunity*, 119.

11. Brittany Kaiser, former director of the political data analysis company Cambridge Analytica, revealed that Bongbong Marcos had approached the company to "rebrand" his "family's image" in social media in time for the vice-presidential elections in 2016. Kaiser calls this "historical revisionism . . . in a data-driven and scientific way." Following a series of scandals, Cambridge Analytica ceased operations in 2018. See "Bongbong Marcos Asked Cambridge Analytica to 'Rebrand' Family Image," *Rappler*, July 15, 2020. See also Jose Santos P. Ardivilla, "The Marcos Memes and the Manipulation of Memory," in *Remembering/Rethinking EDSA*, eds. JPaul S. Manzanilla and Caroline S. Hau (Pasig: Anvil, 2016), 84–105; and Victor Felipe Bautista, "The Pervert's Guide to Historical Revisionism: Traversing the Marcos Fantasy," *Philippine Studies: Historical And Ethnographic Viewpoints* 66, no. 3 (2018): 273–300.

12. In an international conference titled "The Remains of a Dictatorship: An International Conference of the Philippines under Marcos," which was held at Ateneo de Manila University, Quezon City, Philippines, in August 2017, some papers, such as Noahlyn C. Maranan and April Hope T. Castro's "Remembering EDSA 1: A Content Analysis of Millennials' Recall of the People Power Revolution," deal with the lack of the memories among the present generation on the Martial

Law era. Other papers, such as Imelda Veloso-Beltran et al.'s "Narrative Momentum and the Duty of Hearsay Testimony: Second-Generation Stories on Martial Law" and Maria Serena Diokno's "Imprisonment and 'Social' Solitude," discuss the lived experiences of children during Martial Law, exploring how elders explained their activist involvement to their children. Also, there are published works that recount growing up during the Marcos dictatorship. Roland Tolentino and Frank Cimatu's *Mondo Marcos (Writings on Martial Law and the Marcos Babies)* (Pasig City: Anvil Publishing, 2010) is an anthology of works by "Marcos babies" or the generation who spent their childhood during Martial Law. Sandra Nicole Roldan's autobiographical children's book *At the School Gate* (Makati City: Bookmark, 2018) tells of her witnessing her father's arrest and imprisonment.

13. Joel David, "The Cold War and Marcos-Era Cinema in The Philippines," in *Proceedings of the 8th ASEAN Inter-University Conference on Social Development* (Manila: University of the Philippines, Union Network International—Asia and Pacific, Free Trade Alliance, National University of Singapore, 2008), 1.

14. Marianne Hirsch, "The Generation of Postmemory," *Poetics Today* 29, no. 1 (2008): 106–7.

15. Dori Laub and Nanette Auerhahn, "Intergenerational Memory of the Holocaust," in *International Handbook of Multigenerational Legacies Of Trauma*, ed. Yael Danieli (New York: Plenum Press, 1998), 22.

16. See, for instance, Marianne Hirsch, "Past Lives: Postmemories In Exile," *Poetics Today* 17, no. 4 (1996): 659–86; Ken Setiawan, "The Omnipresent Past: Rethinking Transitional Justice through Digital Storytelling on Indonesia's 1965 Violence," in *Civil Society And Transitional Justice In Asia And The Pacific*, ed. Lia Kent, Joanne Wallis, and Claire Cronin (Canberra: ANU Press, 2019), 63–81; and Cara Levey, "Of HIJOS and Niños: Revisiting Postmemory in Post-Dictatorship Uruguay," *History and Memory* 26, no. 2 (2014): 5–39.

17. Hirsch, "Generation of Postmemory," 106–7.

18. Macarena Gomez-Barris, *Where Memory Dwells* (Berkeley: University of California Press 2008), 6.

19. Elected in 2016, now ex-president Rodrigo Duterte was criticized for his human rights violations even by international bodies such as the United Nations and the European Parliament. While running for the presidency, he campaigned for a strong and authoritarian rule akin to the Marcos dictatorship. His administration was known for extrajudicial killings under his "War on Drugs," which encouraged police and vigilantes to gun down illegal drug users without benefit of due process. Duterte created the National Task Force to End Local Communist Armed Conflict (NTF-ELCAC), led mostly by his military men. Even without substantial basis, the NTF-ELCAC accused dissenters and political activists of being recruiters of communist rebels who were seeking to topple the administration through armed means. Some of those who were "red-tagged" became victims of extrajudicial killings. There was a rise in police brutality under the Duterte administration. See "Duterte Administration Needs 'Substantial Improvement' in Human Rights Record,' Inquirer," *The Straits Times*, September 25, 2020; "NTF–ELCAC to Go 'Full Blast' on Legal Offensives after Anti-terror Law Oral Arguments," *Rappler*, May 8,

2021; and "Critics Compare Marcos, Duterte," *Philippine Daily Inquirer*, September 22, 2020.

20. In this chapter, I have used pseudonyms for the safety and privacy of interviewees.

21. Paul John Eakin, "Breaking Rules: The Consequences of Self-Narration," *Biography* 24, no. 1 (2001): 115.

22. Due to differences in political tactics and ideology, the left formalized its split into two camps in the 1990s: the "reaffirmists," or RAs, who reaffirmed their commitment to armed struggle in the countryside and adherence to Marxism, Leninism, and Maoism; and the "rejectionists," or RJs, who rejected the armed struggle and gave primacy to parliamentary struggle.

23. Taken from the Spanish word meaning "disappeared," *desaparecido* means enforced disappearances. The Families of Victims of Involuntary Disappearance (FIND) has recorded 926 *desaparecidos* under the Marcos Sr. administration. See "What You Need to Know about Enforced Disappearances in The Philippines," *Rappler*, August 29, 2018.

24. May, interview by the author, May 23, 2019.

25. Andrew, interview by the author, September 27, 2019. "Ambush" refers to an encounter with the military and the underground New People's Army.

26. Karlo, interview by the author, September 10, 2019.

27. Beth, interview by the author, May 14, 2019.

28. Andrew, interview.

29. May, interview.

30. The tensions between their middle-class status with their left-wing political views and attempts to identify with the masses are a recurring theme in the life stories of middle-class activists during the Marcos dictatorship. This tension is reflected in their memoirs. See Portia Reyes, "Claiming History: Memoirs of the Struggle against Ferdinand Marcos's Martial Law Regime in the Philippines," *Journal of Social Issues in Southeast Asia* 33, no. 2 (2018): 457–98.

31. Andrew, interview.

32. Beth, interview.

33. After the overthrow of the Marcos dictatorship in 1986, the Corazon Aquino administration was also marked by political ambushes of known leftist leaders. Lean Alejandro, secretary general of *Bagong Alyansang Makabayan* (New Patriotic Alliance or BAYAN—an umbrella organization of workers and progressive groups) was murdered in his car in 1987 after attending a press conference. Rolando Olalia of the labor group *Kilusang Mayo Uno* (May First Movement) was killed in November 1986. Bernabe Buscayno, the pardoned leader of the New People's Army who ran for senator under the Partido ng Bayan, was seriously wounded after coming home from a television interview. Polytechnic University of the Philippines president Nemesio Prudente also survived an ambush. These killings, though not solved, were attributed to the disgruntled military who were angered by the Aquino administration's softening stance toward the left. See Marites Danguilan Vitug, "Leandro Alejandro: Thinker-Activist," in *Six Young Filipino Martyrs*, ed. Asuncion David Maramba (Pasig: Anvil Publishing, 1997), 35; and Belinda A. Aquino, "The

Philippines in 1987: Beating Back the Challenge of August," *Southeast Asian Affairs 1988*, 206.

34. Karlo, interview.
35. Andrew, interview.
36. May, interview.
37. Beth, interview.
38. Karlo, interview.
39. Andrew, interview.
40. May, interview.
41. Karlo, interview. *Kampanyang Ahos* or *Kahos* was an anti-infiltration campaign of suspected undercover military agents by the Communist Party of the Philippines and its armed wing, the New People's Army, from 1986 to 1987 in Mindanao.
42. Karlo, interview.
43. May, interview.
44. Cathy Caruth describes the effects of trauma in the form of "belatedness," as one needs the time and distance to process the event. At the same time, trauma is "haunting," as it resides in the deep recesses of memory. See Caruth, *Trauma: Explorations in Memory* (Baltimore: Johns Hopkins University Press, 1995), 6; and *Unclaimed Experience: Trauma, Narrative, and History* (Baltimore: Johns Hopkins University Press, 1996), 4. To access and reclaim these traumatic memories, Dori Laub observes that an attuned "listener" could help the survivor narrate his or her pain, from which the testimony would resurface and assume a life of its own. See Laub, "On Holocaust Testimony and Its 'Reception' within Its Own Frame, as a Process in Its Own Right: A Response to 'Between History and Psychoanalysis' by Thomas Trezise," *History & Memory* 21, no. 1 (2009): 139. In a way, these children have become "secondary witnesses" since they have listened to the testimony of the primary witnesses, who have deep connections to their lives. See Esther Jilovsky, *Remembering the Holocaust* (New York: Bloomsbury Academic, 2015), 11–12. I have also discussed how Martial Law survivors needed time and distance to process their own traumas, which resulted in the publication of their autobiographical narratives decades after the end of the Marcos dictatorship. See Mary Grace R. Concepcion, "Writing the Self and Exigencies of Survival: Autobiography as Catharsis and Commemoration," *Philippine Studies: Historical And Ethnographic Viewpoints* 66, no. 3 (2018): 301–34.
45. Sally, interview by the author, May 11, 2019.
46. Karlo, interview.
47. Karlo, interview.
48. May, interview.
49. Andrew, interview.
50. Beth, interview.
51. Andrew, interview.
52. Andrew, interview.
53. Karlo, interview.
54. May, interview.
55. May, interview.
56. See Hirsch, "Generation of Postmemory," 104.

57. Karlo, interview.
58. Andrew, interview.
59. Karlo, interview.
60. May, interview.
61. Andrew, interview. Educational discussions or EDs are study sessions within the activist movement, usually on Marxist, Leninist, and Maoist theory, history of the movement, and Philippine social issues.
62. Grace Leksana, "Review: Remembering the Indonesian Genocide, 53 Years Later," *Bijdragen Tot De Taal-, Land- En Volkenkunde* 175, no. 1 (2019): 68–78.
63. Kar-Yen Leong, "Speaking across the Lines: 1965, the Family, and Reconciliation in Indonesia," *Kritika Kultura* 37 (2021): 6–16.
64. JPaul S. Manzanilla, "A Season for Remembering: People's Power, Democratization, and the Memories of a Revolution," in Manzanilla and Hau, *Remembering/Rethinking EDSA*, 8–9.
65. Karlo, interview.
66. May, interview. President Joseph "Erap" Estrada was a popular movie actor who won the presidential race with his slogan *Erap para sa mahirap* (Erap for the poor) in 1998. However, an impeachment trial ensued after he was accused of corruption because of his involvement in *jueteng*—a numbers game that is considered a form of illegal gambling. On January 16, 2001, the Philippine senators deliberated on whether to open an envelope containing evidence that a billion-peso bank account labeled "Jose Velarde" actually belonged to Joseph Estrada. Ten of the senators voted "yes" to opening the envelope, while eleven voted "no." This was a decisive moment in the impeachment trial, which triggered a five-day rally along Epifanio de los Santos Avenue (or EDSA) to oust Estrada from his presidency. Estrada stepped down from office and was succeeded by Vice President Gloria Macapagal-Arroyo on January 20, 2001. This event was known as EDSA People Power II, reminiscent of the bloodless protests to end the Marcos dictatorship in EDSA People Power 1986. See "Looking Back at EDSA II: The Political Paths of Estrada and Arroyo," *Rappler*, January 17, 2017. Five years later, President Gloria Macapagal-Arroyo placed the entire country under a state of emergency through Proclamation No. 1017 on February 24, 2006, following a supposed thwarted coup d'état that coincided with the twentieth anniversary of EDSA People Power I. The government claimed that there was a conspiracy between the disgruntled military and the left to overthrow her administration. This was because of her declining popularity due to impeachable offenses such as the "Hello Garci" scandal, which provided evidence that she had cheated in the presidential elections. Rallies were declared illegal, and warrantless arrests were allowed. Even though emergency powers were lifted after seven days, human rights violations and extrajudicial killings continued during her administration. See "States of Rebellion, Emergency under Arroyo Administration," *Philippine Daily Inquirer*, September 4, 2016.
67. Beth, interview.
68. Andrew, interview.
69. May, interview.
70. Beth, interview.
71. Sally, interview.

12 Letter to Granddad

Tracing the Life of a Leftist during the
Malayan Emergency, 1948–60

. . . .

SIM CHI YIN

Four years ago, I gave birth to a little boy.
A day before the peak of COVID-19 deaths in London.
A time when they were issuing no birth but just death certificates.
It was traumatic for all of us.
But perhaps nothing like what you experienced in your time.
I gave him a part of your name.
The "Yi 毅" that you had used in your pen name, when you wrote those anticolonial editorials and speeches.
"Resolute, firm, tenacious, determined."
Yiwei 毅炜
I wonder what else he inherits from our pasts.
What he carried with him into the world.
What he will take into the future.
What of my excavating the stories of you and your compatriots,
The stories of struggle, destruction, sacrifice, idealism, conviction,
Did he get, in utero?
What of my digging in the colonial archive in those final months of the pregnancy
Was he exposed to?
What transpired through my skin into his?
What echoes?
Does history write itself in a line,
Or in circles?
When the family laughs nervously about how your genes "skipped a generation" and passed on to me, maybe they weren't joking.

. . . . . .

There was never a photograph of you in our home. Or in any of your children's houses.

For years, I wondered why they never spoke about you.
Why does grandma's gravestone not bear your name?
Did they really forget?
Could they?

......

I never met you. The family—from the time I was a child—never talked about you.

Except once. Dad mentioned in passing that you had died in China in the 1940s and, for some reason, had a monument built to you.

I thought it was strange that you, having been born in Hong Kong but then taken as a baby to Malaya where you grew up, lived, and worked, would have died back in our ancestral village in China. Your father had left the village at the turn of the twentieth century, along with a wave of migrant Chinese laborers headed for Southeast Asia, America, Australia, and Africa.

And why did the family never talk about you in the sixty years since your death? Why does grandma's gravestone not bear your name?

Years ago, when I was going to be posted to China as a foreign correspondent for a newspaper, I pestered dad and his older brother about you.

They never wanted to talk, even—or perhaps, especially—after sixty years.

One Lunar New Year, on my visit home, my mum handed me a black-and-white photograph. The man in the photograph stood confidently, hands on hips. He was not tall, had a high forehead and full lips. . . . and a camera was slung around his neck.

There had been another photographer in the family? I was intrigued.

Eventually, oldest uncle coughed up a letter from his drawers. It was one of many letters relatives in our ancestral village had written to us over sixty years. But we never replied to them. Grandma had ordered your five children to forget you.

I called the only phone number in the letter and introduced myself as your granddaughter. They thought I was lying and tested me by asking me to name your five children. On New Year's

Day in 2011, I got on a bus in Hong Kong and rode seven hours north to Meizhou city, southern China. I looked around the old town. Are the same roads you walked, the same things you saw?

I took a van back to our village, going past the jetty that great-grandad left China from in the late 1800s, and the same steps you must have walked up when you returned to China in the 1940s.

I met our relatives. I found the house that great-granddad had built and where you had lived when you returned.

I looked for traces of you and observed the rituals in this hundred-year-old house where our relatives farm, live, and gamble, and sometimes eat boiled rat for breakfast. . . .

I asked them how you came back here in early 1949, in the final months of the civil war between the Communists and the Nationalists in China. . . . I heard how you were chased down, surrounded, arrested, and jailed by the Nationalists because you had joined a Communist guerrilla army unit in our home village. . . .

I learned how you were eventually executed in July 1949 by the Nationalists. . . . just two months before the Communists declared victory over China.

I was speechless when I saw the three-meter-high monument obelisk built to commemorate your martyrdom for the Chinese Communists. . . . and your grave tablet at its foot that bore the names of your four faraway sons.

There was no other trace of you here. It had been sixty-two years and no one in your immediate family had returned before.

I started piecing together the fragments of your life, trying to make sense of why you had become taboo in your own family.

A relative ran into one of the rooms in the old house and thrust a tattered photograph into my hand.

He said it was the only thing you had brought back from Malaya.

It took me a while to comprehend.

It was your prison photo. It bears your "detainee number" and your name romanized into English.

I have seen many others since, in the archives and from interviews I have done. It seems the British had every deportee photographed and inoculated against smallpox before putting you all on ships "back" to China.

Your eyes seem to have lost the luster they once had.

. . . . . .

For another two years, your family did not know you were already dead.

I looked in the county archives and found a paragraph recording your role and death. "Propaganda cadre, local guerrilla unit. Executed July 1949, by the Kuomintang army unit."

A few months shy of the Communist "liberation."

Your death was the pivot on which the family's fate turned.

Grandma angrily said you "chose politics over family."

She never spoke about you again. . . .

I don't know if any of your children knew much about your life, about what shaped your ideas, your convictions, your work, about your possible double life as an underground political activist.

There were murmurs of your socialist ideals, the sighting of a pistol one day, but never a smoking gun.

I looked deep in the family photo albums for some clues.

There you were, in your high school volleyball team. In the front row, first from left.

You seemed to self-consciously tuck your left arm far behind your body, in the shadow.

We now know the hairy mole on your upper left arm was the vital clue that helped relatives identify your body from among the corpses in the mass grave you were left in after being executed.

I now know that in the 1930s you had been a school principal and then a leftist journalist and photographer in northern Malaya. You were a community leader.

By all accounts, you were an advocate for social justice.

Like most overseas Chinese who still cared for China, you and grandma did theater in the streets to raise money for the anti-Japanese war in China. You were arrested and waterboarded by the Japanese for this. They hung you from a tree. You survived. And continued being active in politics, culture, and intellectual circles.

When the British returned after the war, you were part of a wave of anticolonial sentiment. You made anti-British speeches. You became the chief editor of a leftist newspaper in northern Malaya and published anti-British editorials.

One of dad's primary school classmates remembers you making fiery anti-British speeches in their town.

Another classmate later teased him about his "Communist father."

As the winds of the Cold War were blowing everywhere around the world, you were arrested by the British who had declared Emergency Rule in Malaya as the communist-led resistance grew.

The guerrillas in the dense jungles across Malaya sabotaged British rule and the tin and rubber supply that the British relied on from its prized colony. The British solution to this was to round up over 30,000 "leftists" like you and deport you all to China, whether you had been born there or not.

That's how you ended up "back" in China.

There are no official records of your arrest, but there is a deportation list with your name on it.

The British offered you "voluntary repatriation" in those times of overcrowded jails.

Some sort of choice that was. You took it anyway.

It was an all-out war in every way but name. The British called it the "Malayan Emergency." It was a war that lasted twelve years, and left families broken and traumatized.

History is written by the victors and this trauma became buried with time. In the bodies of my uncle, and other families like ours.

I wanted to understand this trauma, this amnesia.

I wanted to understand you, the political choices you made, the fire you had in your belly. I traveled around southern China, Hong Kong, Malaysia, Thailand, and Singapore to do oral history interviews with other Malayan leftists whose lives paralleled yours—they fought against the British and got deported or exiled.

I met men and women now well into their nineties who were the foot soldiers of what they saw as a just national liberation revolution—like with so many other places in the Third World.

I asked them why they wanted the British out.

I asked them what it was like to be on those ships, being deported to China.

I met many who were lucky, unlike you, and lived on to find good jobs in Communist China.

I met others who stayed on in Malaya and went into the jungles to fight to establish a communist state for the next thirty years, living in the jungles between Malaysia and Thailand.

They had their own field hospitals, radio station, printing press, made their own weapons.

They went on fighting for the idea and ideal of communism, laying down arms only in 1989.

Some remain exiled today in the jungles of southern Thailand.

They gave their lives to a failed revolution.

Most of them are now fading from the scene. . . .

I drove around northern Malaysia and southern Thailand, in the towns where you'd lived, worked, in the so-called black areas where the communists were active. Where they had ambushed British soldiers, shot British rubber estate managers, where they hid in limestone caves, lived with tigers and elephants in the jungles. I visited old tin mines founded by the British, and that jail where they had kept you. . . .

I went to the cemeteries of Commonwealth soldiers and plantation owners who were killed by "bandits" and "Communist Terrorists."

On the gravestone of a Scottish plantation owner killed in this war, it is inscribed: "One Day We'll Understand."

Will we?

Reflections

13 The Long, Hot Cold Wars of Asia— and Latin America

ALAN McPHERSON

In 1999, I was in Panama interviewing Napoleón De Bernard, one of former president Omar Torrijos's right-hand men. Torrijos had been accused of being both a dictator and a leftist, so I asked De Bernard if he considered himself on the left. His answer surprised me: "No! I've never liked communists. Me, I like to *work*."[1]

I had never heard communists being described as lazy. If anything, US policymakers were notorious for stereotyping Latin American communists, from Guatemala in 1954 to Cuba in 1959 to Chile in 1973, as hard-working schemers ready to pounce on any opportunity to wrest power from woolyheaded moderate leftists. But in Panama, where communists notoriously enrolled in universities only to avoid classes and instead agitate for Stalinist or Maoist political factions, it made sense.[2] Sitting on De Bernard's veranda, as cockatiels squawked and chirped around us, I wondered how Latin Americans may have perceived and investigated the Cold War differently from US citizens. Never could I systematically investigate the topic.

For Asia's Cold War, Masuda Hajimu and his team of collaborators have done just that, and the volume they have produced deserves a hearty *¡felicidades!* Each of the chapters herein features never-before-used sources— especially oral histories—historiographical innovation, and analytical sophistication. The forest is even greener than its verdant trees: the volume as a whole demonstrates that Asians created their own Cold War, adapting ideologies from the West to suit local needs, thus transforming long-running social tensions into polarized political wars. This book proves pathbreaking in its methods and insights. Nothing approaches it in the vast historiography of Cold War Latin American studies.

This reflection will ask what these two scholarships can learn from one another. As Masuda suggests in his introduction, Latin American Cold War studies are also caught in a dilemma: vertiginous growth produces scholarship that is varied and rich but also atomized and disconnected. Asia and

Latin America experienced—and defined—the Cold War in ways that warrant a look at similarities and differences and suggest some advice for the Asianists. Hopefully, having area studies specialists compare and contrast their findings will spark creativity in both regions.

Similarities

The first similarity between Asia and Latin America evident in this volume is one of the more traditional but nevertheless important takeaways of the Cold War: that the East-West struggle intensified and rendered more violent already simmering local conflicts. In both regions, the Cold War was a hot, scorched-earth affair that incinerated millions in its path. "The Cold War as weather" paradigm might feel disempowering, but at times it is apt. To add to the metaphor, the weather of the Cold War mostly manifested as a maelstrom—a mighty whirlpool that sucked toward it everything that approached. The sources of the sucking, however, were not only the United States, the Soviet Union, and China but mostly Asia's and Latin America's own nation-states, which grew more formidable as the Cold War afforded them an increased ability to define the enemy as a monolith and magnify their own powers of repression against that enemy. In almost every case, from Burma to Bolivia, the state took on a Cold War–related identity, usually as anticommunist and, adopting what Latin Americans called the "national security doctrine," repressed any opposition to it.[3]

In his chapter from this book, Imam Muhtarom demonstrates all too well the ease with which, in East Java, the police and death squads, using state resources and benefiting from impunity, collaborated in or at least witnessed torture and repression. In one of the most gruesome uses of oral history, witnesses detail how these forces dehumanized so-called communists and dispensed with even quasi legalities such as mock trials or formalities such as firing squads. They killed leftists like chickens, by snapping their necks. The Cold War's national security state enabled the psychopaths.

Throughout Latin America, Stephen Rabe and others have demonstrated the overwhelming power of the security state to surveil, suppress, detain, torture, and kill—especially when conservatives led that state. In Guatemala, the political right was responsible for 93 percent of the 200,000 or so deaths from 1954 to 1996. In contrast, the armed left's responsibility stood at 3 percent. In El Salvador, the percentages were 85 to 5.[4] Were Asia's proportions similar, or did left-wing massacres and genocide in China, Cambodia, and elsewhere scramble the equation? Regardless,

Rabe's characterization of Latin America as a "killing zone" is eerily close to Asia's infamy as a "killing field," most recently applied by Paul Thomas Chamberlin.[5] Specific studies of right-wing Latin American states' murderous reach are too many to enumerate, but they are concentrated in Guatemala after 1954, the Southern Cone of South America in the 1970s, Central America in the 1980s, and the Andes throughout.[6] In Chile, for instance, the military junta that overthrew an elected Marxist government in 1973 later justified its massacre of over 3,000 leftists by evoking the specter of a "Plan Z," an alleged conspiracy to eliminate conservatives. In reality, the nonexistent "Plan Z" was Plan A of the dictatorship of Augusto Pinochet, and whipping up apocalyptic propaganda against the left went hand in (iron) glove with killings and disappearances.[7]

The second similarity between the regions reflects one of this volume's emphases: that many Asians in the Cold War were concerned largely not with lofty ideology but with day-to-day issues such as land, work, political power, family, and racial identity. In East Java, the Indonesian Communist Party occupied or forcibly harvested rice fields so as to implement agrarian reform, the major source of tension that the Cold War intensified. In his chapter, Bin Yang shows that former Red Guards did not serve in Burma to "export revolution" but rather for "a chance to change their current, seemingly hopeless lives." Vietnamese women volunteers interviewed by Luong Thi Hong cited a range of practical reasons for their commitment: to avoid the fate of deceased family members, to protect families and communities, to satisfy one's anger, to escape underprivileged lives, to avoid forced marriage, or to demonstrate their worthiness. Personal rather than ideological motivations appeared more common with women and should be further investigated by Cold War scholars.[8] In many case studies of this book, the powerless turned to local communist parties to demand justice against government bureaucrats, soldiers, or police.

Local issues, however, could also exacerbate the narcissism of small differences throughout Asia. Cold War ideologies amplified many cleavages: vendettas of one family against another, children versus parents, women versus men, syncretic versus "pure" religions, peasants versus city dwellers, and what Kisho Tsuchiya calls "ancestral, communal, and personal grudges in the names of 'anticommunism' on the one hand, and 'nationalism' on the other." In India, the Naxalite Movement of "radical communists," as Muhammed Kunhi Mahin Udma calls them, sought to equate attacks on the caste system with class warfare and thereby challenge the "feudal exploitation" of lower castes.

For most Cold War Latin Americans—that is, peasants—agrarian reform was also the core issue, and those, such as the early Cuban revolutionaries of 1959, who accelerated it, were greeted as angels by the *guajiros* or peasants and feared as devils by the Dwight D. Eisenhower White House.[9] Latin Americans, too, fought for meaningful pragmatic issues of equality, justice, and power.

A third similarity is that of continuation. Contributors to this volume use the words "predisposed," "preexisting," "continuing," and *"longue durée"* to argue that the Cold War enabled or amplified tensions that had existed long before 1945. Cui Feng, for instance, demonstrates that, while Thailand forced migrating Chinese to assimilate during and because of their association with communism, Chinese immigrants had long before been seen as a "problem" for Thai leaders. He labels the Cold War as "an excuse" to further repress Chinese language and education. Simon Creak illustrates a similar dynamic in Laos: a preexisting anti-Viet xenophobia intensified by the Cold War.

In Latin America, with oral histories and a microhistory of Guatemalan villages, Greg Grandin demonstrated that the Cold War also superimposed itself onto long-simmering struggles between Indigenous Guatemalans and European-descended elites in urban areas.[10] At the macro level, Hal Brands made the case that "Latin America's Cold War was . . . a series of overlapping conflicts," including not only anti-US nationalism and decolonization but also "long-running clashes over social, political, and economic arrangements."[11] Even migrants—to the United States, at least—received different treatment depending on whether they were fleeing a socialist revolution (Cuba) or not (Haiti), yet the shoddy treatment of Latin American immigrants had begun long before World War II.[12]

A fourth and final similarity is that of agency. All the contributors to this volume are steadfast in demonstrating that their actors—whether oral history subjects or others—to a significant extent steered their own ships through the maelstrom of the Cold War. Overwhelmingly, ordinary people appear as the leading figures in these stories; rarely do contributors even use the name of a policymaker in Washington, Moscow, or Beijing. They thus decenter the meaning and therefore the power of the Cold War away from the West. Prasit Leepreecha characterizes the Hmong in Northern Thailand as "active agents who took advantage of the Cold War." While this minority group certainly perceived the Cold War as "weather"—in their case, a "wave of disease"—the Hmong fought on both sides of the conflict, and in return gained education, training, protection, and infrastructure.

Similarly, the returning Okinawans educated in the United States were not merely "pro-American," as Kinuko Maehara-Yamazato argues. Her interviewees refused to be pegged as cold warriors. Some opposed the continuing US occupation or promoted peace movements and other social movements. Even the poignant "Letter to Grandad" by Sim Chi Yin touches on the theme of agency.

Historians of the Western Hemisphere have similarly been exploring its autonomy from one particular hegemon—the United States. In 2003, Max Friedman made the argument that, for an increasing number of historians, Latin Americans were rarely puppets of Washington. Historians since have piled on evidence for the claim.[13] Piero Gleijeses demonstrated that Cuba's revolutionary foreign policy was free not only of US but also largely of Soviet influences.[14] Tanya Harmer used oral history and South American archives to uncover that Brazil and other Latin American nations were as important to Chile's experiment in Marxist governance—and its crushing—as was the United States.[15] Renata Keller explained how Mexico played a careful chess game with its foreign policy during the early Cuban Revolution, and she has more recently "Latin Americanized" the Cuban Missile Crisis.[16] My own first book focused on how Latin Americans insisted on separating anti-Americanism from communism and on Washington's unwillingness to acknowledge the difference.[17] As a collective, the contributors to *Latin America and the Global Cold War* have gone further and traced the region's links outside of the Americas, building on the groundbreaking work of *In From the Cold: Latin America's New Encounters with the Cold War*.[18]

Differences

Of course, Asia and Latin America are distinct in language, religion, history, and other respects. In two key ways those differences marked their experiences of the Cold War at ground level. First, religion seems to have played a larger part in Asians' identification, whether assumed or assigned, with the communist/noncommunist binary, reflecting the recent rise in attention that historians of US foreign relations have paid to religion during the Cold War.[19] In Timor, writes Tsuchiya, the Catholic Church not only opposed communism but also supported any remnant of Portuguese imperialism. Muhtaron and Matthew Woolgar, meanwhile, differ on the clash between Islam and communism in East and West Java, respectively. Woolgar argues that "communism was not inherently incompatible with Islam," yet both authors concur that the perception of incompatibility rose after

1965. Communism tended to attract those interested in achieving modernity, whether via gender equity, peasant rights, or secularism. Traditional religious leaders, to borrow from William F. Buckley Jr., often stood athwart such projects, yelling "Stop!"[20]

In Latin America, in contrast, there seems to have been less animosity between religious groups during the Cold War. No doubt it was because of the preponderance of the Catholic Church in a region that, as late as 1970, was 92 percent Catholic.[21] The church played Cold War politics and so did some religious orders, but mostly against atheistic communism or in favor of human rights—rarely against other faiths. There was some tension between Catholics and Protestants, but nothing near the genocidal religious hatred seen in Asia.[22] If anything, historians have demonstrated that socialists in Latin America, even revolutionaries, went out of their way to demonstrate their tolerance or embrace of Catholicism.[23]

・・・・・・

In Asia, a second difference seems to have been the importance of ethnic identity in assigning Cold War sides. This may stem from the simple fact that Asia is ethnically and linguistically more diverse than Latin America. In 2015, for instance, the Americas (including North America) had 1,064 living languages to Asia's 2,301, and a clear dominance of Spanish and Portuguese over others.[24] Most anti-immigrant sentiment in this volume, for instance, seems premised on racism.

In Latin America, few feared the loss of dominance of European-descended or mixed Spanish- or Portuguese-speaking urban elites vis-à-vis poor, rural Indigenous peasants, who remained minorities everywhere except, at times, in Bolivia and Guatemala. And there seems to have been relatively little overlap between Afro-Latinos and Cold War cleavages, at least in historiography to date.

Advice

Finally, some room for advice, the first item being a caveat. As many contributors to *Cold War Asia* have admitted, oral history has unmistakable but limited value. To be sure, the value of personal testimonies, especially those of ordinary people, is evident. They should become a staple of Cold War histories, especially for the next generation or so while those witnesses are still alive. The stories collected by these contributors are compelling and moving, and the imperative by Masuda to collect them provides a superb methodological unity to this volume that similar works—including those on Latin America—lack. The payoffs are many: Bin Yang demonstrates the patient approach, in his case obtaining the testimonies of former Red Guards through his dozen years of interaction with a local association. In the case of the Hmong, written documents before the 1950s are nonexistent because of a lack of a written language, and so interviews are precious. And Muhammed Kunhi Mahin Udma did what appear to be rare oral histories in Malayalam, helping to show the path for Latin Americanists, who must do more to engage those communities who left no traces in European languages but may have done so in Quechua, Guaraní, Aymara, or Kreyol.

However, one should not be so impressed by these achievements and insights as to set aside the inherent flaws of oral history. Memories are fallible, incomplete, prone to bias and fabrication, and, especially with those who leave little to no paper trail, unverifiable. My own research has involved dozens of oral histories, and too often I was disappointed that Latin Americans whom I knew to have directly taken part in important events were reluctant to discuss their roles. I interpreted their reticence as either evading historic or legal responsibility for past wrongdoings or seeing their roles as peripheral to the sweep of history. Although they provided the occasional gem, their oral histories proved less useful than they could have been. Too many authors in this volume seem to lean on what are only a handful of witnesses who sometimes make sweeping judgments on large swaths of compatriots. Some of these insights may ring true, but they await confirmation either by written sources or by larger numbers of oral histories.

In Latin America, oral testimonies of the Cold War are highly controversial, largely because the issues—and often the leaders—of the Cold War are still with us. If their testimonies come from the left, for instance in Cuba or Nicaragua, remnants of those regimes are still in power. On the right, those who might submit to oral histories, for instance in Argentina or Chile, might rightfully fear retribution were their testimonies to be used against them in court. Which leads to the following questions: Is the Cold War even over in Asia? Will there be a wave of prosecutions for its crimes? Will there be a conflict over its memory?

As suggested above, the absence of archives inflates the value of oral history. This leads to the second piece of advice: one should not assume that archives do not exist in Asia simply because they seem not to. The lesson from Latin America on this score is clear: patience, persistence, political will, and a bit of luck almost undoubtedly will uncover new Cold War documents, probably intact collections, and possibly entire new archives. Some of these might come from personal homes, private offices, or corporations. Some, as Mary Grace R. Concepción demonstrates, will come from oral transmission from parents to children. But there *will* be the occasional discovery that will illuminate the darkest secrets of Asia's hot Cold Wars.

Latin Americans have made leaps forward in historical knowledge—and politics—by discovering, after the Cold War, some of the papers of the most brutal forces of repression. An accidental find in 2005 uncovered the lost 75 million pages of records of Guatemala's National Police, which historian Kirsten Weld has called "the largest collection of secret state documents in Latin American history."[25] Other Latin American "terror archives" had already shown up in Paraguay in 1992, and, by the 2000s and 2010s, heads of state in Uruguay, Brazil, Argentina, and Chile were devoting significant resources to making accessible the records from past dictatorships. Such documents helped spur or confirm reports of Cold War–era atrocities by truth and reconciliation commissions, and Latin Americans have become experts in documenting such horrors. So far, fourteen Latin American countries have produced truth and reconciliation commissions, more than any other region and twice Asia's tally.[26]

Peripheral Thought

Whether one uses quotation marks, pluralizes it, or ~~strikes it through~~, the Cold War is here to stay as a historical topic. The contributors to this volume have added to the fascination that it will long evoke. Perhaps their most lasting impact has been to question the relevance of a core-periphery binary. They have demonstrated that most Asians who lived through the bloody or traumatic events of the Cold War were not primarily moved by what was occurring at the "core." And since they made up the majority of people who lived the Cold War as a daily event, shouldn't *they* be considered as the core? The same quandary hovers over Latin America. Perhaps the most subversive question is, who was at the core of the Cold War? Were not the Indigenous peasants of Guatemala, the female volunteers of Vietnam, the farmers of Cuba, the students of Okinawa, and the human rights proponents of Chile its true core?

Henry Kissinger once enraged a Chilean foreign minister by explaining that "nothing important comes from the South. . . . The axis of history starts in Moscow, goes to Bonn, crosses over to Washington, and then goes to Tokyo. What happens in the South is of no importance."[27] By "what happens," Kissinger no doubt meant *state power*, and in that sense, he had a point, if an exaggerated and cruel one. But if "what happens" is taken more literally as an *everyday experience*, then this volume has laid the groundwork for demonstrating that it was Kissinger and his ilk, rather than those in the Global South, who stood on the periphery of history.

Notes

1. Napoleón De Bernard, interview by the author, Panama City, Panama, October 21, 1999.

2. Daniel Goldrich, *Radical Nationalism: The Political Orientation of Panamanian Law Students* (East Lansing: Michigan State University, 1961).

3. Genaro Arriagada Herrera, *El Pensamiento político de los militares* [The political thought of the military] (Santiago, Chile: Centro de investigaciones socio-económicas, 1981); and David Pion-Berlin, "Latin American National Security Doctrines: Hard and Softline Themes," *Armed Forces & Society* 15, no. 3 (April 1, 1989): 411–29.

4. Stephen Rabe, *The Killing Zone: The United States Wages Cold War in Latin America* (New York: Oxford University Press, 2012), 172, 168; and Rabe, *Kissinger and Latin America: Intervention, Human Rights, and Diplomacy* (Ithaca, NY: Cornell University Press, 2020).

5. Paul Thomas Chamberlin, *The Cold War's Killing Fields: Rethinking the Long Peace* (New York: HarperCollins, 2018).

6. Here is a sample, starting with Guatemala: Richard Immerman, *The CIA in Guatemala* (Austin: University of Texas Press, 1982); Piero Gleijeses, *Shattered Hope: The Guatemalan Revolution and the United States, 1944–1954* (Princeton, NJ: Princeton University Press, 1991); and Nick Cullather, *Secret History: The CIA's Classified Account of its Operations in Guatemala 1952–1954* (Stanford, CA: Stanford University Press, 1999); for the Southern Cone, see Peter Kornbluh, *The Pinochet File: A Declassified Dossier on Atrocity and Accountability* (New York: New Press, 2003); John Dinges, *The Condor Years: How Pinochet and His Allies Brought Terrorism to Three Continents* (New York: New Press, 2004); J. Patrice McSherry, *Predatory States: Operation Condor and Covert War in Latin America* (Lanham, MD: Rowman & Littlefield, 2005); Jerry Dávila, *Dictatorships in South America* (Chichester: Wiley-Blackwell, 2013); William Michael Schmidli, *The Fate of Freedom Elsewhere: Human Rights and U.S. Cold War Policy toward Argentina* (Ithaca, NY: Cornell University Press, 2013); Alan McPherson, *Ghosts of Sheridan Circle: How a Washington Assassination Brought Pinochet's Terror State to Justice* (Chapel Hill: University of North Carolina Press, 2019); and Vanessa Walker, *Principles in Power: Latin America and the Politics of Human Rights Diplomacy* (Ithaca, NY: Cornell University Press, 2020); for Central America in the 1980s, see E. Bradford Burns, *At War in Nicaragua: The Reagan Doctrine and the Politics of Nostalgia* (New York: Harper & Row, 1987); R. M. Koster and Guillermo Sánchez, *In the Time of the Tyrants: Panama: 1968–1990* (New York: W. W. Norton, 1990); Thomas Carothers, *In the Name of Democracy: U.S. Policy toward Latin America in the Reagan Years* (Berkeley: University of California Press, 1991); Mark Danner, *The Massacre at El Mozote* (New York: Vintage

Books, 1993); William M. LeoGrande, *Our Own Backyard: The United States in Central America, 1977–1992* (Chapel Hill: University of North Carolina Press, 1998); Brian D'Haeseleer, *The Salvadoran Crucible: The Failure of US Counterinsurgency in El Salvador, 1979–1992* (Lawrence: University Press of Kansas, 2017); Charles Berguist, Ricardo Peñaranda, and Gonzalo Sánchez G., eds., *Violence in Colombia 1990–2000: Waging War and Negotiating Peace* (Wilmington, DE: Scholarly Resources, 2001); and Thomas C. Field, Jr., *From Development to Dictatorship: Bolivia and the Alliance for Progress in the Kennedy Era* (Ithaca, NY: Cornell University Press, 2014); and finally, more general accounts, some about the left, include Jorge G. Castañeda, *Utopia Unarmed: The Latin American Left after the Cold War* (New York: Knopf, 1993); Martha K. Huggins, *Political Policing: The United States and Latin America* (Durham, NC: Duke University Press, 1998); and Jonathan C. Brown, *Cuba's Revolutionary World* (Cambridge, MA: Harvard University Press, 2017).

7. Steve J. Stern, "Foreward," in *The Politics of Memory in Chile: From Pinochet to Bachelet*, ed. Cath Collins, Katherine Hite, and Alfredo Joignant (Boulder, CO: First Forum Press, 2013), xi.

8. Excellent work has already been done, for instance, by Elizabeth Manley, *The Paradox of Paternalism: Women and the Politics of Authoritarianism in the Dominican Republic* (Gainesville: University Press of Florida, 2017); Victoria Gonzalez-Rivera, *Before the Revolution: Women's Rights and Right-Wing Politics in Nicaragua, 1821–1979* (University Park: Penn State University Press, 2011); Michelle Chase, *Revolution within the Revolution: Women and Gender Politics in Cuba, 1952–1962* (Chapel Hill: University of North Carolina Press, 2015); and Jocelyn Olcott, *International Women's Year: The Greatest Consciousness-Raising Event in History* (Oxford: Oxford University Press, 2017).

9. On agrarian reform in Cuba, see Rafael Menjivar, *Reforma Agraria: Guatemala-Bolivia-Cuba* (San Salvador: Editorial Universario de El Salvador, 1969); Antonio Nuñez Jiménez, *En Marcha con Fidel 1959* (Havana: Letras Cubanas, 1982); and Lillian Guerra, *Visions on Power in Cuba: Revolution, Redemption, and Resistance, 1959–1971* (Chapel Hill: University of North Carolina Press, 2012).

10. Greg Grandin, *The Blood of Guatemala: A History of Race and Nation* (Durham, NC: Duke University Press, 2000); Grandin, *The Last Colonial Massacre: Latin America in the Cold War* (Chicago: University of Chicago Press, 2004); and Grandin and Gilbert M. Joseph, *A Century of Revolution: Insurgent and Counterinsurgent Violence during Latin America's Long Cold War* (Durham, NC: Duke University Press, 2010).

11. Hal Brands, *Latin America's Cold War* (Cambridge, MA: Harvard University Press, 2010), 7.

12. David Lorey, *The U.S.-Mexican Border in the Twentieth Century* (Wilmington, DE: Scholarly Resources, 1999); Paul Ganster and David E. Lorey, *The U.S.-Mexican Border into the Twenty-First Century* (Lanham, MD: Rowman & Littlefield, 2008); Jorge G. Castañeda, *Ex Mex: From Migrants to Immigrants* (New York: New Press, 2007); Deborah Cohen, *Braceros: Migrant Citizens and Transnational Subjects in the Postwar United States and Mexico* (Chapel Hill: University of North Carolina Press, 2011); Torrie Hester, *Deportation: The Origins of U.S. Policy*

(Philadelphia: University of Pennsylvania Press, 2017); S. Deborah Kang, *The INS on the Line: Making Immigration Law on the US-Mexico Border, 1917–1954* (Oxford: Oxford University Press, 2017); and Hideaki Kami, *Diplomacy Meets Migration: US Relations with Cuba during the Cold War* (Cambridge: Cambridge University Press, 2018).

13. Max Paul Friedman, "Retiring the Puppets, Bringing Latin America Back In: Recent Scholarship on United States–Latin American Relations." *Diplomatic History* 27, no. 5 (2003): 621–36.

14. Piero Gleijeses, *Conflicting Missions: Havana, Washington, and Africa, 1959–1976* (Chapel Hill: University of North Carolina Press, 2002); and *Visions of Freedom: Havana, Washington, Pretoria, and the Struggle for Southern Africa, 1976–1991* (Chapel Hill: University of North Carolina Press, 2013).

15. Tanya Harmer, *Allende's Chile & the Inter-American Cold War* (Chapel Hill: University of North Carolina Press, 2011).

16. Renata Keller, *Mexico's Cold War: Cuba, the United States, and the Legacy of the Mexican Revolution* (Cambridge: Cambridge University Press, 2015); "The Latin American Missile Crisis," *Diplomatic History* 39, no. 2 (April 2015): 195–222; and "Responsibility of the Great Ones: How the Organization of American States and the United Nations Helped Resolve the Cuban Missile Crisis," *Journal of Latin American Studies* 51, no. 4 (November 2019): 883–904. See also Eric Zolov, *The Last Good Neighbor: Mexico in the Global Sixties* (Durham, NC: Duke University Press, 2020).

17. Alan McPherson, *Yankee No! Anti-Americanism in U.S.-Latin American Relations* (Cambridge, MA: Harvard University Press, 2003).

18. See Thomas C. Field, Stella Krepp, and Vanni Pettinà, eds., *Latin America and the Global Cold War* (Chapel Hill: University of North Carolina Press, 2020); and Gilbert M. Joseph and Daniela Spenser, eds., *In From the Cold: Latin America's New Encounters with the Cold War* (Durham, NC: Duke University Press, 2008). See also Daniela Spenser, ed., *Espejos de la Guerra Fría: México, América Central y el Caribe* [Mirrors of the Cold War: Mexico, Central America and the Caribbean] (Mexico City: CIESAS, 2004). Monographs in the same vein include Tom Long, *Latin America Confronts the United States: Asymmetry and Influence* (Cambridge: Cambridge University Press, 2015); and James Lockhart, *Chile, the CIA and the Cold War: A Transatlantic Perspective* (Edinburgh: Edinburgh University Press, 2019).

19. Dianne Kirby, ed., *Religion and the Cold War* (Houndmills, UK: Palgrave Macmillan, 2003); Seth Jacobs, *America's Miracle Man in Vietnam: Ngo Dinh Diem, Religion, Race, and U.S. Intervention in Southeast Asia* (Durham, NC: Duke University Press, 2005); Andrew Preston, *Sword of the Spirit, Shield of Faith: Religion in American War and Diplomacy* (New York: Anchor Books, 2012); and Philip E. Muehlenbeck, ed., *Religion and the Cold War: A Global Perspective* (Nashville, TN: Vanderbilt University Press, 2012).

20. Buckley, "Our Mission Statement," *National Review*, November 19, 1955.

21. Pew Research Center, "Religion in Latin America," November 13, 2014.

22. See, for instance, Daniel R. Miller, ed., *Coming of Age: Protestantism in Contemporary Latin America* (Lanham, MD: University Press of America, 1994); Tomás

J. Gutiérrez S., ed., *Protestantismo y política en América Latina y el Caribe* [Protestantism and politics in Latin America and the Caribbean] (Lima: CEHILA, 1996); and Theresa Keeley, *Reagan's Gun-Toting Nuns: The Catholic Conflict over Cold War Human Rights Policy in Central America* (Ithaca, NY: Cornell University Press, 2020).

23. Ernesto Cardenal, *El Evangelio en Solentiname* [The gospel in Solentiname] (San José, Costa Rica: Departamento ecuménico de investigaciones, 1979); Margaret Crahan, "Cuba: Religion and Revolutionary Institutionalization," *Journal of Latin American Studies* 17, no. 2 (November 1985): 319–40; Raúl Gómez Trento, *The Church and Socialism in Cuba*, trans. Phillip Berryman (Maryknoll, NY: Orbis Books, 1988); Phillip J. Williams, *The Catholic Church and Politics in Nicaragua and Costa Rica* (Pittsburgh: University of Pittsburgh Press, 1989); John M. Kirk, *Politics and the Catholic Church in Nicaragua* (Gainesville: University Press of Florida, 1992); and Lillian Guerra, "'To Condemn the Revolution is to Condemn Christ': Radicalization, Moral Redemption, and the Sacrifice of Civil Society in Cuba, 1960," *Hispanic American Historical Review* 89, no. 1 (2009): 73–109.

24. Rick Noack and Lazaro Gamio, "The World's Languages, in 7 Maps and Charts," *Washington Post*, April 23, 2015.

25. Kirsten Weld, *Paper Cadavers: The Archives of Dictatorship in Guatemala* (Durham, NC: Duke University Press, 2014), 2.

26. Wikipedia, "List of Truth and Reconciliation Commissions," https://www.wikipedia.org./wiki/List_of_truth_and_reconciliation_commissions, accessed November 6, 2024.

27. Quoted in Seymour M. Hersh, *The Price of Power: Kissinger in the Nixon White House* (New York: Summit, 1983), 263.

14 An Archipelagic Turn

Islands as Method in Understanding Cold War Asia

....

TAOMO ZHOU

The social isolation related to the COVID-19 crisis makes many people feel like lonely islands. As I write this reflection, I think back with nostalgia about the "Reconceptualizing the Cold War" seminar series, missing the conviviality in the prepandemic world. Stories about the islands of Okinawa, Java, and Timor unfolded through presentations and discussions over coffee, tea, and lunches in Singapore, an island whose birth as an independent city-state took place during the Cold War.

These tales about tropical islands reminded me of an island thousands of kilometers to the north—the Zhenbao or Damansky Island on the Ussuri River. This "unremarkable and uninhabited" island was the key site in the 1969 Sino-Soviet border conflict and occupied a special place in my family's history.[1] When the fighting took place, my maternal grandfather was serving as the party secretary of Hulin County—the administrative unit to which Zhenbao Island belonged—and facing intense political persecution. My grandmother, a high school Russian-language teacher, was forced to shout belligerent slogans in Russian at the local radio station toward the Soviet village across the river. More than half a century later, my mother would recall how on a chilly morning after the skirmish broke out, she was woken up by my grandmother and handed a train ticket to Harbin, where she would hide for safety.

At the seminar, I heard echoes of my personal story of international conflicts, social upheaval, and family separation through chains of islands from the Ussuri River to the Timor Sea. Five years later, as I read the fruition of our intellectual exchanges, a new analytical framework that reconfigures the geography of the Cold War emerges before my eyes. The current edited volume focuses on "Cold War islands" in both physical and metaphorical terms. From the ocean-facing societies in Japan, Indonesia, and the Philippines to inland social pockets such as the Chinese and Hmong minorities in Thailand and Mao's Red Guards in Burma, these seemingly insular communities have been shaped by and helped shape the global Cold War; but they remain largely as the exotic background for superpower contestation in popular perceptions.

This collection breaks the silence, fills the absence, and signals "an archipelagic turn" in Cold War historiography.[2] A focus on islands—as both geographical and social spaces—offers a fresh perspective in wide-ranging discussions in academia and popular culture. As shown in Michael Szonyi's pioneering work *Cold War Island: Quemoy on the Front Line*, the Asian littoral during the Cold War comprised liminal and contested spaces, and the coastal communities' mobility made them appear as vulnerable and unreliable in the official imagination. Islands have long been nodes of connections in maritime exchanges. Across Cold War divisions, the cross-fertilization of cultures and religions, the confluence of politics, and trade in both legal and illicit forms continued.[3] Beyond the field of modern Asia, scholars of the Americas have departed from a continental definition of the United States and advocating instead for the concept of a deterritorialized and networked global power, or "an island empire," with thousands of archipelagic spaces under its domain largely invisible to public view.[4] Outside academia, Lisa See's historical novel *The Island of Sea Women* reveals Jeju Island's ambivalent relationship with the Korean mainland through the story of the friendship between two women, both of their lives altered by the atrocities conducted in the name of anticommunism in the early Cold War.[5] Bruce Sterling's 1988 science fiction novel *Islands in the Net* depicts a twenty-first-century world where the Cold War persists but the power of the United States and the Soviet Union is undermined by a network of data havens in Grenada, Singapore, and Luxemburg.[6]

The twelve chapters in this book, each focusing on a geopolitically marginal and socioeconomically liminal "island" during the Cold War, also formed a network—"a network of stories that intersect and influence each other."[7] In the following two sections, I will first take a bird's-eye view of the book through the lens of fluid ideologies; I will then zoom into a few communities under discussion with a focus on the emotional dimensions of Cold War Asia.

Multifaceted Communism and Anticommunism

During Asia's bipolar era, "What drove polarization? What limited it? Along which axes did polarization occur? And how did different forms of polarization interact?"[8] The questions raised by Matthew Woolgar have a universal reach beyond his focus on rural West Java. Woolgar's and Imam Muhtarom's studies in this volume on communist-Muslim relations in Indonesia in the 1950s and early 1960s reveal how the stereotypical understanding of communism as the antithesis of religion does not hold up under close scrutiny. In the Indonesian setting, the 1965–66 nationwide anticommunist mass killings and the rise of a military-backed authoritarian regime instilled in the public mind-set the image of communists as heartless, murderous atheists. In the film "The Betrayal of the Indonesian Communist Party," a propaganda tool of the Suharto regime that was broadcast annually on the evening of September 30, fanatic communists were shown ambushing Muslims while they were praying.[9] As Muhtarom's and Woolgar's respective studies on East and West Java demonstrate, there had been individuals and organizations that combined left-wing activism with Islamic piety during Indonesia's relatively liberal era under parliamentary democracy. Yet as global polarization intensified and Indonesian domestic politics radicalized, the room for convergence and cooperation shrank. Communist and anticommunist ideologies became weaponized by local individuals to advance their own interests, in forms such as political power, cultural dominance, or command of economic resources.

Besides religion, race or ethnicity serves as another "integral part of the matrix of cultural, social, and political tensions that constituted the Cold War world."[10] Cui Feng's chapter on the Chinese in Thailand and Simon Creak's chapter on the anti-Vietnamese discourse in Laos show the "dynamic and inextricable relationships" among foreign policy, competing racial ideologies, and internationalist agendas in Cold War Asia.[11] Thailand, as argued by Ngoei Wen-Qing, was part of the Southeast Asian "geostrategic arc" that "contained the Vietnamese revolution and encircled China." Together with Singapore, Malaya, the Philippines, and Indonesia, Thailand overcame the mostly Chinese communist parties in the 1970s by "crafting a pro-West nationalism that was anti-communist by virtue of its anti-Chinese bent."[12] The Cold War climate conveniently accelerated the assimilation program promoted by Thailand's powerholders with their preexisting antipathy toward the Chinese diaspora. A similar brand of anticommunist nationalism with a racist tint was also at work in Laos before the rise of the Pathet Lao, when the military-dominated Committee for the Defense of National Interests expressed its anxieties through the portrayals of duplicitous Vietnamese and domineering Chinese in political caricatures.

By identifying racialized anticommunism as a kind of "vernacular ideology" in Cold War Laos, Creak urges historians to "rethink but not remove" our Cold War lens. Kisho Tsuchiya's study on Timor shows a similar case of the ideological fluidity of FRETILIN, "multifaceted Maoists" who borrowed ideas and lobbied for support from across the political spectrum, from Chinese-style propaganda and education campaigns to Sukarno's Marhaenism. Its ideological inclinations were constantly inconsistent. The interesting local-global dynamics in Cold War East Timor is best represented by the FRETILIN's unique vision of international solidarity, which focused mostly on the Lusophone world, including countries such as Angola. While acknowledging the impact of the bipolar structure on the political developments of East Timor, Tsuchiya nevertheless emphasizes that the Cold War was an extraneous, irrelevant force for many people on the margins of global geopolitics.

In the localized social warfare across the globe, how did ideologies influence individual life decisions? Bin Yang's study on the Red Guards in Burma and Luong Thi Hong's on Vietnamese women volunteers reveal the varied individual calculations and complex social mechanisms underneath what seem like classic examples of commitment to world revolution. Why did thousands of Chinese youths cross national borders to join the fierce military battles in the jungles of Burma? What motivated them to risk their lives and, if they managed to survive, to devote the best years of their lives to a political movement in a foreign land? As Yang convincingly shows, revolutionary romanticism played a role, yet pragmatic considerations were more critical. Some of Yang's informants went to Burma to earn political capital that they believed would help them start life anew; others confessed to have joined the insurgency in Burma to escape their boring, repetitive lives in the impoverished countryside where they saw no future. In the havoc of the Cultural Revolution, the fierce military campaigns in Burma seemed more benign and promising than the brutal personal attacks and violent political persecution at home. Similarly, Luong's study shows that the women volunteers in the Vietnam War were ordinary corporeal beings with common desires and dreams, heading to the battlefield with the hopes of reuniting with lovers, escaping from hunger or arranged marriages, elevating their social statuses, and accessing higher education.

The Personal Is Political: An Emotive History of Cold War Asia

"What kinds of emotions were carried through in the form of ideology, whether communism or anticommunism?"[13] Masuda Hajimu's question in the introduction to this volume widens our lens on Cold War Asia. The broader discipline of history has witnessed an "emotional turn" and the study of emotions has become "a legitimate subfield."[14] "Historically positioned as a quintessentially feminine, primitive, and private aspect of human experience," emotion as a topic has received relatively scant attention in studies on Cold War Asia, a field dominated by intellectual concerns about reason and rationality.[15] Masuda's own work looks into how ordinary people's popular sentiments—fear, anxiety, or disdain—played into foreign policy decision-making in the United States, Japan, and China at the time of the Korean War.[16] Rachel Leow's research on the World Peace Congress in Beijing shows how "the emotive expression of solidarity and calls for social justice among ordinary people" was a crucial component of Third World internationalism.[17] Adding to these exciting works, the current edited volume unearths the "political negotiation and social communication" behind everyday expressions of emotion during Asia's bipolar era.[18]

Love, resentment, passions, and remorse—the Cold War climate legitimized and augmented some feelings while suppressing and stigmatizing others. During the Vietnam War, guided by the communist ideal of desexualized women revolutionaries, the young female volunteers abandoned their pursuit of feminine beauty and suppressed their desires for romance and sexual relationships. During the Indonesian mass violence, the perpetrators—backed by the military—felt a kind of righteous anger toward the suspected left-wing activists and took pride in conducting the murders in a "neat" and "orderly" fashion. Yet the gravekeeper who witnessed the execution remained haunted after half a century by the screams of pain from "a man whose ears were cut, a woman whose genitals were stabbed with a sword."[19] These chapters' discussions on emotions allow us to cross the boundaries between the private and the public, the internal experience and the global bipolarity.

Elusive and ephemeral, some feelings nevertheless live on through generations. Several of the book's chapters showcase the afterlife of the Cold War as reflected in stories—told, retold, and untold—about families. Mary Grace R. Concepcion's chapter traces the transmission of Filipino left-wing activists' experiences of the Martial Law era to their children through storytelling in intimate domestic settings, such as during meals or when braiding hair. The narratives transform as the children grow and the parent-child dynamics change. The emotions the parents experienced during the Cold War morphed into the political opinions of their children living in the twenty-first century, many of whom compare the recent Duterte administration—with its anticommunist propaganda, mass disappearances, and extrajudicial killings—to Marcos Sr.'s rule.[20] Sim Chi Yin's letter to the granddad she has never met tackles her family's silence and amnesia over the father and husband who "chose politics over family." Yet the legacy of the absent grandfather somehow "skipped a generation" and passed on to her, as she carves out a career uncovering and presenting the Malayan Emergency in journalistic and artistic forms.[21]

In the industrial world, family is usually regarded as a haven for emotions. The emotional turbulences in the aforementioned Asian families urge historians to reframe the Cold War through the framework of family rupture and agony. At the War Memorial of Korea in Seoul, the iconic Statue of Brothers shows two soldiers in a desperate embrace as they stand on a split dome landscape. Behind the statue is the story of two brothers meeting in a battle during the Korean War: the elder an officer in the army of the Republic of Korea, the younger a North Korean soldier. In his *The Other Cold War*, Heonik Kwon told a similar story: after the end of World War II, many communities in Greece were divided between the supporters of the Communist forces and the supporters of the government's anticommunist drive. In one village, a partisan supporter was arrested in his home and subsequently sent to a prison camp on a remote island. The arrest was carried out by a group of men from outside the village, including one wearing a hood. The villagers later learned that the masked man was the arrested man's brother.[22] Besides atrocities such as the Indochina Wars and the Indonesian Mass Killings of 1965–66, slow-motion violence in forms such as racial discrimination also caused family disintegration. For instance, Thailand's forceful assimilationist policies toward the ethnic Chinese resulted in intergenerational chasms, as shown in the opening story in Cui's chapter. Due to their lack of access to Chinese-language education, a younger generation of Thai-Chinese found it difficult to communicate and emotionally connect with their grandparents.

Back to the Cold War Coasts

Given the heightened political and military tensions between the United States and China, are we now in a "Cold War 2.0"? I was invited to address this question at a webinar hosted by the Long China-US Institute at University of California, Irvine in 2020, and I asked the same question to my students in my Cold War seminar at the Nanyang Technological University, Singapore.[23] In my class, I gave the students three choices: yes, we are in Cold War 2.0; no, we are not; we remain in Cold War 1.0. To my surprise, the majority of my students thought that we are still stuck in the same old Cold War. Puzzled, I turned to my colleague Ang Cheng Guan, the author of *Southeast Asia's Cold War* and *Southeast Asia after the Cold War*. According to Ang, for the "little red dot" of Singapore, the collapse of the Berlin Wall is far away, and the disintegration of the Soviet bloc is less relevant in the regional context than the Sino-US rapprochement and the reorientation of the People's Republic of China's foreign policy and domestic politics in the late 1970s. Southeast Asia's positioning as carefully balancing between the United States and China has been a consistent reality since then. For my students, who represent a segment of well-educated Southeast Asian youths, the broader power structure remains the same between the 1970s and the 2020s: Southeast Asia needs a US presence to counterbalance China; but at the same time, the region does not want to be dragged into unnecessary conflicts between Washington and Beijing.

The usefulness of the historical analogy is connected to the core concern of this book: what shall we do with the very concept of the "Cold War"? As pointed out by many contributors in the volume, the notion of "Cold War" does not belong to Asia, in light of the millions of casualties there that stood in stark contrast with the Western perception of a long peace. In his 2020 blog piece on the Wilson Center website, Covell Meyskens puts forward a bold argument about the absence of a "Cold War" in China: the term "Cold War" was not used in public discourse in Mao's China, as the CCP never viewed the conflict between capitalism and socialism as cold from the late 1940s to the 1970s.[24] However, Meyskens's own work on the military-industrial complexes in China demonstrates that even though the exact phrase "cold war" (*lengzhan*) was not part of the everyday lingua franca, militarization of everyday life on military-industrial construction sites was evident; the participants in these projects might have never been outside of China, but the central leadership's perception of external threats from both the United States and the Soviet Union determined the trajectory of their careers, shaping their mentality and work ethics and how they found meaning in life.[25]

Human experiences always vary; yet to recognize the diversity of Cold War experiences does not mean we should deny the very existence of the global phenomenon of bipolar conflicts. By focusing on marginal communities and liminal spaces, this edited volume shows a new approach to addressing the incongruities and power disparities embedded in the term "Cold War." The twelve chapters examine individuals' emotions and motivations in the global social warfare; trace the battlelines to local particularities of religious, ethnic, economic, and gender divides; and unpack the historicity, contingency, and complexity of local manifestations of communism and anticommunism. Together, they show how people living on the edges of the great powers' spheres of influence actively appropriated and provincialized the East-West Cold War, and how people of these "island societies" leveraged their own marginality and liminality when navigating through the global bipolarity.

Notes

1. Ankur Shah, "China, Russia and the Legacy of Zhenbao Island," *The China Project*, March 3, 2020, https://thechinaproject.com/2020/03/03/china-russia-and-the-legacy-of-zhenbao-island/.

2. I borrow this term from Brian Russell Roberts and Michelle Ann Stephens, eds., *Archipelagic American Studies* (Durham, NC: Duke University Press, 2017).

3. Michael Szonyi, *Cold War Island: Quemoy on the Front Line* (Cambridge: Cambridge University Press, 2008).

4. Ruth Oldenziel, "Islands: The United States as a Networked Empire," in *Entangled Geographies: Empires and Technopolitics in the Global Cold War*, ed. Gabrielle Hecht (Cambridge. MA: MIT Press, 2011), 13–42; and Daniel Immerwahr, *How to Hide an Empire: A History of the Greater United States* (New York: Random House, 2019).

5. Lisa See, *Island of Sea Women* (New York: Simon & Schuster, 2019).

6. Bruce Sterling, *Islands in the Net* (Gettysburg, PA: Arbor House, 1988).

7. Lorenz Luthi, *Cold Wars: Asia, the Middle East, Europe* (Cambridge: Cambridge University Press, 2020).

8. Matthew Woolgar, "Islam and Communism in West Java: The Cold War and Sociocultural Polarization in Indonesia, 1945–1965," chapter 2 in this volume.

9. *Pengkhianatan G30S/ PKI*, directed by Arifin C. Noer, Perum Produksi Film, 1984.

10. Woolgar, "Islam and Communism."

11. Madeline Y. Hsu, *The Good Immigrants: How the Yellow Peril Became the Model Minority* (Princeton, NJ: Princeton University Press, 2015), 8.

12. Ngoei Wen-Qing, *Arc of Containment: Britain, the United States, and Anticommunism in Southeast Asia* (Ithaca, NY: Cornell University Press), 5.

13. See Masuda Hajimu's introductory chapter to this volume, "Reconceptualizing the Cold War: On-the-Ground Experiences in Asia."

14. "AHR Conversations: The Historical Study of Emotions," *American Historical Review* 117, no. 5 (December 2012): 1487.

15. "Historical Study of Emotions," 1490.

16. Masuda Hajimu, *Cold War Crucible: The Korean Conflict and the Postwar World* (Cambridge, MA: Harvard University Press, 2015).

17. Rachel Leow, "A Missing Peace: The Asia-Pacific Peace Conference in Beijing, 1952 and the Emotional Making of Third World Internationalism," *Journal of World History* 30, no. 1–2 (2019): 25.

18. "Historical Study of Emotions," 1490.

19. Imam Muhtarom, "Terror in East Java: The NU versus PKI Conflict before and after September 30, 1965," chap. 1 in this volume.

20. Mary Grace R. Concepcion, "Afterlife of Cold War Memories: Familial Transmission of Martial Law–Era Memories in the Post–Cold War Philippines," chap. 11 in this volume.

21. Sim Chi Yin, "Letter to Granddad: Tracing the Life of a Leftist during the Malayan Emergency, 1948–60," chap. 12 in this volume.

22. Heonik Kwon, *The Other Cold War* (New York: Columbia University Press, 2010), 15–16.

23. "Cold War 2.0? Rethinking Analogies in US-China Relations," featuring Lorenz Luthi, Meredith Oyen and Taomo Zhou, Long China-US Institute, University of California, Irvine, September 16, 2020, via Zoom.

24. Covell Meyskens, "There Never Was a Cold War China," *Sources and Methods*, September 9, 2020, Wilson Center, https://www.wilsoncenter.org/blog-post/there-never-was-cold-war-china.

25. Covell F. Meyskens, *Mao's Third Front: The Militarization of Cold War China* (Cambridge: Cambridge University Press, 2020).

15 The Cold War in Asia

DAVID C. ENGERMAN

What was the Cold War? For the generations that came of intellectual age during the Cold War itself, the answer was easy—undoubtedly, too easy. The Cold War was an ideological conflict between the United States and the Soviet Union. Though it took shape in the late 1940s over the division of Europe into East and West, the Cold War quickly became global in scope, affecting not just the superpowers and their respective European allies but nations and people all over the world. Since the superpowers readily exported books, power plants, and tanks around the world, there was little, in this view, that happened anywhere in the world between (say) 1947 and 1991 that did not fundamentally revolve around this antagonism.

This consensus about what the Cold War was did not, of course, preclude disagreements, either within scholarly communities or among a broader public. Generations of historians, political scientists, journals, and policymakers fiercely disputed the origins and impacts of the Cold War. Over the three decades since the implosion of the Soviet Union in 1991, scholarship has moved in multiple directions, placing the Cold War in a variety of different contexts: trends such as economic transformation, technological change, popular mobilization, and most importantly decolonization. For the most part, these studies have operated on a planetary scale, which generally means that the superpowers—which provide the throughlines linking far-flung cases—remain at the center of the narratives.[1]

Yet even as scholarship on the global Cold War continues apace—and continues to overthrow long-standing conventions—new approaches promise an even more profound rethinking of the Cold War. Two books appearing in the twenty-first century have called for interrogating the connections between the geopolitical tensions of the Cold War and the social tensions at the "local" level (with what constitutes the local being itself up for grabs). Heonik Kwon's *The Other Cold War* and Masuda Hajimu's *Cold War Crucible* differ in important particulars, but share a common aim.[2] Both seek to reinterpret local tensions not as merely as (in W. E. B. Du Bois's felicitous phrase) "local phases of a global problem," but as independently generated social conflicts that may have been energized by the global conflict but certainly were not imported.[3] (Strikingly, Kwon and Masuda also share a focus on Korea in the immediate post–World War II years. In doing so, they carry on a tradition visible in Bruce Cumings's groundbreaking work balancing the local and global origins of that conflict.[4]) Kwon and Masuda's bottom-up approach, unlike Cumings's, refuses to consider individuals "passive entities" just awaiting mobilization for a global conflict by one or another great power. We might call this the "frog prince" scenario, with the princess passively awaiting the revitalizing embrace of the prince; under such a scenario, the prince, whether dressed in red or red, white, and blue, made history, while the princess was a passive, even agentless, figure.

In the wake of these recent works come the essays assembled in the present volume, *Cold War Asia: Unlearning Narratives, Making New Histories*. Guided by Masuda's thoughtful introduction and made possible by his organizational energies, the volume offers an excellent opportunity to reflect on the fruits of the "frog prince" approach. As Masuda outlines, he wants the volume to "reconsider . . . what the Cold War really was" by seeing how it "took shape and materialized through ordinary people's imaginings and appropriations on the ground." Toward that end, Masuda offers five suggestions for future histories of the Cold War—fewer than Anders Stephanson's fourteen notes, and less philosophically inclined—that exhort readers to focus on individuals far from the White House or the Kremlin, Foggy Bottom or the Arbat, while at the same time promoting the use of oral history and "Asia as a method."[5]

Considered alongside this pentalogue, the essays in the volume score some great successes. Foremost among these is demonstrating the value of oral histories. About half of the essays rely heavily—in some cases almost exclusively—on oral history interviews conducted by the volume's contributors. The interviewees range from Okinawans who received US scholarships to study in the United States to women fighting in the North Vietnamese army to a "violent executioner" operating in the Indonesian region of south Siwi. Each oral interview, unsurprisingly, sheds valuable light on individual experiences and perceptions that tended to the proximate over the global or universal; their motivations were often quotidian factors such as desiring material improvement, seeking a degree of independence, pursuing relationships (familial or romantic), and so forth—and distinctly *not* a desire to enter into a global ideological conflict. Taken together, the oral histories provide deeply grounded accounts of the Cold War as it looked from towns, cities, and villages across Asia. The oral histories facilitate the work of scholars who seek to situate ordinary people, far from the levers of power, as agents. I can only hope that Masuda and his fellow contributors are able to create a repository, virtual or otherwise, for these oral histories and other ones to advance their project. Such a repository could also advance the cause of interrogating oral history as a method, exploring the absences, elisions, and outright errors that exist in oral histories as in all other historical sources. Without this work, the silences of the Cold War archive will replicate the silences of the colonial archive.[6]

The volume also makes the case, in essay after essay, for the value of interrogating the links between global and local conflicts. Two central tendencies emerge from the articles' attempts to establish these connections. A number of the authors show how global Cold War tensions became a resource for existing internal disputes. In some cases—the Okinawans able to study in the United States, for instance—the benefits accrued to individuals; in others, such as the Hmong who (in Prasit Leepreecha's words) "actively [took] advantage of the Cold War world," the benefits were communal and political. In these formulations, the Cold War provided opportunities for advancement, protection, or political engagement.[7]

Some of the other authors (for instance, Imam Muhtarom and Matthew Woolgar on Indonesia) see the Cold War as an accelerant, a factor that intensified existing social tensions in the localities they study. In this framing, visible also for instance in Cui Feng's examination of the Chinese in Thailand, ethnic tensions predated the arrival of the Cold War but took more vociferous forms as the long-standing domestic tensions took on the language and the tactics—and more than occasionally the literal and figurative weapons—of Cold War powers. This approach is able to track the deadliness of the Cold War—its own kind of "disease," as Leepreecha quotes from Hmong accounts—by accounting for preexisting conditions. These essays, along with that by Kisho Tsuchiya on Timor, are able to explain how Asian conflicts during the Cold War years took the forms that they did—and, especially in the case of Indonesia, could end up being as deadly as they were.

For all of their insights, though, the essays that focus on preexisting conditions find themselves at the fork of an interpretative dilemma. On the one hand, they ably deploy their regional expertise and deep knowledge of local conditions to show how battles between communists and their opponents (whether Timorese nationalists or Javanese *santri* Islamists) built directly on existing social fissures. On the other hand, these accounts often imply that they are dealing with age-old divisions that have been frozen in time; Tsuchiya makes such implicit claims explicit in his discussion of "ancestral . . . grudges" unleashed in the Cold War–era conflicts. But to see the existing ethnic conflicts as "ancient" runs the risk of what scholars of the Soviet Union have called "primordialism," or the assumption that "age-old" prejudices were simply repressed under Soviet power, rather than exploring the ethnic categories and tensions as constantly evolving phenomena that were not so much repressed by Soviet authorities as reinvented by them.[8] More attention to pre–Cold War, and especially colonial, histories would help us see ethnic divisions, and possibly even ethnicities themselves, as historical products rather than timeless essences.[9]

Ethnic tensions are a recurring theme in the volume, present if not predominant in at least half of the essays. From Simon Creak's analysis of anti-Vietnamese sentiment in Laos to Cui Feng's account of anti-Chinese sentiment in Thailand, the "on-the-ground" Asia depicted in this volume was a cauldron of chauvinism and bigotry. Cold War geopolitics opened up new fronts, then, in old battles; Thai Sinophobia, to take but one example, was hardly new but during the Cold War gained new license for freer expression in a Cold War idiom of communism and anticommunism. Seen from outside the localities, the process looked like the ethnicization of politics; xenophobia directed against the Vietnamese became, in Creak's felicitous phrase, the "vernacular expression of anticommunism."

Judging by the accounts in this book, anticommunism was the predominant Cold War ideology; at least three essays try to see how anticommunism was translated into the vernacular while only one looks at the local origins of communism. That essay, by Muhammed Kunhi Mahin Udma, shows how a Maoist movement in the southern Indian state of Kerala fared in the late 1960s. Udma credits a long period of caste exploitation as the reason for the initial success of the so-called Naxalites, a movement named after a village in West Bengal that was its first military success. But Udma also shows how more recent events shaped the nature of anti-Naxalite sentiment; by associating the radical insurgency with Chinese Communism, the Indian authorities tarred the movement with the brush of being antipatriotic, especially given the humiliation of the Indian armed forces at the hands of the People's Liberation Army in a brief, one-sided battle in the Himalayas in 1962. Udma's double-barreled approach, relying on local expertise to explain both sides of Kerala's Cold War, is an especially effective strategy.

Udma's essay is also unusual for its locale; it is the book's only essay on South Asia. While the book ranges as far East as Korea, Japan, and the Philippines, its center of gravity is in Southeast Asia. The volume convincingly shows how Southeast Asia offers particularly rich material for the "bottom-up" approach that Masuda promotes (and that the book's authors provide). Varied experiences of European colonialism, though only briefly alluded to in most essays, left impoverished and ethnically divided nations, new and old. The ongoing crisis in Vietnam looms large over the region, even well beyond the essays (e.g., Luong Thi Hong's) that focus directly on the American War. The region's Cold War experience is also shaped profoundly by the roles of China—the People's Republic on the one hand and the Chinese diaspora across Southeast Asia on the other. No wonder that this region of Asia provides so much of the material used to reconceptualize the Cold War.

The focus on Southeast Asia offers significant insight but also runs up against certain limits. For instance, in the essays on the region—and indeed, throughout the volume—the United States and the People's Republic of China play the starring roles in the Cold War drama, with the Soviet Union at best a supporting actor. This, in itself, offers a useful reminder that the Sino-Soviet split complicated the nature of the Cold War conflict as it evolved over time.[10] Yet the de-emphasis on the Soviet Union itself merits attention—and the role that the Soviet Union played in the region also deserves fuller explication.

The heavy emphasis on Southeast Asia, furthermore, comes at the cost of attention to South Asia. Udma's essay, however well rounded and persuasive, cannot stand in for a region in constant turmoil over the decades of the Cold War. Not all of the region's deadly violence of the post–World War II years can be traced back to the Cold War—take for instance, the bloody Partition of India in 1947. Yet Indo-Pakistan tensions in the subsequent decades were constantly exacerbated by their imbrication in superpower conflict. Or, to put it differently, India and Pakistan drew on Cold War powers as resources for their ongoing dispute, one that erupted in military conflict in 1965 and 1971 and fed a nuclear arms race.[11]

More attention to South Asia, with its divergent colonial histories and different Cold War alignments relative to Southeast Asia, could add an important dimension to reconceptualizing Cold War Asia. Masuda calls on readers to consider "Asia as a method"—a familiar phrase in multiple fields but not (yet) in Cold War history—and so the geographic bounds and regional antinomies of the large and diverse continent become all the more important.[12] It is premature to speculate on how consideration of South Asia would affect the broader implications of this volume, but it is worth noting that the connections between the regions were themselves being transformed over the course of the Cold War. Some of these changes came at the macro level of economic and political transformation—the "Korean War boom," for instance, affected all of Asia, albeit in many different ways.[13] These macro trends undoubtedly combined with highly variegated local conditions to create Cold War Asia.

In sum, *Cold War Asia* offers a template and some exemplars of a new generation of history, one that centers the Cold War in Asia and locates the Cold War in everyday life in villages, towns, and cities. Most importantly, the book invites us to take advantage of historical distance to find not just new sources but new perspectives on a dominant element of the twentieth-century world—one whose legacies we are still reckoning with some three decades after its end.

Notes

1. Odd Arne Westad, *The Global Cold War: Third World Interventions and the Making of Our Times* (Cambridge: Cambridge University Press, 2005); Lorenz M. Luthi, *Cold Wars: Asia, the Middle East, Europe* (Cambridge: Cambridge University Press, 2020); Jeremy Friedman, *Ripe for Revolution: Building Socialism in the Third World* (Cambridge, MA: Harvard University Press, 2021); and Paul Thomas Chamberlin, *The Cold War's Killing Fields: Rethinking the Long Peace* (New York: HarperCollins, 2018).

2. Masuda Hajimu, *Cold War Crucible: The Korean Conflict and the Postwar World* (Cambridge, MA: Harvard University Press, 2015); and Heonik Kwon, *The Other Cold War* (New York: Columbia University Press, 2010). For an earlier effort to emphasize local dimensions—"effects"—and focused primarily on the North Atlantic world, see *Local Consequences of the Global Cold War*, Cold War International History Project Series (Washington, DC: Woodrow Wilson Center Press, 2007).

3. The phrase comes from W. E. B. Du Bois via Robin D. G. Kelley, "'But a Local Phase of a World Problem': Black History's Global Vision, 1883–1950," *Journal of American History* 86, no. 3 (1999): 1045–77.

4. See Bruce Cumings, *The Origins of the Korean War*, 2 vols. (Princeton, NJ: Princeton University Press, 1981).

5. Anders Stephanson, "Fourteen Notes on the Very Concept of the Cold War," *H-Diplo* essay, February 2007 (originally published May 1996).

6. Interrogating the archive, and especially the colonial archive, has produced a fruitful vein of scholarship. See for instance, Michel-Rolph Trouillot, *Silencing the Past: Power and the Production of History* (Boston: Beacon Press, 1995); Ann Laura Stoler, *Along the Archival Grain: Epistemic Anxieties and Colonial Common Sense* (Princeton, NJ: Princeton University Press, 2009); and Bernard S. Cohn, "History and Anthropology: The State of Play," *Comparative Studies in Society and History* 22, no. 2 (1980): 198–221.

7. My own work has explored the Cold War as a resource for postcolonial Indian makers of economic policy—David C. Engerman, *The Price of Aid: The Economic Cold War in India* (Cambridge, MA: Harvard University Press, 2018).

8. See, for instance, Terry Martin, *The Affirmative Action Empire: Nations and Nationalism in the Soviet Union, 1923–1939* (Ithaca, NY: Cornell University Press, 2001); and Ronald Grigor Suny, "Constructing Primordialism: Old Histories for New Nations," *Journal of Modern History* 73, no. 4 (2001): 862–96.

9. Nicholas B. Dirks, *Castes of Mind: Colonialism and the Making of Modern India* (Princeton, NJ: Princeton University Press, 2001).

10. Austin Jersild, *The Sino-Soviet Alliance: An International History* (Chapel Hill: University of North Carolina Press, 2014); Lorenz M. Luthi, *The Sino-Soviet Split: Cold War in the Communist World* (Princeton, NJ: Princeton University Press, 2008); and Sergey Radchenko, *Two Suns in the Heavens: The Sino-Soviet Struggle for Supremacy, 1962–1967* (Stanford, CA: Stanford University Press, 2009).

11. From a predominantly Anglo-American perspective, see Robert J. McMahon, *The Cold War on the Periphery: The United States, India, and Pakistan* (New York: Columbia University Press, 1994); and Paul M. McGarr, *The Cold War in South Asia: Britain, the United States and the Indian Subcontinent, 1945–1965* (Cambridge: Cambridge University Press, 2013). From an Indian perspective, see Srinath Raghavan, *War and Peace in Modern India: A Strategic History of the Nehru Years* (Delhi: Permanent Black, 2010); and *1971: A Global History of the Creation of Bangladesh* (Cambridge, MA: Harvard University Press, 2013). There is less scholarship on Cold War South Asia from the Soviet perspective, but see Vojtech Mastny, "The Soviet Union's Partnership with India," *Journal of Cold War Studies* 12, no. 3 (2010): 50–90.

12. See especially Kuan-Hsing Chen, *Asia as Method: Toward Deimperialization* (Durham, NC: Duke University Press, 2010).

13. See the ongoing work by Sandeep Bhardwaj, "India and the Making of Political and Economic Order in Eastern Asia" (PhD diss., Ashoka University, 2024).

Contributors

MARY GRACE R. CONCEPCION is associate professor in the Department of English and Comparative Literature at the University of the Philippines Diliman. Her research interests are autobiographical writing, memory studies, and literature under Philippine Martial Law. Her recent articles include "Writing and Rewriting the Self: Narrative Projection and Transformation in Martial Law Autobiographies," *Humanities Diliman* (2021).

SIMON CREAK is a historian of modern Southeast Asia and associate professor of history at the National Institute of Education, Nanyang Technological University, Singapore. He is the author of *Embodied Nation: Sport, Masculinity, and the Making of Modern Laos* (University of Hawai'i Press, 2015), coauthor of *Historical Dictionary of Laos, Fourth Edition* (Rowman & Littlefield, 2023), and has published articles in the *Journal of Asian Studies, Journal of Contemporary Asia*, and *Asian Studies Review*.

CUI FENG (family name Cui) is a lecturer in the School of Sinology at Mae Fah Luang University (MFU). His areas of concentration are the history of China's foreign relations, Sino-Southeast Asian interactions, and the Cold War in Southeast Asia, with particular attention toward the communist movement in Thailand.

DAVID C. ENGERMAN, Leitner International Interdisciplinary Professor in the Department of History and the Jackson School of Global Affairs at Yale University, is a scholar of twentieth-century international history. He is the author of *Modernization from the Other Shore: American Intellectuals and the Romance of Russian Development* (Harvard University Press, 2003); *Know Your Enemy: The Rise and Fall of America's Soviet Experts* (Oxford University Press, 2009); and *The Price of Aid: The Economic Cold War in India* (Harvard University Press, 2018). His next book, *Apostles of Development: Six Economists and the World They Made* will appear in 2025.

PRASIT LEEPREECHA is senior lecturer in the Department of Social Science and Development at Chiang Mai University. In English, he has coedited two anthologies: *Living in the Globalized World: Ethnic Minorities in the Greater Mekong Subregion* (University of Washington Press, 2008) and *Challenging the Limits: Indigenous Peoples of the Mekong Region* (University of Washington Press, 2008).

LUONG THI HONG (family name Luong) is a research fellow in the Institute of History at the Vietnam Academy of Social Sciences. She specializes in the contemporary history of Vietnam since 1945, especially the wars in Vietnam and Vietnam's connections with other socialist countries during the Cold War. She has coauthored several books in Vietnamese, in addition to articles appearing in *Journal of Southeast Asian Research* and *The International History Review*.

MUHAMMED KUNHI MAHIN UDMA (family name Mahin Udma) is a postdoctoral fellow in the Department of History at the National University of Singapore. He is the author of "The Image of China in Indian Public Discourse During the 1962 War," *Culture, Society and Law* (2016), and "Technology and Work Opportunities for the Poor: An Analysis of Challenges in Developing a Sustainable Urban Solid Waste Management System in China," *Institute of Chinese Studies Occasional Paper* (2019).

MASUDA HAJIMU (family name Masuda) is a historian of Modern Japan, twentieth-century Asia, and US foreign relations, and associate professor of history at the National University of Singapore. He is the author of *Cold War Crucible: The Korean Conflict and the Postwar World* (Harvard University Press, 2015), which is translated into Japanese, Korean, and Chinese. In 2022, he established an online archive of oral history collections, "Reconceptualizing the Cold War: On-the-Ground Experiences in Asia," https://rcw-asia.com/.

ALAN McPHERSON is the Thomas J. Freaney Jr. Professor of History at Temple University, and the author of *Yankee No! Anti-Americanism in US-Latin American Relations* (Harvard University Press, 2003); *The Invaded: How Latin Americans and their Allies Fought and Ended US Occupations* (Oxford University Press, 2014); *The World and U2: One Band's Remaking of Global Activism* (Rowman & Littlefield, 2015); *A Short History of US Interventions in Latin America and the Caribbean* (Wiley-Blackwell, 2016); *Ghosts of Sheridan Circle: How a Washington Assassination Brought Pinochet's Terror State to Justice* (University of North Carolina Press, 2019); and *The Breach: Iran-Contra and the Assault on American Democracy* (University of North Carolina Press, 2025).

IMAM MUHTAROM teaches Indonesian literature at Universitas Singaperbangsa Karawang and is completing a PhD at Universitas Indonesia. He writes fiction, nonfiction, book reviews, literary criticism, and translations, as well as art and theater reviews. He is a curator of the Borobudur Writers and Cultural Festival. He has published two books: *Rumah yang tampak Biru oleh Cahaya Bulan* [A house that looks blue in the moonlight] (2007); and *Kulminasi: Teks, Konteks, dan Kota* [Culmination: Text, context and city] (2013).

SIM CHI YIN (family name Sim) is an artist from Singapore whose research-based practice uses artistic and archival interventions to contest and complicate historiographies and colonial narratives. She works across photography, film, installation, performance, and bookmaking. She was an artist fellow in the Whitney Museum's Independent Study Program (2022–23) and has a PhD in War Studies from King's College London. She has exhibited at the Venice Biennale 2024 and her work is in the collections of the Singapore Art Museum, M+ Hong Kong and The J. Paul Getty Museum, among others.

KISHO TSUCHIYA is assistant professor in the Center for Southeast Asian Studies at Kyoto University. He is the author of *Emplacing East Timor: Regime Change and*

Knowledge Production, 1860–2010 (University of Hawai'i Press, 2024). He specializes in transnational intellectual history, Modern Southeast Asian History, ethnography, war, and social history.

ODD ARNE WESTAD, Elihu Professor of History and Global Affairs at Yale University, is a scholar of modern international and global history. He is the author of *The Global Cold War: Third World Interventions and the Making of Our Times* (Cambridge University Press, 2006); *Restless Empire: China and the World since 1750* (Basic Books, 2012); *The Cold War: A World History* (Basic Books, 2017); *Empire and Righteous Nation: 600 Years of China-Korea Relations* (Harvard University Press, 2021), and (with Chen Jian), *The Great Transformation: China's Road from Revolution to Reform* (Yale University Press, 2024). He has also coedited (with Melvyn P. Leffler) *The Cambridge History of the Cold War* (Cambridge University Press, 2010).

MATTHEW WOOLGAR is lecturer in international history at the University of Leeds, and the author of *Communism, Cold War, and Revolution: The Indonesian Communist Party in West Java, 1949–1966* (forthcoming from Oxford University Press). He has also coedited *A Graveside Ritual: Contemporary Indonesian Short Stories* (Katarsis, 2020).

KINUKO MAEHARA-YAMAZATO is associate professor of American studies at the University of the Ryukyus, Okinawa, Japan. Her work examines the life stories of Okinawans and the Okinawan diaspora, exploring the impact of the US military occupation and its continuous presence in identity construction and negotiations.

BIN YANG, professor in the Department of Chinese and History at City University of Hong Kong, is the author of *Between Winds and Clouds: The Making of Yunnan—Second Century BCE—Twentieth Century CE* (Columbia University Press, 2008); *Cowrie Shells and Cowrie Money: A Global History* (Routledge, 2019), and *Discovered but Forgotten: The Maldives in Chinese History, c. 1100–1620* (Columbia University Press, 2024). He is one of the founding members of the Asian Association of World Historians, which, since 2008, has worked to promote world history teaching, research, and graduate training in and for Asia.

TAOMO ZHOU is associate professor in the Department of Chinese Studies and Dean's Chair in the Faculty of Arts and Social Sciences, National University of Singapore. Her first book, *Migration in the Time of Revolution: China, Indonesia and the Cold War* (Cornell University Press, 2019), won a *Foreign Affairs* "Best Books of 2020" award and an Honorable Mention for the 2021 Henry J. Benda Prize from the Association of Asian Studies.

Index

Italic page numbers refer to illustrations.

Abadilla, Rolando, 275
abangan, 47–48, 62n26
Abdullah, Kyai, 50
Adivasis (tribal groups), 117, 126, 130, 138n7
Agent Orange, 243–44
agrarian reform, 25–27, 28, 42n14, 57, 309, 310. *See also* farming communities
Aguinaldo, Rodolfo, 275
Aidit, D. N., 27, 49
AITUC (All India Trade Union Congress), 122
Ajitha, Kunnikkal, 124, 127, 130–31
Akha (tribal group), 92, 109n2
Alejandro, Lean, 296n33
Amaral, Xavier do, 153, 156, 157
Amornsiripanich, Tonglaw, 81–82, 83, 84–85
Anakhod Mai (New Future) party, 109
Anshary, Isa, 52
Ansor (The Helpers; organization), 27
anti-Chinese sentiments, 8, 73, 74, 77–79, 84–86
anticommunism, 46, 57, 60, 174–98, 202n59, 320–22. *See also* communism; *names of specific organizations*
anti-Vietnamese xenophobia, 10, 174–98
APODETI (Timorese Popular Democratic Union), 151, 152, 153, 163
ASDT (Timorese Social-Democratic Association), 151
assimilados (term), 153, 171n30
Associated State of Laos, 182. *See also* Laos

Auerhahn, Nanette, 276
Aung San, 253

Bangkok dynasty, 75
Bank of the Ryukyus, 213
Banser (Barisan Ansor Serbaguna; Ansor Multi-Purpose Brigade), 28–29, 33–39, 55–56
barlaque, 158, 172n49
Battle of Okinawa (1945), 209, 210, 216, 220
Battle of Saipan (1944), 222–23
BAYAN (*Bagong Alyansang Makabayan*), 296n33
beiryu-gumi (term), 205. *See also* Okinawan students in US universities
The Betrayal of the Indonesian Communist Party (film), 321
bidi, 141n38
Blitar Regency, 23–24
Bonaparte, Muki, 158
Booth, Donald, 213
BTI (Barisan Tani Indonesia), 23, 27, 51, 56–57. *See also* Indonesia
Bua Haw Yang, 97
Buckley, William F., Jr., 312
Buddhism, 175, 191
Burma, 11, 252–71, 322
Burmese language, 264
Burmese Way to Socialism, 254
The Burning Forest (Sundar), 117

Cao, Mr., 257–60
Caraway, Paul, 213, *214*, 216, 218–19
Carnation Revolution, 143, 163

cartoons, 183–89
caste system, 9, 116–24, 134, 137, 138nn7–8, 147, 309, 331
Catholics, 163, 164, 166, 311, 312
CCP (Chinese Communist Party), 78–80, 100–101, 123, 125, 252, 253–58, 260, 267, 270–71, 272nn6–7, 325. *See also* Mao Zedong
CDIN (Committee for the Defense of National Interests), 190–91
Central Committee of the Vietnam Youth Union, 234, 235
Central Organization of Indonesian Workers. *See* SOBSI
Chakkri dynasty, 75
Chang, Mr., 260–62
Chatib, Haji Tubagus Ahmad, 54
Chiang Kai-shek, 77
Chiến dịch Biên giới (Border Campaign), 234
China, 74–75, 115, 190. *See also* anti-Chinese sentiments; CCP (Chinese Communist Party); Mao Zedong; Red Guards
Chinese Communist Party. *See* CCP (Chinese Communist Party)
Chinese language, 264
Chinese Nationalist Party (Kuomintang), 77–78, 261, 302
Chinese origin in Thailand, 73–87
Chinese Revolution (1911), 74–75
Christianity, 48, 82, 94, 105, 164, 167–68, 237, 311–12
Chua Chai Yang, 106
CIA (Central Intelligence Agency), 123, 139n19
civilizados (term), 153, 171n30
Cold War (term), 44, 325. *See also* Cold War lens
Cold War Asia vs. Cold War in Asia (analytical framework), 14–15. *See also* Cold War lens
Cold War Crucible (Masuda), 119, 328–29
The Cold War in South Asia (McGarr), 119

Cold War International History Project (CWIHP), 18n2
Cold War Island (Szonyi), 320
Cold War lens: Cold War Asia, analytical approach, 14–15; "Cold War as weather," analytical approach, 3, 18n10; from Cold War to C̶o̶l̶d̶ War, 144–57, 167–68; Connelly on removing, 12, 146, 147, 176, 195, 196; Kwon on, 202n64; on US military in Okinawa, 206–9. *See also names of specific countries and conflicts*
Cold War studies, 1–7, 12–17, 44–45, 324–25
Committee for the Defense of National Interests, 321
Committee on Anti-Filipino Activities (CAFA), 274
communism: in Burma, 252–71; in China, 78–80, 100–101, 123, 125, 252, 253–58, 260, 267, 270–71, 272nn6–7, 325; in India, 115–26; in Indonesia, 8, 26–41, 45–59, 289; multifaceted, 320–22; in Philippines, 274, 294n2; in Thailand, 79–80, 91, 95–109, 111n22; in Vietnam, 234. *See also* anticommunism; *names of specific organizations*
Communist Party of Burma (CPB), 252–71, 309
Communist Party of India. *See* CPI (Communist Party of India); CPI (M) (Communist Party of India)
Communist Party of Indonesia. *See* PKI (Partai Komunis Indonesia; Indonesian Communist Party)
Communist Party of the Philippines, 274, 278, 294n2
Communist Party of Vietnam (CPV), 234–35
Concepción, Mary Grace R., 11, 274–98, 314, 323
Connelly, Matthew, 12, 146, 176, 195
containment rhetoric, 149, 155–57
Corazon Aquino, María, 296n33
Coughlin, Richard J., 73

CPB (Communist Party of Burma), 252–71, 272n2, 309
CPI (Communist Party of India), 119–20
CPI (M) (Communist Party of India), 123–32, 140nn27–28
CPT (Communist Party of Thailand), 79–80, 91, 95–109, 111n22
CPV (Communist Party of Vietnam), 234–35
Creak, Simon, 10, 174–202, 310, 321–22, 331
The Crown and the Capitalists (Wongsurawat), 74
Cuba, 310
Cuban Missile Crisis, 311
Cuban Revolution, 310
cultural nationalism in Laos, 177
Cultural Revolution (China; 1949), 182, 252, 255–56, 272n9, 322. *See also* China
Cumings, Bruce, 329

Da Costa Guterres, Joaquim (Elder), 164–65
Da Costa Guterres, Joaquim (Junior), 164, 166
Dai (ethnic group), 265, 269
Dalit movement, 136
Damahapan, Charoen, 82–83
Dang Miangong, 256
Darul Islam uprising, 47, 51–52, 58, 67n83, 72n147
De Bernard, Napoleón, 307
decolonization, 149–51
Decree of Keeping Jobs (1952), 81
Democratic Republic of Timor-Leste, 143. *See also* Timor
Democratic Republic of Vietnam (DRV), 190. *See also* Vietnam
Deng Xiaoping, 255
Desai administration, Morarji, 132
Diliman Commune, 274
disease, 93, 108, 244, 264, 310, 330
diversification in Cold War studies, 1–4
Đồng Lộc Junction, Vietnam, 232

Du Bois, W. E. B., 328–29
Dutch colonialism, 26
Duterte, Rodrigo, 277–79, 295n19. *See also* Philippines

Eaksittipong, Sittithep, 73–74
East Java, Indonesia, 23–40, 47, 49–51, 56–58, 308, 309, 311, 321. *See also* Indonesia
East Timor, 143, 148–73
Echo de la liberté (newspaper), 192, 193
EDs (educational discussions), 298n61
EDSA Revolution, 275
Eisenhower, Dwight D., 310
El Salvador, 308–9
emotive expression, 13, 191, 322–24
enemy (label), 162–64, 167
Engerman, David C., 328–34
Estrada, Joseph, 291, 298n66
ethnic Chinese in Thailand, 8, 73–87, 321
Etsujiro Miyagi, 207

FALINTIL, 172n55
farming communities, 25–26. *See also* agrarian reform
Fealy, Greg, 53
Feng Cui, 8, 73–90, 310, 321, 330, 331
F. H., 222–23
First Indochina War (1945–54), 191, 231, 324
First Quarter Storm, 274
"Five Principles (Panca Sila)," 49–50
Five Principles of Peaceful Coexistence (Burma-China), 253
FNLA, 156
"Foho Ramelau" (anthem), 158–59
folk poem, 242–43
Foreign Exchange Control Law (1953; Thailand), 81
fractionalization in Cold War studies, 2–4
Franco-Lao Convention (1949), 179
Free Lao (Lao Issara) movement, 174, 179, 182

Free Lao Front (Neo Lao Issara) movement, 180, 181, 182
Freire, Paulo, 159–60
FRELIMO, 152
French colonialism, 92, 178–79
FRETILIN (Revolutionary Front for an Independent East Timor), 143–44, 148–68, 170n21, 322. *See also* Timor
From the Mud Houses (Kunnath), 118
"The Future of the Ryuku Islands" (speech), 213

GARIOA (Government Aid and Relief in Occupied Areas), 206, 210
Gari-Wai village, Timor, 161–62
Geertz, Clifford, 46, 47
gender politics, 158
Geneva Accords (1954), 189
Gerwani (Gerakan Wanita Indonesia; Indonesian Women's Movement), 23. *See also* Indonesia
global confrontation (phrase), 3, 60n1, 145, 148, 169n15
Golden Gate Club, 213, *214*, 215, 216, 227
Gopalan, Ayillyath Kuttiari, 122, 135
Grandin, Greg, 310
great men's narrative, 3–4
GROW (Gwailor Rayons Workers' Organization), 120
Guatemala, 314
Guizhou laobing, 253–54
Guskin, Alan Edward, 73
Gustiallah Mantu (God Performs Marriage; play), 29

Haiti, 310
Hansip (Pertahanan Sipil; Civil Defense Guards), 27
Harmer, Tanya, 311
Hà Tĩnh Transport Company, 238
He Gao, 255
Hirsch, Marianne, 276
Hizbullah, 48–49
Hmong, 8, 91–109, 109n1, 109n7, 177
Ho (ethnic group), 177

Hồ Chí Minh, 95, 234, 245. *See also* Vietnam
Hồ Chí Minh Trail, 190–91, 194, 233, 243
Hồ Chí Minh Youth Union, 232
Hongxuan, Lin, 48
H'tin (ethnic group), 109n2
Huachiew Chalermprakiet University, 82
Huk Rebellion (Philippines), 274

India, 9, 115–37. *See also* Naxalite Movement
Indonesia: Banser's work in, 37–39; communism and Islam in, 46–52; 1950s PKI and Islamic parties in, 52–55, 289; 1960s and growing conflict in, 55–58; 1965–66 massacres of, 7–8, 23–25, 32–41, 324; social and cultural tensions in, 28–32; south Siwi conflicts, 25–28, 32–37; Timor occupation by, 149–55. *See also* East Java, Indonesia; Sukarno; West Java, Indonesia
Indonesian Communist Party. *See* PKI (Partai Komunis Indonesia; Indonesian Communist Party)
Indonesian Mass Killings (1965–66), 7–8, 23–25, 32–41, 324
Indonesian Peasant's Front. *See* BTI (Barisan Tani Indonesia)
Indonesian Revolution (1945–49), 48
Indonesian Women's Movement. *See* Gerwani (Gerakan Wanita Indonesia; Indonesian Women's Movement)
inductive analytical approach, 13–14
Institute of People's Culture. *See* Lekra (Lembaga Kesenian Rakyat; Institute of People's Culture)
intergenerational memory, 276–77
International Monetary Fund, 274
ISDV (Indische Sociaal-Democratische Vereeniging; Indies Social Democratic Association), 48
Islam, 25, 29–30, 39, 45

Islamic League. *See* PSII (Partai Sarekat Islam Indonesia; Indonesian Islamic League Party)
Islamized communism, 46–52. *See also* Indonesia
The Island of Sea Women (See), 320
Islands in the Net (Sterling), 320

Janmis, 9, 117, 126, 127, 130, 131–36, 138n7
Java, Indonesia, 25–41
Javanese culture, 25, 39, 43n53. *See also* Indonesia
Java War (1825–30), 25
Jeju Island, 320
"The Jews of the East" (article), 75
Jingpo (ethnic group), 253, 255, 256, 264, 265, 269, 271
Jingpo language, 255, 264

Kaeo Vietminh, 183–89, 201n41
Kammen, Douglas, 162
Kampanyang Ahos (Kahos), 284, 297n41
Kang Sheng, 255
Karen (tribal group), 92, 109n2, 264
Kartawinata, Yati Aruji, 54
Katay Don Sasorith, 180–81
Katsunori, Yamazato, 208
Kayin language, 264
Keller, Renata, 311
Ke Ming, 255
Kerala Student Federation (KSF), 134
Kerdphol, Saiyud, 80
Khamu (ethnic group), 109n2
Khu Vang Yang, 103, 104
Kilsung Mayo Uno, 296n33
Kissinger, Henry, 314–15
Klein, Christina, 206
KM (*Kabataang Makabayan*), 274
KMT (Kuomintang; Chinese Nationalist Party), 77–78, 261, 302
Koramil (Military District Command), 33–34
Korean War (1950–53), 182, 324
Krishnan, Kunnel, 134, *135*, 136

Krushchev, Nikita, 190, 191
Kwon Heonik, xii, 144, 324

Lahire Gustiallah (Birth of God; play), 29
Lahu (ethnic group), 109n2
Lao Hakxa Sat (newspaper), 190, 191, *192*
Lao Issara (Free Laos) movement, 174, 179, 182. *See also* Free Lao Front (Neo Lao Issara) movement
Lao National Army, 182
Lao Nhay (Great Laos) renovation movement, 178
Lao People's Democratic Republic, 92
Laos, 109n7, 174–98, 254, 321–22
"Lao-Viets," 175, 186
Laub, Dori, 276
La Yi Lee, 104–5
Leepreecha, Prasit, 8, 85, 91–111, 310, 330
Lekra (Lembaga Kesenian Rakyat; Institute of People's Culture), 23, 30–31. *See also* Indonesia
Le Laos, pivot idéal de la lutte contre le Communisme dans le Sud-Est Asiatique (pamphlet), 180
Leong Kar-Yen, 290
Leow, Rachel, 323
Lesbumi (Lembaga Seni-Budaya Muslim Indonesia; Indonesian Moslem Art-Culture Institute), 29–30
letrados, 153, 171n30
Lisu (tribal group), 92, 109n2, 269
Liu Shaoqi, 255
local imaginings (analytical framework), 6, 9, 119
Logevall, Frederik, 2
Lua (ethnic group), 109n2
Luong Thi Hong, 10–11, 226, 231–51, 309, 322, 332
Luo Xian, 253, 255

Macapagal-Arroyo, Gloria, 291, 298n66
Madiun Affair, 49, 52, 59
Maehara-Yamazato, Kinuko, 10, 205–30, 311

Index   343

Mahin Udma, Muhammed Kunhi, 9, 115–42, 309, 313, 331–32
Makarabis, 34–35
Malayan Emergency (1948–60), 299–304
Malaysia, 299–304
Maneepruek, 98
Mao Zedong, 140n36, 252, 253, 254–55, 261, 268, 269. *See also* CCP (Chinese Communist Party); China
Marcos, Ferdinand "Bongbong," Jr., 274–76, 294n11, 295n19. *See also* Philippines
Marhaenism, 27, 156, 172n45, 322
Martial Law in Philippines, 274–93, 298n66
Martinho, Jose, 161–62
Marxist Publications (company), 123
Masahide Ota, 227
massacre. *See* Indonesian Mass Killings (1965–66)
Masuda Hajimu, 1–20, 24, 93, 144, 207, 307
Masyumi, 49, 52–53, 55
Matine Gustiallah (Death of God; play), 29
maubere, 156–57
Mau Kali, Timor, 161–62
May First movement, 296n33
McCoy, Alfred, 275
McPherson, Alan, 15, 307–18
Melvin, Jessica, 47
Melvin Price Report (1956), 218
memory and memorialization, xii–xiii, 15
Meo (ethnic group), 177
Meo (term), 109n1
mertelu system, 26
mestizos (term), 153, 171n30
Meyskens, Covell, 325
Miao (term), 109n1
Mien (Yao), 106, 177. *See also* Red Meo soldiers
Miyara Chyogi, 217
Mlabri (ethnic group), 109n2

M. O., 219–22. *See also* Okinawan students in US universities
mobilization campaigns, 157–61
Moh Daeng, 103
Mottin, Jean, 92
MPLA, 152, 156
MRPP party, 152
Muhtarom, Imam, 7, 13, 23–43, 51, 57–58, 308, 321, 330
M. Y., 216–19. *See also* Okinawan students in US universities
Myanmar. *See* Burma

Nak Rop Lao (newssheet), 183–89
Nao Bee Lao, 100, 101
Narayanan, Kunnikkal, 123, 124–26
Nationalist Party of Indonesia. *See* PNI (Partai Nasional Indonesia; Nationalist Party of Indonesia)
National Revolution of Vichy France, 178
Naxalite Movement, 9, 116–19, 124–37, 309, 331
Nayar, Narayan Kutti, 133
Nehring, Holger, 4, 196
Nehru, Jawaharlal, 191
Neo Lao Issara (Free Laos Front) movement, 174, 179, 182
neutralism, 202n59
new Cold War studies, 1–7, 12–17, 44–45
Ne Win, 254
Ngô Thị Hoa, 242–44
Nguyễn Thị Mùi, 244–46
Nguyễn Thị Thảo, 238
Nihonn Fukki, 209
nongchang zhiqing, 257
NTF-ELCAC (National Task Force to End Local Communist Armed Conflict), 295n19
NU (Nahdlatul Ulama; Revival of the Ulama), 23, 27–40, 53–56. *See also* Indonesia

Office of the High Commissioner, 210
Okinawa, 205–14

Okinawan students in US universities, 10, 205, 206–7, 209–19, 224–26; M. O., 219–22; M. Y., 216–19; Y. A., 222–24
Okinawa Relief and Rehabilitation Foundation, 210
Olalia, Rolando, 296n33
"On the Possibility of an Autonomous History of Modern Southeast Asia" (article), 146
Operation Rolling Thunder, 239–40
OPMT (Organização Popular das Mulheres Timorenses), 158
oral history, 5–6, 15, 94, 246–47. See also research methods
ordinary people's experiences (analytical framework), 13, 14
The Other Cold War (Kwon), 119, 324, 328–29

PAIGC, 152
Pa lom muang strategy, 91, 95
Panca Sila. See "Five Principles (Panca Sila)"
Pancha-Shila, 191
Paraguay, 314
Parempett, Mani, 136
Pathet Lao movement, 174, 175, 179, 180, 189, 194, 202n59, 321
Pedagogy of the Oppressed (Freire), 159–60
Pemuda Marhaen (Marhaen's Youth), 27
Pemuda Rakyat (People's Youth), 23, 27
Peng Qinglong, 84
Peng Shantan, 84
People Power Revolution, 275, 278, 283
People's Republic of China (PRC), 190, 253. See also China
People's Revolutionary Party (LPRP), 194
Perks, Robert, 94
Phetsarath, 179
Phibun Songgram, 76–77, 80–81, 88n30. See also Thailand

Philippines, 274–93, 294n2, 296n33, 297n41, 298n66. See also Marcos, Ferdinand "Bongbong," Jr.
Phomvihane, Kaysone, 179
Phoumsavanh, Nouhak, 179
Phukong Laoyee, 108–9
Pinochet, Augusto, 309
PKI (Partai Komunis Indonesia; Indonesian Communist Party), 8, 26–41, 45–59, 289. See also Indonesia
PLA (People's Liberation Army), 254, 331
Plan Z, 309
Plato, 144, 168n3, 169n13
PNI (Partai Nasional Indonesia; Nationalist Party of Indonesia), 23. See also Indonesia
political cartoons, 183–89
Portuguese Communist Party, 170n21
Portuguese language, 157–58
Portuguese Maoist movement, 170n21
Portuguese Public Institution for Education, 165
Portuguese Socialist Party, 170n21
Portuguese Timor, 143–73
Power and Diplomacy (study), 119
Pradesh, Andhra, 122
Pratthachariya family, 83
"Prisons for APODETI and UDT Members" (FRETILIN document), 165
PSII (Partai Sarekat Islam Indonesia; Indonesian Islamic League Party), 48, 54–55
Pulpally, India, 126–28, 135

Rabe, Stephen, 308–9
racism. See xenophobia
Raid, Hasan, 48–49
Rama VI (king), 74, 75–78, 89n43
Ramon, Foam, 73
RA-RJ split, 279, 288–89, 296n22
reactionary (label), 162–64, 167
Rebel Publications (company), 123
"Reconceptualizing the Cold War" project, 5–6, 146–47
"Red Guard" (*Renmin Ribao*), 125, 140n36

Index 345

Red Guards, 11, 252, 255–58, 267, 268, 270–71, 272n9, 309, 313, 319–20, 322. *See also* China
Red Meo soldiers, 96–109. *See also* Mien (Yao)
research methods, xii–xiii, 5–6, 215–16, 252. *See also* oral history
Ricklefs, Merle, 46–47
Riem Eng, 183–89
Rochet, Charles, 178
Romero, Frederico, 4, 196
Royal Lao Government (RLG), 179–80
Ryuku Islands, 209–14. *See also under* Okinawa

Sakini, 36
San Francisco Peace Treaty (1951), 209
Sani, 27–28
santri, 62n26
Sarjoti, 30–31, 32, 35, 38
Scott, James C., 93
shihan gakko, 210, 219
Shimabuku, Annmaria, 208
Siam. *See* Thailand
Sichuan laobing, 253
Sim Chi Yin, xiiin5, 11–12, 299–304, 311, 324
simulcrum (concept), 9, 144, 162, 166
Sino-Indian Border Conflict (1962), 115. *See also* India
Sino-Japanese War (1937–45), 267
Sison, Jose Maria, 274, 294n2
Siwi, Java, 25–26
Skinner, G. W., 73
Smail, John R. W., 146
SOBSI (Sentral Organisasi Buruh Seluruh Indonesia; Central Organization of Indonesian Workers), 23. *See also* Indonesia
social revolution (concept), 149
social warfare (analytical framework), 12–13, 14, 74, 175
Solo (kingdom), 25
Souphanouvong (prince), 179, 181
Statue of Brothers, Seoul, 324

Stephanson, Anders, 329
Student Corps of Blood and Iron for Emperor (*Tekketsu Kinnotai*), 219–20
study-abroad program. *See* Okinawan students in US universities
Sudi Subidi, 30, 32–33
Suharto, 23, 24, 143, 154, 166–67, 289–90, 321. *See also* Indonesia
Sukarno, 26–27, 49–50. *See also* Indonesia
Sukhothai dynasty, 75
Syamsul, 35

Tablo (play), 30
Taiping Rebellion, 177
Taiwan, 78, 79, 216, 226
Taylor, Sandra, 231
Tetun language, 157–58
Thailand: communist movements in, 95–109; ethnic Chinese in, 8, 73–87, 321; Hmong in, 91–109. *See also* Phibun Songgram
Thai nationalism, 75, 76, 81
Thakin Ba Thein Tin, 254–55
Thakin Than Tun, 254
Thakin Zin, 254
Thalassery, India, 126–29, 135, 141n37
Theravada Buddhism, 175
Thirunelli-Thrissileri revolt (1969), 131–32, 136
Thomson, Alistair, 94
Tibet, 191
Timor, 143, 148–73. *See also* FRETILIN (Revolutionary Front for an Independent East Timor)
Timorese elite (phrase), 153, 171n30
Torrijos, Omar, 307
Toru Maeda, 165
Towi, 31
traitor (label), 162–64, 167
Trần Thị Lan, 239–41
trauma processing, 297n44
Tsuchiya Kisho, 6, 9, 143–73, 309, 311, 322, 331
T. Y., 226

Udma, Muhammed Kunhi Mahin, 331–32
UDT (Timorese Democratic Union), 151, 153–54, 163
UNITA, 156
United Front, 124
United War State Party, 272n2
University of the Ryukyus, 216, 222, 224–25
UNRRA (United Nations Relief and Rehabilitation Administration), 267
Up-to-Mountain and Down-to-Countryside movement, 256–57, 268
US Army, 209
USCAR (US Civil Administration of the Ryuku Islands), 210, 212. See also Ryuku Islands
US Department of Defense, 212
US-educated Okinawans. See Okinawan students in US universities
US-Japan Status of Forces Agreement, 209
US military occupation of Okinawa, 205–14
US Navy, 209
US study-abroad program. See Okinawan students in US universities
UUBH (Undang-Undang Bagi Hasil; Production Sharing Law), 26–27, 28
UUPA (Undang-Undang Pokok Agraria; Basic Agrarian Law), 26–27, 28

Vajiravudh. See Rama VI (king)
Va Long Lee, 98–100
Vasu, Ayinnor, 120, *121*, 122
Venu, K., 136
vernacular expressions, 189–94
Vietminh, 175, 183–89
Vietnam, 190, 254. See also Hồ Chí Minh
Vietnamese women volunteers in Vietnam War, 10–11, 231–48, 249n8; Ngô Thị Hoa, 242–44; Nguyễn Thị Mùi, 244–46; Trần Thị Lan, 239–41
Vietnam War (1954–75), 10–11, 92, 231–48

Võ Nguyên Giáp, 235
Vũ Kỳ, 234

Wa (ethnic group), 253, 256, 271
Wan Siang Puen Taek (1965), 95
Weld, Kirsten, 314
Wen-Qing Ngoei, 321
Westad, Odd Arne, xi–xiii, 145
Western-centric narratives, 3–4
West Java, Indonesia, 8, 44–60. See also Indonesia
Wolfson-Ford, Ryan, 174, 180, 182, 190
women volunteers, 231–48, 249n8; Ngô Thị Hoa, 242–44; Nguyễn Thị Mùi, 244–46; Trần Thị Lan, 239–41
Wongsurawat, Wasana, 74
Woolgar, Matthew, 8, 44–72, 311, 320–21, 330
World Peace Congress, 323
world revolution (concept), 149, 155–57
World War II, 92–93
Wu, Mrs., 262–64

xenophobia: anti-Chinese, 8, 73, 74, 77–79, 84–86; anti-Vietnamese, 10, 174–98
xiaxiang zhiqing, 256–57
Xinhai Revolution (1911), 74

Y. A., 216, 222–24. See also Okinawan students in US universities
Yang Bin, 11, 252–73, 309, 313, 322, 337
Yao (ethnic group), *106*, 109n2, 177
Yogyakarta (kingdom), 25
Yoshino Kozen, 217
Youth Volunteer Union, 234–39, 245, 247
Yunann Zhiqing Lianyihui, 257

Zhenbao (or Damansky) Island, 319
zhiqing, 252
Zhou Enlai, 191, 255, 269
Zhou Taomo, 17, 319–27
Zhu, Mr., 266–69
Zhuang, Mr., 264–66
Zhu De, 269

www.ingramcontent.com/pod-product-compliance
Lightning Source LLC
Chambersburg PA
CBHW020320240426
43673CB00039B/871